Foreign Direct Investment

A National Bureau
of Economic Research
Project Report

Foreign Direct Investment

Edited by **Kenneth A. Froot**

The University of Chicago Press

Chicago and London

KENNETH A. FROOT is professor of business administration at Harvard University's Graduate School of Business and a research associate of the National Bureau of Economic Research.

The University of Chicago Press, Chicago 60637
The University of Chicago Press, Ltd., London

© 1993 by the National Bureau of Economic Research
All rights reserved. Published 1993
Printed in the United States of America
02 01 00 99 98 97 96 95 94 93 1 2 3 4 5
ISBN: 0-226-26621-4 (cloth)

Library of Congress Cataloging-in-Publication Data

Foreign direct investment / edited by Kenneth A. Froot.
    p. cm.—(National Bureau of Economic Research project report)
  Includes bibliographical references and index.
  1. Investments, Foreign. 2. Investments, Foreign—United States. 3. Investments, American. 4. Investments, Asian—United States. 5. International business enterprises—United States. I. Froot, Kenneth.
II. Series.
HG4538.F618   1993
332.6'73—dc20   93-27230
                                                     CIP

Relation of the Directors to the
Work and Publications of the
National Bureau of Economic Research

1. The object of the National Bureau of Economic Research is to ascertain and to present to the public important economic facts and their interpretation in a scientific and impartial manner. The Board of Directors is charged with the responsibility of ensuring that the work of the National Bureau is carried on in strict conformity with this object.

2. The President of the National Bureau shall submit to the Board of Directors, or to its Executive Committee, for their formal adoption all specific proposals for research to be instituted.

3. No research report shall be published by the National Bureau until the Prsident has sent each member of the Board a notice that a manuscript is recommended for publication and that in the President's opionion it is suitable for publication in accordance with the principles of the National Bureau. Such notification will include an abstract or summary of the manuscript's content and a response form for use by those Directors who desire a copy of the manuscript for review. Each manuscript shall contain a summary drawing attention to the nature and treatment of the problem studied, the character of the data and their utilization in the report, and the main conclusions reached.

4. For each manuscript so submitted, a special committee of the Directors (including Directors Emeriti) shall be appointed by a majority agreement of the President and Vice Presidents (or by the Executive Committee in case of inability to decide on the part of the President and Vice Presidents), consisting of three Directors selected as nearly as may be one from each general division of the Board. The names of the special manuscript committee shall be stated to each Director when notice of the proposed publication is submitted to him. It shall be the duty of each member of the special manuscript committee to read the manuscript. If each member of the manuscript committee signifies his approval within thirty days of the transmittal of the manuscript, the report may be published. If at the end of that period any member of the manuscript committee withholds his approval, the President shall then notify each member of the Board, requesting approval or disapproval of publication, and thirty days additional shall be granted for this purpose. The manuscript shall then not be published unless at least a majority of the entire Board who shall have voted on the proposal within the time fixed for he receipt of votes shall have approved.

5. No manuscript may be published, though approved by each member of the special manuscript committee, until forty-five days have elapsed from the transmittal of the report in manuscript form. The interval is allowed for the receipt of any memorandum of dissent or reservation, together with a brief statement of his reasons, that any member may wish to express; and such memorandum of dissent or reservation shall be published with the manuscript if he so desires. Publication does not, however, imply that each member of the Board has read the manuscript, or that either members of the Board in general or the special committee have passed on its validity in every detail.

6. Publications of the National Bureau issued for informational purposes concerning the work of the Bureau and its staff, or issued to inform the public of activities of Bureau staff, and volumes issued as a result of various conferences involving the National Bureau shall contain a specific disclaimer noting that such publication has not passed through the normal review procedures required in this resolution. The Executive Committee of the Board is charged with review of all such publications from time to time to ensure that they do not take on the character of formal research reports of the National Bureau, requiring formal Board approval.

7. Unless otherwise determined by the Board or exempted by the terms of paragraph 6, a copy of this resolution shall be printed in each National Bureau publication.

(Resolution adopted October 25, 1926, as revised through September 30, 1974)

Contents

Preface   ix

Introduction   1
Kenneth A. Froot

1.   **The Surge in Foreign Direct Investment in the 1980s**   13
Edward M. Graham and Paul R. Krugman
Comment: Kenneth A. Froot
Discussion Summary

2.   **New Perspectives on Foreign Direct Investment**   37
Rachel McCulloch
Comment: Karl P. Sauvant
Discussion Summary

3.   **Where Are the Multinationals Headed?**   57
Raymond Vernon
Comment: Richard E. Caves
Discussion Summary

4.   **Japan's Low Levels of Inward Investment: The Role of Inhibitions on Acquisitions**   85
Robert Z. Lawrence
Comment: Richard C. Marston
Discussion Summary

5.   **Foreign Direct Investment in the United States: Changes over Three Decades**   113
Robert E. Lipsey
Discussion Summary

6.   **Mobile Exporters: New Foreign Investors in
           East Asia**   173
           Louis T. Wells, Jr.
           Comment: Peter A. Petri
           Discussion Summary

7.   **Foreign Direct Investment in Semiconductors**   197
           David B. Yoffie
           Comment: S. Lael Brainard
           Discussion Summary

8.   **International Corporate Equity Associations:
           Who, Where, and Why?**   231
           Paul M. Healy and Krishna G. Palepu
           Comment: Michael Adler
           Discussion Summary

9.   **Foreign Mergers and Acquisitions in the
           United States**   255
           Deborah L. Swenson
           Comment: Donald Lessard
           Discussion Summary

           Biographies   285

           Contributors   287

           Author Index   289

           Subject Index   293

Preface

This volume presents the proceedings of a conference, "Foreign Direct Investment Today," sponsored by the National Bureau of Economic Research and held in Cambridge, Massachusetts, on May 15–16, 1992.

For their help in collecting these writings in one place, I would like to express my appreciation to the authors, discussants, and participants whose papers, views, and comments are presented in this book.

On behalf of the National Bureau of Economic Research, I would also like to thank the Ford Foundation and the Starr Foundation. I am indebted to Kirsten Foss and Lauren Lariviere for their usual efficiency in distributing materials and running the conference and for the charm and cheer they displayed all the while. I also thank Jane Konkel and Deborah Kiernan for their very effective management of the manuscript during the publication process. Finally, I thank Martin Feldstein and Geoffrey Carliner of the National Bureau of Economic Research for their encouragement and support of this project from the outset.

Introduction

Kenneth A. Froot

Foreign direct investment (FDI) has grown dramatically as a major form of international capital transfer over the past decade. Between 1980 and 1990, world flows of FDI—defined as cross-border expenditures to acquire or expand corporate control of productive assets—have approximately tripled. FDI has become a major form of net international borrowing for Japan and the United States (the world's largest international lender and borrower, respectively). Direct investment has grown even more rapidly of late within Europe.

To what extent is this sudden worldwide surge in FDI explained by traditional theories? These theories predict the scale and scope of multinational enterprises by looking to differences in competitive advantage, across firms or countries, that might lead to the extension of corporate control across borders. So, for example, better technology, management capability, and product design; stronger consumer allegiance; and greater complementarities in production or use of technology can allow a domestic firm to control foreign assets more productively than would a foreign firm and could therefore predicate direct investment. In many cases, these theories also explain why an enterprise's alternatives to FDI—domestically based production or licensing of foreign-based production—are less efficient than direct control of foreign-based operations (see, e.g., Caves 1982; Vernon 1966).

Traditional theories are very useful for explaining basic long-term patterns of FDI. For example, they help understand the behavior of U.S. firms during the post–World War II period (the experience on which these theories were honed). At that time, advanced U.S. firms were superior in technology and well established in foreign markets. U.S. firms tended to move overseas to retain competitive access (or to preempt competitors' access) to those markets and, in the process, met with relatively little competition.

These theories also help us understand why the tide of U.S. FDI flows has slowly turned. The evolution of the United States from a home for domestically

1

based multinationals to a host for foreign-based multinationals is probably the single most obvious sign of change in FDI today. This development basically coincides with the waning (and even disappearance) of U.S. firms' former competitive advantages. It is obvious to today's consumer that European-, Japanese-, and Canadian-based firms have developed advantages that allow them to control certain assets in the United States more efficiently than would U.S.-based firms.

In spite of their successes, however, the traditional theories leave many recent features of FDI unexplained. First, it is hard to believe that the tide of underlying competitive advantage followed closely (or at all) the behavior of total FDI flows over the last decade: very rapid increases from 1979 through 1981, strong declines from 1982 through 1985, and then increases of unprecedented size from 1986 through 1990. One would have expected changes in national competitive advantages to be reflected in more steady trends. Second, to the extent that any developments happen quickly, one might have expected that they would occur in a single industry at a time—say, the automobile producers of Japan—as shocks to competitive ability come to be reflected in world ownership patterns. Yet the surges of the past fifteen years take place across virtually all industries simultaneously.

The recent FDI surges in U.S. inflows and Japanese outflows illustrate these two features. Japanese FDI overall, which historically was small, exploded across all industries in the latest surge, experiencing in the aggregate a sevenfold increase from 1985 to 1989. During this surge, both U.S. inflows and Japanese outflows were particularly large and fast-growing in real estate and financial services. In these industries, however, there was little evidence of meaningful change in competitive advantage. Particularly puzzling is the case of Japanese banks, which during the latest surge went on a much-publicized binge in acquiring foreign affiliates. Many of the involved banks were actually noted for their apparently *in*efficient operations and low profitability in comparison with U.S. and European companies. These facts suggest that existing theories do a good job of explaining neither the timing or magnitude of surges nor their broad cross-industry composition.

Another group of theories, less well established, may help us understand the timing and cross-sectional behavior of surges. Tax changes may have had sudden, large (sometimes unintended) across-the-board effects on the relative (foreign versus domestic) profitability of asset control. Such effects are unlikely to be sustained for decades.

Changes in corporate borrowing capacity and availability of internal funds may also help explain why some firms can invest or purchase assets more "cheaply" than others can even without a perceptible change in competitive advantage. Follow-the-leader tendencies, even if not completely rational, may influence corporate location decisions in the short run (although in the long run such decisions will presumably be more consistent with the underlying economics of production). Strategically oriented location decisions (in goods and factor markets which display imperfect competition) might be driven by conjectures about other firms' propensity to invest abroad and might therefore lead to rational herdlike behavior. Actual or existing trade barriers are also an important consideration (and are also stressed by more traditional theories).

The essays in this volume assess these newer explanations as well as other, older theories. The chapters are grouped in order to attack the issue from a variety of perspectives. The first group comprises overview essays (by Paul Krugman and Monty Graham, Rachel McCulloch, and Raymond Vernon) that look at the broad FDI experience during the most recent period and contrast it with earlier trends. The papers define the main issues and areas of change in FDI patterns and assess the performance of macrotheories. The second group deals with specific-country experiences. There are essays on Japan (Robert Lawrence), on the United States (Robert Lipsey), and on East Asian developing countries (Louis Wells). One chapter analyzes the FDI experience along a different dimension, evaluating how the developments within a specific industry—semiconductors—match up with those seen on a country or worldwide basis (David Yoffie).

Another important characteristic of recent FDI is the mode by which it is accomplished. In the past, greenfield investment was the rule, but today the vast majority of FDI is done through mergers and acquisitions (M&A). Why the sudden change? Older theories say little about the mechanics of FDI transactions; perhaps changes in financing technologies made acquisitions easier and resulted in a surge in M&A (domestic as well as foreign).

The growth in international merger and acquisition transactions has led researchers to study M&A on its own terms. One advantage of looking at acquisitions data is that purchase prices are flexible and, because they often are the result of competitive bidding, are meaningful as well. By contrast, the "costs" of doing greenfield investment are rarely recorded and rarely reflect the investor's eagerness to proceed. By analyzing M&A transactions, we can learn something about foreign investors' reservation prices and can compare them with the reservation prices of domestic investors. This can give us another independent measure of the propensity of foreigners to gain control of domestic assets.

The last group of papers (Paul Healy and Krishna Palepu, and Deborah Swenson) investigates developments in international M&A. The authors focus on both the size of cross-border flows and the price that foreigners tend to pay in such transactions.

Overview Papers

Graham and Krugman provide an overview of the late-1980s surge in worldwide foreign direct investment and survey the conceptual issues that it raises.

During the 1985–1989 period, they estimate, FDI grew at a rate of 27 percent per year, amounting to $3.6 trillion of business assets acquired or built by foreign owners during that time. While Graham and Krugman discuss the ambiguities in these overall numbers, all measures of FDI paint a generally similar story for the period. Furthermore, there is little disagreement that this period was characterized by the rapid emergence of Japan into the process of investment abroad (although not into that of investment at home), a diminution in the importance of U.S. FDI outflows and a shift toward the United States as a dominant recipient for FDI, a decline in the relative magnitude of North-South flows compared to North-North flows, and a dramatic shift in the nature of FDI away from greenfield and toward merger and acquisition.

What do we understand about the causes and effects of this late-1980s surge in FDI? The first issue concerns the most fundamental determinants of FDI, which almost by definition involve the determinants of the boundaries of the firm. Perhaps the growth in the importance of FDI may be interpreted as a widening of the boundaries of the firm. Graham and Krugman look at two basic approaches for thinking about this question. The first suggests that the boundaries of the firm are defined by the tension between costs of transacting and costs of institutional rigidities. While this view is intriguing, its ability to predict the large increase in FDI during the 1980s seems questionable. Factors such as improvement in communication and information technology probably help improve the flexibility of large organizations and hence may help to explain the surge in FDI. But these factors probably also help firms economize on arm's length transaction costs, which predicts a tendency toward more-restrictive firm boundaries.

A second view focuses on the behavior of enterprise scale rather than scope. For example, a firm might grow "too" big as a result of the incentives of managers (agents), which differ from those of owners (principals). Using these views, Graham and Krugman go on to suggest four reasons that multinational enterprises might be growing: increasing integration of world markets, growing similarity of national markets, improved communications and control technology, and growing symmetry in international technological capabilities.

Even if economists were in complete agreement about the factors governing long-run growth of multinationals, there still would be a need to explain the surge of FDI in the 1980s. Graham and Krugman discuss three theories that might help explain the timing of FDI: valuation effects, tax changes, and trade barriers. They stress the first (the valuation story originally discussed by Froot and Stein 1991), in which internally generated funds are cheaper than those raised externally, so that fluctuations in internal funds can help explain fluctuations in FDI. The behavior of exchange rates and stock prices over the late 1980s seems to help explain the surge in Japanese outward and U.S. inward investment. Graham and Krugman also propose that agency problems similar to those that U.S. savings and loans experienced during this period led to a more aggressive corporate attitude toward risk and to heightened levels of FDI.

In her paper, Rachel McCulloch relates the changing role of the United States in world FDI to changes in the firm-specific competitive advantages required for successful global expansion. McCulloch reminds us that the eco-

nomics of comparative advantage is an unrefutable force for explaining country trade but that no similar force exists for explaining company trade. Firm-
specific advantages and how they determine scope and scale of firm activities
are still poorly understood.

McCulloch considers two economywide influences on FDI: exchange rates
and trade barriers. Exchange rate movements have a clear effect on relative
production costs; dollar depreciation, all else equal, makes producing traded
goods in the United States more profitable. However, low production costs do
not necessarily guarantee inward FDI; domestic firms may be the ones to grow
and exploit the enhanced opportunity. McCulloch argues that when exchange
rate fluctuations are large and unpredictable (as they were in the 1980s), multinational corporations (MNCs) may have an advantage over purely domestic
firms because of their flexibility in shifting marginal production and sales in
response to exchange rate changes. Import barriers ought also to have an
important trade-substituting effect on FDI. However, the empirical evidence
on the importance of trade barriers is much weaker than that for the exchange
rate. It may be that domestic firms are better suited to take advantage of actual
trade barriers through domestic investment.

McCulloch also argues that one can easily put too much emphasis on the
importance of location per se. Even if all production locations are perfect substitutes, a firm with a good idea will expand rapidly and hence is likely to
generate FDI. There are good reasons to think that FDI has an ambiguous
impact on both trade, domestic employment, and industry competitiveness.

McCulloch notes that FDI often occurs in markets which display imperfect
competition. As in the "new" trade literature, a government may find that it
can exploit these imperfections to the advantage of its domestic residents. It
can garner more of the world's taxable profits by encouraging the most profitable companies to locate domestically (especially those that can compete most
profitably with a domestic location). McCulloch asks whether the United
States will deviate from its former role of advocating limitless host country
FDI. Now that the United States is the world's foremost FDI host, there will
be pressures to change this policy.

Raymond Vernon explores the major changes in multinational corporations
over the last forty years and then uses that history as a platform for forecasting
future developments. Vernon first explores the reasons why U.S. firms early on
took the multinational framework to heart. He suggests several motivations.
The first—that MNCs were necessary for vertical integration—was an important factor before World War II for companies involved in extracting and
processing raw materials. With relatively few players in the business, markets
could not be counted on, and quantity or strategically induced rationing was a
concern. A second motivation Vernon discusses is that of "animal spirits," in
which presumably there is little economic gain (and perhaps some loss) for the
foreign investment behavior of U.S. firms. Third comes the more rational desire of these firms to defend their export markets against foreign firms. During

the late 1950s and the 1960s, foreign competitors gradually acquired the ability to compete effectively with U.S. leaders. These U.S. firms were then motivated to move abroad in order to better design their products for local markets and to avoid the protectionist pressures which can crop up when indigenous industries attempt to grow. Finally, firms moved abroad for purposes of risk management. Implicit collusion among competitors may be better facilitated if firms precommit to having similar sources of revenues and costs. Thus, once a single competitor moves abroad (regardless of the reasons), other firms have an incentive to follow.

Vernon also looks at the more recent period, in which European and Japanese firms have taken their place along with U.S. companies as innovators and leaders. These firms (Europeans first and now the Japanese) have experienced stages similar to those of U.S. firms. Vernon argues that much of their FDI can be interpreted as an attempt to prevent overseas markets from being competed away by local enterprises. Vernon also discusses the conflicts emerging in Europe as to whether local firms will retain their national character in the unified market. Japanese firms, he argues, are in an initial catch-up phase in the internationalization of their production. It is too early to tell whether differences in their practices (e.g., using Japanese managers to run foreign affiliates) will disappear as the affiliates age.

Vernon also speculates on the future of the MNC. He argues that past trends point toward continued growth in the importance of MNCs in world trade. He suggests that the influence of individual governments on MNCs is on the decline, as competition among governments and the substitutability of different locations of production grow.

Country Papers

Robert Lawrence's paper looks at FDI in Japan. He begins by noting that Japanese inbound FDI is an interesting topic because there is so little of it: the foreign-owned share of Japanese domestic production is approximately 1 percent of industrial assets, compared with an average of about 20 percent foreign controlled in other developed countries. Recently, net inflows of FDI into Japan have actually been negative. There is no sign that foreign acquisitions in the local market are picking up.

Most of Lawrence's chapter is devoted to examining the evidence for barriers to foreign acquisitions of Japanese firms. He argues that the low levels of inbound FDI point toward barriers to entry rather than toward low foreign demand.

Lawrence presents several kinds of evidence that supply rather than demand considerations have combined to keep FDI low. First, U.S. receipts from royalties and fees paid by unaffiliated foreigners worldwide come disproportionately from Japan. Because of high entry and market costs, foreigners choose to license in Japan rather than to invest directly. Second, in the presence of barriers to foreign entry, one would expect the percentage of majority foreign-owned FDI would be low and that an unusually large share of FDI would need to be devoted to wholesale trade. This implication seems to be borne out: the fraction of U.S. FDI in Japan that is majority owned by a U.S. parent (34 percent)is very low in comparison with comparable shares worldwide (76 percent). Also, the fraction of U.S. FDI in wholesale trade in Japan is unusually high compared to similar fractions worldwide.

These considerations suggest that distribution and entry into the Japanese market are more difficult than elsewhere and that, as a result, foreigners will have an unusually high demand to acquire (rather than build) enterprises in Japan. However, foreign acquisitions in Japan remain extremely low (in absolute terms and also relative to greenfield FDI activity). Cross-shareholding practices by Japanese firms and rules discriminating against foreign acquirers seem to explain this tendency. Evidence of liberalization is lacking: in recent years, Japanese firms have accelerated their acquisitions of both Japanese and non-Japanese firms, yet acquisitions of Japanese firms by foreigners have barely held constant. Lawrence finds that the low level of acquisitions relative to greenfield investment in Japan explains almost entirely the low absolute amount of total FDI into Japan. Finally, he finds that *keiretsu* affiliations in an industry have a dampening affect on FDI, even when controlling for both capital intensity and concentration. He concludes that many of these features of Japanese FDI support the conclusion that there remain substantial barriers to foreign entry and operation.

Robert Lipsey's paper studies the experience of the country that virtually defined FDI during most of the postwar period, the United States. Indeed, until the mid-1970s, the United States was responsible for more than half of the world's FDI outflows and owned more than half of the developed world's stock of direct investment. Only one other country accounted for more than 6 percent of the world's stock of FDI (the United Kingdom) with about 16 percent). On the inflow side, the United States absorbed on average only about 10 percent of inflows to developed countries through the mid-1960s. World FDI was pretty well characterized as the move of U.S. companies to produce abroad.

By the mid-1980s, of course, these figures had changed dramatically. U.S. outflows had fallen to about 15 percent of world FDI; at the same time, inflows into the United States accounted for 46 percent of world flows. By 1990, the FDI stock in the United States had already risen to a level about as large as the stock of U.S. FDI abroad. Lipsey argues that while these numbers overstate the relative size of the FDI stock in the United States (assets are carried at historical cost, which tends to understate the value of relatively older U.S. assets held abroad), they nonetheless provide a rough gauge for how rapidly foreign ownership in the United States has grown.

Lipsey shows that growth of foreign ownership has been particularly rapid in manufacturing, where the FDI stock has quadrupled over the past fifteen years and now accounts for over 10 percent of employment. Naturally this increase was led by the Japanese, who went from insignificant owners to the second-largest investor in the United States (after the British), accounting for 20 percent of the stock of U.S. FDI.

Lipsey points to another important change in inbound FDI: the means by which it is financed. Over half of the investment which took place in the 1950s and 1960s was financed through retained earnings. By the 1980s, this fraction had dropped to almost zero. It is well known that this increase was at least partly due to the increased viability of cross-border mergers and acquisitions. What is less well known is that the profitability of foreign affiliates in the United States declined dramatically in the 1980s, so that foreign investors had little to retain. These low returns may reflect increases in affiliates' financial leverage and/or poorer choices of investment targets.

Louis Wells focuses on an important recent trend in world FDI, done by companies he calls "mobile exporters." Typically these are companies from relatively high-income developing countries seeking low-cost installations to access third-country markets. The rate of growth of mobile-export FDI in some developing countries is quite astonishing. Wells takes Indonesia as his primary example. There the FDI approved during the 1987–90 period is 150 percent of *all* the FDI which occurred in that country from 1967 to 1987. The lion's share of this growth is associated with an increase in the role of export-oriented FDI from other developing countries. For instance, from 1977 to 1985, the share of FDI into Indonesia that came from developing countries was only 6 percent. During this period, Japanese investment dominated. By the first half of 1991, however, other East Asian developing countries *alone* accounted for 56 percent of projects approved for FDI (in manufacturing alone, the fraction rises to 65 percent). Wells points out that while the Japanese are widely thought of as dominating FDI in Southeast Asia, other developing countries in the region have in fact invested 3.5 times as much in Indonesia.

Wells identifies three major rounds of developing-country to developing-country FDI. The first round was also export oriented, driven by the desire to avoid import quotas in third-country markets (common industries included textiles and shoes). The second round consisted of trade-substituting FDI—developing-country companies came to Indonesia fearing that present or future trade barriers would block their access to Indonesia's domestic markets. The third round has come from companies seeking lower-cost export bases for their products. Firms from South Korea, Taiwan, Singapore, and Hong Kong have faced currency appreciations, wage increases, and labor shortages. They have chosen Indonesia and Thailand over other low-cost locations such as Africa or other local developing countries (such as Vietnam, China, and the Philippines). Ease of doing business, input access, tax considerations, and assurances of property rights seem to promote investment when the investor is searching for a low-cost location. Wells suggests that countries such as Mexico are increasingly suitable hosts; he cites political considerations as well as Mexico's strengthening access to U.S. markets.

Industry Studies

David Yoffie investigates FDI in the semiconductor industry. Semiconductors are perhaps the world's most highly tradable manufactured product. Yoffie distinguishes three "waves" of FDI in semiconductors. In the first wave, which took place in the late 1960s and early 1970s, firms (most U.S.-based) moved assembly and test functions (the relatively labor-intensive portion of production) to take advantage of low overseas wage costs. Also during this time, U.S. firms invested in foreign fabrication facilities in order to avoid existing and likely future trade restrictions. Thus, the first wave included both trade-complementing and trade-substituting FDI.

During the mid-1970s, a second wave of FDI began. The mode shifted from greenfield investment *by* U.S. firms to mergers and acquisitions *of* U.S. firms. The motivation for this change was the need for technology transfer to another generation of both U.S. and non-U.S. firms.These firms were more capable of expending the large amounts of money needed to innovate in the face of the industry's rising capital intensity and scale economies. Indeed, as the labor share in costs plummeted, a motivation behind the first wave of FDI was undermined.

The third and most recent wave of FDI in semiconductors became prevalent around the time that the boom in U.S. mergers and acquisitions subsided. (The watershed event was the political intervention that blocked the purchase of Fairchild Semiconductor by Fujitsu.) This wave is a continuation of the first—active greenfield investment in fabrication facilities—but the investment is now being undertaken in Europe and the United States by firms from all three major country blocks (the United States, Europe, and Japan). Investment in Japan by non-Japanese companies is noticeably absent, reinforcing the trend which emerges in the macrodata. The third wave is distinguished from the first in that labor costs have become less important than other factors (tax breaks, local infrastructure, etc.).

In describing these waves, Yoffie notes three features which appear puzzling. The first is that history in location choice seems to matter, especially in the third wave. The increased capital intensity of all phases of production has made labor costs essentially irrelevant, yet new, trade-enhacing investment inflows continue in countries with low labor costs. This pattern suggests that accumulated knowledge or other specific factors at the plant or affiliate level are important economically. Second, new greenfield investments have not followed the Silicon Valley model, in which firms choose to invest near one another. Any agglomeration effects or externalities in the production and testing processes must therefore be difficult to realize across firms. Third, both greenfield and investment and acquisition activity in Japan remain limited, even though formal restrictions have been removed. Of the FDI that does take place, most comes in the form of joint ventures with Japanese partners.

Investigations of Mergers and Acquisitions

Paul Healy and Krishna Palepu examine international mergers and acquisitions among eleven major industrialized countries for the period 1985 to 1990. These cross-border M&A deals account for fully 30 percent of all cross-border equity purchases (direct plus portfolio investment). The worldwide patterns are similar to those seen in balance-of-payments measures of FDI (of which cross-border M&A is but one component): the United States now accounts for a large portion of world inflows, with over 60 percent on average during the period; Japan's foreign acquisitions account for 14 percent of such flows over the period, with a large increase in the final few years; foreign acquisitions done in Japan are essentially zero over the period; the United Kingdom is the most active acquirer nation (controlling 26 percent of world M&A expenditures) and also one of the most aggressive; and Spain appears to have witnessed rapid growth in inflows (as has Europe overall) during the sample period.

Healy and Palepu look at two possible determinants of the level of cross-border M&A: the regulation of intercorporate investments, and the typical ownership structure of corporations. The authors find that regulations of intercorporate investment (particularly those regulations which discriminate against foreigners) reduce cross-border flows. For example, Australia, France, Sweden, and Japan (Japan requires government notification and approval) all have relatively low levels of international M&A and restrictions on foreign investment.

The authors also examine some possible determinants of the recent changes in cross-border acquisitions. These changes do not appear to be explained well by regulation and ownership structure, which evolve only slowly over time. Healy and Palepu find little explanatory power in lagged real exchange rate changes, changes in economic growth in the target and acquirer countries, and changes in the level of domestic M&A activity in the target country. Only the latter of these factors is significant. The importance of changes in domestic M&A for explaining changes in international M&A suggests that some underlying causes—changes in the technology of doing acquisitions (such as in the United States in the late 1980s) or changes in the strategic importance of large scale operations in a country (such as Spain at the end of the 1980s)—may be driving both.

Deborah Swenson explores foreign-led mergers and acquisitions which took place in the United States between 1974 and 1990. She finds that foreign M&A activity in the United States has risen even faster than inward FDI and that it has become the most common form of FDI in the United States. Japan is the country which seems to do the least amount of acquisition (versus greenfield) FDI, although recently its acquisition share has risen dramatically. Swenson reports evidence that only a small fraction of foreign acquisitions can be explained by domestic M&A activity. Thus, domestic acquisitions, which

Healy and Palepu find useful for understanding cross-border M&A in the cross section, are not particularly useful for understanding foreign M&A over time.

Swenson also investigates a number of specific features of foreign-led M&A in the United States. She finds that, in acquiring U.S. companies, a foreigner tends to pay a premium of about 10 percent over what is typically paid when another U.S. company is the acquirer. This price differential remains when one controls for variables that have been found to influence the premium paid in domestic acquisitions (i.e., the method of payment, the degree of industry concentration, and the presence of government or target-management resistance).

The premium paid by foreigners has other interesting features. For example, foreigners tend to purchase firms with higher growth potential (as measured by price-earnings ratios) than domestics. When mounting an acquisition, foreigners are considerably less likely to face competition from other bidding firms or challenges from government agencies than are domestics. In addition, it appears that the premiums paid on foreign acquisitions are highly sensitive to the exchange rate (premiums paid by domestic acquirers are not exchange rate sensitive) and to foreign stock prices. This may be evidence to support theories of FDI that rely on wealth effects generated by imperfections in capital markets.

References

Caves, Richard E. 1982. *Multinational enterprise and economic analysis.* Cambridge: Cambridge University Press.

Froot, Kenneth A., and Jeremy Stein. 1991. Exchange rates and foreign direct investment: An imperfect capital markets approach. *Quarterly Journal of Economics* 106 (November): 1191–217.

Vernon, Raymond. 1966. International investment and international trade in the product cycle. *Quarterly Journal of Economics* 80 (May): 190–207.

1   The Surge in Foreign Direct Investment in the 1980s

Edward M. Graham and Paul R. Krugman

From the early 1970s until the mid-80s, most measures suggested that the role of multinationals in the world economy had largely stabilized. In particular, U.S. firms in Europe were no longer growing much faster than the European economy as a whole, while many Third World countries, finding bank lending available as an alternative source of finance, tightened restrictions on investment by multinationals. Except for a gradually rising share of foreign ownership in the U.S. economy, there was little indication of a broad trend toward further globalization of firms' activities. Beginning around 1985–86, however, firms began a new wave of foreign direct investment (FDI)—that is, foreign investment aimed not simply at securing future income but also at establishing control.

The United Nations Center on Transnational Corporations (UNCTC), using International Monetary Fund data, has estimated that during the five years 1985–89, world FDI flows totaled over $630 billion on a balance-of-payments basis. FDI on a balance-of-payments basis is a measure of changes in owners' equity in business organizations or real assets that these owners control. The $630 billion figure cited above thus is far short of the total value of assets that came under foreign control as a result of FDI. If the ratio of owners' equity to total asset value of all FDI worldwide is equal to this ratio for FDI in the United States, then upwards of $3,580 billion of business assets came under foreign control during the 1980s' FDI boom. During the period 1983–89, world FDI flows (expressed in U.S. dollars at current prices) grew at annual compound growth rates of 28.9 percent; world income grew at about one-fourth this rate (7.8 percent), and world trade at less than one-third (9.4 percent) (U.N. Center on Transnational Corporations 1991).

The surge in FDI after 1985 was largely a surge in investment flows among industrialized nations. The UNCTC data show that the G5 nations (France, West Germany, Japan, the United Kingdom, and the United States) were the

13

home (source) nations of almost 70 percent of FDI flows during this time, while nations classified by the United Nations as "developed market economies" were home to most of the remaining FDI flows. The G5 nations were also host (recipient) nations to 57 percent of these flows, and developed market nations in total were host to 81 percent. The share of FDI flows going to developing nations thus was only about 19 percent, a low share by the standards of earlier decades. Of this share, an overwhelming majority went to a small group of nations, notably Mexico, Brazil, and the Asian newly industrializing countries (NICs). (See table 1.1).

Why is the late-80s surge in direct investment important? Most immediately, FDI came to play a key role in financing international current account imbalances: in 1989, nearly half of the U.S. current account deficit was financed by inflows of direct investment rather than by more conventional short-term and portfolio investment, whereas Japan used more than two-thirds of its current account surplus for direct investment. In effect, the U.S. raised the money to pay for its imports by selling foreigners companies instead of bonds. Japan similarly used much of the revenue from its exports to acquire overseas subsidiaries instead of passive assets.

Beyond its immediate financial role, foreign direct investment implies a rising share of foreign ownership in those economies that have been its main recipients. To the extent that foreign-owned firms behave differently from those with domestic owners, this may have important long-term economic implications. Equally important, concern over how foreign firms *might* behave has inevitably become an important political issue.

Finally, the surge in direct investment is an indicator of other changes now taking place in the world economy. To the extent that we can understand this investment, it may provide valuable clues to other economic trends as well.

This paper provides some background information on and a conceptual framework for the growth of direct investment. The intention is to stimulate discussion that can be used to guide subsequent study.

The paper is in four parts. The first part reviews briefly some evidence on the growth of direct investment in the 1980s. The second part then lays out a conceptual framework for thinking about the causes and possible consequences of direct investment. The third part identifies a series of central questions regarding FDI. Finally, the last section briefly sketches some possible directions for future study.

1.1   Trends in Direct Investment

1.1.1   Measurement Issues

In principle, firms could become multinational or increase their operations abroad without any international movement of capital per se. For example, a British firm could acquire a U.S. firm with funds borrowed in the United

Table 1.1   **Stocks and Flows of FDI Inward and Outward, by Region ($ billions)**

Region	Outward Stock		Rate of Growth	Inward Stock		Rate of Growth
	1980	1988		1980	1988	
United States	$ 220	$ 345	5.6%	$ 83	$ 329	17.2%
European Community (EC)	203	492	11.1	188	399	9.4
EC (excluding intra-EC)	153	332	9.7	143	239	6.4
Intra-EC	50	160	14.5	45	160	15.9
Japan	20	111	21.4	3	10	15.0
Rest of world	81	86	0.7	235	481	9.0
World total (including intra-EC)	524	1,034	8.5	509	1,219	10.9

Sources: Unpublished estimates by the United Nations Center on Transnational Corporations (UNCTC); UNCTC (1991), *World Investment Directory* (New York: United Nations); UNCTC (1991), *World Investment Report 1991* (New York: United Nations). The estimates are derived from national government sources, which use somewhat differing accounting standards. For example, Japan and several European nations do not count retained earnings by affiliates of foreign firms as FDI, whereas most other nations do. Hence, reported total inward flows do not equal reported total outward flows.

States; a Japanese firm could acquire a U.S. firm via an exchange of stock with an already existing subsidiary. In either case, there would be an increase in the share of the U.S. economy controlled by foreign firms, but no inflow of capital. Ideally, therefore, the analyst should measure the growth of multinational enterprise by looking directly at the share of each economy controlled by foreign firms rather than by looking at capital movements. Trends in globalization could then be measured from these shares.

Unfortunately, numbers on the share of economies controlled by foreign firms are spotty and lag well behind actual events. Efforts have been made to create such numbers: table 1.2 contains illustrative figures on the share of G5 economies that foreign firms control by a variety of measures. We will discuss some of the implications of these numbers below. For now, however, the important point to note is that direct information on control is both too difficult to calculate and too tardy to be useful in tracking rapid changes. In particular, the most recent available data on foreign control tend to lag from three to five years behind actual events; because other measures show a sudden increase in FDI since about 1985, this is a fatal defect.

As a result, it is necessary to rely on other measures to track recent developments. The most commonly used measure is flows of foreign direct investment, as appear in national balance-of-payments accounts.

The balance-of-payments accounts define direct investment as that part of capital flows that represents a direct financial flow from a parent company to an overseas firm that it controls. Accounting standards vary from country to country, resulting in some problems of consistency when national figures are aggregated. By International Monetary Fund (IMF) standards, however, FDI

Table 1.2   Role of Foreign-Owned Firms in G5 Economies, 1977 and 1986

	Percentage Share Held by Foreign-Owned Firms	
G-5 Country	1976	1986
United States		
Sales	5%	10%
Manufacturing employment	3	7
Assets	3	9
Japan		
Sales	2	1
Manufacturing employment	2	1
Assets	2	1
West Germany		
Sales	24	27
Manufacturing employment	18	21
Assets	N.A.	N.A.
France		
Sales	17	18
Manufacturing employment	14	13
Assets	17	17
United Kingdom		
Sales	22	20
Manufacturing employment	15	14
Assets	N.A.	14

Source: Dee Anne Julius and Stephen Thomsen (1988), Foreign-owned firms, trade, and economic integration, Tokyo Club Papers 2 (1):151–74.

Note: N.A. = not available.

consists of the sum of (1) new equity purchased or acquired by parent companies in overseas firms they are considered to control (including establishment of new subsidiaries), (2) reinvestment of earnings by controlled firms, and (3) intracompany loans from parent companies to controlled firms. The often reported *stock* of direct investment is simply not the cumulation of these flows over time.

The balance-of-payments measure of direct investment contains a number of well-known defects:

1. *Control*: The definition of a controlled firm is ambiguous. Majority control is clearly too strict a criterion, since a smaller stake may be sufficient to give effective operating control. In U.S. data, 10 percent ownership of equity by a single foreign owner is deemed to make a U.S. firm foreign; this leads to a few obvious misclassifications in the opposite direction, of which the best known is DuPont, considered foreign because of Seagram's 23 percent stake.

2. *Debt*: Only intracompany debt is counted as direct investment. Thus, if British Petroleum's U.S. subsidiary borrows directly from its U.K. parent, this

is considered a direct investment; borrowing directly on the Eurodollar market, however, is not, even if the debt is guaranteed by the parent firm. More generally, investment financed by anything other than intracompany debt or equity does not count as direct investment even if it effectively increases the share of the economy controlled by foreign firms. The assets of foreign-controlled firms in every country, even measured at book value, are thus much larger than the balance-of-payments–based measures of the stock of direct investment.

3. *Book versus market value*: While retained earnings are counted as part of direct investment, capital gains (including pure inflation) are not. In effect, direct investment is counted as historical cost. This leads to an understatement that varies substantially depending on the age of the investments; U.S. direct investment abroad is widely viewed as much more understated than foreign investment in the United States simply because it is of older vintage.[1]

Because of these defects, direct investment numbers from the balance of payments are unreliable guides to either the actual extent of foreign control in any economy or the value of a country's assets abroad. Conversely, the balance-of-payments numbers have two great advantages: they are available on a reasonably comparable basis for many countries, and they usually become available within a few quarters of actual events.

The best compromise seems to be to use, where available, direct evidence on the role of foreign-controlled firms to provide a baseline, then to use balance-of-payments data as an indicator of recent developments. That is the approach followed below.

1.1.2 Trends in Direct Investment

As already noted, table 1.2 contains comparisons of share measures of foreign ownership for 1977 and 1986. Several points should be noted about these numbers. First, the numbers lag well behind events. The most recent numbers are for 1986. Since, as stated above, other evidence points to a surge in direct investment that began in 1985–86, this evidence completely misses the developments that are at the center of this paper's concern. We therefore need to use other data to infer what must have been happening more recently. Second, the numbers show no upward trend in the foreign share of either the European or the Japanese economies. The only notable change is a rise in the foreign-controlled share of the U.S. economy. The suggested conclusion is that "globalization" did not show any general upward trend before the late 1980s. We will show below that the U.S. rise may be attributed largely to a brief surge in the period 1978–81, which can be viewed as a forerunner to the later, post-1985 surge. Third, Japan has remarkably little foreign penetration. This observation will be confirmed from other data later on.

---

1. The U.S. Department of Commerce has recently begun to publish estimates of the stocks of U.S. inward and outward investment at current market value and current replacement cost, as well as at historical value.

Aside from the rise in foreign ownership in the United States, the data in table 1.2 provide little indication of the recent surge in foreign direct investment. Table 1.3 shows why. It provides data on flows of foreign direct investment from and to developed countries, as measured by the balance of payments. It shows that these flows were actually quite low in 1982–84; only after 1985 did the surge take place.

An even clearer picture emerges if we look at the balance-of-payments numbers in three crucial directions (table 1.4): first, the flow of direct investment into the United States; second, the flow out of Japan; third, the flow into Spain, the largest recipient of North-South direct investment within Europe. We see a brief surge in investment into the United States in 1978–81; then, a second, larger wave of investment into the United States, out of Japan, and (smaller in dollar terms) into Spain began.

Who are the foreign direct investors, and where are they investing? Table 1.5 presents a crude tabulation of the cumulative outward and inward direct investment flows from 1981 through 1988, both in dollar terms and as a share of 1988 gross national product (GNP), for a number of countries. These numbers yield five observations:

1. In dollar terms, foreign direct investment flows are dominated on both the outward and the inward side by transactions among the large, advanced nations. That is, the rise in direct investment has been primarily a North-North issue between countries at similar levels of development, rather than a North-South issue.

2. The United States has emerged as the largest destination for direct investment. This is not simply a matter of relative size; the United States has been a

Table 1.3   **FDI Flows of Developed Countries, 1981–1990 ($ billions)**

	Outward	Inward
1981	$ 46	$ 32
1982	18	22
1983	23	23
1984	31	31
1985	50	27
1986	86	64
1987	135	108
1988	161	129
1989	201	165
1990	217	152
1981–85	168	134
1986–90	800	618

Sources: 1981–85 data: Organization for Economic Cooperation and Development (OECD) unpublished etimates: 1986–90 data: United Nations Center on Transnational Corporations (1992), *World Investment Report 1992* (New York: United Nations), 12.

Table 1.4   **Key FDI Flows, 1975–1988 ($ billions)**

	Into United States	Into Spain	Out of Japan
1975	$ 2.6	$ 1.8	$ 0.7
1976	4.3	2.0	0.5
1977	3.7	1.6	0.6
1978	7.9	2.4	1.2
1979	11.9	2.9	1.4
1980	16.9	2.4	1.5
1981	25.2	1.7	4.9
1982	13.8	1.8	4.5
1983	12.0	1.6	3.6
1984	25.4	1.8	6.0
1985	19.0	1.9	6.5
1986	34.1	3.4	14.5
1987	42.0	4.5	19.5
1988	42.2	N.A.	34.2

Source: Unpublished estimates by the Organization for Economic Cooperation and Development.
Note: N.A. = not available.

Table 1.5   **Direct Investment by Country, 1981–1988**

	Outward		Inward	
	$ Billion	% of GNP	$ Billion	% of GNP
Canada	$ 29.4	6.2%	$ 3.7	0.7%
France	40.6	4.3	24.1	2.5
West Germany	47.7	3.9	8.7	0.7
Greece	0+	0+	3.5	2.5
Italy	18.8	2.3	16.1	1.9
Japan	93.7	3.3	2.6	0.1
Portugal	0+	0+	1.5	4.8
Spain	2.7	0.7	16.9	5.0
United Kingdom	120.2	14.7	53.9	6.6
United States	121.2	2.7	213.7	4.8

Source: Unpublished estimates by Organization for Economic Cooperation and Development.

substantial *net* importer of direct capital, and it ranks high even when inflows are measured as a share of GNP.

3. Japan has become a major direct investor abroad (in 1988, its direct investment exceeded that of the United Kingdom). While gross direct investment flows are still a somewhat smaller share of GNP than are those of European nations, these numbers represent a dramatic shift from Japan's earlier strong preference for short-term and portfolio investment. At the same time, Japan

remains a strikingly small host nation to inward direct investment. During the 1980s, the huge Japanese economy was the recipient of less inward investment than the tiny economy of Greece!

4. The United Kingdom apparently presents a striking picture of globalization through two-way investment flows. The country was simultaneously the largest outward direct investor and the second-largest destination; as a share of GNP, the United Kingdom's FDI ranks at the top in both categories.

5. Finally, direct investment flows to the nations of southern Europe, while minor from a global point of view, have been very significant relative to the size of those economies.

1.1.3. Direction and Composition of Direct Investment

In any attempt to interpret the aggregate trends just described, it will be important to have some sense of where the money is going. A brief look at some U.S. and Japanese data helps provide guidance.

Perhaps the most important point to make is that one should be careful about stereotyping the pattern of direct investment. Much casual discussion seems to view Japanese direct investment in the U.S. auto industry as the norm—that is, foreign direct investment is seen largely as a matter of Japanese firms with superior production skills building new manufacturing plants abroad. While this does happen, it is not the typical case. Most recent direct investment in the United States is not from Japan; most takes the form of acquisition of existing firms, not construction of new plants; and most of it is not in manufacturing.

Table 1.6 compares the sources of recent U.S. direct capital inflows and the destinations of recent Japanese outflows. While the flows from Japan to the United States are indeed large, the United States has also been a major host to FDI from Europe and Canada. At the same time, Japan has sharply increased its investment in Europe as well as in the United States.[2]

Information on the form of direct investment cannot be presented this simply. However, U.S. data clearly shows that greenfield plants are a quite minor part of the story. Acquisitions such as Bridgestone-Firestone or Sony-Columbia have been more prevalent than Honda-style plant openings.

Finally, direct investment is not exclusively or even primarily a manufacturing issue. For example, while manufacturing accounts for a significant share of the total inward investment into the United States and outward FDI from Japan, it is rivaled by banking and real estate. U.S. data (not shown here) reveals that while the share of the United States manufacturing sector controlled by foreign firms exceeds that for the economy as a whole, the share of banking controlled by foreign firms is much larger.

---

2. Although we do not show this, Europe has also become the host to significant new flows of FDI from the United States, and intra-European FDI flows have also been substantial.

Table 1.6   **Percentage Distribution of FDI, 1988**

Japan's Outflow		U.S. Inflow	
North America	47.5%	Canada	5.9%
Europe	19.4	Europe	53.2
United Kingdom	8.4	United Kingdom	39.0
East Asian NICs	6.9	Japan	31.9

Sources: For Japan's outflow: Ministry for International Trade and Industry. For the United States' inflow: U.S. Department of Commerce, *Survey of Current Business,* various issues.

1.1.4   Keys to Thinking about Trends

At the risk of oversimplifying, we would suggest four key facts about foreign direct investment that should guide our thinking:

1. The growth of direct investment does not look like a steady trend; instead, extended periods of slow growth are punctuated by occasional surges. Any explanation of FDI growth must explain why.

2. Direct investment flows have not simply paralleled international capital flows, either in timing or in direction. The post-1985 surge in direct investment took place at a time of stabilizing or narrowing of imbalances in current accounts; it was not simply a matter of flows from surplus to deficit countries.

3. Direct investment has mostly taken the form of acquisitions rather than of construction of new facilities.

4. Manufacturing is only a fraction, albeit a large one, of the direct investment story. The service sector is of comparable importance. Indeed, foreign-owned firms play a larger role in U.S. banking than in manufacturing.

1.2   Conceptual Issues

1.21   FDI and the Economic Theory of the Firm

Foreign direct investment is, in essence, the creation or expansion of firms that operate across national boundaries. In principle, then, the first part of economic theory that should be consulted in thinking about FDI is not the theory of international trade and capital movements but rather the theory of the firm per se. That is, the key question ought to be, why does it sometimes make sense for two factories to be under common ownership? (And why is it sometimes *not* a good idea?) If we have a clear answer to this question, it is not much of a jump to extend the answer to the case in which the two factories happen to be in different countries.

Unfortunately and somewhat surprisingly, economists have relatively little to say about why the economy is organized into firms and why the boundaries between firms are drawn where they are. For example, economists have not been very successful at explaining why some industries are strongly vertically integrated while others are not. Why did General Motors absorb Fisher Body, while IBM has not tried to do the same for Microsoft? It turns out that this sort of question is both a deep issue and a controversial one and that existing economic analysis provides, at best, suggestive guidance.

This is too bad, because ultimately the assessment of both the prospects for and the effects of FDI depends on the economics of industrial organization. For example, Ford has reached an arrangement with Mazda (in which it owns a large stake) under which Mazda has largely taken over the design function for Ford's small cars. Will this joint dependence eventually equire the merger of the two firms? If so, how will the behavior of the merged firm differ from that of the two firms from which it is created? These questic 's are on one side, obviously similar to issues involved in purely domestic mergers and acquisitions and, on the other, clearly unanswerable simply by looking at balance-of-payments questions.

Because the economics of the firm are so crucial to the whole issue of foreign direct investment, it is necessary to begin a conceptual discussion with a brief review of existing theory—even though this theory tends to be vague and to lack operational content. Only then can the discussion turn specifically to multinational firms and FDI.

There are two main strands in the economic theory of the firm. On one side is a set of propositions surrounding the question of the appropriate boundaries of the firm. On the other is consideration of where and how firms may expand.

Optimal Boundaries of the Firm

Market transactions have costs: the seller and buyer may have to spend time bargaining, one or the other may cheat, they may be reluctant to reveal information that would help the other, and so on. Thus, there is always some incentive to remove dealings from the marketplace and conduct them within a hierarchical organization. On the other hand, hierarchies have their own problems: rigidity and the dilution of incentives for individuals.

The standard economist's theory of the firm, originally proposed by Coase (1937) and elaborated by such modern theorists as Williamson (1975) and Hart (1989), is that firm boundaries are drawn in ways that achieve the best possible tradeoff between transaction and rigidity costs.[3] Thus, by this reasoning, General Motors acquired Fisher Body because it had determined that the difficulties of doing business with an independent supplier were greater than the erosion of incentives and flexibility that would occur when Fisher was absorbed by a much larger organization; IBM has not tried to acquire Microsoft because it judges that the reverse would be the case.

When are transaction costs high enough to justify removing transactions from the market? Since transaction costs are elusive, this is a difficult question

3. Buckley and Casson (1976) pioneered the application of Coasian logic to multinational firms.

to answer. One consideration that has received emphasis, however, is that transaction costs are likely to be higher if firms must make investments that are specific to each other. Suppose that Fisher must install expensive machinery suitable only for GM cars and that GM must design cars that can only be built if Fisher delivers the agreed-on components. Then, any dispute or failure of communication between the parties will be very costly. Suppose, on the other hand, that a supplier firm's investments can be used to service any of a number of customers and that each customer can turn at any point to several suppliers. Then the costs of dispute will be low, and it will make sense to avoid creating a large, bureaucratic firm.

This logic suggests that optimal firms should group closely related activities that are strongly dependent on one another and for which effective competition does not take place at any given moment. Grain merchants do not acquire control of wheat farms; because a merchant and a farmer can always turn to other partners in the event of a dispute, the transaction costs are low. Conglomerates consisting of more or less unrelated activities do not make sense, because there are no transaction costs to save. But auto manufacturers own their stamping plants.

A clear dichotomy does not necessarily exist between market activities among firms and hierarchical organization within firms. Long-term contracts and other relationships between firms with different owners may bear little relationship to freewheeling auction markets, while marketlike incentive and control schemes exist within many firms. One economic view holds that a firm is simply a particular kind of "nexus of contracts" (see Jensen and Meckling 1976) that has proved so useful that it has become a standard form. The point of this view is that other kinds of long-term business relationships may be as durable and significant as the particular structure of firms visible at a given time. This may be an important issue in considering the impact of foreign direct investment, particularly by Japanese firms.

Finally, there is not necessarily a one-way link between technological progress and the optimal size of firms. Improvements in telecommunications and computing, to take the most obvious example, cut both ways: they make it possible for large organizations to be more flexible, reducing the disincentive to extend firm boundaries; but they also reduce transaction costs and increase the flexibility of small firms, making market arrangements more effective as well. It is an entirely open question whether firms in the year 2020 will be larger or smaller than they are today.

The Growth of Firms

While most economic analysis of firms has focused on their optimal size and activities, managers may simply be trying to make the firms they run grow. They can, of course, decide that growth is not profitable and return earnings to stockholders; or they can decide that rapid growth will be profitable even if it must be financed by large debt issues. There is overwhelming evidence, however, that corporate management is ordinarily reluctant both to part with retained earnings and to borrow; that is, they view internally generated cash flows as cheaper than funds raised on the market.

This suggests a perspective on the firm that is somewhat different from the economic analysis described above. Firm boundaries may be pushed out not so much because of efficiency gains but because the money is available.[4]

In the 1960s, the preference of firms for investment out of internally generated funds was often used as a justification for the creation of conglomerates of seemingly unrelated activities. By combining a business that yielded high earnings but offered few investment opportunities (a "cash cow") with one that presented opportunities but low earnings (a "star"), conglomerate builders hoped to create gains. This strategy is now out of fashion: the problems with combining unrelated businesses are now apparent, and firms are enjoined to "stick to their knitting." International expansion, however, offers firms a possible way to stick to the businesses they know while opening up new investment opportunities.

Emphasizing the role of cash in the determination of firm growth is also important in trying to explain the timing of changes in firm strategies. As we will argue below, it is difficult to make sense of the suddenness of the surge in FDI without appealing to some influence from the wealth of firms.

1.2.2 Long-Run Trends in Multinational Enterprise

Economists generally believe that there is a long-term trend toward an increasing role of multinational firms in the world economy. From the early 1970s to the mid-1980s, as seen above, there was an apparent pause in that trend—if it exists. But it is worth asking what factors might underlie a growth in cross-country ownership of firms over time.

At varying levels of generality, we might suggest four reasons for long-term growth in multinational enterprise: increasing integration of world markets, growing similarity of national markets, improved communication and control technology, and growing symmetry in the international generation of technology.

Growing Integration

Both the logic of the economic theory of the firm and experience suggest a close connection between the long-term growth of international trade and that of international direct investment. On logical grounds, if a firm is essentially a device for economizing on transactions costs, then multinational firms will normally be created to facilitate international transactions. In practice, the growth of multinational firms since World War II has accompanied a general growth in trade.

Perhaps more interestingly, the rise and decline of FDI in the pre-World War

---

4. Penrose (1956) emphasized the role of growth in fostering the international spread of firms.

II era paralleled the rise and decline of international trade. It is not generally realized that the trend of international trade over time has not been uniformly upward. The world economy was already highly integrated by 1914; the United Kingdom actually had a larger share of trade in national income at that time than it does today. During the interwar period, however, protectionism led to a general decline in international trade as a share of world income. Estimates by economists such as Arthur Lewis (1978) indicate that the growth of international trade from the 1940s until about 1970 simply represented a recovery to 1914 levels as a share of income and that only since then has trade risen to new heights.

The interesting point then becomes that much the same is true of foreign direct investment. Multinational enterprise played a surprisingly large role in the pre-World War I world. Many pioneering manufacturing firms quickly went multinational. In its early years, for example, Singer produced sewing machines from one plant in New Jersey and one in Scotland. At the same time that Standard Oil was integrating crude production, refining, and distribution within the United States, it was also establishing control over distribution systems and oil fields abroad. When economic nationalism fragmented the world economy in the interwar years, the importance of foreign direct investment declined. The book value of the stock of U.S. direct investment abroad was 7.3 percent of GNP in 1914. It was only 3.4 percent in 1946 and had recovered only to 6.9 percent by 1970 (see Wilkins 1970, 1989).

Since both theory and experience suggest that growth in trade should lead to growth in the role of multinationals, we would expect the continuing rise in integration of the world economy since 1970 eventually to be reflected in more multinational enterprise. In the United States, in particular, the share of imports in GNP doubled from 1970 to 1989, while the share of exports increased almost as much. One would expect this to be matched, other things equal, both by greater U.S. direct investment abroad and by greater foreign direct investment in the United States.

Again, the growth of multinational firms does not necessarily have anything to do with overall movements of capital. Consider the following example. Suppose that there is some industry (not necessarily manufacturing) that in 1975 contained five U.S. and five European firms. Further suppose that, owing either to new technological developments or to deregulation, this industry now becomes truly global, with firms able to operate and compete in all markets. This more competitive world market may be big enough to accommodate more firms than could either separate market alone, but it will probably not allow for the continued existence of ten firms; more likely it will only have room for, say, seven. Integration of the market, then, will necessarily be accompanied by a process of consolidation through mergers and acquisitions. These mergers and acquisitions will create multinational firms, and some of the associated transactions will be recorded as foreign direct investment for balance-of-payments purposes. But what is really happening is corporate restructuring, not international capital movement.

Growing Homogeneity of Markets

One factor that on casual observation seems to be a reason for growing globalization of companies is a convergence in demand patterns and other economic conditions among advanced nations. Even in 1970, the differences in wage rates, living standards, and culture among advanced nations were large enough so that a good deal of natural segmentation of markets occurred for both producer and consumer goods. For example, Europeans demanded much smaller cars and appliances, European factories slower but more flexible capital goods, than their U.S. counterparts. With the convergence since then, economies of scope from multinational operation are greater: Ford can design and market (or arrange with Mazda to develop) a world car, one sold in essentially the same form in a variety of markets. Like the increase in integration generally, convergence creates an incentive for cross-border acquisitions and mergers that reduce the number of firms in the world as a whole.

Communication Technology

This is a double-edged issue. Clearly it is easier in 1992 for a firm to coordinate the activities of a manufacturing subsidiary on another continent than it was in 1970. It is also easier, however, for the firm to coordinate activities with another firm ten thousand miles away. It is possible though not certain that technological effects have, on balance, fostered multinational operation.

Symmetry of Technology

Until the mid-1970s, the United States was in a very asymmetric position with regard to multinational enterprise: while the country had extensive investment abroad, foreign direct investment in the United States was limited. The main reason for this was probably the country's leading position in technology. Multinational firms are disproportionately concentrated in sectors with large R&D budgets and large numbers of technical personnel, presumably because transactions costs of selling and licensing technology are particularly high. It was therefore natural that the country that generated most of the world's new technology should also be the country in which most multinationals were based.

Whatever the global trend of FDI, this observation suggests that there should have been a trend toward growing foreign ownership of U.S. firms as the dominance of U.S. technology faded from 1970 to 1990. That this trend was not more apparent before 1985 should perhaps be surprising.

For some or all of these reasons—and certainly because of the growth of world integration on other dimensions—a long-term trend toward greater cross-country ownership of firms is not a surprise. What needs explaining is why, instead of a steady trend, we have seen pauses alternating with surges, especially the great surge after 1985.

1.2.3 Surges in FDI

While there may have been a long-run trend toward increasing FDI flows, the most apparent feature of the data is the existence of two huge surges in investment, one from 1978 through 1981 and the second since 1986. Whatever the long-run factors underlying the growth of FDI, any explanation of recent events must cope with this apparent tendency toward sudden surges.

Three main explanations have been proposed for these surges in FDI: fluctuations in relative cost of capital, associated in particular with exchange rate fluctuations; changes in taxation; and actual or prospective changes in tax policy.

Valuation Explanations

World financial markets have become increasingly integrated since the 1970s. In two major ways, however, this integration has fallen short of completion. First, for reasons still unclear, *equity* markets are not all that closely tied together; international diversification of stock portfolios remains limited. Second, firms continue to regard internally generated money as cheaper than external borrowing (which also remains true in domestic markets). As a result, the valuation of a given asset can differ substantially for firms based in different countries. Above, we argued that, to some extent, the growth of firms is driven not by considerations of optimal organization but by the efforts of managers to find a use for available funds. Systematic differences in valuation between countries can therefore play a role in determining the pace of foreign direct investment.

How does this help make sense of surges in FDI? Because particular shocks that differentially affect the prices that firms based in different countries are willing to pay for assets, or that affect the ability of firms in one country to buy assets abroad out of available cash, can lead to surges in FDI even if there is no deeper reason for a further extension of multinational enterprise. We look for such shocks.

The U.S. experience suggests one obvious candidate shock: the exchange rate. Both the 1978–81 and the post-1986 surges of direct investment into the United States coincided with periods of dollar weakness. While a weak dollar may make U.S. assets attractive, it should do so for both foreign and domestic firms. Thus, in principle, it need not encourage foreign direct investment. If firms are cash constrained, however, a fall in the dollar means that yen and pounds go further in buying U.S. assets; the fall thus encourages a wave of inward investment. Froot and Stein (1991) provide both a simple theoretical model that justifies a role for the exchange rate and some rough empirical work that confirms a strong correlation between dollar fluctuations and FDI into the United States. The surge in Japanese direct investment abroad since 1986 also corresponds to a record high for the yen.

Other factors may also affect direct investment via valuation effects. The high Japanese stock market pre-1990 may have made it easier for Japanese firms to invest abroad. Also, international differences in savings rates, which are generally understood to drive overall capital flows, may have some influence on direct investment via the cost of capital. There is a crude correlation between current accounts and FDI: the United States became the world's largest destination for FDI in the same decade (though not at the same time) that it became the largest-deficit nation; after a lag, Japan's emergent current surplus was followed by large FDI. On the other hand, the peculiar position of the United Kingdom and the general presence of large two-way flows in Western Europe argue against a general emphasis on savings rates and the overall cost of capital.

Tax Changes

Scholes and Wolfson (1990) have pointed out that shifts in U.S. tax laws during the 1980s first acted to discourage foreign ownership, then removed this bias. The argument runs as follows: The accelerated depreciation introduced in 1981 was generally worth more to a U.S. based firm than to a U.S. subsidiary of a foreign firm, because most foreign governments tax repatriated income of firms, with a credit for taxes paid to foreign governments. A tax break from accelerated depreciation, which is a pure benefit to a domestically owned firm, is partially offset by the reduced future tax credit for a foreign-owned firm. So accelerated depreciation, other things being equal, discouraged foreign ownership. U.S. tax reform in 1986 removed this bias. Scholes and Wolfson point out that the timing of these changes helps explain the end of the 1978–81 FDI surge and the onset of the post-1986 surge.

If this explanation has any validity, it should have some explanatory power across industries. For a variety of reasons, effective rates of corporate taxation vary considerably across industries; the Scholes-Wolfson argument says, counterintuitively, that foreign ownership should be larger in industries with relative *high* effective tax rates. Work by Swenson (1989) confirms that this is true for the U.S. manufacturing sector.

It is probably true that taxation plays an important role in multinational enterprise more generally. Unfortunately, international corporate taxation is an extraordinarily complex subject that yields few clear answers.

Trade Policy

Obviously, at least some FDI is motivated by actual or prospective changes in trade policy. On one side, some direct investment is clearly aimed at avoiding actual trade barriers or forestalling prospective barriers. Japanese television firms set up operations in the United States in the late 1970s in response to a voluntary export restraint (VER); Japanese auto manufacturing operations in both the United States and Europe have been motivated at least to some extent by actual and prospective trade restraints. On the other side, actual or prospective improvements in access to markets have motivated direct investment; manufacturing investment in southern Europe has clearly been stimulated by the combination of EC enlargement and the Europe 1992 program.

Can changes in views about trade policy be a major explanation of the surges in FDI since 1985? It seems unlikely. The most telling counterargument is that trade policy issues apply most obviously to manufacturing, while the surge is not concentrated in manufacturing investment.

Summary

Conceptual discussion of FDI trends tends to be unsatisfying, for a good reason: the central conceptual issues in FDI are the same as those of corporate restructuring in general and are equally elusive and problematic. The discussion yields three main points.

First, direct investment should be thought of primarily as an issue in industrial organization, not in capital flow. That is, analysis should focus more on the reasons why multinational firms exist and have advantages than on the international flows of money per se.

Second, it is relatively easy to explain a long-term trend toward greater cross-border ownership of firms. It is not clear that technological change per se necessarily encourages further growth of multinational enterprise, but the growing integration of the world economy certainly does. In fact, explaining a long-term trend is, in a way, too easy, since the observed history since 1970 has been less of a steady trend than of occasional surges.

Third, then, explaining these surges is the biggest conceptual and, in turn, empirical problem. That is, observation of broad trends toward globalization is easy; it is explaining why these trends suddenly came to a head in the third quarter of 1986 that is hard.

1.3   Key Questions Regarding Foreign Direct Investment

What questions most need to be answered about foreign direct investment? We would propose three, all of which are, of course, interrelated. First, why now? Why were the late 1980s marked by so much increase in FDI? Second, what are the prospects for further FDI? Will the boom continue? Will it move in new directions (e.g., to Eastern Europe and the Third World)? Finally, what are the effects of foreign direct investment? Are there any risks that will require or, at any rate, provoke a policy response?

1.3.1   Why Now?

This question, already reviewed in the previous section, is deliberately posed as a question about recent events rather than a more general one. Explaining a long sweep of multinational expansion is easy and has probably been overdone. What we confront instead is the problem of explaining a rapid growth in a fairly short period. Was it the exchange rate movements following the Plaza Accord? Was it the prospective formation of regional trading blocs? Tax reform? Or did ongoing gradual trends simply reach some kind of critical mass?

An unsettling possibility is that foreign direct investment may to some extent reflect irrational follow-the-leader behavior. Think of FDI for a moment as financial restructuring, not that different from domestic waves of corporate realignment. Then ask how well economists understand the wave of conglomerate formation in the 1960s or the wave of acquisitions and buyouts of the 1980s. The era of conglomerates in particular looks like a case of financial fashion, which is now condemned as misguided. Is the enthusiasm for buying U.S. firms any better grounded?

A related, equally unsettling possibility is that the wave of FDI in the late 1980s was a symptom of a worldwide epidemic of moral hazard in financial markets. It has become increasingly clear that financial deregulation after the late 1970s, while eliminating one set of distortions, led to new and perhaps worse ones. Financial institutions found themselves free to take risks with funds that were explicitly or implicitly guaranteed by their governments and, at the same time, found that they were no longer deterred from risk taking by the desire to safeguard the valuable "franchises" formerly created by barriers to entry. The best-known example of the new incentives to questionable risk taking is, of course, the U.S. thrift industry. It is arguable, however, that Japanese financial markets, led by thinly capitalized banks exposed to new competition, represent an even bigger case of moral hazard at work. In that case, much of the surge in foreign direct investment may have represented not an efficient movement toward globalization but a kind of side effect of the unraveling of the world financial system.

1.3.2 Prospects?

Our guess at the prospects for FDI is closely related to our assessment of its causes.

Two of the most influential proposed explanations of the surge in FDI since 1985 strongly suggest that some of that surge may have represented a temporary bulge and that the pace was inevitably going to slacken. If the valuation story is right, the combination of a low dollar, a high yen, and a sky-high Nikkei played a major role in generating large FDI flows into the United States and out of Japan. Even if these conditions had persisted, there would have been a natural slowing of the flow as the more obvious investment opportunities were exhausted. Given the financial developments of 1990 to date, we should have expected a sharp cutback in foreign direct investment—and indeed we have.

The tax story also suggests a limit. It basically posits a pent-up demand for ownership of U.S. firms from 1981 to 1986, held back by discriminatory tax treatment, and then a wave of investment when the tax laws were changed.

Once opportunities have been exploited, however, one would expect to see the pace slow.

On the other hand, if there are deeper trends that simply happened to come to a head in the late 1980s, the surge in FDI could resume.

Prospects for North-South and potential East-West FDI are equally problematic. Consider the following two plausible arguments:

1. Large FDI flows to southern Europe represented a one-time shift of production in anticipation of increased access to the European market and will not be repeated.

2. The growing unity of Europe and multinational operation of its firms will lead to a continuing shift of manufacturing to lower-wage areas on Europe's periphery, implying high rates of direct investment in southern and perhaps eastern Europe for a number of years.

Either of these arguments could be right; they have very different implications.

To make an assessment of prospects, it is necessary to answer the first key question about the reasons for the recent surge in FDI, then use that answer together with other information to make a forecast.

1.3.3 Effects?

The balance-of-payments implications of foreign direct investment are relatively straightforward. FDI flows have helped finance the U.S. current account deficit and recycle the Japanese surplus. They have actually posed a dilemma for Spain and Portugal, which have tried to maintain stable exchange rates while controlling inflation and have found the job difficult in the face of direct capital inflows.

Beyond the balance-of-payments effects, the longer-term question is whether and how foreign-owned firms will behave differently from domestic ones. The fear once expressed in Europe about U.S. firms and now expressed in the United States about Japanese and (to some extent) European firms is that these firms will use their operational control to the detriment of the host country. Accusations by critics such as Prestowitz (1988) and Tolchin and Tolchin (1988) are that foreign-owned firms in the U.S. will shift high-wage jobs and high value-added production to the parent company and shift sophisticated activities such as R&D abroad. The result will, so these critics assert, be to reduce the growth rate of the host economy.

Such concerns are not absurd in the light of theoretical analysis. Multinational firms are created for a reason; they are more than the sum of their parts, and their subsidiaries therefore ought to behave differently from purely domestic firms. It is not implausible that this difference in behavior might include hiving off some high-level activities to the parent firm. On the other hand, it is not certain either: the conceptual foundations of discussion about FDI are fuzzy enough to allow many hypotheses.

Available empirical evidence does not confirm the critics' fears. Studies by Graham and Krugman (1991) and by Julius (1990) basically find that foreign-owned firms behave very similarly to domestically owned firms in the same industry. They pay similar wages, engage in similar amounts of R&D, and so on. The only clear difference is a tendency to buy inputs from home suppliers, leading to a higher import propensity on the part of foreign-owned manufacturing firms. This tendency, however, appears to decline as investments become more mature.

Will this similarity in behavior continue? This question would of course be easier to answer if we knew why so much investment is now taking place and what its future prospects are.

1.4   Studying the Issue

What approach is most likely to help us answer the key questions just described? The standard answer is theoretical analysis of the basic motives for multinational enterprise, backed by econometric testing of hypotheses. There are, however, two difficulties with this standard approach.

First, the theoretical analysis of the boundaries of the firm—what the question of multinational enterprise is really about—is a deep issue, one on which economists have made only modest progress. In a fundamental way, it involves concerns about bounded rationality that are at present beyond the limits of our formal understanding. So it is unlikely that theorists will produce really convincing models of FDI anytime soon.

Second, econometric work is also likely to be difficult, in part because the theoretical base is limited. There are also practical difficulties. Aside from problems with the data, there are simply limits to how much can be accomplished via statistical inference—especially when subtle issues regarding the restructuring of firms are involved. Clearly, room exists for an alternative approach.

The immediately apparent alternative is, to *ask* them what they are doing and why, instead of trying to infer the motives and behavior of firms from poorly suited data. There are some known problems with this approach, but in conjunction with the ongoing process of more formal analysis, it could be very useful.

References

Buckley, Peter J., and Mark C. Casson. 1976. *The future of multinational enterprise.* London: Macmillan.
Coase, Ronald H. 1937. The nature of the firm. *Economica* (New Series) 4: 386–405.
Froot, Kenneth, and Jeremy Stein. 1991. Exchange rates and foreign direct investment:

An imperfect capital markets approach. *Quarterly Journal of Economics* 106 (November): 1191–217.

Graham, Edward M., and Paul R. Krugman. 1991. *Foreign direct investment in the United States.* Washington, D.C.: Institute for International Economics.

Hart, Oliver. 1989. An economist's perspective on the theory of the firm. *Columbia Law Review* 89: 1757–74.

Jensen, Michael C., and William H. Meckling. 1976. Theory of the firm: Managerial behavior, agency costs, and ownership structure. *Journal of Financial Economics* 3: 305–10.

Julius, Dee Anne. 1990. *Global companies and public policy.* London: Royal Institute of International Affairs.

Lewis, W. Arthur. 1978. *The evolution of the international economic order.* Princeton, N.J.: Princeton University Press.

Penrose, Edith T. 1956. Foreign investment and the growth of the firm. *Economic Journal* 66: 220–35.

Prestowitz, Clyde V., Jr. 1988. *Trading places: How we allowed the Japanese to take the lead.* New York: Basic Books.

Scholes, Myron, and Mark Wolfson. 1990. The effects of changes in tax laws on corporate reorganization activity Part 2. *Journal of Business* 63, no. 1 (January): s141–64.

Swenson, Deborah. 1989. The impact of U.S. tax reform on foreign investment in the United States. Cambridge, Mass.: MIT Department of Economics. Mimeo.

Tolchin, Martin, and Susan Tolchin. 1988. *Buying into America: How foreign money is changing the face of our nation.* New York: Times Books.

U.N. Center for Transnational Corporations. 1991. *World investment report 1991.* New York: United Nations.

Wilkins, Mira. 1970. *The emergence of multinational enterprise: American business abroad from the colonial era to 1914.* Cambridge, Mass.: Harvard University Press.

———. 1989. *The history of foreign investment in the United States.* Cambridge, Mass.: Harvard University Press.

Williamson, Oliver E. 1975. *Markets and hierarchies, analysis and antitrust implications: A study in the economics of internal organization.* New York: Free Press.

Comment   Kenneth A. Froot

Monty Graham and Paul Krugman have provided a useful overview of broad direct investment issues. Their most penetrating point is that temporary surges in FDI are more puzzling than the long-term trends in FDI. They consider three possible explanations for these surges: valuation effects, taxation, and trade policy. I want to comment briefly on this list and add several other explanations which I think are also important.

One plausible way that valuation effects might affect foreign investment behavior is discussed by Froot and Stein (1991). They argue that if external sources of finance are more expensive to corporations than are internal sources, negative shocks to relative domestic wealth can raise the cost of capital to domestic bidders for corporate control. This in turn leads to a decline in domestic reservation prices relative to those of foreigners. As Graham and Krugman mention, the exchange rate is merely one among many variables which can transmit changes in relative wealth. Increases in internal liquidity (due, for example, to past profits) or increases in stock market value can also raise relative corporate financial slack and thereby lessen a corporation's reliance on expensive external financing.

Unfortunately, there is relatively little systematic testing of this hypothesis outside of that using the exchange rate. Since the FDI time-series samples are so short, exchange rates alone probably cannot provide convincing evidence that valuation stories are correct. Nevertheless, as Graham and Krugman suggest, the fall in both Japanese outward FDI and Japanese stock prices during the 1990–92 period provides additional casual evidence that wealth effects do matter.

Another possible explanation of the recent surge in worldwide FDI—one which Graham and Krugman do not consider—is the dramatic change in corporate financing techniques. In particular, during the late 1980s, the junk bond market matured and then partially collapsed. Bank lending for the purposes of acquisitions and mergers also increased significantly over this period. Is it possible that these innovations actually had a substantial influence on worldwide FDI?

To answer this question, let us look at the most conspicuous features of the recent FDI surge. First, the fraction of direct investments which took the form of a merger or acquisition increased, particularly in countries such as the United States. Second, the decline in importance of greenfield FDI in part made FDI an increasingly North-North phenomenon, as North-South flows grew considerably more slowly. Third, the fraction of the acquisition price raised externally by the foreign acquirer increased substantially over this period. These facts are all consistent with the hypothesis that there have been important innovations in the corporate capital markets which have allowed takeovers to occur more easily and to rely more heavily on external financing. Corporate control is now a traded asset as never before. Indeed, the same capital market innovation hypothesis is frequently used to explain the rise of U.S. domestic takeover activity during the late 1980s. Foreign multinational firms are likely to have similar access to these financing innovations.

The financial-innovation story is interesting in that it does not necessarily lead to a temporary surge in takeover activity—FDI may be permanently increased as a result. While there may have been some pent-up demand released when these innovations were initially popularized, junk bonds and highly leveraged financing are here to stay as corporate financing alternatives. As a result, companies will remain likely to undergo a takeover whenever management systematically underperforms or whenever other bidders have some reason to value an ongoing business more highly. The hope is that a permanently higher level of M&A activity (domestic as well as foreign) may increase the average level of efficiency across the corporate sector.

A second issue, which Graham and Krugman touch upon only briefly, is that surges may be caused by follow-the-leader behavior. It is important to emphasize that such herding outcomes can be the result of rational decision making and that they may lead to multiple equilibria. For example, if Coca-Cola decides to pursue direct investment opportunities in the Third World, Pepsi-Cola may rationally follow. Even if the investment is a risky one, Pepsi's managers may wish to follow Coke. By following the leader, Pepsi's risks remain about the same as Coke's, which may help minimize the *relative* risk of underperformance of Pepsi's managers vis-à-vis Coke's. Managers may attempt to achieve outcomes correlated with a benchmark when their skill (and ultimate pay) is evaluated relative to that benchmark. (For a model along these lines, see Scharfstein and Stein 1990). Naturally, such correlated choices create the possibility of multiple herding equilibria.

Another reason that management may rationally herd is that firm value may be maximized through correlated strategic choices. If firms minimize costs by smoothing production over time, then strategies which involve large fluctuations in output may be dominated by strategies which offer a lower return but a more predictable level of output. Thus, a firm may follow the leader for many types of foreign investment strategies (even when the strategy offers relatively low return). However, this hypothesis also implies that there are limits to the herding: firms do not follow a leader who chooses a very "risky" strategy which has highly variable output over time.

References

Froot, Kenneth, and Jeremy Stein. 1991. Exchange rates and foreign direct investment: An imperfect capital markets approach. *Quarterly Journal of Economics* 106 (November: 1191–217.

Scharfstein, David, and Jeremy Stein. 1990. Herd behavior and investment. *American Economic Review* 80 (June): 465–79.

Discussion Summary

Karl Sauvant began by questioning whether the recent experience reflects a sustainable increase or just a surge. Recent liberalization of policy toward investment, especially in services, may explain the recent increase and, if so, this will continue. He made several other points about FDI. First, it is a cumulative process: the stock of $1.7 trillion at book value means that just the reinvestment of earnings will generate substantial continued FDI. Second, the LDC share has declined from 30 percent to 20 percent, but this may reverse because Mexico, Argentina and India have become more open; also, some LDCs such as Taiwan and South Korea have become FDI exporters. Finally, the recent decline in the flow of FDI may be due to the fact that the inflow to the United States has declined because of the recession in the United States.

Robert Feenstra asked whether high U.S. interest rates in the early 1980s could have hurt FDI in the United States.

Robert Lipsey then cautioned about the use of balance-of-payments data on FDI. Those data may record an outflow even as the stock of FDI is increasing.

Rachel McCulloch suggested that the apparent follow-the-leader pattern may reflect rational learning from the experience of the firms that went earlier. She cautioned that the annual flow variations can be dominated by the experience of a small number of firms.

Martin Feldstein observed that national governments may adopt market access policies that cause foreign firms to invest that would not do so if they could produce elsewhere and import. This is particularly true for firms in the pharmaceutical industry, but it can extend to any industry where firms want to sell to the government. FDI may be the price of access to certain domestic markets. *Feldstein* believes that much of the two-way FDI can be explained by the fact that the firms involved are selling intermediate products and have to go where their customers are because of the nature of supplier-buyer relations. This is true whenever it is advantageous to be near the buyer to participate in ongoing design activities or to provide product on a just-in-time basis.

Edward Graham stated that 80 percent of FDI in the United States is financed locally in the United States.

Raymond Vernon added that multinationals' share of current account transactions has increased substantially and is now an overwhelming share of total U.S. exports.

2   New Perspectives on Foreign
Direct Investment

Rachel McCulloch

Foreign direct investment is hardly a new subject for controversy, whether among policymakers or among economic analysts. Until the 1980s, the controversy centered primarily on outward investments of U.S. multinationals. Indeed, so great was the perceived dominance of the United States as quintessential source country, that the emergence of significant two-way flows of direct investment has required a fundamental shift in both analytical perspective and policy stance.

Statistics on inward direct investment document a dramatic turnaround in the U.S. position. As a host country, the United States was barely on the map during the 1960s, when less than 3 percent of direct investment globally came to the United States. In 1987, shortly after the United States had overtaken Canada as the leading host in terms of book value of accumulated direct investment, the U.S. share of total annual inflows peaked at nearly 50 percent.

In terms of outward investment, the U.S. position also changed substantially as firms based elsewhere became important players. During the 1960s, U.S. firms accounted for nearly two-thirds of all direct investment flows globally. By 1987, the U.S. share in total outward investment had dropped to less than one-quarter. However, the United States remained a top source country for outward direct investments. In fact, it was still the leading source country for the decade of the 1980s; in terms of annual flows, Japan did not replace the United States as the leading source until 1988.[1]

When the United States assumed its new role as the world's leading host to inward direct investment and Japan took its place as the leading source for new

<hr />

1. Flow data are from Lipsey (1984) for the 1960s and from the International Monetary Fund's *Balance of Payments Yearbook* (1991 and earlier issues) for the 1980s. Shares are based on total balance-of-payments flows that include local reinvestment of subsidiary profits but exclude expansion financed through subsidiaries' local borrowing. On adequacy and interpretation of direct investment data, see Stekler and Stevens (1991).

outward direct investment, U.S. policy retained the nationalistic "us versus them" orientation of earlier decades. Where analysts once probed the consequences for U.S. trade and employment of U.S.-controlled investments abroad (e.g., Bergsten, Horst, and Moran 1978), the same questions have instead been raised about the growing domestic role of foreign subsidiaries of companies based in Europe, Canada, and especially Japan.

There is, however, one striking difference. Where the debate of the 1960s and 1970s often lumped U.S. multinationals with the foreign "them," the 1990s debate prominently includes the impact on U.S.-based firms with the domestic "us." Formerly quoted more as an ironic commentary on U.S. corporate greed, Charles Wilson's dictum, "What's good for General Motors is good for the United States," now merely reflects the conventional wisdom of many U.S. policymakers.[2] Rather than the earlier battle of U.S. organized labor against footloose U.S.-based multinationals, the recent motif pits beleaguered U.S. companies (capital perhaps even more than labor interests) against rapacious foreign-based multinationals.

This paper reviews the changing composition of global direct investment flows and relates these developments to contemporaneous changes in global competition. My theme is that direct investment is an integral part of large firms' overall strategy for global production and sales. The emergence of significant two-way direct investment flows signals that U.S. companies no longer have a monopoly on the firm-specific competitive advantages required for successful global expansion.

2.1 Why Firms Invest Abroad

It comes as no surprise when successful firms expand their operations. Indeed, along with profitability, growth is often a yardstick for measuring success among firms in an industry. Substantial increases in *domestic* market share rarely come without some geographic expansion, first of sales and service operations, later of production facilities. However, it is the initial success that drives the expansion, both through lower costs associated with the learning curve and through increased access to and thus lower cost of financial capital.

Sooner or later—usually later for firms located in large domestic markets such as the United States, earlier for firms located in small markets such as Switzerland—the expansion process spills over into foreign markets (Caves 1982, 44). In manufacturing, exports typically come first, accompanied or followed by investments in sales and service facilities (Bergsten, Horst, and Moran 1978, chap. 3). After a successful trade initiative, establishment of pro-

2. According to Webber and Taylor (1992), Wilson's actual words and meaning were somewhat different. In 1953 hearings on his nomination to become secretary of defense, Wilson was asked whether he would be willing to make a decision with adverse consequences for General Motors. Wilson replied that he would but that he could not conceive of a need to do so, "because for years I have thought that what was good for our country was good for General Motors—and vice versa."

duction facilities close to the new markets is often the next step. Depending on cost conditions, some subsidiary production may eventually replace domestic production even in supplying the home market. This process can entail plant closings, but firms have an incentive to take the less conspicuous approach of sourcing only increases in domestic sales from foreign subsidiaries.[3]

In this account, both trade and foreign direct investment (FDI) are simply aspects of competition among (large) firms. During the early postwar period, burgeoning U.S. exports and the contemporaneous expansion abroad of U.S. companies were reflections of the same underlying circumstance, namely that most of the world's highly competitive companies were American. Trade statistics for the subsequent decades chronicle a steady deterioration in the relative attractiveness of the United States as a site for export production, as measured by the share of total world manufactured exports produced in the United States.

Over the same period, U.S.-based multinationals also lost ground, as measured by their share (U.S. plus foreign subsidiary production combined) in total world exports, although the loss was not as large as for on-shore production alone.[4] A similar picture emerges from statistics on production for the U.S. domestic market. For manufacturing as a whole and for almost every manufacturing industry taken individually, both imports and foreign-controlled domestic production have increased as a share of total domestic sales.

Trade theory provides a reasonably coherent explanation for postwar changes in the global pattern of production and, thus, for the associated changes in trade flows. Broad trends in the world pattern of production can be linked to observed changes in relative factor abundance worldwide as predicted by the dominant Heckscher-Ohlin paradigm. But the standard neoclassical theory has little to say about the very large firms that carry out much of the world's production and even more of the world's trade, nor about the ongoing process of entry and exit that characterizes most international markets. Trade theory is thus relatively good at explaining why *country* shares of world production are what they are but less good at explaining *company* shares, or why so much production in virtually every nation is controlled by companies based elsewhere.[5]

Foreign direct investment has no place in a strictly neoclassical world. Un-

3. For the service-sector activities that now account for a large part of direct investment, exports in the sense of production in one country for sale in another are less often an option; sales may require establishment of local facilities. On international competition in services, see McCulloch (1988).

4. On the distinction between the competitiveness of U.S.-based multinationals and that of the United States as a location for production, see Lipsey and Kravis (1986). Franko (1991) documents the declining position of U.S.-based companies as measured by share of total industry sales worldwide. This measure differs from the one used by Lipsey and Kravis, who look at shares in world exports rather than total sales.

5. Although many in the United States are apprehensive about the increasing share of foreign-controlled production, the U.S. ratio still looks low in relation to other industrial nations, with the significant exception of Japan (Graham and Krugman 1991, chap. 1).

der "perfect" competition, atomistic firms all enjoy equal access to technology and markets, with none large enough to influence prices of inputs or outputs The growth of any one firm's production beyond the minimum efficient size of a single plant requires an explanation, because coordination of activities in multiple locations imposes additional costs. A firm will incur these costs only when they are more than offset by associated benefits from internalizing activities that could, alternatively, be carried out through market transactions. The associated benefits must be larger still if the multiple locations span several nations, as this entails still higher coordination costs. In part, these costs reflect the need to deal with several legal systems, tax codes, cultural environments, and perhaps languages. Moreover, no host country applies strict national treatment; operations of foreign-based firms are invariably subject to some types of discriminatory policies.

Foreign direct investment is most prominent in industries where the competitive paradigm fits least well. Old-style multinationals populated oligopolistic natural-resource-based industries such as oil and aluminum. Modern multinationals thrive in fast-moving Schumpeterian sectors such as pharmaceuticals and electronics, where products are differentiated, reputation is vital, and technology is firm specific and constantly improving. The competitive advantage of these multinationals is created through large investments in advertising and in research and development (R&D). Multinational firms typically earn above-average rates of return, in relation both to the average for all industries and to nonmultinational firms in the same industry. The extra return can be seen as rent earned by the intangible assets that constitute the firm's competitive advantage.[6]

Firms possessing a competitive advantage such as superior technology, managerial know-how, established brands, or efficient channels for product distribution can exploit that advantage in a variety of ways, including but not limited to establishment of foreign subsidiaries. The most obvious choice is through trade, with all markets sourced from domestic production. Most manufacturing firms at least begin with this approach. Why do some choose to incur the extra expense of establishing production facilities abroad? Direct investment will be chosen instead of, or as an adjunct to, trade only to the extent that the location itself confers a substantial advantage to the company. This advantage may result from the usual elements of comparative advantage as reflected in lower production cost. Barriers to imports or other host-country policy inducements

---

6. From an industrial-organization perspective, these firm-specific advantages are barriers to entry. Empirical studies of several periods and host countries indicate a close relationship between seller concentration and the importance of direct investment (Caves 1982, chap. 4). This finding does not necessarily imply that seller concentration promotes direct investment, since entry barriers may affect both seller concentration in a given market and propensity of firms to establish foreign production. Morck and Yeung's (1991) study linking q-ratios to firm characteristics concludes that companies with firm-specific intangible assets created through R&D and advertising gain additional benefits from multinationality.

also play a role in determining the most advantageous location for production.[7]

Because expansion through direct investment means higher cost of management, advantageous location is not enough to explain the establishment of foreign subsidiaries. Unless multinationals possess an advantage over local firms sufficient to offset the cost of international coordination, the benefits of location will be captured instead by indigenous firms. In the latter case, the foreign company's advantage may be shared with indigenous firms in the preferred location through licensing or other types of long-term contracts.

How a given firm-specific advantage is exploited thus depends on the balance, for each potential mode, between the benefits to be derived and the costs to be incurred. Relative to direct investment, exports or licensing will typically provide lower benefits but entail lower costs. However, coordination costs vary across firms; those already large in the home market reveal a firm-specific advantage of intrafirm coordination. Small high-technology firms are more likely to use exports or licensing agreements to exploit innovations where larger companies find internalization (i.e., establishment of production subsidiaries) profitable.

2.2 Exchange Rates and Direct Investment

Since exchange rate movements are an important determinant of ex post rates of return on many types of internationally traded assets, anticipated *movements* in currency values play a significant role in shaping international capital transactions. Currency *levels* may serve as a proxy for anticipated future movements toward a trend value such as purchasing power parity. This implies an essentially speculative investment motive and should thus be more important for portfolio than for direct investment, which generally involves a longer planning horizon. But even if anticipated currency movements do not affect firms' overall plans for expansion abroad, they may influence timing of flows associated with those plans.

Other things equal, a weaker currency makes a country's products a better buy in world markets. Is the same true for its productive assets? An asset (a factory or a hotel, for example) is a claim to a stream of future domestic-currency-denominated profits. If those profits will be converted back into the currency of the foreign investor at the same exchange rate, the level of the exchange rate does not affect the present discounted value of the investment; neither a permanently strong nor a permanently weak currency alters the antic-

7. Some advantages of multinational activity are associated with being multinational rather than with any specific host location. A global production network permits the firm to diversify risk and, more generally, increases its potential for optimizing responses when conditions are volatile (Kogut 1983). Enhanced opportunities for tax avoidance are an additional benefit; multinational firms raise global after-tax profits by using advantageous transfer prices to shift profits to lower-tax jurisdictions.

ipated return. When an activity requires imported inputs or results in exports to other markets, the domestic-currency value of the profits will not typically be independent of the exchange rate. However, the direction of the effect is ambiguous–some investments will become more profitable, others less so, as the exchange rate falls.[8]

The most important effect of exchange rates on local-currency profits is through production costs. By raising production costs relative to those elsewhere, an appreciation of the source country's currency might shift direct investors' locational preference toward other regions. Even so, an advantage of integrated global management is still required to make direct investment a profitable response to the new currency values. Otherwise, local firms will be better able to exploit the locational advantage of lower production costs.[9] Moreover, lower production costs are obviously not the sole determinant of expected profitability. During the U.S. recession of the early 1990s, a weak dollar has not been enough to entice foreign investors.

Given the large swings in key rates during the 1980s, from apparent undervaluation to apparent overvaluation and back again, the explanation for increases during the late 1980s in both inward U.S. investments and direct investments worldwide may lie less in the specific level of the exchange rate at the time of the investment than in the high probability of future large movements. Here the benefit of global management plays a key role. Firms with multinational production and sales networks enjoy greater flexibility in shifting marginal production and marginal sales in response to future exchange rate realignments.[10]

2.3   The Role of Import Barriers

International trade theory predicts that restriction of trade flows will stimulate compensating factor flows. If a nation limits imports of autos, for example, it seems almost self-evident that frustrated foreign suppliers ought to establish domestic production facilities.[11] The automobile and electronics industries

8. See Caves (1989). Another argument appeals to a wealth effect on firms facing imperfect capital markets. Other things equal, a fall in the dollar increases the wealth of foreign firms and thus allows them to outbid their domestic counterparts (Froot and Stein 1991). Long-range corporate planning of investment expenditures in terms of the home currency would have a similar qualitative effect on observed dollar flows.

9. Aliber (1987, 302) cites an overvalued dollar as one factor explaining the dominance of U.S. firms among multinationals: "U.S. firms were obliged to invest and produce abroad if they were to be competitive in foreign markets." But the strong dollar merely favored a foreign production location. Other advantages of U.S. firms must be invoked to explain why these firms could make money in head-to-head competition with local competitors.

10. Lipsey (1991) finds trade of foreign-owned U.S. manufacturing firms more responsive to exchange rate movements than is trade of U.S.-owned firms.

11. Investments can also be the implicit price paid by foreign firms to avoid the imposition of new trade barriers. Bhagwati (1985) has coined the term *quid pro quo investment* to describe this link.

seem to offer visible support worldwide for the proposition. Yet statistical analyses do not always confirm a strong systematic relationship.

One likely reason for the weak empirical findings is that protection creates a locational advantage by raising the cost of serving the market through trade. In some cases, this locational advantage does promote foreign investment; in others, it affects mainly domestic entry and exit. When there is no firm-specific competitive advantage best exploited through integrated global management, domestic producers should be better able than subsidiaries of foreign companies to capture the benefits of local production.[12]

The conspicuous cases of autos and electronics, important though they are in their own right, may not point to a general rule. In these industries, technological and managerial know-how provides advantages that allow foreign producers to compete effectively with established domestic firms. By contrast, the highly protected apparel and footwear industries have seen relatively little direct investment from abroad. For these low-technology industries, firm-specific advantages are apparently too small to offset the greater costs incurred by foreign investors.[13]

Evidence at the country rather than the industry level also casts doubt on the role of protection as a strong magnet for inward direct investment. Among developing countries, open export-oriented economies such as Hong Kong have been more successful than nations pursuing import substitution strategies in attracting new investment. Among the industrial nations, the most important host countries have been Canada, the United Kingdom, the United States, and Germany, all with relatively liberal trade regimes.

2.4   What Firms Do When They "Invest Abroad"

Direct investment, particularly in the manufacturing sector, is often discussed under the heading "location of production," implying that the central issue affected by investment decisions is where production is located. As suggested above, the focus on location is misleading. Foreign direct investment is, by definition, the acquisition by a firm in one country of *control* over business activity in a second country. This may or may not be associated with a change in the location of production, but it is necessarily associated with a change in *which firm* controls production in that location. In particular, for the significant fraction of direct investment that entails acquisition of an existing local busi-

---

12. A separate explanation of weak results in cross-sectional studies relating direct investment to tariffs is that tariff rates change over time and many other economic developments also affect the level of subsidiary activity at any given date. Thus, current activity and current tariff rate may not be closely related "even if that relationship was originally a potent one" (Caves 1982, 41).

13. Changing cost conditions and extension of the Multi-Fiber Agreement to new production locations have given rise to short-lived direct investments based mainly on firm-specific advantages in the marketing of apparel. Such foreign operations, established, for example, by Taiwanese and Korean firms in Thailand and Malaysia, later pass into the hands of local investors.

ness, the transaction can alter control while leaving location of production unchanged.

Foreign direct investment is an intrinsic element of competition for market share within an industry. The typical pattern for U.S. companies in the 1960s, as well as for Japanese companies in the 1980s, was for global market share to grow simultaneously through exports and through direct investment abroad.[14] Viewing foreign investment mainly in terms of relocation of production begs the central issue.

A production site can become more attractive because of factors such as proximity to a growing market, changing cost structure, host-region incentives, or trade barriers; each of these has the potential to alter a firm's decision regarding location of production. However, such location factors do not explain why a foreign-based firm is able to increase its *share* of control over production in that location. A focus on location thus ignores the question of why particular firms are best able to exploit the advantages of that location.

Although it is crucial in understanding foreign direct investment, the distinction between location and firm-specific advantage may be easier to see in the more familiar case of domestic competition. The success of Houston-based Compaq in the market for IBM-compatible computers was primarily news about Compaq's growing share—at IBM's expense—in the U.S. market, not about the relocation of computer production facilities to Texas. In the many business press stories analyzing Compaq's rise, the Houston location was rarely if ever mentioned as a factor. The reason is obvious. Unlike other clone manufacturers, Compaq's success was due primarily to superior product rather than low cost. The Texas location may have been an advantage, but not *the* advantage. (Any Texas advantage was clearly not sufficient to save Texas Instruments, which dropped out of the market for PCs and other consumer products in the early 1980s.)

Compaq's growth was due primarily to a firm-specific competitive advantage over its rivals, an advantage that allowed it to increase market share while selling its products at a premium over other clone manufacturers. But, for the same reason, Compaq's initial success could not last. As other companies came closer to, or even exceeded, Compaq's quality standard while offering a substantially lower price, erosion of market share became inevitable.

At this later stage, where no one producer enjoys a significant product advantage (lower-end PCs are now described as having reached "commodity" status), location of production may appear to become the critical issue. Costs

14. The resulting positive correlation between exports and controlled foreign production led some analysts in the 1960s to conclude that firms' global expansion *caused* the growth of U.S. exports. The reality was, as suggested, more complex. Both types of growth were manifestations of the competitive strength of U.S.-based companies. Nonetheless, some level of direct investment abroad in the form of distribution and service facilities is almost a requirement for strong export performance. Until the mid-1980s, much Japanese investment in the United States was of this export-facilitating type.

in, say, Singapore or Taiwan are lower than in Houston; costs in Malaysia and China are even less. But all potential competitors, including firms already established in those regions, have the option to locate production so as to benefit from the lower costs. The interesting question from an analytical perspective still is: who controls the production, and why?

The numbers reveal that both Compaq and IBM are losing market share in the commodity environment, even though both now produce much of their output offshore. The firm-specific advantages that allowed first IBM and then Compaq to dominate the market are now insufficient to offset their *disadvantage* relative to the clones, presumably the disadvantage of higher costs of co-ordinating global production and sales. Who has lower coordinating costs? The answer may be, literally, no one. As firm-specific product or service advantages become less important, the market itself may provide a more efficient alternative to coordination within *any* multinational firm. The benefits of expansion, whether domestic or international, must be balanced against costs. Some costs decline with size; others grow exponentially. Bigger, as both IBM and General Motors amply illustrate, is not always better.

2.5   Trade and Employment Impact

Most economists agree that the extent of direct investment has minimal consequences for a nation's aggregate employment, yet both enthusiasts and critics focus their attention on the assumed impact on trade and associated changes in employment opportunities. Direct investment *can* have significant trade and employment effects at the industry or regional level. Anticipated trade and employment effects are important in shaping policy, but actual impacts are complex to identify, even ex post, and tend to be offset at the country level by induced changes elsewhere in the economy.

Direct investments can take one of two forms. A greenfield investment entails construction of new physical plant. Alternatively, investment may be carried out through merger with or acquisition of an existing domestic producer.[15] Greenfield investments are eagerly sought by host regions because they are perceived to provide a net increase in capital stock, with corresponding implications for regional trade and employment. In particular, greenfield investments are assumed to expand output of the domestic industry, thus allowing reduced imports or increased exports; more production is anticipated to mean new jobs, at least for the industry. Typically more controversial are investments that entail merger with or acquisition of an existing local business, as these are less obviously a source of positive trade effects and new jobs. (The associated change of management is also often bad news for incumbent executives, who may have considerable political influence at the local level.)

15. Actual investments often combine the two basic types, so that a merger or takeover may also include substantial additions to plant. In some cases, a takeover transfers ownership from one foreign parent to another.

Missing from the standard interpretation is an explicit statement of the counterfactual: that is, what would have happened in the absence of the investment. Without the greenfield investment, an existing producer might have added to domestic capacity; given the foreign investor's presence, another producer may decide to exit from the industry. The presumption of a net addition to industry capacity thus rests on the implicit and questionable assumption that other firms already established do not change their own investment decisions in response to the new circumstances.

Standard inferences for trade and for industry employment rest on even shakier ground. The prediction of favorable trade balance effects relies on the assumption that total domestic output expands relative to demand. Since it is unlikely that overall demand for the product rises significantly as a consequence of new investment, new production mainly replaces reductions elsewhere. The key question is thus whether that "elsewhere" is at home or abroad—whether the new output substitutes mainly for other domestic production or for foreign production (goods otherwise imported or goods otherwise produced abroad for other markets).[16]

Even one-for-one substitution of domestic production for foreign production is unlikely to translate into equal changes in trade flows. Foreign-controlled producers typically use a higher percentage of imported intermediate inputs.[17] Positive trade balance effects in the first industry will then be offset at least in part by corresponding changes in the trade positions of the industries producing these inputs. Induced exchange rate movements or other associated macroeconomic developments are a further offset to any impact beyond the industry level. Working in the opposite direction is the possibility that foreign-based firms may, especially in the longer run, prove to be more adept than their domestic counterparts in exporting to markets elsewhere. But again, this is likely to be offset in the aggregate by other induced changes economywide.

Although it is reasonable to assume that a favorable trade impact will translate into an increase in industry jobs, the effect will be diluted if the investor's competitive advantage includes higher efficiency in production. In this case, the investment is desirable precisely because it does raise productive efficiency; the emphasis on industry job creation thus distracts from the real gains from upgrading productive efficiency.[18]

Even ex post empirical data cannot be used to settle this issue. For example, further deterioration in an industry's trade position or employment tells only

16. To the extent that direct investment increases efficiency and competition in the industry, total sales should rise relative to what they would otherwise have been. In most cases, however, this effect will be small relative to the substitution among alternative sources of supply.

17. On this point and the relationship between foreign ownership and trade performance more broadly, see Lipsey (1991).

18. Empirical evidence for the United States suggests that foreign owners pay roughly the same wages as domestic owners in the same industry but have higher output per worker. For comparisons of U.S.-controlled and foreign-controlled U.S. companies, see Leonard and McCulloch (1991) and Graham and Krugman (1991, chap. 3).

what did happen, not what would have happened in the absence of an investment. The 1960s debate concerning the domestic trade and employment consequences of U.S. direct investments abroad produced predictions of sectoral effects that ranged from strongly negative to strongly positive. The large discrepancies arose mainly from contradictory assumptions concerning the substitution among alternative locations of production.[19] In light of the prevailing U.S. view that Japanese-controlled U.S. factories import too much of their intermediate inputs, it is interesting that the relatively high reliance of U.S. subsidiaries abroad on imported inputs was cited in the 1970s as one reason to expect favorable effects on domestic employment from foreign expansion of U.S. multinationals.[20]

The same qualification applies to the standard presumption concerning industry trade and employment impact of investment via merger or acquisition. The critical assumption is that domestic output remains the same. Yet such transactions often involve a domestic competitor too weak to survive on its own. In this case, the investment may *add* industry jobs to the ones that would have remained had the acquired firm exited instead.[21] This may be true even when actual firm and industry employment fall, as might be expected if the takeover raises productivity.

2.6   Impact on Industry Competition and Profits

Like expanded imports, ownership of local operations is basically a way for highly competitive foreign firms to expand their presence in a given market. As long as this expansion does not reduce the number of active competitors serving the market, its most predictable effect is to reduce profits of firms already in that market. This should hold both for domestic firms and for foreign firms that have previously entered the market through exports or direct investment, and the typical behavior of established firms in the affected industry is consistent with this outcome. As with competition from imports, beleaguered domestic firms are apt to label the activities of their foreign-controlled rivals as unfair or detrimental to the national interest.

Yet, as with other forms of entry, the net effect is not always to increase the number of active competitors. Takeovers of existing firms may leave the num-

19. Researchers in the early 1970s estimated net U.S. employment impacts ranging from losses close to half a million jobs to gains of a similar magnitude. OECD (1987, 212) compares six major studies.

20. A quaint echo of the earlier debate can be found in chapter 7 of the *1991 Economic Report of the President,* which cites increased demand for exports of U.S. production inputs among the likely benefits of expansion abroad of U.S. multinationals. The discussion asserts that if U.S. firms did not produce abroad, the markets would typically be lost to other suppliers—in other words, that controlled foreign production rarely substitutes for exports.

21. On the other hand, even an infusion of whatever foreign investors bring may not be enough to save a weak domestic firm, as with Renault's majority interest in the now-defunct American Motors.

ber constant or even reduce it; also, as suggested above, greenfield investment may induce exit by one or more incumbent firms. Moreover, some analysts in the 1970s suggested that entry via direct investment could help to maintain a stable pattern of oligopoly.[22]

Direct investments can also influence profits of firms that do not compete directly. The new entrants' operations change demand for productive inputs and for other outputs, thus affecting profits of related industries. Investments also affect regional and national tax revenues[23] and public expenditures. Opposition to locally provided inducement packages often comes from established firms in unrelated industries. These firms anticipate unfavorable effects on their own profits via higher future taxes and increased competition for skilled workers. In the longer run, foreign ownership is likely to affect—for better or for worse—even the legal structure within which the industry operates, as new owners lobby for advantageous legislative and regulatory action.

2.7 Policy toward Direct Investment

Nearly all countries make efforts to attract inward direct investment; at the same time, most also impose limits on access and otherwise restrict the activities of foreign-controlled companies within their borders. This carrot-and-stick approach can have important consequences for the location of economic activity and for the efficiency of that activity in any given location. In particular, investment policies can have predictable effects on trade flows, effects similar to those of policies aimed explicitly at trade: reducing imports, expanding exports, or both. Along with other nontariff measures that influence trade, investment policies have become more conspicuous in recent decades. As successive rounds of negotiations within the General Agreement on Tariffs and Trade (GATT) have reduced the importance of tariffs, a major unanticipated result has been expanded use of investment measures and other "opaque" forms of protection.

The Uruguay Round is the first GATT round to attempt negotiations on policies toward foreign direct investment. Some past agenda items (e.g., subsidies) have been comparable in importance to members' perceived ability to control domestic economic activity, but none has been such a core issue in terms of national sovereignty. In the case of direct investment, the national policies in question aim specifically at regulating the extent and character of foreign-controlled production *within the nation's own boundaries.* Moreover, as discussed above, direct investment tends by its very nature to be concentrated in sectors of the economy that conform least well to the paradigm of perfect

---

22. For example, Graham (1978). On the general issue of direct investment as a form of entry, also see Caves (1982, chap. 4).

23. Despite the notorious tax-avoidance techniques of multinationals, tax revenue remains the best-documented benefit of inward direct investment.

competition. Thus, standard efficiency arguments for laissez-faire are unlikely to hold without significant qualification.

2.8   A "New" Investment Theory?

The nature of direct investment implies that firms engaging in it will typically earn what might be considered supernormal profits. As the "new" trade theory dealing with imperfect competition has suggested, the existence of such rents creates an additional class of arguments for intervention. The basic theme is that a nation can use trade policy to garner a larger share of the industry's worldwide rents. However, this new class of arguments has met with a cool reception. The theoretical case for any particular policy prescription is highly sensitive to modeling assumptions. Those with practical bent note that conditions in few, if any, real-world industries remotely resemble those required to make the case for national-welfare-enhancing policies along these lines; moreover, the policy process is unlikely to be endowed with the pinpoint accuracy required to ensure national welfare gains rather than losses. Most believe that this new literature, like the older one based on infant industries and other market distortions, yields little guidance for policymaking; adherence to free trade is still seen as the best practical advice.[24]

Is the rent-grabbing motive more persuasive for investment than for trade? As with policies toward trade, national policies aimed at investment tend in practice to reduce global efficiency via suboptimal allocation of resources in production and via associated rent-seeking activities. An important difference, however, is that investment policies are less likely to reduce the country's *own* aggregate welfare than are those aimed directly at trade flows. International cooperation to avoid a "prisoner's dilemma" situation may therefore be more important than in the case of trade.[25]

For a country small enough to have no appreciable effect on world prices, the cost of tariff protection is borne almost entirely by the county itself. Even for large countries, the net effect of protection on national welfare is typically negative. But when a tariff creates an incentive for import-substituting direct investment and investment policies are then used to extract some part of the rents generated by foreign-controlled production for the local market, the country may in fact gain.[26] However, the foreign investor will also gain (or

24. For example, Pomfret (1991) argues that the new case for protection is deficient even for jet aircraft, the real-world industry closest to satisfying the conditions of the models.

25. The policy process itself and the attempts of firms to shape policy and to maximize their benefits within any policy environment also use resources. Even when the location and operation of a footloose investment is, in the end, unaffected by competition among rival would-be hosts, the rent-seeking process may entail a substantial social cost.

26. The most obvious channel is via the host country taxation of multinational profits (see Caves 1982, chap. 10). However, profits may also be taxed implicitly through performance requirements imposed on foreign-controlled firms. Labor employed by subsidiaries can also capture part of the rent in the form of above-market wages.

expect to gain), at least relative to the situation of protection but no investment.

For example, assume that a monopoly producer would otherwise serve the local market through imports from plants elsewhere at a fixed marginal cost, but a sufficiently high tariff barrier makes local production the monopolist's preferred alternative. Although less profitable for the monopolist than the laissez-faire situation, local production is likely to mean a lower *marginal* cost of serving the market. Thus, the monopolist will maximize profits by selling a larger volume of output at a lower price than before the tariff was imposed. The host thus gains relative to free trade.[27] This gain is augmented by any local tax revenue generated or rents incorporated in wages paid to local workers.[28]

Corresponding losses, although potentially larger in the aggregate, will be spread among other nations (in the example, the main loser is the alternative production site)[29] but may be small for any one of them. An important implication is that the "problem" of investment policies is at least in part of problem of incomplete liberalization of trade that creates a locational advantage. Without tariffs, quotas, and other important barriers, there would be less rent to extract and thus less scope for performance requirements. Likewise, harmonization of taxation across potential hosts would reduce the scope for rent-shifting via tax incentives.

Efforts to bring investment policies under GATT discipline have come principally from the United States, propelled by the perceived interests of some U.S.-based multinational firms. Yet, while there is no question that many U.S.-based firms have been affected by investment policies of host countries, the evidence is far from conclusive that source countries such as the United States have been harmed significantly by the use of these policies. In some instances, as illustrated in the example above, the host country and the source country can both benefit on net at the expense of numerous "third" nations, each of which, however, bears only a small part of the cost.

Moreover, there is still less evidence to suggest that trade-related investment policies currently exert an important independent influence on global patterns of production and trade, especially in relation, say, to the remaining egregious

27. Free trade is not the optimal policy for a small country facing a monopoly producer (see Grossman 1990). However, implementation of the optimal policy requires extensive cost information as well as an enforcement capability. The second-best approach of forcing the monopolist to produce locally may be, from a practical point of view, the more attractive option.

28. In the example, a tariff provides the inducement to relocate. An alternative inducement could be favorable tax treatment. In this case, even the multinational may be better off relative to the initial equilibrium. The potential gains to the firm and the host region come in part from increased sales in the host market and in part from a shift in rents to the host (as taxes or wages) and to the firm (as higher after-tax profits).

29. Although the existence of monopoly implies that efficiency may be raised by intervention, the benefits to the host and firm reflect mainly the transfer of rents that would have accrued to a different region under laissez-faire.

and well-documented barriers in textiles and apparel and in agriculture.[30] The main effect of most investment measures, at least in the medium term, is to shift rents between the source and the host country.[31]

2.9   What Role for the United States?

The greatly increased extent of two-way foreign direct investment and even of two-way flows within a given industry has blurred the distinction, at least among industrial nations, between host and source countries. In the 1960s, the United States was the preeminent source country and thus also the most conspicuous potential beneficiary of international limits on nationalistic policies of host countries. In the 1990s, the United States remains a major source country as well as the strongest voice for international action to regulate investment policies. Yet it has also become the world's most important host to direct investment, with all the new political pressures that entails. Correspondingly, the European Community, Canada, and Japan have gained a new stake in placing limits on host country investment policies, particularly those of the United States.[32]

A key policy question on foreign investment for the United States in the 1990s is analogous to the one raised by the national debate on trade policy a decade earlier: whether the United States is willing and able to champion global goals even when this requires some sacrifice of perceived national needs. Specifically, is the United States willing and able to continue its leadership role in combating investment policies that achieve nationalistic objectives at the expense of global efficiency? Or will it instead join other host countries by adopting its own nationalistic policies? And should the United States opt for the route of nationalism, will any other country be willing and able to assume the responsibility of global leadership on this issue?

30. The decision to tackle investment measures primarily on the basis of their presumed role as nontariff trade distortions neglects important interactions between trade restriction and direct investment as *joint* determinants of the global pattern of production. Changes in trade policies have implications for foreign investment decisions; conversely, the effects of trade policies on productive efficiency and income distribution within and across countries depend crucially on the extent of induced changes in foreign investment. National investment policies can thus have an important though typically *indirect* influence on the consequences of protection and of trade liberalization. National investment policies may therefore be critical to the success of the GATT even though these policies in themselves do not constitute important distortions of trade.

31. Longer-run effects are more complex. If rents are the return to past research and development, policies that reduce the share going to the innovative firms can be expected to discourage future innovation.

32. The convergence of interests may have created a temporary window of opportunity for fruitful international negotiations on trade-related investment measures (TRIMs). On the likely elements of a bargain, see Graham (1991) and Lawrence (1992).

References

Aliber, Robert Z. 1987. *The international money game.* New York: Basic Books.

Bergsten, C. Fred, Thomas Horst, and Theodore H. Moran. 1978. *American multinationals and American interests.* Washington, D.C.: Brookings Institution.

Bhagwati, Jagdish N. 1985. *Investing abroad.* Esmee Fairbairn Lecture, University of Lancaster.

Caves, Richard E. 1982. *Multinational enterprise and economic analysis.* Cambridge: Cambridge University Press.

————. 1989. Exchange-rate movements and foreign direct investment in the United States. In *The internationalization of U.S. Markets,* ed. David B. Audretsch and Michael P. Claudon. New York: New York University Press.

Franko, Lawrence G. 1991. Global corporate competition II: Is the large American firm an endangered species? *Business Horizons* 34, no. 6 (November–December): 14–22.

Froot, Kenneth A., and Jeremy C. Stein. 1991. Exchange Rates and foreign direct investment: An imperfect capital markets approach. *Quarterly Journal of Economics* 106 (November): 1191–217.

Graham, Edward M. 1978. Transatlantic investment by multinational firms: A rivalistic phenomenon? *Journal of Post Keynesian Economics* 1, no. 1 (Fall): 82–99.

————. 1991. Multilateral discipline on foreign direct investment: Beyond the TRIMs exercise in the Uruguay Round. In *The Uruguay Round and beyond: Problems and prospects,* ed. Robert E. Baldwin and J. David Richardson. Cambridge, Mass.: National Bureau of Economic Research.

Graham, Edward M., and Paul R. Krugman. 1991. *Foreign direct investment in the United States.* Washington, D.C.: Institute for International Economics.

Grossman, Gene M. 1990. Promoting new industrial activities. *OECD Economic Studies* 14 (Spring).

Kogut, Bruce. 1983. Foreign direct investment as a sequential process. In *The multinational corporation in the 1980s,* ed. Charles P. Kindleberger and David B. Audretsch. Cambridge, Mass.: MIT Press.

Lawrence, Robert Z. 1992. Futures for world trade and investment and their implications for developing countries. Paper prepared for presentation at the United Nations Center on Transnational Corporations Symposium. The Hague, Netherlands.

Leonard, Jonathan S., and Rachel McCulloch. 1991. Foreign-owned business in the United States. In *Immigration, trade, and the labor market,* ed. John M. Abowd and Richard B. Freeman. Chicago: University of Chicago Press.

Lipsey, Robert E. 1984. Recent trends in U.S. trade and investment. In *Problems of advanced economies,* ed. Nagasada Miyakawa. Heidelberg: Springer-Verlag.

————. 1988. Changing patterns of international investment by and in the United States. In *The United States in the world economy,* ed. Martin Feldstein. Chicago: University of Chicago Press.

————. 1991. Foreign direct investment in the United States and U.S. trade. *Annals of the American Academy of Political and Social Science* 516 (July): 76–90.

Lipsey, Robert E., and Irving B. Kravis. 1986. The competitiveness and comparative advantage of U.S. Multinationals, 1957–1983. NBER Working Paper no. 2051. Cambridge, Mass.: National Bureau of Economic Research, October.

McCulloch, Rachel. 1988. International competition in services. In *The United States in the world economy,* ed. Martin Feldstein. Chicago: University of Chicago Press.

Morck, Randall, and Bernard Yeung. 1991. Why investors value multinationality. *Journal of Business* 64, no. 2 (April): 165–87.

OECD. 1987. *International investment and multinational enterprises: Recent trends in international direct investment.* Paris: Organization for Economic Cooperation and Development.

Pomfret, Richard. 1991. The new trade theories, rent-snatching and jet aircraft. *World Economy* 14, no. 3 (September): 269–77.

Stekler, Lois, and Guy V. G. Stevens. 1991. The adequacy of U.S. direct investment data. In *International economic transactions: Issues in measurement and empirical research,* ed. Peter Hooper and J. David Richardson. Chicago: University of Chicago Press.

Webber, Alan, and William Taylor. 1992. Is what's bad for General Motors bad for the USA? *Boston Globe,* 1 March.

Comment   Karl P. Sauvant

Rachel McCulloch's paper raises a number of intriguing questions; in particular, the policy issues on which it ends are very important. She presents three basic propositions, namely that the emergence of significant two-way flows of foreign direct investment (FDI) requires a fundamental shift in both analytical perspective and policy stance and that firms consider FDI as part of an overall international strategy. I will deal with each of these propositions separately.

1. Emergence of Significant Two-way Flows of FDI Requires Fundamental Shift in Analytical Perspective.

It is true that the relative position of the United States as a home country has decreased and that, as far as FDI outflows are concerned, there is a rough parity between the EC, Japan, and the United States, the three areas that make up the Triad (together, they account for about 80 percent of world FDI outflows) (See UNCTC 1991.) It is also true that the United States, as part of the triad that accounts for some 70 percent of world FDI inflows, has become the principal host country. And it is true that this raises all sorts of issues for the United States as host country, including those raised in the paper (e.g., impact on trade, employment, industry competition, and profits). But these issues are not new—there is a large literature that looks at these issues from the perspective of host countries in Western Europe or the developing world. Hence, it is not clear why the decline of the United States as a home and its size as a host country should require a fundamental shift in analytical perspective.

On the other hand, the rise of FDI inflows into the United States should stimulate analysis that revisits the work on FDI impact and systematically reviews the impact of FDI inflows on the economic growth of host countries. Given some changes in the world economy (e.g., the globalization of firms and industry, the importance of new technologies, the importance of the services sector, regionalization), such a reexamination could indeed be quite useful.

2.   Firms Consider FDI as Part of Overall International Strategy for Global Production and Sales

I agree with the second proposition. Firms do indeed, regard exports, production abroad (i.e., FDI), licensing, and other forms of nonequity linkages as alternative ways to deliver goods and services to foreign markets. But it should be noted that the alternative of export versus production abroad does not apply to many services because these are not tradable. A good part of the text reads as if it dealt with *all* FDI, while in reality some of the discussion (e.g., the progression from exports to foreign production) only applies to the industrial sector. The paper would benefit from an explicit discussion of the manner in which this proposition holds in the services sector. In this respect, the increasing tradability of some services would deserve attention.

But the approach that FDI should be seen as an integral part of a firm's overall global strategy is a promising one and deserves further investigation. The focus of analysis would become *international production:* the emergence of a system of value-added activities across national boundaries that integrates international, capital, trade, technology, and training flows within the framework of firms. Is such an international production system actually emerging? If so, what is its nature? In which industries is it particularly important? How important is it? And so on.

3.   Emergence of Significant Two-way Flows of FDI Requires Fundamental Shift in Policy

I agree with the final proposition but for reasons other than those developed in the paper. McCulloch suggests that, because the United States is now both a significant home country and host country, it may waver in the future in its commitment to an open, multilateral FDI regime. She also suggests that the United States is the "strongest voice for international action to regulate investment policies." The first point is well taken. Now that FDI is becoming relatively more important in the U.S. economy (although it is still considerably less important than in, say, the United Kingdom or Canada), there are voices that urge a restriction in inward investment. Such a course could have unfortunate implications for efforts to build an international regime for FDI and must therefore be carefully watched. As to the second point, it is necessary to specify that support for international action means support for an open system— that is, a system that defines primarily the rights of foreign investors and the responsibilities of governments and is fairly silent about the responsibilities of investors and the rights of governments. To be equitable and durable, a multilateral system ought to be balanced and hence address the rights and responsibilities of both foreign investors and governments. The current international situation offers a window of opportunity to establish such a system, but it does not look as if major steps are being made to seize that opportunity.

That does not mean, however, that no progress is being made. Most important in this respect are the achievements of the Uruguay Round in the areas of services (the General Agreement on Trade and Services, or GATS, if adopted, will cover FDI in services) and TRIMs. But some progress has been made in the Development Committee of the IMF and the World Bank, which have adopted guidelines; progress is being made by the OECD, where efforts have begun to devise an investment regime incorporating, among other things, the liberalization codes and the guidelines for transnational corporations (TNCs); and of course there is the United Nations Draft Code of Conduct for Transnational Corporation. All this, however, does not necessarily involve a new policy stance but rather is a continuation of old policies.

But a new policy stance *is* needed, because FDI is now probably the most important form of international economic transaction; as Raymond Vernon put it in the discussion: "The proportion of current account transactions attributable to TNCs has gone up dramatically." This has happened as a result of the absolute growth of FDI, its relative importance (e.g., foreign production is more important than exports in bringing goods and services to foreign markets), and the interlinkages of FDI and other international transactions (e.g., a good part of trade is intrafirm trade). As a result, as mentioned earlier, an international production system is emerging.

No international policy framework exists, either for FDI or for international production, in the same way as it exists, for instance, for trade. The framework ought to approach international economic transactions from the perspective of FDI, given the importance of FDI per se and the way in which it shapes a significant share of international trade and technology flows. (Transnational Corporations and Management Division [1991] addresses some of these issues.) Such a framework would, for instance, address strategic FDI policy—which is referred to in the paper but only from a rent-snatching perspective, not as a strategic, long-term approach. It would deal with investment-related trade measures (IRTMs), in the same way in which the GATT framework deals with TRIMs. It could make provisions for transparency regarding FDI policies and institute FDI policy review, patterned on GATT's trade policy review. It would also have to address the question of maintaining competition in the face of globalizing firms and industries and perhaps establish an international competition authority as a focal point for international policies in a world in which international production is assuming importance.

References

UNCTC. 1991. *World investment report 1991: The triad in foreign direct investment.* New York: United Nations.

Transnational Corporations and Management Division. 1992. *World investment report 1992: Transnational corporations as engines of growth.* New York: United Nations.

Discussion Summary

Michael Adler started the discussion by asking whether the main issue addressed by the literature on direct investment could be more clearly identified. He suggested one candidate: an evaluation of the contribution of FDI to economic development in host countries. In the current environment, an important issue is the possibility that FDI might substitute for the official and private portfolio investment that has dominated capital flows to developing countries in recent years.

Rachel McCulloch observed that the conventional wisdom in host countries has come full circle. Their preference had been for portfolio investment inflows and local ownership, but host country preferences seem to have shifted toward direct investment. There is now a widespread view that FDI involves imports of knowledge and efficiency as well as capital.

Ray Vernon observed that the theory of FDI is concerned with patterns of corporate control rather than with net financial transfers from direct investors to host countries. He would emphasize, for example, incentives for firms in oligopolistic industries to match direct investments by competitors, in order to ensure access to markets and inputs.

Robert Lipsey reminded participants that hostility to direct investment had a long history, not just in developing countries, but also in the United States in the nineteenth century. What is quite different today is that developing countries are encouraging and even subsidizing FDI.

Michael Adler asked whether subsidies to FDI could be efficient policies and, if so, what form would they take?

Ann Harrison pointed out that, in practice, FDI was often attracted by offering protection or was concentrated in protected industries. It is not clear this is an efficient policy.

Rachel McCulloch argued that in cases where FDI involved a valuable technology transfer, a small tariff could be optimal for the host country.

3 Where Are the Multinationals Headed?

Raymond Vernon

Four decades ago, the multinational enterprise was widely regarded as a peculiarly American form of business organization, a manifestation of the existence of a pax Americana. Today, every industrialized country provides a base for a considerable number of multinationals, which collectively are becoming the dominant form of organization responsible for the international exchange of goods and services. Indeed, by the end of the 1980s, even the larger firms in some of the rapidly industrializing countries of Asia and Latin America had joined the trend (UN Commission on Transnational Corporations 1990; Lall 1991).

For scholars who want to understand the factors affecting international trade in goods and services, these changes are of consummate importance. In the past, whenever the international behavior of multinationals appeared at odds with a world regulated by comparative advantage and capital market theory, the deviation could be treated as idiosyncratic, the basis for a footnote in passing. But today, with multinationals dominating the international traffic in goods and services, the question of what determines their behavior takes on considerable significance.

I cannot pretend to provide a definitive answer to this central question in the pages that follow; that is a labor which will take many minds over an extended period of time. But I have two goals in mind which contribute to that central task. The first is to persuade the reader that explanations of the behavior of multinational enterprise which draw on the national origins of the enterprise as a major explanatory variable are rapidly losing their value, to be replaced by an increased emphasis on the characteristics of the product markets in

The author is indebted to Ernest Chung and Subramanian Rangan for their research support in preparing this paper and to Richard Caves and Lawrence H. Wortzel for their incisive comments on a earlier draft.

which the enterprises participate. The second is to plant a few ideas regarding the motivations and responses of the multinational enterprise that I believe must figure in any rounded explanation of the behavior of these enterprises in the various product markets they face.

3.1   U.S. Firms Ascendant

The sudden growth of U.S.-based multinational networks after World War II was in fact some time in the making. Many decades earlier, the first signs that large enterprises might find themselves pushed to develop a multinational structure were already beginning to appear. Setting the stage for the development of these multinational networks were the dramatic improvements in the technologies of transportation and communication, coupled with the vastly increased opportunities for scale economies in industrial production. Operating with high fixed costs and low variable costs, a new crop of industrial giants felt especially vulnerable to the risks of price competition. And by the beginning of the twentieth century, these risks were beginning to be realized; the country's industrial leaders, including firms in machinery, metalworking, and chemicals, were coming into bruising contact not only with rivals from the United States but also with some from Europe.

Facing what they perceived to be dangerous and destructive competition, the leaders in many U.S. industries went on the defensive. By the beginning of the century, many of the new industries of the country had organized themselves in restrictive market-sharing arrangements and were reaching out to their European competitors to join agreements that were global in scope.

From the first, however, it was apparent that these restrictive arrangements were fragile responses to the threat of competition, especially for firms based in the United States (Hexner 1945; Stocking and Watkins 1946; 1948). The diversity and scope of the U.S. economy, coupled with a hostile legal environment, made it difficult for U.S. leaders to stifle the appearance of new firms inside the country; those same factors put a brake on the leaders' engaging in overt collusion with European rivals. Nevertheless, global market-sharing agreements persisted at times, especially when patents and trademarks provided a fig leaf for the participants. By and large, though, the role of U.S. firms in these restrictive arrangements was cautious and restrained.

While participating in the international division of markets in a number of products before World War II, many large firms also established the first of their subsidiaries in foreign locations during that period. Commonly, however, large firms used these subsidiaries to implement their restrictive agreements with other firms, as in the case of the Du Pont–ICI subsidiaries located in Latin America. Often, too, firms established such subsidiaries as cautionary moves against the possibility that competitors might be in a position to cut them off from raw materials in times of shortage or from markets in times of glut. U.S. firms that were engaged in extracting and processing raw materials, for instance, typically developed vertically integrated structures that covered the chain from wellhead or mine shaft to the final distribution of processed products; and because other leading firms shared the same fear, partnerships among rivals commonly appeared at various points in these vertical chains, in the form of jointly owned oil fields, mines, and processing facilities. Meanwhile, other U.S. firms, such as General Motors, Ford, and General Electric, established subsidiaries in Europe, to serve as bridgeheads in the event of warfare among industry leaders. Such bridgeheads, consistent with their function, were usually allowed to operate with considerable independence and autonomy (Chandler 1990, 38–45, 205–33; Wilkins and Hill 1964, 360–79; Wilkins 1970, 93–96).

For a decade or two after World War II, the defensive responses of U.S.-based firms to their perceived risks in world markets were a little less in evidence. The reasons were too obvious to require much comment. The proverbial "animal spirits" of U.S. business were already at an elevated level as a result of the technological lead and financial advantages that U.S. firms enjoyed over their European rivals. Dramatic advances in communication and transportation were enlarging the stage on which those spirits could be released. The real cost of those services was rapidly declining; and with the introduction of containerized freight, airborne deliveries, and the telex, the range of those services was widening. These improvements expanded the business horizons of U.S.-based firms, allowing them to incorporate more distant locations in the marketing of their products and the sourcing of their needed inputs.

The first reaction of most U.S. firms to their expanding product markets was to meet demands by increasing exports from the home base. But, as numerous case studies attest, the establishment of local producing subsidiaries soon followed. Almost all of the first wave of manufacturing subsidiaries established in foreign countries after World War II were dedicated principally to serving the local markets in which they were placed.[1] As a consequence, about four-fifths of the sales of such subsidiaries during the 1960s were directed to local markets (Lipsey and Kravis 1982, 3).

The motives of the firms in serving local markets through producing subsidiaries rather than through exports were usually complex. In some cases, for instance, the establishment of a producing subsidiary was simply perceived as a more efficient means for serving the foreign market, a consequence of the fact that sales in the market had achieved a level sufficient to exploit the existing economies of scale in production. But other factors contributed to the scope and timing of these decisions as well. There were indications, for instance, that the decisions taken to establish subsidiaries abroad, whether for the marketing of products or for the production of required materials and com-

---

1. Even as late as 1975, about two-thirds of the manufacturing subsidiaries of U.S.-based firms were engaged almost exclusively in serving their local markets (Curhan, Davidson, and Suri. 1977, 393).

ponents, were often reactive measures, stimulated by and intended as a hedge against some perceived threat. Once a U.S. firm lost its unique technological or marketing lead, as seemed inevitable in most products over the course of time, governments might be tempted to restrict imports in order to encourage domestic production. In that case, the foreign subsidiary served to protect existing market access.

But even without the threat of action by governments, U.S.-based firms frequently faced threats posed by rivals in the product markets in which they operated. And some rich anecdotal evidence strongly suggests that foreign subsidiaries were often created as a hedge against such threats.

That hypothesis may help to explain why, in the first few decades after World War II, U.S.-based firms were engaged in follow-the-leader behavior in the establishment of new producing subsidiaries abroad. Once a U.S.-based firm in an oligopolistically structured industry set up a producing subsidiary in a given country, the propensity of other U.S.-based firms in the oligopoly to establish a subsidiary in the same country was visibly heightened (Knickerbocker (1973, 22–27; Yu and Ito 1988, 449–60). Such a pattern, of course, does not conclusively demonstrate that the follower is responding defensively to the behavior of the leader. Alternative hypotheses also need to be entertained, such as the possibility that both follower and leader were responding to a common outside stimulus or that the follower was responding in the belief that the leader had done a rational analysis equally applicable to both their situations.

However, stimulated by my reading of various individual cases, I am strongly inclined to attribute such follow-the-leader behavior in many cases to the follower's desire to hedge a threat posed by the leader. Although the follower may be unsure whether the leader has properly analyzed the costs and benefits of its move in establishing a foreign subsidiary, the follower is understandably fearful of allowing a rival to enjoy the benefits of undisturbed exploitation of its foreign opportunities. As long as the number of rival producers in the market is small, therefore, following the leader often seems to entail smaller downside risks than failing to follow. Failing to follow a leader that was right in making its move would give that leader an unrivaled opportunity to increase its competitive strength, whether by increasing its marketing opportunities or by reducing its production costs; if the leader was wrong, the follower's risks from committing the same error would be limited by the leader's having shared in it.

If the hedging of a threat was sometimes necessary for the growth of U.S.-based multinational enterprises, however, it was certainly not sufficient for such growth. Still to be explained was why in so many cases U.S.-based firms chose to establish producing subsidiaries rather than to exploit their strengths through licensing or other contractual arrangements with a local firm. In some cases, the high transaction costs associated with searching out and dealing with local firms may provide an adequate explanation. But here too, I am inclined to put heavy weight on explanations that see the establishment of a subsidiary in part as a hedge against various risks. Whenever licensing agreements are negotiated, both parties face the uncertainties generated by asymmetrical information; the licensee is uncertain of the value of the information it is to receive, while the licenser is uncertain of the use to which the licensee proposes to put the information. Moreover, enforcing the provisions of any licensing agreement carries both parties into areas of major uncertainty, based partly on the difficulties of monitoring the agreement and partly on the difficulties of enforcing its provisions.

In any event, the late 1960s registered a high watermark in the spread of the multinational networks of U.S.-based industrial enterprises, as the number of foreign affiliates added annually to such networks reached an all-time high (UN Commission on Transnational Corporations 1978, 223). For at least a decade thereafter, the number of foreign affiliates added annually was much reduced. Without firm-by-firm data of the kind compiled by the Harvard Multinational Enterprise Project for the period up to 1975, it is hard to know more precisely what was going on at the firm level during the succeeding years. But the rate of growth of these networks appeared to pick up again in the late 1980s.

The high rate of growth in recent years, however, appears to be based on somewhat different factors from those that prevailed in earlier decades. Anecdotal evidence indicates that U.S.-based firms continue to use their multinational networks to transfer newly generated products and processes from the United States to other countries. But with the U.S. lead greatly diminished in the generation of new products and processes, it is doubtful that the transmission of new products and processes from U.S. parents to foreign subsidiaries plays as important a role in the business of U.S.-based enterprises as it did some decades ago. Indeed, by the 1990s, the ostensible purpose of some U.S.-based firms in establishing foreign subsidiaries in Japan was not to diffuse existing skills but to acquire new skills for their multinational network in the hope that their Japanese experience would strengthen their competitive capabilities in markets all over the world.[2] With Japanese and European firms acquiring subsidiaries in the United States at the same time for the same purpose, it was apparent that the distinctive characteristics of U.S.-based multinational networks were beginning to fade.

Another factor that began to change the behavior of U.S.-based enterprises was the increasing familiarity of their managers with the problems of operating in foreign environments. At least until the 1970s, in their decisions when and where to establish subsidiaries in foreign countries, U.S.-based firms had been

2. See "American Business Starts a Counterattack in Japan," *New York Times,* Feb. 24 (1992, p. 1). A survey conducted by Japan's Ministry for International Trade and Industry in January 1990 reports that 38 percent of the foreign direct investors in Japan responding to the survey listed "engineering skill is high" as a reason for their investment, while 18 percent listed "collection of technical information and market information." Reproduced in *Nippon 1991* (1992, 109).

giving a heavy preference to the familiar. Careful analyses of the geographical sequence by which these firms established manufacturing facilities abroad demonstrated a historically heavy preference for setting up the first foreign production unit in Canada, with the United Kingdom taking second place and Mexico third.[3] By the 1960s, U.S.-based firms were bypassing Canada for Europe and Latin America as the first point of foreign manufacture; by the 1970s, although Europe and Latin America continued to provide the principal first-production sites, Asian sites were beginning to turn up with increasing frequency[4] (Vernon and Davidson 1979, 52, 134–35).

The role played by experience during these early postwar decades could be seen even more directly by trends in the reaction times of U.S.-based firms in setting up foreign production facilities. Where new products were involved, U.S.-based firms characteristically set up their first production sites within the United States. Eventually, however, they set up production sites abroad as well; as these firms gained experience with producing in a given country, the time interval involved in setting up production facilities in the country for new products showed a marked decline. Moreover, as the number of foreign production sites in any product increased, the time interval in setting up another facility in a foreign country also declined. By the 1970s, therefore, U.S.-based firms were beginning to show less hesitation in setting up production subsidiaries abroad for their new products and were scanning a rapidly widening circle of countries for their production sites.

The pattern toward which U.S.-owned multinational networks seem to be moving, therefore, is one in which the parent firm in the United States is prepared to survey different geographic locations on their respective merits, with a much reduced presumption in favor of a U.S. location. Instead, when assigning tasks to the various units of their multinational networks, U.S. business managers are increasingly likely to discount the distinction between home-based and foreign facilities, except as governmental restraints compel them to recognize that factor. This does not mean that the role played by geography is altogether obliterated. U.S.-based firms, for instance, continue to rely on Latin America more than on Asia to provide their low-cost labor needs, while the reverse is true for Japanese firms.[5] But the sense of uncertainty associated with producing outside the home economy has substantially declined, and the pref-

3. The generalizations are based on an unpublished study of the manufacturing subsidiaries of 180 U.S.-based multinational enterprises as of 1964. The 180 firms, whose multinational networks are covered in the computerized files of the Harvard Multinational Enterprise Project, were all large U.S.-based firms with substantial foreign manufacturing facilities (Vaupel 1971).

4. The study is based on the same multinational enterprises as those in Vaupel (1971). Conclusions in the two paragraphs following are based on data in the same study.

5. United Nations data affirm the preferences of U.S.-based and Japan-based firms for direct investment in nearby locations during the years 1971 to 1986, as well as the tendency of these geographical preferences to decline over time (UN Centre on Transnational Corporations 1988, 518–20. table A.5).

erence for nearby production locations such as those in Latin America over more remote locations such as those in Asia has declined as well.

For enterprises operating in oligopolistic markets, however, a major source of uncertainty remains. Even when such enterprises are fully familiar with the foreign environments in which they are obliged to operate, they are still exposed to the predatory and preemptive tactics of their rivals in the oligopoly. The reasoning that led the international oil and minerals firms to develop vertically integrated structures before World War II, therefore, can be glimpsed in more recent decades in the behavior of U.S.-based firms operating in oligopolistic markets. For instance, U.S.-based oil companies, having been separated from some of their captive crude oil supplies by the nationalizations in the 1970s, remain unwilling to rely upon the open market for the bulk of such supplies despite the existence of a large public market for the product. Facing the latent threat posed by the vertical integration of the Saudi and Venezuelan state-owned oil companies, U.S.-based firms are repairing and strengthening their upstream links.[6]

Such cautionary behavior is not confined to the raw materials industries. Similar behavior is apparent among U.S. firms in the electronics industry: under pressure to reduce the costs of labor-intensive components, firms such as IBM and Texas Instruments have chosen to manufacture a considerable part of their needs within their own multinational networks rather than to rely upon independent suppliers. A major factor in that decision, according to many observers, has been the fear that predatory rivals might withhold the most advanced versions of those components from competitors while incorporating them in their own products. (U.S. Congress 1991, 97–100; Schwartz 1992, esp. 149; Teece 1987, 65–95.)

For some U.S.-based enterprises, it was only a small step from using their foreign subsidiaries as feeders for manufacturing facilities in the United States to using those facilities to fill requirements arising anywhere in the network; by the 1980s, it had become apparent that this process was well advanced (Lipsey 1988). Of course, in practically every multinational network, the parent unit in the United States typically continued to occupy a unique position: characteristically, the parent's U.S. sales still accounted for the bulk of network sales, its U.S. facilities were responsible for the most important research and development work in the network, and its U.S. offices still coordinated some of the network's functions that might benefit from a centralized approach, such as the finance function. But the direction was clear. Although the centralized functions of the network would presumably remain in the United States indefinitely, the historical and institutional forces that resisted the geographical

---

6. For an account of the downstream movements of the various state-owned oil companies, and of new upstream ties forged by Gulf Oil, Sun Oil, Citgo, and Texaco, see *Business Week* 1988.

diffusion of other functions to locations outside the United States were growing weaker.

A more novel trend, however, has been the growing propensity of U.S.-based firms to enter into alliances of one kind or another with multinational networks based in other countries—typically, in other highly industrialized countries. Such alliances, for instance, sometimes take the form of a joint subsidiary established to perform a specified function or of an exchange of licenses in a specified field. At times, the arrangements link suppliers to their customers; at other times, the parties involved in such limited linkages appear to be direct rivals. A considerable literature is already developing regarding the operation of these alliances (Contractor and Lorange 1988; Gomes-Casseres 1989; Lewis 1990; Lynch 1989; Parkhe 1991). Although the definitions are muddy and the data far from complete, such alliances seem to be concentrated in industries in which barriers to entry are high and technological change is rapid and costly.

Part of the motivation for these alliances is apparent: an effort of each of the participating firms to reduce the risks associated with lumpy commitments to new research and development projects and to ensure that they are abreast of their competitors in their research resources. The alliances, therefore, are not much different in function from the jointly owned mines and oil fields that rival refiners and marketers shared in decades gone by, such as ARAMCO in Saudi Arabia, Southern Peru Copper in Peru, and HALCO in Guinea. Moreover, with common interests linking rivals to their suppliers and to one another in these new alliances, the likelihood that any one of the rivals might steal a technological lead on the others is obviously reduced. As with the partners in the raw material subsidiaries, therefore, there may well be a sense among some of the partners in the new alliances that their ties with rivals and suppliers could be used to reduce the harshness of future competition among them.

In one respect, however, many of the new alliances differ from those in the raw material industries. In industries with rapidly changing technologies and swiftly changing markets, the interests of the participants in any given alliance are likely to be relatively unstable; such firms will be constantly withdrawing and regrouping in order to satisfy their rapidly shifting strategic needs. Nevertheless, the possibility remains very real that these arrangements will serve at times to take the edge off the competition in some product markets.

For all the evidence that defensive motivations have been dominating the behavior of U.S.-based enterprises, there are various signs that the animal spirits of some U.S. managers can still be roused. One sign of such spirits is the global spread of U.S.-based firms in various service industries, including fast foods, advertising services, and management consulting. Some of these service-oriented firms developed multinational networks simply by following their multinational clients abroad in an effort to maintain an existing relationship; others, relying on a technological or managerial capability that their foreign rivals had not yet matched, bravely set out to master new environments without any apparent defensive motivation. Such initiatives, it appears, depend on the extent to which enterprises feel protected by some unique firm capability, such as a technological or managerial lead, or a patent or trademark.[7] But whether such situations are common or not in the future, defensive responses can be counted on to compel many large firms in the United States to maintain and extend their multinational networks.

3.2 Emergence of the Europeans

European industry often enjoys a reputation among Americans for sophistication and urbanity that equips them especially for the role of global entrepreneurs. But their performance as a group after World War II presents a very mixed picture.

In the decades just prior to World War II, the principal strategy of the leading European firms was to protect their home markets from competition, not to seek out new foreign markets. When they established subsidiaries in foreign countries, they tended to concentrate on countries to which their home governments had close political ties (Franko 1976, 81). And their typical reaction to the threat of international competition in those decades was to develop market-sharing arrangements along national lines.

In the immediate postwar period, European firms continued to cling to their home markets. Absorbed in the rebuilding of their home economies and saddled with the need to catch up technologically, they had little slack to devote to the establishment of new foreign facilities. True, enterprises headquartered in some of the smaller countries that possessed a technological edge, such as the pharmaceutical companies of Switzerland and the Netherlands and the machinery firms of Sweden, often felt compelled to set up subsidiaries outside their home countries in order to exploit their technological lead and to finance their ongoing innovational efforts; and the subsidiaries they set up in foreign countries typically operated with greater autonomy in foreign locations than did subsidiaries of some of their U.S. rivals. Moreover, manufacturing firms headquartered in the larger European countries were not altogether averse to establishing producing subsidiaries in areas over which their home governments still exercised strong political or economic influence. Between 1945 and 1965, for instance, British parents established about four hundred manufacturing subsidiaries in Australia, Canada, and New Zealand. (Harvard Multinational Enterprise Project data banks).

The disposition of European firms to identify closely with their home governments has some of its roots in history. Until recently, many were family-owned enterprises, with a long history of dominance in some given city or

---

7. The reader will recognize this theme as a major element in John H. Dunning's "eclectic theory." For his view of U.S. foreign direct investment trends in relation to the theory, see Dunning (1985, 66–70).

region. Some were so-called national champions, accustomed to especially favorable treatment by their governments in the provision of capital and the purchase of output (Michalet 1974, 105–25). The idea of maintaining close ties to their home government when operating abroad therefore represented an easy extension of their relationship at home.

After 1960, the emergence of a common market on the European continent began to affect the strategies of European firms. At first, however, these developments did little to encourage European firms to set up subsidiaries in other countries within the area. For one thing, the promise of a duty-free market among members of the European Community actually served to eliminate one of the motivations for creating such subsidiaries, namely the threat that frontiers might be closed to foreign goods. And with land distances relatively small and national markets relatively limited in size, the economic reasons for establishing such subsidiaries often did not appear compelling.

On the other hand, by the 1960s, U.S.-based companies were beginning to set up their subsidiaries in Europe in large numbers. Data from the Harvard Multinational Enterprise Project show that whereas, in the fifteen years between 1945 and 1959, U.S. parents had established some three hundred manufacturing subsidiaries in Europe, between 1960 and 1975 these parents established nearly two thousand manufacturing subsidiaries in Europe. Typically, the first landing of the U.S. invaders was in the United Kingdom, despite that country's delay in entering the European Community; but the U.S.-based firms were not long in establishing subsidiaries on the continent as well.

One might have expected the appearance of these subsidiaries to stimulate moves to renew the restrictive market-sharing agreements of the prewar period, but the environment following the end of World War II was much less conducive to such agreements. For one thing, rapidly expanding markets and swiftly changing technologies generated an environment that made agreements difficult. In addition, although enforcement of U.S. antitrust laws had grown lax in the postwar period, the European Community itself had adopted and was occasionally enforcing some exemplary measures aimed at preventing enterprises from dividing up the European market (Goyder 1988, esp. 71–133).

Eventually, however, most large European firms were led through the same defensive cycle that some U.S.-based firms had already experienced. Having reestablished export markets for their manufactured goods in many areas, including the Middle East and Latin America, they faced the same kind of threat that had moved their U.S. counterparts to set up producing subsidiaries abroad, namely the fear of losing a market through import restrictions. By 1970, manufacturing firms based in Europe were adding affiliates to their multinational networks in numbers over twice as high as those recorded by their U.S. counterparts (Harvard Multinational Enterprise Project data).

Moved largely by defensive considerations, European firms were adding rapidly to their holdings in the United States. There they showed a strong preference for investing in existing firms rather than in wholly new undertakings, and a strong disposition to team up with a U.S. firm in the process.[8] Such entries, some European managers supposed, would give them exposure to the latest industrial technologies and marketing strategies, thus strengthening their ability to resist the U.S. onslaught in their home markets and in third countries.

By the end of the 1960s, however, the Europeans had begun to have less reason to fear the dominance of U.S.-based firms. The differences in technological achievement between U.S. firms and European firms had obviously shrunk, and access to capital no longer favored the Americans. Not surprisingly, then, some of the motivations that lay behind the expansion of the European networks grew more nearly akin to that of the Americans—that is, largely defensive moves aimed at protecting a foreign market from import restrictions or copycat responses to the initiatives of rivals in setting up a subsidiary abroad (Flowers 1976).[9] In an apparent response to such stimuli, the number of European-owned subsidiaries appearing in various parts of the world increased rapidly (Harvard Multinational Enterprise Project data).

These new transborder relations have not wholly obliterated the distinctive national traits that have characterized European firms. German enterprises, for instance, continue to huddle in the shelter of their big banks, French companies in the protective cover of their national ministries. Moreover, despite the existence of the European Community, European firms continue to owe their existence to their respective national enabling statutes, which reflect wide differences in philosophical values and political balance. The United Kingdom, for instance, cannot agree with its continental partners on such fundamental issues as the responsibilities of the corporation to its labor force; whereas the British tend to see corporate managers primarily as the agents of their stockholders, continental governments generally take the view that labor has a quasi-proprietary stake in the enterprise that employs it, which stake managers are obliged to recognize. Differences such as these have served to block projects for the creation of a European company under the European Community's aegis.

Nevertheless, cross-border mergers are growing in number in Europe. In 1987, among the large industrial enterprises based in the community, only 75 cases were recorded in which a firm based in one EC country gained control of a firm based in another, but by 1990 the number had risen to 257 (European Commission 1991, 228). Indeed, in this universe of large industrial firms, the number of such transborder acquisitions in 1990 for the first time exceeded the number of like acquisitions involving firms in a single member country.

8. In the period from 1960 to 1970, about 80 percent of the manufacturing subsidiaries established by European parents in the United States were through acquisition or mergers with U.S. firms. The comparable figure for manufacturing subsidiaries of U.S. parents in Europe for the same period was 67 percent (Harvard Multinational Enterprise Project data).

9. The assumption that the spread of European networks was due in part to follow-the-leader behavior, at least until the 1970s, is fortified by some unpublished studies undertaken by Fred Knickerbocker (1973), whose analysis of the behavior of U.S.-based manufacturing subsidiaries is cited elsewhere in this chapter.

In part, the trend toward cross-border mergers is a consequence of the many liberalizing measures that the member countries of the European Community have taken with regard to capital flows. In addition, however, there appears to be a visible weakening of the family conglomerate, a distinctly national form of big business. In Italy, for instance, where that kind of structure has been particularly prominent in the private sector, the country's leading family conglomerates have fallen on especially hard times.[10]

The disposition of many firms to cling to the shreds of their national identity will lead many of them to hesitate over transborder mergers and consolidations in which they are not the surviving entity or, when they finally succumb to the pressures for merger, to insist on retaining a minority interest in the subsidiary that has been joined to the network of the foreign-based firm. That same disposition suggests why European firms appear to give a heavier preference to consortia and alliances as a way of combining their strengths with a foreign firm than U.S.-based competitors would do. But, because I see such arrangements as fragile over time, I see transborder mergers as the preferred vehicle in spite of the obstacles. Such mergers may still generate resistance and hostility in some countries.[11] A few decades from now, however, the national differences in Europe's business communities are likely to prove no more important than the differences between Texas-based enterprises and Massachusetts-based enterprises in the United States.

In explaining the growth of the networks of firms based in Europe, then, I return to some of the same themes that were stressed in the case of U.S.-based firms. The summary of the factors that have pushed U.S.-based enterprises to develop and expand their multinational networks in the past decades stressed the continuous improvements in the technology of communication and transportation as the powerful exogenous factor; the decisions of the U.S.-based firms to expand their enterprises were seen in large part as a response aimed at reducing the uncertainties and countering the threats that accompanied such developments. I feel sure that these generalizations will carry the observer a considerable distance in understanding the behavior of Europe-based firms as well.[12] Over time, the differences that heretofore have distinguished U.S.-based from Europe-based multinational networks are likely to diminish as the conditions of their founding and early growth begin to lose their original importance.

3.3 Latecomer Japan

Studying the factors behind the growth of multinational enterprises based in Japan, a phenomenon of the past two or three decades, will bring us back to

---

10. For an account of the troubles of the Agnelli and Pirelli family conglomerates, see *Financial Times* (1992a).

11. For a rich account of such hostilities in France's reactions to the Agnelli family's efforts to acquire control over Perrier, see *Financial Times* (1992c).

12. A study of European banking confirms the existence of each of the major tendencies identified above. See Campayne (1992).

the same defensive motivations, including the need of Japanese enterprises to protect their interests against the hostile acts of foreign governments and business competitors, and their desire to build up competitive strengths by exposing themselves to the most challenging technological and marketing environments.

Indeed, the defensive motivations that commonly lie behind the creation and spread of multinational enterprises are likely to act even more powerfully on the Japanese than on their U.S.-based and Europe-based competitors. To see why, it helps to review briefly the evolution of Japan's industrial structure (see, e.g., Wilkins 1990, 585–629).

From the earliest years of the Meiji restoration in the last decades of the nineteenth century, the industrial structure of Japan exhibited some distinctive national characteristics. Dominating the core of Japan's modern economy were half a dozen conglomerate organizations, each with its own captive bank, trading company, and portfolio of manufacturing and service enterprises. The conglomerate structure, well developed before World War II, was modified only a little by Japan's loss of its foreign territories and by the ensuing occupation. Japanese firms lost their investments in the territories its armies had occupied, but these investments had largely been controlled by the so-called new zaibatsu, companies that depended for their existence on Japan's foreign conquests and that had very little stake in the home economy itself.

In Japan proper, the holding companies that sat at the apex of each conglomerate were liquidated during the occupation. But the member firms of the conglomerates maintained their old ties by cross-holdings of stock and by shared memories of past loyalties. And in the 1960s and 1970s, as foreign enterprises began to show some interest in acquiring control over Japanese firms, member firms within each conglomerate systematically built up their cross-holdings even further as a means of repelling foreign boarders (Ito 1992, 191).

From the early emergence of these conglomerate organizations, a fierce rivalry existed among them—but a rivalry based much more on comparative rates of growth and market shares than on nominal profits. Within each conglomerate, the financing of the contest was left to the conglomerate's captive bank rather than to public capital markets. But the general scope and direction of the lending by these banks to their affiliates were largely determined by continuous consultation with key government agencies, especially the Ministry of Finance, the Bank of Japan, and the Ministry for International Trade and Industry (MITI).

By the 1980s, however, it was becoming apparent that major changes were taking place in the conglomerate structures. Perhaps the most obvious change was the dramatic shift in the financing practices of the industrial firms. As the rate of growth of the Japanese economy slowed up a little in the 1980s and as the need to finance capacity expansion grew less urgent, Japanese firms found that internally generated cash was going a much longer way toward meeting their capital needs.

At the same time, under pressure from foreign sources and from Japan's own financial intermediaries, the Ministry of Finance was gradually relaxing its tight controls over the development of internal capital markets, thereby providing Japanese companies for the first time with a real option for raising their capital needs through the sale of securities in public markets. Concurrently, Japanese firms were being granted permission to raise capital in foreign currencies by selling their securities abroad or borrowing from foreign banks. Japanese banks, trading houses, and other service facilities, therefore, were strongly represented in the outflow of direct investment from Japan to major foreign markets.[13] And because Japanese manufacturing firms were always a little uncomfortable when dealing with foreigners as service suppliers, the existence of those service facilities in foreign markets eased the way for the manufacturers to establish their foreign subsidiaries outside of Japan (Gittelman and Dunning 1992, 237–67).

In accounting for the changes in the character of the multinational networks based in Japan, however, one must place particularly heavy emphasis on the increasing technological capabilities of these enterprises. In the very first stages of the development of multinational networks by Japan-based firms, in the 1960s and 1970s, some scholars entertained the hypothesis that these firms would develop a pattern of foreign direct investment quite different from that pioneered by U.S.-based and Europe-based firms (Kojima 1978, 85–87). At that stage, Japan's penetration of foreign markets for manufactured goods was most in evidence in South and Southeast Asia and was heavily concentrated in relatively simple items such as batteries, noodles, radios, and other consumer goods—items in which Japan's comparative advantage was already fading. Given the unsophisticated nature of the products and the lack of a need for after-sales services, Japanese producers usually used their affiliated trading companies as their agents in these foreign markets; indeed, in many cases, the Japanese producers were not large enough even to consider marketing their own products abroad and so had no choice but to rely on trading companies.

In these cases, when the risk that the government might impose restrictions became palpable, the trading company typically took the lead in establishing a local production facility, often through a three-way partnership that combined the trading company with a local distributor and with the erstwhile Japanese exporter (Yoshino 1976, 95–126). From this early pattern, it appeared that the Japan-based multinational enterprise might root itself much more deeply in its foreign markets than did the U.S.-based and Europe-based companies, with results that might prove more benign from the viewpoint of the host country.

By the 1980s, however, the patterns of foreign direct investment by Japanese firms were converging toward the norms recorded by their U.S. and European rivals (Encarnation 1992, 9–35). As with U.S.- and Europe-based firms, the

---

13. In the 1980s, the relative importance of services in the outflow of foreign direct investment from Japan was substantially higher than for FDI outflow from the United States, the United Kingdom, West Germany, or France (UN Centre on Transnational Corporations 1991, 16, table 6).

object of Japanese firms in establishing a producing subsidiary in a foreign country was commonly to protect a market in a relatively differentiated product that originally had been developed through exports from Japan.

Compared with U.S.-based or Europe-based firms, however, the stake of Japanese firms in the export markets of other industrialized countries soon grew very large.[14] The spectacular growth of Japanese exports to the markets of such countries exposed Japanese firms once more to threats of restrictive action on a major scale. At this advanced stage, however, the markets to be protected were considerably different in character from those that the first generation of Japan-based multinationals had developed. One difference was in the identity of the markets under siege, now located mainly in the United States and Europe. Another was the nature of the products involved; these were relatively sophisticated products, such as automobiles, camcorders, and computer-controlled machine tools. And a third was the channels of distribution involved; such sophisticated products were usually marketed through channels under the direct control of the manufacturers rather than through trading companies.

The networks that Japan-based firms created in response to the new threats came closer to emulating those of the U.S.-based and Europe-based firms with multinational networks. Moreover, as with their European rivals, many of the foreign acquisitions by Japan-based firms were explained by a desire to acquire advanced technological skills; this motive was especially apparent in the acquisition of various medium-sized high-tech firms in the United States (Kester 1991; Kogut and Chang 1991).

Although the multinational networks that Japan-based firms produced in this second generation bore a much greater resemblance to the networks of their counterparts from other advanced industrialized countries, some characteristic differences remained. One such characteristic was the high propensity of Japan-based multinationals to control their producing subsidiaries tightly from Japan. Symptomatic of that fact was the near-universal use of Japanese personnel to head their foreign subsidiaries.[15] A striking illustration of the same desire for control was the limited leeway allowed subsidiaries in the acquisition of capital equipment. Australian subsidiaries of Japanese firms, for instance, possessed far less leeway in the selection of new machinery than did the subsidiaries of U.S.-based or Europe-based firms (Kreinin 1988). Some signs existed in the 1990s that a few Japanese firms were breaking away from their traditional controls and giving their foreign subsidiaries greater leeway, but the illustrations were still exceptional (*Economist* 1992).

14. Data on the identities of the world's leading multinationals in the latter 1980s, with partial statistics on their respective stakes in foreign markets gleaned primarily from annual reports, appear in UN Commission on Transnational Corporations (1978, 287–316).

15. For instance, a study of the U.S. subsidiaries of Japanese electronic firms reports that only 2 percent of Japanese electronics firms in the United States had U.S. chief executive officers (U.S. Congress 1991, 99).

The early reluctance of Japan-based firms to develop a multinational network and the tendency of the foreign subsidiaries of such firms to rely upon their established sources in Japan have been attributed to a number of different factors. They have been variously explained as a consequence of the relative inexperience of Japanese firms with the novel problems of producing abroad, as a result of the heavy reliance on the consensual process in firm decision making, or as a consequence of the extensive use of just-in-time producing processes, which demand the closest coordination between the firms and their suppliers (Kester 1991, 109). Introducing strangers into the system, according to the argument, entails major modifications in firm practices that cannot be achieved overnight.

Nevertheless, by the end of the 1980s, Japan-based firms were expanding their multinational networks at an unprecedented rate. What is more, their manufacturing affiliates in the United States and Europe were drawing a considerable fraction of their inputs from sources located in the host country (Gittelman and Dunning 1992, 40). Moreover, it appeared that some of the very factors that had slowed the growth of Japan-based multinational networks in the past could be expected to reinforce the expansion rather than to slow it down. For example, the desire of Japanese firms to rely on Japanese sources means that the foreign subsidiaries of major Japanese firms are pulling large numbers of satellite suppliers with them into foreign locations. While this has not been an unknown phenomenon in the establishment of the multinational networks of firms based in the United States, it appears to be an especially powerful force in the case of Japan-based firms (Wilkins 1990, 612–16).[16] Moreover, if one pair of authoritative observers is to be believed, Japanese firms already are being drawn into Europe by the conviction that they must assimilate some distinctive regional emphases if they are to be successful in major industries, such as automobiles and electronic equipment (Gittelman and Dunning 1992). Finally, given the intense rivalry of Japanese firms, with their stress on market share, it is not unreasonable to expect a pattern of copycat behavior even stronger than that observed with respect to firms based in other countries.

Whether the Japanese government will seek at some point to restrain the overseas movement of its firms through administrative guidance is unclear; but even if it makes such an attempt, there is no certainty that the attempt would prove effective. The growing financial independence of Japanese firms means that the Ministry of Finance and MITI have lost one of their principal sources of coercion. The Japanese firms' commitment of a large proportion of their assets to foreign locations means that they will be exposed to stimuli not strik-

---

16. A hint of the strong tendency of Japanese firms to buy from enterprises with which they have close links appears also in Gittelman and Dunning (1992). See also *Financial Times* (1992a), an account of Nissan's impact on northeast England.

ingly different from those affecting their U.S. and European rivals. Developments such as these promise to contribute to the movement of Japan-based multinationals toward the norms typical of multinationals based in other countries (Lipsey 1991, 87).

3.4   Patterns of the Future

International Business

In the future as in the past, some powerful exogenous factors will influence the spread of multinational enterprises, including changes in the technologies of transportation, communication, and production. But it is not easy to project the consequences of such changes. For instance, if just-in-time manufacturing takes on added strength, the clustering tendency of related enterprises should grow stronger; but if flexible manufacturing processes gain in strength, smaller and more self-contained plans could dominate, reducing the tendency toward clusters (Auty 1992; Dunning 1992, esp. 158–62). Despite uncertainties of this sort, however, I anticipate that multinational networks and transborder alliances, already a major factor in international economic flows, will grow in importance.

3.4.1   The Response of Governments

How governments will respond to that situation is a little uncertain. Although globalization and convergence may prove to be major trends defining the behavior of multinational enterprises in the future, it is implausible to assume that national governments will stand aside and allow such behavior to develop as it may. With jobs, taxes, payment balances, and technological achievement seemingly at stake, governments are bound to act in an effort to defend national interests and respond to national pressures. Their efforts, involving carrots in some cases and sticks in others, will continue to pose threats and offer opportunities to the multinationals.

Some governmental responses will take the form of restrictions, unilaterally adopted, aimed at holding inbound and outbound foreign investment in check. But from all the signs, political leaders in the major industrialized countries seem aware that national autarky is not an available option unless a country is prepared to absorb some overwhelming costs. That recognition explains why so many countries now eye the possibility of developing regional blocs—areas large enough to satisfy the modern requirements of scale and scope, and small enough to promise member countries that they will exert some influence in shaping their joint economic policies.

There is surface plausibility to the idea that such blocs may figure importantly in the future, a plausibility reflected in the preeminence of Japanese interests in South and Southeast Asia, European interests in Africa, Eastern Europe, and the Middle East, and U.S. interests in Latin America. But it is easy to misinterpret the significance of those concentrations. As already suggested, they may reflect little more than the myopic learning process of business managers, and increasing experience may push them toward scanning over a wider geographical range.

In any case, when seen through the eyes of the managers of multinational enterprises based in the industrialized areas, the managers' principal stake by far lies in other industrialized areas, not in the hinterlands of their respective "regions." That has been the case for decades, and it has shown no signs of changing in recent years. To be sure, such enterprises will not hesitate to use the influence of their respective governments to promote their interests in these regions. But from the viewpoint of the firms, such efforts will be a sideshow compared to their respective stakes in other industrialized economies.

At the same time, the influence that individual governments are in a position to exert over their respective multinational enterprises appears rapidly on the decline. Although governments have been known to remain blind to the obvious for remarkably prolonged periods of time, that ineluctable fact should eventually lead them to limit their unilateral efforts at control. Where control of some sort still seems necessary or desirable, the option remaining will be to pursue mutually agreed-upon measures with other countries. In the decades ahead, the United States, Europe, and Japan are sure to find themselves addressing the feasibility and desirability of international agreements that define more fully the rights and obligations of multinational enterprises. Although most other countries may be slower to address the issue, a few such as Singapore and Mexico along with the non-European members of the Organization for Economic Cooperation and Development (OECD) are likely to be involved as well. Already some of the elements of an international system are in place with respect to a few functional fields, such as the levying of corporate income taxes. It does not stretch the imagination very much to picture international agreements on such subjects as the competition of governments for foreign direct investment, the threats to market competition posed by restrictive business practices and mergers, the rights and obligations of multinational enterprises in national political processes, and other issues relating to the multinational enterprise.

3.4.2   The Development of Theory

In the past, as multinational networks appeared and grew, some researchers concerned with understanding the causes of their behavior found it useful, even indispensable, to distinguish such enterprises according to their national base. If I am right in seeing strong tendencies toward national convergence, distinctions based on the national origin of the network are likely to lose their analytic and descriptive value, and distinctions on other dimensions are likely to grow in importance. Even more than in the past, distinctions based on the characteristics of the product market and the production process are likely to prove particularly fruitful.

As I observed earlier, many multinational enterprises created global networks in response to perceived threats and operated under circumstances in which ignorance and uncertainty were endemic. For the most part, the enterprises operated in product markets with significant barriers to entry, including static and dynamic scale economies, patents and trademarks. With the passage of time, however, a considerable proportion of these multinational enterprises overcame their sense of acute uncertainty in foreign markets, especially as the products and their related technologies grew more stable and standardized.

These tendencies often reduced barriers to entry, increased the number of participants, and elevated the role of price competition. In the production and sale of metals and petroleum, for instance, the number of sellers on world markets inexorably increased, and the role of competitive pricing grew. In big-ticket consumer electronics, an intensification of competitive pricing among multinational enterprises also has become commonplace, despite the persistent efforts of sellers to differentiate their products. In such cases, there is considerable utility in models that cast the participants as fully informed actors operating in a market in which their choices are known, under conditions in which some scale economies exist (Helpman and Krugman 1985, 225–59; Grossman and Helpman 1991, 197–200). I see no reason why models based on these assumptions should not generate useful first approximations to the behavior of multinational enterprises in a considerable number of industries.

Other models may also have something to contribute, such as those that view multinational networks as the consequence of decisions by firms to internalize certain types of transactions. The international market for the sale of technology and management skills, for instance, is a grossly inefficient market from the viewpoint of both buyer and seller (Teece 1986; Galbraith and Kay 1986). Internalization can be viewed as a response to those inefficiencies, in a setting in which the enterprises are otherwise fully aware of the set of choices they confront and of the facts bearing on those choices (Casson 1987, 1–49; Williamson 1971).

Models based on the internalization hypothesis therefore fit comfortably into the structure of the models described earlier, which are based essentially on a neoclassical framework driven by costs and prices. But they have tended to crowd out the analysis of other motivations that seem at least as important in explaining the behavior of the managers of such enterprises. For instance, various measures taken by the firm to create a multinational network may be driven by another motive, namely a desire to avoid being exposed to the predatory behavior of rivals, including the risk that such rivals might cut off needed supplies or deny access to a distribution system during some future contingency.

That possibility pushes the modeler in a very different direction in attempting to explain the behavior of multinational enterprises. Such enterprises continue to figure prominently in many product markets that have not yet attained a stable middle age. In such markets, the number of producers is often sharply limited, products and related services are often highly differentiated, technologies are in flux, and price differences are not the critical factor in competition. Moreover, externalities of various kinds commonly play a dominant role in locational decisions, as when enterprises try to draw on various national environments to produce the stimuli they think will improve their competitive strengths. Firms engaged in producing microprocessors, aircraft engines, and wonder drugs, for instance, are strongly influenced by one or another of these factors.

Needless to say, where the number of rivals in a market is low, that fact fundamentally conditions the strategies of the participants. Some of them may long for the security of a market-sharing arrangement and may even take some tentative steps in that direction, such as entering into partnerships with some of their rivals. But developing an effective market-sharing arrangement is usually difficult and dangerous.

In any event, when a limited number of participants are involved in a product market, theorists must entertain the possibility that the firms that are engaged in such markets see any given transaction as only one move in a campaign stretching across time. In each transaction, the principal objective of the firm is to strengthen its position in relation to its rivals or to neutralize the efforts of its rivals to steal a march; with that objective paramount, share of market becomes a critical measure of success. In such circumstances, invading a rival's principal market may prove a useful defensive strategy, aimed at reducing the rival's propensity for warfare elsewhere. And, given the imperfect knowledge under which each firm is assumed to operate, a policy of following a rival into new areas of supply and new markets may be seen as a prudent response to the rival's initiatives.[17]

Of course, by shedding many of the assumptions underlying the neoclassical model, models built on such behavioral assumptions relinquish the support provided by a comprehensive body of well-explored theory. Instead, the analyst is thrown into a world of uncertain outcomes, explored so far largely by game theorists, specialists in signaling theory, and others outside the neoclassical mainstream. It is hardly surprising, therefore, that most of the scholars who have sought to model the behavior of the multinational enterprise have avoided the implications of high uncertainty and limited numbers, preferring instead to concentrate on hypotheses that require less radical departures from neoclassical assumptions.

Nevertheless, any serious effort to project the behavior of multinational enterprises in the future will have to recognize that the players in many major product and service markets will see themselves as engaged in a campaign against specific adversaries in a global market, with individual decisions being shaped in light of that perception. At different times and places, there will be

---

17. Casson (1987, 53–83) and Bower (1992) omit any reference to such possibilities. See also Graham and Krugman (1989), where such possibilities are presented not in the theory section of the report but in an annex entitled "Industrial-Organization Explanations of Foreign Direct Investment."

efforts to call a truce, efforts to weaken specific adversaries, and efforts to counter the aggressive behavior of others. The behavior that emerges will not be easily explained in terms of models that satisfy neoclassical conditions. Therein lies a major challenge for those who are attempting to cast light on the behavior of multinational enterprises through systematic modeling.

References

Auty, Richard M. 1992. *Changing competitiveness of newly industrialized countries in heavy and chemical industry: Effects of the product cycle and technological change.* Amsterdam: University of Amsterdam.

Bower, Anthony G. 1992. Predicting locational decisions of multinational corporations. N-3440-CUSTR. Santa Monica, Calif.: Rand Corporation.

Business Week. 1988. Why kings of crude want to be pump boys. 21 March, pp. 110–12.

Campayne, Paul. 1992. Cross investment in the European banking sector. In *Multinational investment in modern Europe: Strategic interaction in the integrated community,* ed. J. Cantwell. London: Edward Elgar.

Casson, Mark. 1987. *The firm and the market: Studies on multinational enterprise and the scope of the firm.* Cambridge, Mass.: MIT Press.

Chandler, Alfred D. 1990. *Scale and scope: The dynamics of industrial capitalism.* Cambridge: Belknap Press.

Contractor, F. J., and Peter Lorange, eds. 1988. *Cooperative strategies in international business.* Lexington, Mass.: Lexington Books.

Curhan, Joan P., William H. Davidson, and Rajan Suri. 1977. *Tracing the multinationals: A sourcebook on U.S.-based enterprise.* Cambridge, Mass.: Ballinger Publishing.

Dunning, John H. 1992. The competitive advantage of countries and the activities of transnational corporations. *Transnational Corporations* 1, no. 1 (February): 135–69.

———, ed. 1985. *Multinational enterprises, economic structure and international competitiveness.* New York: John Wiley and Sons.

Economist. 1992. Japan's less-than-invincible computer makers. 11 January, pp. 59–60.

Encarnation, Dennis J. 1992. *Rivals beyond trade: America versus Japan in global competition.* Ithaca, N.Y.: Cornell University Press.

European Commission. 1991. *20th report on competition policy.* Brussels: European Commission.

Financial Times. 1992a. Leaders that have lost their way. 21 January, p. 18.

———. 1992b. Benefits beyond the automotive sector. 18 February, p. 28.

———. 1992c. Dynastic hopes fall flat in France. 25 March, p. 14.

Flowers, E. B. 1976. Oligopolistic reactions in European and Canadian direct investment in the United States. *Journal of International Business Studies* 7 (3): 43–55.

Franko, Lawrence G. 1976. *The European multinationals.* New York: Harper and Row.

Galbraith, Craig S., and Neil M. Kay. 1986. Towards a theory of multinational enterprise. *Journal of Economic Behavior and Organization* 7 no. 1 (March): 3–19.

Gittelman, Michelle, and John H. Dunning. 1992. Japanese multinationals in Europe and the United States: Some comparisons and contrasts. In *Multinationals in the new Europe and global trade,* ed. Michael W. Klein and Paul J. J. Welfens. Berlin: Springer-Verlag.

Gomes-Casseres, Benjamin. 1989. Joint ventures in the face of global competition. *Sloan Management Review,* 30, no. 3 (Spring): 17–26.

Goyder, D. G. 1988. *EEC competition law.* New York: Clarendon Press.

Graham, Edward M., and Paul R. Krugman. 1989. *Foreign direct investment in the United States.* Washington, D.C.: Institute for International Economics.

Grossman, Gene, and Elhanan Helpman. 1991. *Innovation and growth in the global economy.* Cambridge, Mass.: MIT Press.

Helpman, Elhanan, and Paul R. Krugaman. 1985. *Market structure and foreign trade.* Cambridge, Mass.: MIT Press.

Hexner, Ervin P. 1945. *International cartels.* Chapel Hill: University of North Carolina Press.

Ito, Takatoshi. 1992. *The Japanese economy.* Cambridge, Mass.: MIT Press.

Kester, W. C. 1991. *Japanese takeovers: The global quest for corporate control.* Boston: Harvard Business School Press.

Knickerbocker, Frederick T. 1973. *Oligopolistic reaction and multinational enterprise.* Boston: Harvard University, Graduate School of Business Administration, Division of Research.

Kogut, Bruce, and Sea Gin Chang. 1991. Technological capabilities and Japanese foreign direct investment in the United States. *Review of Economics and Statistics* 73, no. 3 (August): 401–13.

Kojima, Kiyoshi. 1978. *Direct foreign investment: A Japanese model of multinational business operations.* London: Croom Helm.

Kreinin, Mordechai E. 1988. How closed is Japan's market? Additional evidence. *World Economy* 11, no. 4 (December): 529–42.

Lall, Sanjaya. 1991. Direct investment in South-East Asia by the NIEs: Trends and prospects. *Banca Nazionale del Lavoro Quarterly Review* 179: 463–80.

Lewis, Jordan D. 1990. *Partnerships for profit: Structuring and managing strategic alliances.* New York: Free Press.

Lipsey, Robert E. 1988. Changing patterns of international investment in and by the United States. In *The United States in the world economy,* ed. Martin Feldstein, 475–545. Chicago: University of Chicago Press.

———. 1991. Foreign direct investment in the United States and U.S. trade. *Annals of the American Academy of Political and Social Science* (July): 76–90.

Lipsey, Robert E., and Irving B. Kravis. 1982. U.S.-owned affiliates and host-country exports. NBER Working Paper no. 1037. Cambridge, Mass.: National Bureau of Economic Research.

Lynch, Robert Porter. 1989. *The practical guide to joint venture and corporate alliances.* New York: John Wiley and Sons.

Michalet, Charles-Albert. 1974. France. In *Big business and the states,* ed. Raymond Vernon. Cambridge, Mass.: Harvard University Press.

New York Times. 1992. American business starts a counterattack in Japan. 24 February.

Nippon 1991: Business facts and figures. 1992. New York: JETRO.

Parkhe, Arvinde. 1991. Interfirm diversity, organizational learning, and longevity in global strategic alliances. *Journal of International Business Studies* (4): 579–601.

Schwartz, Jacob T. 1992. America's economic-technological agenda for the 1990s. *Daedalus* 121, no. 1 (Winter): 139–65.

Stocking, George W., and Myron W. Watkins. 1946. *Cartels in action: Case studies in international business diplomacy.* New York: 20th Century Fund.

———. 1948. *Cartels or competition?* New York: 20th Century Fund.

Teece, David J. 1986. Transaction cost economics and the multinational enterprise. *Journal of Economic Behavior and Organization* 7 no. 1 (March): 21–45.

———. 1987. Capturing value from technological innovations: Integration, strategic partnering and licensing decisions. In *Technology and global industry: Companies and nations in the world economy,* ed. Bruce R. Guild and Harvey Brooks. Washington, D.C.: National Academy Press.

UN Centre on Transnational Corporations. 1988. *Transnational corporations in world development: Trends and prospects.* New York: United Nations.

―――. 1991. *World investment report 1991: The triad in foreign direct investment.* New York: United Nations.

UN Commission on Transnational Corporations. 1978. *Transnational corporations in world development: A re-examination.* New York, E/C. 10/38, based on data from the Harvard Multinational Enterprise Project.

―――. 1990. *Non-conventional transnational corporations.* New York: United Nations.

U.S. Congress, Office of Technology Assessment. 1991. *Competing economies: America, Europe and the Pacific Rim.* OTA-ITE-498. Washington, D.C.: U.S. Government Printing Office.

Vaupel, James W. 1971. Study of manufacturing subsidiaries of 180 U.S.-based multinational enterprises as of 1964. Paper presented at June conference, Turin, Italy.

Vernon, Raymond, and W. H. Davidson. 1979. *Foreign production of technology-intensive products by U.S.-based multinational enterprises.* Report to the National Science Foundation, no. PB 80 148638.

Wilkins, Mira. 1970. *The emergence of multinational enterprise.* Cambridge, Mass.: Harvard University Press.

―――. 1990. Japanese multinationals in the United States: Continuity and change, 1879–1990. *Business History Review* 64 (Winter): 585–629.

Wilkins, Mira, and Frank Ernest Hill. 1964. *American business abroad: Ford on six continents.* Detroit: Wayne State University Press.

Williamson, Oliver E. 1971. The vertical integration of production: Market failure considerations. *American Economic Review* 61 (May): 112–23.

Yoshino, Michael Y. 1976. *Japan's multinational enterprises.* Cambridge, Mass.: Harvard University Press.

Yu, C. J., and K. Ito. 1988. Oligopolistic reaction and foreign direct investment. *Journal of International Business Studies* 19 (3): 449–60.

Comment   Richard E. Caves

Raymond Vernon writes about the changing activity patterns of multinational enterprises from a long and intense involvement with the subject. His observations cover important trends or attributes in three areas of their operations: (1) multinationals based in different countries become more similar over time, just as U.S.-based leviathans grow less dominant and the national sources of multinationals more diffuse; (2) public policies remain important constraints and threats affecting multinationals' decisions; (3) foreign investment is influenced importantly by strategic considerations such as denying tactical advantage to oligopolistic rivals. I shall comment on each of these areas.

That the activities of multinationals based in different countries grow more homogeneous is clearly correct and rests on a number of underlying trends. As noted by Vernon, one of these is that, among different countries' largest firms, institutional differences that differentially affect their potential performance (such as predominant family ownership) are dying out. This is true for the simple Darwinian reason that inefficient institutions tend not to survive forever, although institutional differences can coexist that do not differentially affect firms' performance as foreign investors.

A second source of reduced difference lies in increasingly similar comparative-advantage patterns, broadly defined, of the major industrial countries. With labor-intensive manufacturing gravitated to the newly industrializing countries, the developed nations that are the principal homes of multinational firms exhibit increasingly similar patterns of comparative advantage in trade. This similarity is evidenced by the large increase in intraindustry trade among the OECD countries that has occurred since World War II. This increased similarity in comparative-advantage patterns translates (it can be argued) into increased similarity in nations' patterns of foreign investment.

A third factor, harder to pin down, is greater homogeneity of both tastes and technology among the industrial countries. *Homogenization* is perhaps not quite the right word: the operative force is awareness of differences in consumption sets and ways of doing things that translates into selective adoption of foreign ways and things, driven by greatly reduced costs of international communication and travel. For potential multinational firms, this trend lowers many components of the fixed cost of adaptation to a foreign environment. This trend is especially evident in the development of Japan's multinational firms. Japanese foreign investment in the United States during the 1970s and 1980s was driven by its complementarity with Japanese exporting activities and Japan's growing research capability, as one would expect. In the 1980s, it also came to be positively related to industries' advertising intensities, as Japanese firms demonstrated the capability to steer around the national style differences that seem to prevail in most advertising-intensive products (Drake and Caves 1992).

Regarding countries' interventions in multinationals' activities, Vernon argues in essence that the trend is more of the same. Significant amounts of foreign investment take place, he feels, to avert profit losses caused by the importing country's restrictions on the foreign firm's exports. Governments are certainly growing no less solicitous about preserving substantial (if limited and inexplicit) property rights of workers in their jobs. Because domestic firms' property rights in their rents are much less secure, foreign investment that threatens only investors' rents is viable where exports that threaten both investors' rents and employees' job opportunities are not. (The glorious confusion surrounding this public policy preference is illustrated by the debate in the United States over what is a foreign automobile.)

Although I basically agree with Vernon's *plus ça change* . . . judgment, I suggest that invasive public policies have been somewhat muted by the increased symmetry of the industrial countries' positions as sources and hosts of foreign direct investment. Xenophobic reactions to foreigners, as suppliers of imports, investors, owners of property, and so on, can be taken for granted. Those familiar with other countries' complaints about U.S. multinationals two and three decades ago can only regard with bemusement the rise of exactly the same complaints about foreign multinationals in the United States during the past decade. Nonetheless, when xenophobia clamors for translation into public policy, the interests of multinationals based in the afflicted country demand to be weighed in the balance. The result, I suggest, is an important damper on restrictive policies analogous to the one on trade policies that Milner (1988) documented, which was due to increasing symmetries of trade positions. Independently, the developing countries have chosen less restrictive policies since the 1960s, part of their more general recognition of the productivity-raising effects of market-based incentive structures. That a code of conduct toward multinational enterprises was even on the table for discussion in the Uruguay Round under the General Agreement on Tariffs and Trade testifies to the increased similarity of nations' policy preferences; a quarter-century ago, broad international agreement on the treatment of multinationals would have been inconceivable.

Statistical research has shown that much of the variance in the activity levels of multinational enterprises can be explained by transaction cost factors that call for internalization within the enterprise to avert what would otherwise be contractual failures in arm's-length transactions. This explanation for multinationals and their activity levels is nonstrategic in the sense that expansion abroad by one firm does not directly affect the payout in reduced transaction costs to a parallel expansion by its market rival. Vernon urges, however, that a large amount of foreign investment is strategic and influenced specifically by oligopolistic interaction of competing firms. (I am not sure how he would define *large:* the criterion might be the proportion of foreign investment decisions ranked in some upper tier by dollar amount.) In view of the great interest that industrial economics has recently taken in game theory and strategic interactions, this position merits close examination.

Vernon starts by noting the familiar evidence of the extent of international collusion and market-sharing agreements in important industries between World Wars I and II. It might be attractive for researchers to revisit this evidence in light of modern game theory, in order to characterize more precisely what processes were at work. The role of foreign investment in this process has always, to me, seemed problematic, because the division of markets involves a pledge to forgo investing in some nations. If the deployment of subsidiaries as threats or hostages was indeed involved, the evidence would make excellent grist for modern students of industrial organization who are oriented toward game theory.

The pattern that Vernon finds prevalent, however, is the one discerned by Knickerbocker (1973): parallel and imitative foreign investments by competing firms in a U.S. oligopoly in the same host country markets and period of time. The mechanism seems to be the following. The oligopolists are few enough that they can sustain a price exceeding marginal cost in any market where they operate, and scale economies are (implicitly) not sufficiently large to inflict substantial losses if all firms invest in a given foreign market and period of time. A firm that does not join the investment race suffers a certain loss of profits on its exports to that market (local production is assumed to convey a substantial marketing advantage); that firm also takes the risk that, by virtue of experience in the foreign market, a rival might acquire some new competitive asset that could be used to improve its competitive position in the home market.

This model seems coherent in identifying imitative foreign investments as a prisoners' dilemma game; it conveys the interesting implications that the direct profits of foreign investments could be negative and that such unprofitable rounds of advantage-seeking investments could continue until the oligopoly's core excess profits were eliminated. Knickerbocker claimed to confirm the model empirically by showing that imitative foreign investment bouts occur more commonly in U.S. industries that are concentrated and therefore prone to the recognition of oligopolistic interdependence.

The theoretical coherence and empirical validity of this model strike me as issues that remain important. One reason why they deserve attention is the apparent prevalence in recent years of races among large international firms to undertake mergers that cross national borders but stay largely within a narrowly defined product or service market. Such international horizontal mergers, creating or extending multinational enterprises, seem to have occurred in pharmaceuticals, branded food products, major home appliances, and the entertainment (motion pictures, recordings) and publishing industries, among others.

These mergers pose an interesting problem for industrial economics, because they contain elements not fully explained either by the Knickerbocker-type model summarized previously or by the models of horizontal mergers that are standard in the literature of industrial organization. The latter models focus on the incentives that might exist for mergers between direct competitors in a homogeneous market, with the nonnourishing conclusion that the incentive is pervasive if the firms are price competitors (Bertrand behavior) and almost nonexistent if they are quantity competitors (Cournot). None of these industrial-organization models explain merger waves or races, nor do they explain why (as apparently happens) the short-run supply strategy of the acquired firm or business is often left independent of the acquirer's supply decisions. Knickerbocker's model is also insufficient to explain the absence of coordinated policies.

I have argued (Caves 1991) that an explanation might lie in extension of the theory of real options, constructed along the following lines. Consider an international horizontal merger in an industry whose national product markets are independent for purposes of short-run price or quantity competition but potentially interdependent in the application of innovations, design changes, or other such investment-type forms of nonprice competition. Assume that Nature periodically reveals new opportunities for such investments; assume also that the speed with which a firm can seize an opportunity depends on its having in place an appropriate coalition of resources. Assume finally that an international horizontal merger extends this coalition of resources and therefore increases the number of possible opportunities that the firm can seize. The international horizontal merger then becomes analogous to the purchase of a portfolio of real options.

The value of such an acquisition does not depend on any immediate redeployment of the assets of the acquired unit, so that apparently passive acquisitions can be explained. Furthermore, one firm's improvement of its response capability is adverse to the expected profits of its competitor; possibly (though not necessarily), the competitor's best reply is to make a similar acquisition in order to shrink or nullify the rival's conditional advantage. The occurrence of waves of similar acquisitions can thus be explained. The normative implication is not that horizontal mergers point toward monopolistic restriction of output but that they represent strategic rent-seeking in oligopolistic markets.

My effort to test this model in a way similar to Knickerbocker's yielded negative results, perhaps because it was not targeted closely enough on those internationally concentrated industries for which the model is a priori plausible. Nonetheless, the approach does seem useful for extending Vernon's (and Knickerbocker's) insight concerning strategic foreign investments with the theory of horizontal mergers in industries that give scope for strategic behavior.

References

Caves, Richard E. 1991. Corporate mergers in international economic integration. *European financial integration,* ed. Alberton Giovannini and Colin Mayer, 136–60. Cambridge: Cambridge University Press.

Drake, Tracey A., and Richard E. Caves. 1992. Changing determinants of Japanese foreign investment in the United States. *Journal of the Japanese and International Economies* 6 (September): 228–46.

Knickerbocker, Frederick T. 1973. *Oligopolistic reaction and multinational enterprise.* Boston: Harvard Business School, Division of Research.

Milner, Helen V. 1988. *Resisting protectionism: Global industries and the politics of international trade.* Princeton, N.J.: Princeton University Press.

Discussion Summary

Robert Feenstra questioned *Raymond Vernon's* conclusion that the patterns of foreign direct investment now coming from the industrialized Asian economies would be increasingly harmonized with the former patterns from the United States. He noted that the trade patterns from the Asian countries show marked differences from those of the United States and Europe, partly in response to the differences in market structure of the countries. In addition, the market structures of the Asian countries are not explained well by the transactions cost theories developed in a U.S. contest. On this basis, *Feenstra* suggested there should be some interesting differences in the patterns of direct investment from the Asian and western economies, rather than harmonization.

Donald Lessard and *Kenneth Froot* questioned why firms might follow each other in establishing production facilities in a foreign market. There was some agreement that this action depended on an "option value" from establishing overseas facilities or merging with foreign firms. *Edward Graham* described a model of this type, with two countries (A and B) and two firms (1 and 2), both of which are initially located only in country B. If firm 1 moves into country A, then firm 2 might choose to follow because it believes A has some superior information about market conditions there: the "option value" reflects the possibility that demand might be especially high or costs low in that country.

There was some discussion of the model described by *Graham,* with *Feenstra* asking whether firm 2 would have entered country A in any case and *Froot* arguing that there must be some initial distortion present for this "leader-follower" behavior to occur. *Lael Brainard* noted that there was not a good model of this behavior in the industrial organization literature, but she suggested two approaches that might help. First, there has been increased attention recently to locational choices within a country (such as the agglomeration of firms), and these factors might help to explain locational choices across borders. Second, it has been empirically established that transportation costs and distance are important determinants of trade patterns, and we might expect them to also be determinants of foreign investment.

In response to the last point, *Peter Petri* argued that "distance" can reflect many different factors, so we should be wary about its interpretation. *Richard Caves* suggested that cement production, a good example of an industry in which transportation costs are obviously important, was now experiencing some international mergers, so a case study might be useful. *William Zeile* noted that the latest data on foreign investment in the United States would be available from the Bureau of Economic Analysis, U.S. Department of Commerce in July 1992 and would include information on the cement industry.

4   Japan's Low Levels of Inward Investment: The Role of Inhibitions on Acquisitions

Robert Z. Lawrence

The 1980s have seen a dramatic increase in global foreign direct investment (FDI) within the Center on Transnational Corporations triad (UN 1991). In particular, both Japanese and European firms have rapidly increased their holdings in the United States, while U.S. and Japanese investments in Western Europe have expanded considerably. Foreign direct investment into Japan, however, remains the weakest link, with flows much smaller than those into the United States and Europe, even when the relatively smaller size of the Japanese economy is accounted for (Transnational Corporations and Management Division 1992, 20, table I.4). The result is that foreign firms play an unusually small role in the Japanese economy. As noted by Edward Graham and Paul Krugman (1991, 33), compared with other major economies such as Germany, France and the United States, in which between 14 percent and 26 percent of industrial assets are controlled by foreigners, the 1 percent share controlled by foreigners in Japan is minuscule. Other data indicate a similarly low share of FDI in Japanese employment, sales, and domestic capital formation.

Should one be surprised at these low levels of FDI in Japan? What do they tell us about the nature of the Japanese market? The official Japanese interpretation is that foreigners can readily succeed in Japan, although it takes considerable effort. Indeed, publications of government agencies (e.g., JETRO 1989) proclaim the success of firms such as IBM, Texas Instruments, Procter and Gamble, and Coca-Cola. According to the *Japan Economic Journal* (1990, 1), "As numerous examples of successful foreign ventures testify, [Japan] may not be an easy market, but it certainly is an open one."

The author is grateful to Dara Menashi for her contributions and her superb research assistance and for comments and assistance from Richard Marston, Mark Mason, Karl P. Sauvant, Louis Wells, and participants in presentations at the National Bureau of Economic Research and the Graduate School of Business Administration, Harvard University. In addition he thanks Dan Crisafulli, Paula Holmes, and John Park for their assistance.

But the success stories seem to be the exception rather than the rule. The relatively low FDI stock in Japan is partly the result of a history of official inhibitions on FDI. As Dennis Encarnation (1992) and Mark Mason (1992) describe, inward FDI was heavily restricted for much of the postwar period. Officially, however, at least since the early 1980s, the Japanese market has been open to FDI.[1] Indeed, JETRO (1989, 1) disseminates reports by the American Chamber of Commerce in Japan and by the European Business Community which state that "government regulations are no longer an obstacle to foreign investment in Japan."[2]

4.1   Recent Foreign Direct Investment in Japan

One might have expected that FDI would surge in the 1980s as firms compensated for their previous exclusion from Japan. According to Japan's Ministry of Finance, which records notifications rather than actual transactions, the pace of inward FDI has accelerated. The Japan Economic Institute (1991a, 3) reports that between 1980 and 1990 the Ministry of Finance was notified of $12.6 billion as additions to equity capital. This raised the total of postwar FDI from 8,826 cases valued at $3 billion at the end of 1980 to 42,900 cases valued at $15.5 billion at the end of 1990.

Ministry of Finance data, however, overstate FDI since they refer to notifications and not to actual investments and do not include loan repayments or liquidations of assets. In fact, in recent years, major withdrawals, particularly from minority-owned ventures, have been significant. These include the much publicized sales of equity by General Motors, Chrysler, Honeywell, Avon, and Southland Corporation (7-Eleven). According to estimates made by the United States Department of Commerce using balance-of-payments data reported by the Bank of Japan, the value of the total stock of inward FDI (valued at historical cost) in Japan at the end of 1989 was a mere $9.2 billion (to be sure, a threefold increase over the value in 1980), an amount that implied no increase in the global share of inward FDI of Japan over the decade.[3]

The estimates of the Bank of Japan understate FDI in Japan because they exclude reinvested earnings. An indication of the importance of this omission

1. In 1980, the Foreign Exchange and Foreign Trade Control Law allowed FDI in all but four industries (petroleum, leather, mining, and agriculture). Notification of investments was still required, and the government retained the right to object to any investment deemed a threat to national security or to "the smooth performance of the Japanese economy." Japan also retained the right to reject investments "from the viewpoint of reciprocity." Nonetheless, in principle, such objections were supposed to be rare. In 1992, the diet enacted provisions to remove the government's authority to block FDI deemed a threat to the smooth performance of the economy (Mason, forthcoming).

2. The U.S. government argued in the Structural Impediments Initiative talks that the notification process involved delays. In 1991, the Japanese diet shifted to ex post facto reports; in March 1992, the government of Japan actually passed a law designed to encourage FDI.

3. It is striking that just two acquisitions, one of MCA Inc. by Matsushita Electric Industrial Co. Ltd. in late 1990 ($6 billion) and the other of Columbia Pictures by Sony Corporation ($3.4 billion), are roughly equal to the entire value of the stock of inward FDI in Japan.

can be gleaned from the data reported by the United States, which is the largest foreign investor in Japan. (On a cumulative basis, Minister of Finance data suggest that, as of March 1991, United States investors held 47 percent of the total book value of reported FDI.) U.S. balance-of-payments data show a significant increase in the value of the FDI position of the United States in Japan, valued at historical cost. Between 1982 and 1990, for example, this position tripled, from $6.4 billion to $21 billion. This represents a considerably faster rise than the twofold increase in the global stock of U.S. FDI valued at historical cost over the same period. However, the data also reveal that the growth was dominated by the activities of enterprises that were already in Japan. Valuation adjustments (which occur, for example, when a U.S. affiliate is sold to another U.S. owner), reinvested earnings, and intercompany debt flows more than account for the growth. On balance, changes in equity capital were actually negative. Apparently, liquidations outweighed new injections of capital.[4] In sum, therefore, it appears that the foreign stake in Japan is growing, but primarily through the reinvested earnings of the firms already resident in Japan. New inflows have been offset by increased exit. As a result, compared with that of other economies, the overall FDI stock in Japan remains unusually low. In 1990, assets held by U.S. foreign affiliates in Japan accounted for 12.8 percent of the total assets held by all U.S. foreign affiliates abroad. However, these data include U.S. minority stakes in firms such as Mazda, Mitsubishi Motors, and Isuzu. Japan accounted for only 5.7 percent of the assets in United States majority-owned foreign affiliates worldwide and only 5.5 percent of the majority-owned manufacturing affiliates.

This paper argues that the difficulties of acquiring existing Japanese firms help explain the low level of FDI in Japan. Indeed, the distribution system and other unusual entry barriers to the Japanese market suggest that the demand for acquisitions by foreigners contemplating FDI should be unusually high. In fact, however, most foreign entry into Japan occurs through greenfield operations. Obstacles to acquisition on the supply side, therefore, dominate entry patterns. The low levels of FDI in Japan reflect the need to rely on greenfield entry in a market in which entry barriers would normally induce entry through acquisition. One of the major barriers to foreign acquisitions of Japanese firms are the stock cross-holdings of Japanese corporate groups. Statistically significant evidence suggests, indeed, that *keiretsu* linkages inhibit FDI in Japan. The final section of the paper considers some implications of this finding.

4.2   The Demand for Acquisitions

Foreign firms may face higher market entry costs than their domestic counterparts. Some of these simply reflect a lack of familiarity with the domestic

---

4. New inflows of equity capital were not a major source of the overall growth of the United States FDI position worldwide. Between 1982 and 1990, only 4 percent of the growth in the historical-cost position reflects net equity flows.

economy; others may be permanent and reflect official and/or private discrimination against foreign-owned firms. Much of FDI theory rests on the recognition of these disadvantages and the insight that, to compete abroad, a firm must have compensating advantages in the form of specialized product, process, or marketing assets. But establishing a majority-owned foreign operation is not necessarily the optimal means of exploiting firm-specific assets. One alternative is to service the foreign market through exports. If foreign production is advantageous (e.g., because of trade barriers, transportation or production costs, or the benefits of market proximity), then licensing, franchising, and joint ventures could be attractive alternatives to majority-owned FDI. Of course, these methods of market entry could be complementary. However, it is instructive to consider the factors that determine choices between them, since it helps to evaluate the characteristics of FDI in Japan.

4.2.1   Foreign Direct Investment versus Licensing

Consider first the choice between FDI and licensing without equity. Licensing has the advantage of saving the firm the costs of manufacture and market entry. On the other hand, licensing requires formulating and monitoring a contract relating to the foreign use of the specific assets of the licensing firm. As Edward John Ray (1989, 59) points out, the licenser faces risks of opportunistic behavior by the licensee and difficulties of assessing the value of the assets being licensed. In addition, where specific assets of a firm are not easily reduced to a formula or a blueprint, the licensee faces the risk that the know-how will not be readily assimilated. Foreign direct investment, by contrast, allows a firm to internalize these contracting, informational, and transference difficulties, although it requires incurring the costs associated with foreign entry and operation. As Ray notes, the desire to invest directly is positively related to these licensing contract costs and negatively related to the market entry and operating costs of the investing firm. A reliance on licensing suggests the dominance of entry and marketing costs over contracting costs.

The propensity to license could also rise with the presence of domestic monopolies.[5] Foreign firms could prefer to take advantage of domestic monopoly power of a local firm rather than enter into head-to-head competition with it. Indeed, a domestic firm with existing market power may be prepared to pay more for a license than would firms that are forced to compete.

The government of Japan has historically induced foreign firms to grant licenses by placing severe restrictions on FDI. Officially, the Ministry of International Trade and Industry (MITI) is no longer engaged in such activities. Nonetheless, it is clear that, compared with other nations, a disproportionate amount of United States know-how continues to be exploited in Japan through licensing rather than through export sales or FDI. In 1990, for example, the $1.2 billion U.S. companies earned from royalties and licensed fees from Japan

---

5. I thank Kenneth Froot for this point.

accounted for 35 percent of U.S. receipts from royalties and fees from unaffiliated foreigners worldwide.[6] By contrast, in 1990, U.S. receipts from Japan from foreign affiliates in the form of income and royalties and license fees were only 5.5 percent of total U.S. receipts from affiliates worldwide. Indeed, U.S. earnings from royalties and license fees from unaffiliated Japanese firms were 33 percent of all U.S. receipts from their foreign affiliates in Japan in the form of income and royalty fees. By contrast, worldwide, total U.S. receipts from payments of royalties and fees by unaffiliated foreigners amounted to just 5.2 percent of total U.S. receipts (income plus royalties) from affiliates.

Over the 1980s, as restrictions on FDI were removed, the role of licensing might have been expected to diminish. Yet, in 1980, the $354 million paid by unaffiliated Japanese firms to the United States in the form of fees and royalties equaled 40 percent of FDI income—considerably smaller than the corresponding ratio of 61 percent in 1990. In 1980, Japan accounted for 30 percent of all U.S. income from fees and royalties; in 1990, its share was 35 percent. To be sure, more research is required to determine how much of the rapid growth in Japanese fees and royalties reflects recent licensing and how much simply reflects a historical legacy.

4.2.2 Joint Ventures

Consider next the choice between minority positions in joint ventures and majority-owned FDI. Joint ventures represent a compromise between licensing and full control. They may be more advantageous to foreign firms than licensing is, because they permit a foreign firm to exploit its specific assets while economizing on the costs of operation in a foreign environment and avoiding some of the contract costs associated with licensing; they may be more advantageous to the domestic firm in ensuring an effective transfer of the specific foreign assets. Joint ventures, nonetheless, retain the risks associated with the loss of know-how to foreign partners and with the lack of complete operating control. Both partners in joint ventures may fear the creation of formidable future competitors. In general, one would expect joint ventures to predominate over FDI in those cases in which operating in a foreign environment presented unusually large problems for foreign-owned firms, because of entry barriers and/or operating difficulties (e.g., nationalistic discrimination against foreign-owned firms). Indeed, often sanctioned by law, joint ventures predominate in FDI in developing countries following protectionist policies. Joint ventures could also be a means of collusion when ventures have monopoly potential.

Generally, however, U.S. firms prefer to invest abroad in majority-owned ventures. In 1990, majority-owned companies accounted for about 78 percent of the FDI assets of U.S. firms. By contrast, only 34 percent of the FDI assets in Japan and only 26 percent of the assets in manufacturing were in majority-

---

6. In 1990, Japanese firms earned only $185 million in payments from unaffiliated U.S. firms for royalties and license fees. This is less than one-sixth of the corresponding receipts from unaffiliated Japanese firms earned by U.S. firms.

owned companies. Indeed, there is a relationship between countries that have generally discriminated against FDI and the share of majority-owned firms in FDI assets. While in developed countries that ratio averaged 76 percent, the conspicuous outliers are the Republic of Korea (18 percent), India (14 percent) and Japan (34 percent).

There is evidence, however, that the U.S. FDI position in Japan is becoming more concentrated in majority-owned firms. In 1977, for example, majority-owned U.S. affiliates accounted for only 16 percent of the assets of U.S.-affiliated firms in Japan. One source of that shift is the actual decline in the activity associated with minority-interest U.S. affiliates in that country. Indeed, as reported in table 4.1, employment and sales (adjusted for exchange rates and inflation) in minority-interest U.S. affiliates in Japan actually declined by 28 percent and 36 percent, respectively, between 1977 and 1990. The second source of the shift is the rapid growth in real assets (increasing by 91 percent) and real employment (increasing by 70 percent) of majority-owned ventures. Thus, while the U.S. stake in majority-owned affiliates in Japan remains unusually small, it is a growing component of the overall U.S. FDI position.

4.2.3 Investment in Wholesale Trade

As emphasized in particular by Encarnation (1992), U.S. majority-owned investment in Japan has been heavily directed toward wholesale trade. Valued at historical cost, worldwide U.S. investment in wholesale trade accounted for just 11 percent of the U.S. global FDI position in 1990. A similar valuation of the U.S. position in Japan indicates that wholesale trade has an 18 percent share in the U.S. position. Similarly, the value of assets in majority-owned affiliates involved in wholesale trade account for 18 percent of all assets held by majority-owned U.S. Japanese affiliates. By contrast, only 10 percent of majority-owned affiliate assets worldwide are in wholesale trade. Also, unlike other forms of investment in Japan, U.S. FDI in wholesale trade is predominantly majority owned. Indeed, in 1990, 49 percent of all U.S. assets in wholesale trade were in majority-owned firms. These data strongly suggest either unusual profit opportunities in this industry or the importance of such investment for making sales.

In sum, the continued dependence on licensing, the heavy reliance on minority-interest ventures, and the relatively large investments in majority-owned wholesale trade ventures support the argument that the marketing and distribution of foreign products in Japan are unusually difficult or that current inflows have been too small to offset the impact of earlier policies. (The data on U.S. licensing and wholesale trade investment could also indicate a lack of competition.)

A study conducted by the U.S. International Trade Commission (1990) singled out:

• Legal restrictions on retailing, wholesaling, and investment as limiting entry. These include a weak enforcement of the antimonopoly law of Japan, the

Table 4.1   **U.S. FDI: Japan versus Developed Countries in 1977 and 1990**

Type of Affiliate	1977	1990	Percentage Change
Japan			
Majority owned (%)			
Employment	16.8	32.4	70.4
Sales	25.5	37.4	12.3*
Assets	16.1	33.8	91.4*
Minority interest (%)			
Employment	83.2	67.6	−28.1
Sales	74.5	62.6	−35.8*
Assets	83.9	66.1	−28.4*
Total			
Employment (number)	389,123	344,300	−11.5%
Sales ($ billions)	$51.9	113.4	−23.5%*
Assets ($ billions)	$41.8	108.3	− 9.2%*
Developed countries			
Majority owned (%)			
Employment	76.7	75.1	
Sales	75.4	77.5	
Assets	71.3	76.2	
Minority interest (%)			
Employment	23.3	24.9	
Sales	24.6	22.5	
Assets	28.7	23.8	
Total			
Employment (number)	4,980,691	4,308,500	
Sales ($ billions)	$449.0	$871.1	
Assets ($ billions)	$359.6	$843.2	

Sources: International Monetary Fund, *International Financial Statistics,* various issues; U.S. Department of Commerce, National Trade Data Bank; U.S. Department of Commerce (1981).

Note: In 1977, $1 in U.S. = 268.5 yen. In 1990, $1 U.S. = 144.8 yen.

*Real sales/assets adjusted for inflation and exchange rate changes. The consumer price index in Japan rose by 54 percent during the period 1977–1990.

Large Retail Store Law (which limits expansion of large retailers), and other regulations and entry fees.

- Business practices used by manufacturers to exert vertical control over distribution channels and to reduce horizontal competition.
- The high costs associated with setting up independent distribution systems (land rent, warehousing, transportation), partly as a result of government tax and land use policies.
- Social customs that emphasize long-term relations, resulting in less willingness by purchasers to switch suppliers or retailers.

4.2.4   Greenfield versus Acquisitions

Once the decision to invest has been made, a firm has the choice of either starting a greenfield operation or acquiring an existing operation. In equilibrium, one would expect to see firms priced at their replacement cost—that is, for Tobin's q (the ratio of the firm's market value to its replacement costs) to equal unity. However, when $q = 1$ for domestic entrants, foreigners, if their costs of entry are systematically higher, should be prepared to pay more than domestic firms do for existing firms. Indeed, except in cases where the specific assets can only be transferred to new ventures, one would expect to see acquisition as a more common means of entry in FDI than in domestic investment. In general, the foreign preference for acquisitions over greenfield investments reflects the disadvantages faced by foreigners in establishing domestic operations. The more costly it is for foreigners, as compared with domestic firms, to enter new markets, the higher the demand for acquisition over greenfield entry.

In terms of our theoretical analysis, the evidence on licensing, joint ventures, and investment in majority-owned wholesale trade operations is strongly suggestive of unusual barriers to entry, operation, and marketing in Japan. This evidence suggests that, ceteris paribus, foreign demand for acquiring existing Japanese firms as a means of entry should be unusually high. Ex post, however, the share of entry accounted for by foreign acquisitions also reflects the relative supply of acquirable assets to foreigners. This supply is related to the overall level of economic development. In addition, however, it reflects the market for corporate control in general, as well as official and unofficial discrimination against foreigners. Indeed, it will be argued below that all factors limiting the supply of acquirable assets have played a role in constraining FDI in Japan.

4.3   The Supply of Acquirable Assets to Foreigners

Data gathered by the Japan Economic Institute (1990) show that the number of mergers and acquisitions in Japan is actually quite similar to that in the United States, but the typical Japanese deal appears to be smaller (table 4.2). However, this finding could simply reflect a bias in the samples; the Japanese data, which are based on reports to the Fair Trade Commission, are comprehensive, while the U.S. data may not be. In both countries, merger and acquisition activity has increased rapidly in recent years. Although megadeals appear to be more rare in Japan, they are not unknown. In fact, the Mitsui Bank merger with Taiyo Bank in 1990 was actually the largest in the world in terms of market capitalization (Holloway 1990, 41).

4.3.1   Hostile Takeovers

The more striking differences between Japan and the United States, however, relate to the feasibility of hostile takeovers and of takeovers involving foreign firms. In part, hostile takeovers are rare because the Japanese concept of a firm places less emphasis on the role of stockholders and more emphasis on the rights of other stakeholders—in particular, employees and management. According to the Japan Economic Institute (1990, 13), the Japanese word for "takeover bid" (*nottori*) can also mean "hijack." Moreover, the loyalty felt by

Table 4.2   **U.S. and Japanese Merger and Acquisition Activity, 1981–1988**

Year	Number U.S.	Number Japan	Value ($ billions) U.S.	Value ($ billions) Japan*	Average Value ($ billions) U.S.	Average Value ($ billions) Japan*	Number of Large Deals U.S.†	Number of Large Deals Japan‡
1981	2,395	1,815	$ 82.6	$ 10.1	$ 34.49	$ 5.58	113	50
1982	2,346	919	53.8	13.3	22.93	14.50	116	47
1983	2,533	1,722	73.1	8.9	28.86	5.14	138	63
1984	2,543	1,886	122.2	10.4	48.05	5.52	200	81
1985	3,001	1,920	179.8	15.0	59.91	7.80	270	79
1986	3,336	2,083	173.1	27.2	51.89	13.06	346	112
1987	2,032	2,299	163.7	24.0	80.56	10.42	301	131
1988		2,364		27.2		11.49		

Sources: Japan Economic Institute (1990).

*The dollar values of Japanese deals were calculated using current exchange rates from the International Monetary Fund, *International Financial Statistics* (various issues); Japanese data are for fiscal years.

†Deal of $100 million–plus.

‡Deals of ¥50 billion–plus; ¥50 billion = $220 million, $210 million, and $346 million in 1980, 1985, and 1987, respectively.

employees and management to large firms in a system (often characterized by lifetime employment) stands in the way of even friendly mergers in which companies lose their identity.

In part, however, hostile takeovers are more difficult because many Japanese firms have large percentages of their stock held either by stable shareholders (such as insurance companies and trust and pension funds), who have close relations with the management of the company, or by *keiretsu* members (that is, members of a corporate group characterized by extensive cross-shareholdings). In many cases, these two groups account for two-thirds of all outstanding shares of a company and therefore can prevent hostile takeovers.

The practice of cross-shareholdings was originally a response to the prohibition on holding companies that was implemented in Japan in the early 1950s to prevent the reconstitution of the large prewar zaibatsu conglomerates. Despite these strictures, the three former zaibatsu groups—Mitsubishi, Mitsui and Sumitomo—and other large groups of diverse companies (horizontal *keiretsu*) centered on major banks have developed more subtle mechanisms of collaboration, a feature of which is extensive cross-holdings of stock. In addition, other groups, centered on such large manufacturing companies as Nippon Steel and Toyota (vertical *keiretsu*), have developed close links that involve an exchange of equity. For the six largest horizontal groups, the average percentage of stock of a group held by other group members ranged from 7 percent to 14.3 percent in 1963 and had risen to between 12.2 percent and 26.9 percent in 1988 (fiscal year).

Nonetheless, hostile takeovers are not unknown in Japan. For example,

Aaron Viner (1988, 89–90) noted that Takami Takahashi (president of the Minebea ball bearing company) has masterminded takeovers in both Japan and the United States. Minebea was also the object of a takeover attempt by foreigners, who acquired stocks through convertible bonds and warrants that are traded anonymously in the Euromarket. However, a foreign participant in the effort, Charles Knapp (a Los Angeles financier), "could not find a single Japanese bank or securities house to help in any capacity with his bid" (p. 90), and Takahasi successfully fought off the bid by merging his company with another and thereby diluting Knapp's stake.

Some suggest that possibilities for hostile mergers have increased recently. In part, this reflects increased experience of Japanese firms with acquisitions abroad. In addition, Japanese courts that formerly frowned upon hostile takeovers have modified their stance in recent rulings. In a particularly noteworthy case in 1989 (Shuwa versus Chujitsuya), the court found that efforts to dilute Shuwa's shares by an exchange of stocks at low prices between two targets was unfair. This was the first time a court declared antitakeover practices unfair.

In addition, Japan has seen a nascent debate over shareholders' rights, sparked in part by the ill-fated efforts of T. Boone Pickens, who tried to claim a seat on the board of Koito Manufacturing Company.[7]

4.3.2   Foreign Acquisitions

Japan's other striking difference from the United States relates to its treatment of foreign investors. As mentioned above, FDI in Japan was severely restricted during the 1950s and 1960s (Encarnation 1992, chap. 2). By 1973, however, Japan was officially complying with the Organization for Economic Cooperation and Development (OECD) Code of Liberalization of Capital movements. However, although the official policy was that Japan was open, less formal policies undermined this commitment.

Mason (1992, 205–7) described how a revision of the Commercial Code of Japan in 1966 made it easier for Japanese firms to issue shares to third parties of their choice. He detailed how firms belonging to industrial groups took advantage of these regulations over the following decade to insulate themselves from foreign companies. In addition, an amendment of the Securities Exchange Law in 1971 introduced a system of notification of takeover bids. In 1972, as described by Viner (1988, 88), the Bendix Corporation made a tender offer for some of the equity in the small firm Jidosha Kiki. This created concerns and prompted a deliberate effort to prevent foreign firms from initiating takeovers of domestic companies. To render foreign takeovers virtually impossible,

7. According to the Japan Economic Institute (1991b), on 13 June 1991, a study group of the Ministry of International Trade and Industry urged the ministry to promote mergers and acquisitions through various regulatory and legal changes. However, the report also called on the ministry to provide legal aid to firms facing hostile buyouts.

hundreds of corporations (with unofficial Ministry of Finance encouragement) which were not members of *keiretsu* systematically expanded their mutual shareholdings. Companies within *keiretsu* increased mutual shareholding to the legal limit. As a direct result . . . the total percentage of shares held by corporations rose 12.7 percent in just one year, 1971/2. [Indeed] the redistribution was so effective that between 1978–84, the number of foreign acquisitions of Japanese companies numbered just 20. Of these only two were of substantial size (BOC takeover of Osaka Gas and Banyu-Merck). (Viner 1988, 88)

In general, foreign firms contemplating Japanese acquisitions do not enjoy national treatment. As of mid-1989, as noted in "Mergers and acquisitions" (1989), takeover bids from foreigners had to be carried out through a domestic securities house, which gave the Ministry of Finance ten days notice of its intentions—"i.e., enough time to organize a rescue operation to be mounted to keep the target in Japanese hands" (p. 68). If a foreign firm managed to clear that obstacle, it was allowed just twenty to thirty days to complete the acquisition. Japanese firms were not subject to these rules.

Recent data confirm that foreign involvement in merger and acquisition activity within Japan, though increasing, remains rare. According to data collected by Yamaichi Securities (table 4.3), between 1985 and 1989, foreign purchases of Japanese firms were in the range of about twenty per year; however, these data include purchases outside of Japan. By contrast, there was a dramatic increase in Japanese purchases of foreign firms and Japanese purchases of Japanese firms. Data on foreign sellers collected by Merrill Lynch (table 4.4) confirm the paucity of sales of Japanese companies to foreign firms; these averaged about 3 per year. By comparison, averages were 52, 15, 14, and 6 per year for British, West German, French, and Swiss firms, respectively.

Table 4.3   **Number of Mergers and Acquisitions Involving Japanese Firms: 1981, 1985–1990**

Year	Japanese Firms Acquire Japanese Firms	Japanese Firms Acquire Foreign Firms	Foreign Firms Acquire Japanese Firms	Total
1981	122	48	6	176
1985	163	100	26	289
1986	226	204	21	451
1987	219	228	22	469
1988	223	315	17	555
1989	240	405	15	660
1990	293	440	18	751

Source: Yamaichi Securities Co., Ltd., cited in Japan Economic Institute (1991a).

Table 4.4   Foreign Sellers: Number of Transactions, by Country, 1982–1991*

Country of seller	1982	1983	1984	1985	1986	1987	1988	1989	1990	1991	Ten-year Cumulative
Australia	6	3	6	7	7	5	4	13	19	10	80
Austria	1	1	0	0	0	0	1	0	0	1	4
Belgium	2	1	3	3	6	2	1	1	2	4	25
Canada	30	35	24	42	54	31	32	41	41	49	379
Denmark	0	1	2	0	0	2	0	1	2	1	9
Finland	0	1	0	0	0	1	0	0	2	1	5
France	8	8	15	16	12	9	14	16	21	18	137
Greece	1	0	0	0	0	0	0	0	2	1	4
Ireland	0	0	0	0	2	1	1	0	3	1	8
Italy	2	6	6	13	4	10	7	15	10	6	79
Japan	3	3	7	7	2	0	1	2	4	3	32
Luxembourg	1	0	0	0	0	0	0	0	0	0	1
Netherlands	3	8	3	7	5	7	5	4	11	17	70
New Zealand	0	0	2	1	0	1	0	3	7	3	17
Norway	0	0	1	0	0	1	2	0	1	3	8
Portugal	0	0	0	0	0	0	0	1	1	0	2
Spain	0	3	6	3	4	2	2	3	5	2	30
Sweden	0	1	3	3	2	5	2	8	7	2	33
Switzerland	10	11	3	5	5	2	2	7	7	3	55
Turkey	0	0	0	1	0	0	0	1	1	0	3
United Kingdom	30	39	45	44	50	41	48	71	80	72	520
West Germany	12	13	13	15	13	11	12	17	25	16	147

Sources: Mergstat Review 1991; Merrill Lynch Business Brokerage and Valuation, Shaumberg, Ill.
*Foreign sellers reflect nationality of ownership, not necessarily location of company. Transaction measures reflect announced transactions only and include acquisitions of both controlling and minority interest in a company.

4.4   Acquisition versus Greenfield Entry

It was established earlier that, ceteris paribus, one would expect that in general the foreign demand for entry via acquisition would tend to be high. Indeed, this is confirmed by the data compiled by James W. Vaupel and Joan P. Curhan (1973) on the ways used by affiliates of U.S.-owned manufacturing firms to enter foreign markets between 1900 and 1968 (table 4.5). More specifically they found that, on average, direct acquisitions dominated newly formed ventures in entries into foreign markets of subsidiaries in which U.S. firms had at least a 5 percent stake. In countries in which acquisitions are made with relatively ease (such as Canada and the United Kingdom), only 35 percent of entries involved newly established operations. In France and West Germany, newly established ventures accounted for 39 percent and 42 percent of all new entries, respectively. Weighted by the number of firms entering, newly formed entrants accounted for 43 percent of all new entries in the sample.

As might be expected, entry into developing countries (in which the supply of acquirable assets is limited) is more dependent on new ventures. The share of new ventures has also been high in some less developed industrialized countries, such as Turkey (86 percent were new establishments), Portugal (81 percent), and Greece (78 percent). Furthermore, data on entry into the United States between 1981 and 1990 indicate, as in the earlier cases of Canada and the United Kingdom, a high dependence on acquisitions rather than greenfield operations. For these years, acquisitions accounted for 79 percent of all entries. While Japanese firms have tended to prefer greenfield entry and plant expansions more so than firms from other countries have, they have not been reluc-

Table 4.5   **Manufacturing Foreign Affiliates of U.S.-based Companies, 1900–1968***

A. By Method of Entry into Foreign Country

Country	Newly Formed	Reorganization	Acquired Directly
Australia	47.0%	2.1%	50.0%
Austria	59.0	0.0	41.0
Belgium	49.0	0.0	51.0
Canada	35.0	2.8	62.0
Denmark	48.0	0.0	52.0
Finland	60.0	0.0	40.0
France	39.0	3.5	57.0
Greece	78.0	0.0	22.0
Ireland	45.0	3.2	52.0
Italy	50.0	0.5	50.0
Japan	64.0	0.7	35.0
Luxembourg	49.0	0.0	51.0
Netherlands	53.0	1.1	46.0
New Zealand	58.0	2.3	30.0
Norway	50.0	0.0	50.0
Portugal	81.0	0.0	19.0
Spain	43.0	0.8	57.0
Sweden	62.0	0.0	38.0
Switzerland	48.0	0.0	52.0
Turkey	86.0	0.0	14.0
United Kingdom	35.0	3.3	62.0
West Germany	42.0	2.3	56.0
Weighted average	43.3	2.1	54.5

B. By Time Period When U.S. Firms Entered into the Japanese Market

	Pre-1946	1946–1957	1958–1967
Percentage of total	6.4	16.7	76.9

Source: Vaupel and Curhan (1973), chap. 4, 256.

*Data cover foreign affiliates formed between 1900 and 1968. the study covers approximately 40 percent of the total number of all foreign manufacturing affiliates of U.S. companies and approximately 70 percent of the value of U.S. manufacturing investment in foreign affiliates. Data include minority-interest and majority-owned affiliates.

Table 4.6   Foreign Direct Investment in the United States: Method of Investment by Source Country, 1989*
(percentage)

Method	All Countries	Canada	France	United Kingdom	Japan	Netherlands	Switzerland	West Germany
Mergers and acquisitions	79.21%	86.85%	90.53%	97.53%	56.20%	99.07%	91.68%	86.72%
Equity increases	3.98	0.51	0.00	0.02	5.45	0.00	8.11	0.00
Joint ventures	3.13	4.33	1.50	0.66	6.47	0.00	0.21	0.00
New plants	4.94	4.47	6.32	1.20	10.23	0.18	0.00	5.24
Plant expansion	3.57	0.89	0.00	0.29	9.28	0.00	0.00	7.94
Real estate	4.59	2.94	1.44	0.24	11.34	0.74	0.00	0.00
Other	0.57	0.00	0.21	0.04	1.03	0.00	0.00	0.10
Total value known ($ million)	$74,715.4	$3,691.3	$3,324.8	$24,955.1	$22,977.7	$3,824.1	$4,306.8	$2,381

Source: U.S. Department of Commerce (1991).

*The data include only investments for which the value of the transaction is known. Foreign direct investment is defined as ownership of 10 percent or more of a company.

tant to engage in acquisitions. In 1989, for example, 56 percent of Japanese FDI involved acquisitions, and 11 percent involved purchases of real estate (table 4.6).

Uniquely among developed countries, entry into Japan historically also involved a relatively large number of greenfield investments. For the entire sample, the ratio was 64 percent. For the period 1957 to 1968, the ratio was 68 percent. Thus, while a priori reasoning suggests that the demand for acquisitions as a mode of entry should be high in the case of Japan, ex post acquisitions appear to be unusually low. The foreign direct investment entry data confirm that there are obstacles on the supply side.

The *24th Survey of Foreign Affiliates in Japan,* undertaken by MITI in 1991, provides an even more overwhelming impression of the degree to which entry into majority-owned firms in Japan has occurred through greenfield operations. As reported in table 4.7, only 7 percent of the firms in which foreigners have more than a 50 percent equity stake started through the acquisition of Japanese firms. Some 49 percent started with new establishments, and the remainder began as joint ventures.

The ex post data on the share of new entry taking the form of greenfield operations can be used to explore whether there is a relationship between the overall quantity of FDI and the mode of entry. These regressions are reported in table 4.8. Regression 1 shows that the level of assets in majority-controlled U.S. affiliates in Japan is 41 logarithmic percentage points lower than one would expect on the basis of Japanese population and per capita purchasing power parity (GDP) gross domestic product. Despite the large standard errors of the equation, the coefficient on the Japanese dummy is almost insignificant. However, as shown in regression 2, inserting the variable GREEN in the regression confirms a negative association between greenfield operations and FDI that is significant at the 90 percent level. The addition of this variable has a large impact on the Japanese dummy variable: it is reduced by 60 logarithmic percentage points. As might be expected, the measure of tariff and nontariff barriers is not significant in explaining overall FDI (equations 4 and 5). It is, however, more significant in manufacturing (equations 6 and 7) and confirms that trade barriers can induce FDI. These regressions, which explain assets in majority-controlled manufacturing FDI, also suggest the importance of mergers and acquisitions for FDI. In this case, the dummy variable on Japan in equation 6 run without GREEN is -103 logarithmic percentage points. However, when GREEN is introduced into the regressions, the coefficient of the Japanese dummy falls to only -16 logarithmic percentage points. The coefficient on the greenfield variable, which is almost significantly different from zero, confirms the negative relationship between reliance on greenfield investment as a mode of entry and overall FDI. Ex post, therefore, the supply of acquirable assets appears to be an important factor in encouraging FDI. Conversely, the lack of such supplies inhibits FDI.

Table 4.7   **Majority-owned Foreign Direct Investment in Japan, by Industry and Method of Entry, 1991 (percentage of total number of firms)**

Industry	Creation of Joint Venture	Creation of New Company (greenfield)	Capital Participation (M&A activity)	Total Number of Firms that Responded
Total investment	43.7%	49.3%	7.1%	1,234
Manufacturing	51.0	40.3	8.7	576
Manufacturing, except oil	51.5	40.7	8.2	562
Food processing	52.4	33.3	14.3	21
Textiles	57.1	42.9	0.0	7
Wood products	42.9	57.1	0.0	7
Pulp and paper	20.0	80.0	0.0	5
Publishing and printing	33.3	66.7	0.0	12
Chemicals	62.3	29.8	7.9	114
Pharmaceuticals	44.4	44.4	11.1	45
Oil	50.0	21.4	28.6	14
Rubber	50.0	41.7	8.3	12
Leather	50.0	50.0	0.0	2
Clay and ceramics	50.0	50.0	0.0	14
Steel and iron	0.0	0.0	0.0	0
Nonferrous metals	35.7	50.0	14.3	14
Processed steel	40.0	50.0	10.0	10
General machinery	52.4	37.8	9.8	82
Electric machinery	50.5	45.9	3.7	109
Transportation machinery	59.1	22.7	18.2	22
Precision machinery	38.3	51.7	10.0	60
Weapons	0.0	0.0	0.0	0
Other manufactured	61.5	26.9	11.5	26
Commerce	38.0	56.0	6.0	502
Oil sales	0.0	0.0	0.0	0
Services	34.3	61.1	4.6	108
Other	35.4	60.4	4.2	48
Oil-related services	50.0	21.4	28.6	14

Source: Ministry of International Trade and Industry (1991). The survey was sent to all business enterprises that had a foreign capital ratio of 50 percent or more as of 31 March 1991. The survey was sent to 2,463 companies.

4.5   *Keiretsu,* FDI, and Mergers in Japan

Few issues in U.S.-Japanese relations are more controversial than the *keiretsu* relationships among Japanese firms. For many firms in the United States, *keiretsu* are the best example of the invisible barriers that make U.S.-Japanese investment and trade unfair. Japanese investors can buy any U.S. firm they choose, but it is almost impossible for U.S. investors to obtain control of most major Japanese firms because of substantial cross-holdings of stock held by *keiretsu* members. Similarly, Japanese exporters can readily sell their goods in the United States, but U.S. exporters find extraordinary barriers in Japan created by the close links between suppliers and assemblers and between manufacturers and distributors. Some believe that these asymmetries in access make free trade with Japan undesirable; thus, they advocate managed trade. Others are calling for antitrust measures and changes in rules that will make *keiretsu* relationships more transparent and Japanese markets more open to foreign exporters and investors.

In the recent Structural Impediments Initiative between Japan and the United States, particular attention was paid to the role of *keiretsu*. The government of the United States argued that *keiretsu* linkages made foreign entry into Japan especially difficult. The Structural Impediments Initiative talks ended with an agreement by the government of Japan to strengthen the monitoring of transactions among *keiretsu* firms by its Fair Trade Commission and to take steps to eliminate any restraints on competition that might arise from their business practices. The United States called for, among other things, streamlined rules for mergers and acquisitions, stronger rights of shareholders, and disclosure requirements against management. However, the relevance of *keiretsu* remains hotly contested, and the Japanese defend it with two diametrically opposed arguments (Yoshitomi 1990).

One argument is that *keiretsu* do not actually have significant economic ef-

Table 4.8   Foreign Direct Investment in OECD Countries, 1990 (*t*-statistics in parentheses)

FDI	ln(POP)	ln(GDP/C)	BAR	JPN	GREEN	Corr. R^2	Standard Error
1. ln(MAJDFI)	0.84	3.05		−1.4		0.70	0.94
	(5.00)	(5.87)		(1.32)			
2. ln(MAJDFI)	0.81	2.4		−0.81	−0.032	0.78	0.88
	(5.10)	(4.00)		(0.77)	(1.90)		
3. ln(MAJDFI)	0.76	2.24			−0.036	0.74	0.88
	(5.30)	(4.00)			(2.20)		
4. ln(MAJDFI)	0.86	3.06	0.02	−1.26		0.69	0.95
	(5.00)	(5.83)	(0.79)	(1.15)			
5. ln(MAJDFI)	0.82	2.44	0.01	−0.074	−0.03	0.65	0.90
	(5.05)	(3.95)	(0.54)	(0.69)	(1.72)		
6. ln(MAJMAN)	0.94	4.85	0.07	−1.03		0.65	1.49
	(3.63)	(5.92)	(1.89)	(0.61)			
7. ln(MAJMAN)	0.88	3.79	0.06	−0.16	−0.05	0.70	1.39
	(3.53)	(4.01)	(1.69)	(0.10)	(1.89)		

Sources: (1) U.S. Department of Commerce, Bureau of Economic Analysis.
    (2) OECD main economic indicators.
    (3) Saxonhouse and Stern (1989).
    (4) Vaupet and Curhan (1973).

Notes: Constant term not reported. Definitions (source number in parentheses): MAJDFI (1) = Assets of U.S. majority-owned affiliates. MAJMAN (1) = Assets of U.S. majority-owned affiliates in manufacturing. POP (2) = Population in 1990. GDP/C (2) = 1991 purchasing power parity per capita gross domestic product. BAR (3) = Sum of tariff rates and tariff equivalents of nontariff barriers. JPN = Dummy = 1 for Japan. GREEN = Percentage of U.S. FDI entries in greenfield establishments.

fects. Foreign concerns about *keiretsu* simply reflect "misunderstandings." *Keiretsu* are really no different from arrangements in other countries, such as vertical integration, conglomerates, and close links between firms and banks. There is no need for new policies, because the Japanese economy is highly competitive. If firms actually made decisions based on *keiretsu* loyalties rather than on economic grounds, they would lose money and soon be driven from the market. Often cited in support of this view is evidence gathered by the Japanese Fair Trade Commission, which indicated that intragroup transactions account for only a small share of total transactions by *keiretsu* members, as well as evidence that *keiretsu* firms are not particularly profitable (Yoshitomi 1990, 13).

The other argument is that *keiretsu* linkages are very important—indeed they are the heart of Japanese success. It is no coincidence that the best firms in Japan are typically members of *keiretsu*. *Keiretsu* provide members with benefits through sharing risk and information. Close links between assemblers and suppliers enhance the transfer of technology. *Keiretsu* linkages are more efficient than vertical integration, because they permit reliable supply while preserving corporate flexibility. Stock cross-holding permits *keiretsu* managers to concentrate on long-term investment decisions. It frees them from pressures of the stock market and fears of takeovers, which have made U.S. managers short-sighted (Yoshitomi 1990, 12).

Proponents of the second argument acknowledge that *keiretsu* create problems for new foreign entrants, but they still defend it on efficiency grounds. According to their view, Japan is confronted with a painful dilemma: if it becomes more open, it will be less efficient. In other words, those who want Japan to become more open are asking it to be less successful.

Robert Lawrence (1991) evaluated these views by examining Japanese trade, using a model developed by Peter Petri (1992). Trade by industry was explained on the basis of such variables as factor intensity, tariffs, transportation costs, and concentration. In addition, variables were used that were drawn from data developed by Dodwell Marketing Associates, which measured the share of sales accounted for by firms belonging to *keiretsu,* by industry. Statistically significant evidence that *keiretsu* were associated with reduced imports was found. The analysis of Japanese exports, however, gave mixed results. The vertical *keiretsu* of major producers and suppliers in a single industry had a positive effect on exports, although it was not statistically significant. However, *keiretsu* of firms drawn from the former zaibatsu groups and those from other horizontal groups had no beneficial effect on exports. It was concluded that the results provided some support for the claim that vertical ties enhance efficiency. On the other hand, no support was found for claims that horizontal *keiretsu* improve performance, and it was therefore concluded that the efficiency benefits from cross-holdings may be exaggerated.

This work on *keiretsu* can now be expanded to explore, in a preliminary fashion, the relationship between *keiretsu* and the activities of majority-owned foreign affiliates in Japan. The dependent variable is the share of industry sales in 1991 accounted for by majority-owned foreign affiliates, as indicated by the data collected for the twenty-fifth annual survey of MITI. The independent variables are taken from the Petri model. In particular, variables have been used that measure concentration (Herfindahl index) and technological intensity (share of scientists and engineers in sectoral employment). Foreign direct investment is expected to be positively associated with both variables. A variable was added to indicate capital intensity and the share of industry sales by *keiretsu* firms in 1987. In a second specification, that variable was separated into the share in sales of firms in horizontal and in vertical *keiretsu*. The results, reported in table 4.9, suggest that *keiretsu* are indeed negatively associated with FDI. As indicated in equation 1, the *keiretsu* variable is statistically significant and negatively signed. The coefficients on concentration and technological intensity are both positive. When separate variables measuring vertical and horizontal *keiretsu* are introduced, they are insignificant and with negative coefficients. While not significantly different from each other, the coefficient of horizontal *keiretsu* is larger than that of vertical *keiretsu*. This suggests that each percentage increase in sales by horizontal *keiretsu* firms is associated with a relatively larger restraining impact than a percentage increase by firms in vertical *keiretsu*.

It should be stressed that the data sample is inordinately small; observations are available for only ten industries. In addition, one cannot be sure that the classification schemes used for measuring sales by industry are all consistent. Moreover, questions have been raised about the classification scheme used by

Table 4.9   **Sales and Mergers and Acquisitions by Industry (*t*-statistics in parentheses)**

Dependent Variable	CAPINT	HERF	TECH	KRETS	VERT9	HORIZ8	Corr. R^2
1. SALESMOF	0.03	0.002	0.42	−0.09			0.77
	(0.39)	(1.79)	(2.31)	(3.45)			
2. SALESMOF	0.097	0.002	0.327		−0.08	−0.12	0.79
	(1.11)	(2.24)	(1.75)		(3.29)	(3.31)	
3. JPNMERG	−15.34	−0.15	113.85	6.82			0.17
	(0.65)	(0.53)	(1.89)	(0.90)			
4. JPNMERG	−28.17	−0.23	123.82		6.19	13.04	0.03
	(0.87)	(0.71)	(1.86)		(0.75)	(1.04)	

Sources: (1) Japanese Ministry of Finance, corporate business statistical annual report; Ministry of International Trade and Industry. (2) Japan Economic Institute (1990). (3) Petrie (1992). (4) Dodwell Marketing Consultants (1986).

Notes: Constant term not reported. Definitions (source number in parentheses): SALESMOF = Share of foreign affiliates in industry sales, FY1991. JPNMERG (2) = Value of mergers and acquisitions, by industry, 1984–88. CAPINT (3) = Capital intensity. HERF (3) = Herfindahl index. TECH (3) = Technology intensity. KRETS (4) = percentage sales by all *keiretsu*. VERT9 (4) = Percentage sales by vertical *keiretsu*. HORIZ8 (4) = Percentage sales by horizontal *keiretsu*.

Dodwell. Nonetheless, there is no reason to believe that the data are particularly biased toward finding significantly negative relationships between *keiretsu* and foreign sales by industry.

To be sure, it is quite possible that *keiretsu* and low FDI are both correlated with an omitted variable that has a causal link with both. However, this variable must operate separately from the effects of both capital intensity and concentration, which were controlled for in the regressions. One argument worth considering, for example, is that *keiretsu* enjoy a lower cost of capital, have lower hurdle rates of return and can therefore outbid foreigners interested in acquiring Japanese companies. It may also be the case that, if exports and FDI are complements, the difficulties experienced by foreign firms in entering industries in which *keiretsu* predominate help to explain the finding in Lawrence (1991) that *keiretsu* have a negative impact on imports.

Finally, the data have also been used to explore whether the existence of *keiretsu* constitutes a barrier to domestic mergers and acquisitions. Indeed, while *keiretsu* may inhibit mergers outside the group, they may actually help to promote such activities between members. Data on mergers and acquisitions (most of which were relatively small) reported to the Japan Free Trade Commission for nine industries over the period 1988 and 1989, showed that merger and acquisition activity is more prevalent in technology-intensive industries (table 4.9, equations 3 and 4). However, no effects associated with the *keiretsu* variables could be found. Apparently, *keiretsu* do not inhibit domestic merger and acquisition activity. Indeed, the coefficients of the *keiretsu* variables are positive (although not statistically significant). The effects of *keiretsu* appear to operate on FDI but not on domestic merger and acquisition activity.

4.6   Conclusions and Policy Implications

During the 1980s, inward FDI in Japan grew primarily through the reinvested earnings of existing firms. In fact, foreign withdrawals, particularly of minority-interest positions, have outweighed new equity capital investments. Apparently, the high values on the Tokyo stock market during the late 1980s not only discouraged new entrants but also encouraged existing foreign participants to liquidate some of their positions.

Several features of foreign activity in Japan support the anecdotal accounts of barriers to foreign entry and operation. These include the high share of U.S. receipts from Japan that take the form of license payments from unaffiliated Japanese firms, the high share of FDI accounted for by joint ventures, and the high share of majority-owned FDI in wholesale trade. Given these entry barriers, one would expect the ex ante demand for acquisitions as a mode of entering Japan to be relatively high.

Mergers and acquisitions in Japan, even under friendly conditions, are difficult. Acquisitions involving foreign firms and/or hostile takeovers are rare. In other developed countries, by contrast, the majority of FDI entries occur through acquisitions. However, a disproportionate share of entries in Japan involves joint ventures and greenfield versus acquisition) and the level of FDI internationally helps to explain the low levels of FDI in Japan.

The expansion of stock cross-holdings among *keiretsu* members and other Japanese firms during the 1970s was an explicit device to prevent foreigners from buying Japanese companies. It appears to have worked. The presence of *keiretsu,* whether horizontal or vertical, is associated with particularly low levels of FDI. Market entry could be hindered by practices that are explicitly collusive (situations in which long-term relationships are the norm), by difficulties associated with making acquisitions of *keiretsu*-related firms because of stock cross-holdings, or by inherent cost-of-capital advantages enjoyed by *keiretsu* members. Additional research is needed to determine the precise mechanism that brings about this negative association. While one cannot be clear on precisely which mechanism is at work, the results represent additional evidence refuting the claim that *keiretsu* linkages are economically insignificant. Although *keiretsu* do not appear to discourage domestic merger and acquisition activity, they are associated with less FDI.

Is the environment for FDI in Japan changing? The 1992 recession in Japan, combined with significant declines in stock and land prices, could herald a change in the environment for merger and acquisition activity in Japan in general and for acquisitions of Japanese firms by foreign companies in particular. Foreigners are likely to find deals more attractive as prices fall. *The Economist* ("Biter Bitten" 1992) noted that though present economic conditions will require considerable restructuring through mergers, most deals are likely to occur between firms within the same *keiretsu.* However,

> Japanese banks are increasingly unwilling to play their traditional role of arranging marriages with healthier Japanese companies. Many just want to get their money back as soon as possible, even if that means selling to a foreign company. [Nonetheless], there is still a huge cultural divide that deters many outsiders from acquisitions in Japan. (p. 85)

The major differences in the ease with which foreigners can acquire domestic companies in Japan and in other developed economies are likely to persist for the time being.

As the world economy becomes increasingly integrated, institutional differences, such as those that exist between Japan and other countries, are coming under particular scrutiny. One view holds that pluralism and diversity are beneficial to the global economy and that, as long as border barriers are removed, a high degree of national sovereignty is warranted. Certainly, since no global investment code exists, Japanese practices do not represent a violation of its international legal obligations. On the other hand, there is a growing recognition that globalization requires mechanisms for deeper integration than that achieved by the removal of border barriers and the adherence to the formal legal obligations of national treatment. At certain times, as the preparation for the single European market has made clear, this may require harmonization; at other times, mutual recognition may suffice. Regardless, efforts to negotiate measures to reconcile institutional differences are likely to continue.

A cost-benefit analysis of these institutional practices is beyond the scope of this article. Foreign direct investment will generally confer benefits on both the host and home countries. The relatively closed Japanese market for corporate control reduces foreign profits. It also reduces domestic competition and may reduce technology transfer to Japan. However, restrictions on FDI could also increase Japanese welfare (and reduce foreign welfare) if it shifts rents from foreign to Japanese-owned firms by forcing foreign firms to license their products rather than to enter the Japanese market directly.

Increasingly, firms recognize that effective global strategies require a major presence in each region of the triad (UN Center on Transnational Corporations 1991). Since access to Japan is more difficult than access to the United States or Europe, Japanese firms could gain a strategic advantage. Indeed, in the long run, firms headquartered in Japan could become more competitive than those headquartered in the European Community or in the United States. As Japanese companies become more important rivals and as they avail themselves of the opportunities to invest in other nations, these asymmetries in market access between Japan and other countries are likely to become an increasing source of friction. It is unclear whether the asymmetries will be closed by a Japanese movement toward foreign practices or by restraints that seek to give Japanese firms investing abroad access that is equivalent to that granted foreign firms in Japan. It is hard, however, to imagine that the current asymmetries will be maintained.

References

Dodwell Marketing Consultants. 1986. *Industrial Groupings in Japan.* Tokyo: Dodwell Marketing Consultants.

Mergers and acquisitions in Japan: Lifting a barrier or two. 1989. *Economist,* 12 August, p. 68.

Biter bitten: Japanese companies once looked able and eager to acquire the rest of the world. Times have changed. 1992. *Economist,* 25 April, p. 85.

Encarnation, Dennis. 1992. *Rivals beyond trade: American versus Japan in global competition.* Ithaca, N.Y.: Cornell University Press.

Graham, Edward M., and Paul R. Krugman. 1991. *Foreign direct investment in the United States.* Washington, D.C.: Institute for International Economics.

Holloway, Nigel. 1990. How Japan takes over. *Far Eastern Economic Review,* 11 January, pp. 40–44.

Japan Economic Institute. 1990. Japan and mergers: Oil and water? *JEI Report,* 6 April.

———. 1991a. Foreign direct investment in Japan. *JEI Report,* 20 September.

———. 1991b. Mergers and acquisitions debate. *JEI Report,* 21 June, p. 23B.

Japan Economic Journal. 1990. *A will and a way: How foreign companies are making it in Japan.* Tokyo: Nihon Keizai Shimbun.

JETRO. 1989. *A survey of successful cases of foreign-affiliated companies in Japan.* Tokyo: Japan External Trade Organization.

Kester, W. Carl. 1991. *Japanese takeovers: The global contest for corporate control.* Boston: Harvard Business School Press.

Lawrence, Robert Z. 1991. Efficient or exclusionist? The import behavior of Japanese corporate groups. *Brookings Papers on Economic Activity* 1: 311–41.

Mason, Mark. 1992. *American multinationals and Japan.* Cambridge, Mass.: Harvard University Press.

———. Forthcoming. United States direct investment in Japan: Trends and prospects. *California Management Review.*

Ministry of International Trade and Industry. 1991. *24th survey of foreign affiliates in Japan.* News Release no. 386 (91-4).

Petri, Peter. 1992. Market structure, comparative advantage, and Japanese trade under the strong yen. In *Trade with Japan: Has the door opened wider?* ed. Paul R. Krugman, 51–84. Chicago: University of Chicago Press.

Ray, Edward John. 1989. The determinants of foreign direct investment in the United States, 1979–85. In *Trade policies for international competitiveness,* ed. Robert C. Feenstra, 53–85. Chicago: University of Chicago Press.

Saxonhouse, Gary R., and Robert M. Stern. 1989. An analytical survey of formal and informal barriers to international trade and investment in the United States, Canada, and Japan. In *Trade and investment relations among the United States, Canada, and Japan,* ed. Robert M. Stern, 302–8. Chicago: University of Chicago Press.

Shimada, Kunio. 1990. Comparisons of the U.S. merger and acquisitions with Japanese one through some examples. Master's thesis. Cambridge, Mass.: Harvard Law Library.

Transnational Corporations and Management Division, Department of Economic and Social Development. 1992. *World investment report 1992: Transnational corporations as engines of growth.* Sales no. E.92.II.A.19. New York: United Nations.

UN Center on Transnational Corporations. 1991. *World investment report 1991: The triad in foreign direct investment.* Sales no. E.91.II.A.12. New York: United Nations.

U.S. Department of Commerce. 1981. *U.S. direct investment abroad, 1977.* Washington, D.C.: U.S. Government Printing Office.

———. 1991. *Foreign direct investment in the United States: 1989 transactions.* Washington, D.C.: U.S. Government Printing Office.

U.S. International Trade Commission. 1990. *Phase 1: Japan's distribution system and options for improving U.S. access.* Publication no. 2291. Washington, D.C.: USITC.

Vaupel, James W., and Joan P. Curhan. 1973. *The making of multinational enterprise: Sourcebook of tables.* Cambridge, Mass.: Harvard University, Graduate School of Business Administration.

Viner, Aaron. 1988. *Inside Japanese financial markets.* Homewood, Ill.: Dow Jones–Irwin.

Yoshitomi, Masaru. 1990. *Keiretsu:* An insider's guide to Japan's conglomerates. *International Economic Insights* 1, no. 2 (September–October): 10–14.

Comment   Richard C. Marston

In his essay, Robert Lawrence provides an interesting and provocative look at foreign direct investment in Japan. He argues that, because of informal and formal barriers, all forms of foreign direct investment (FDI) in Japan are much lower than in other comparable countries. When FDI occurs, moreover, it typically takes the form of joint ventures or greenfield investments rather than the acquisition of existing firms, because foreign corporations are discouraged by Japanese practices from acquiring majority control of Japanese firms.

Lawrence marshalls a variety of evidence to support these two propositions. The evidence on the first point is strong. Graham and Krugman (1991) show that the share of foreign-owned firms in total sales is 1 percent in Japan, but 10 percent in the United States and 18 percent or higher in Britain, France, and Germany. The Bank of Japan's (BOJ) balance-of-payments data indicate that in 1989 the stock of inward FDI is only $9.2 billion in Japan, in contrast to $400 billion in the United States and $100 billion in Canada. U.S. data on direct investment in Japan, which unlike the BOJ data take into account reinvested earnings, show that FDI in Japan in 1989 was $21 billion, still a remarkably low figure.

Lawrence also presents interesting evidence on the importance of licensing as an alternative to FDI. In 1990, 33 percent of U.S. receipts of direct investment income and royalties from Japan were in the form of royalties and fees from licensing. In contrast, only 5.2 percent of U.S. receipts worldwide were in the form of royalties and fees. So a disproportionate amount of U.S. activity in Japan is in the form of licensing rather than direct investment. This evidence is consistent with the view that the Japanese market is difficult to penetrate (for example, because the distribution system is complex), although it does not indicate necessarily that Japanese companies deliberately excluded foreigners.

One piece of evidence is difficult to reconcile with the rest. Table 4.8 examines FDI in countries belonging to the Organization for Economic Cooperation and Development (OECD). In an equation explaining FDI as a function of variables such as population and GDP per capita, a dummy variable representing Japan has no significant effect on FDI (at conventional levels of significance). That's a little surprising, given the other evidence showing that Japan is an outlier.

Lawrence's second proposition is more provocative: that the Japanese system blocks acquisitions by foreign firms. Much of FDI, when undertaken, takes the form of joint ventures or greenfield investments, not acquisitions of majority ownership in Japanese firms. According to Lawrence, FDI does not take the form of acquisitions because the Japanese system actively discourages acquisitions by keeping shares in friendly hands (with stable shareholdings by insurance companies and pension funds and with cross-holding of shares by other corporations). In industries dominated by *keiretsu,* any attempt to buy into the industry will induce defensive reactions in which firms within the *keiretsu* buy the shares of the targeted company. Ministry of Finance rules further thwart potential acquirers by requiring that takeover bids by foreigners be delayed by ten days—time enough to mount a rescue effort. Domestic firms are not subject to these rules.

I will review the evidence Lawrence provides to support his view that foreign acquisitions are restricted in Japan. Then I will offer an alternative explanation for the same phenomena.

What evidence can be marshalled about foreign acquisitions? Table 4.7 presents the results of a MITI survey of foreign-owned firms completed in 1991. This survey shows that only 7.1 percent of these firms were the result of acquisition. In contrast, 49.3 percent were established through greenfield investments, while 43.7 percent were joint ventures between foreign and Japanese firms. So it is true that foreign acquisitions constitute a remarkably low percentage of FDI in Japan. Table 4.2, however, shows that overall merger and acquisition activity, by Japanese as well as foreign firms, is much smaller in value in Japan than in the United States (one-sixth as large). So it may truly be difficult for any firm, Japanese or foreign, to acquire a Japanese firm. Table 4.3, on the other hand, shows that in the last half of the 1980s there was a large surge in acquisition activity by Japanese firms acquiring both Japanese and foreign firms. Japanese acquisition of other Japanese firms almost doubles between 1985 and 1990. And Japanese acquisitions of foreign firms increases fourfold during this same period. Yet there is no increase in foreign firms' acquisitions of Japanese firms.

Let me suggest an explanation of these facts that does not rely on a conspiracy theory involving Japanese firms systematically shutting out foreign acquisitions. The boom in FDI across the world occurred in the last half of the 1980s. That was also a period of unparalleled increases in real estate values and stock market values in Japan—increases which exceeded those in other countries by a considerable amount. Is it possible that Japanese firms were able to outbid foreign firms in acquisitions of Japanese firms during this period?

In a perfectly functioning capital market, of course, all firms should bid the same amount for any given anticipated cash flow. But if firms are *capital constrained,* then firms with large real estate holdings in Japan and cross-holdings of Japanese equity will be able to outbid other firms—including those firms from abroad who are not sharing in the Japanese boom. This is a variation on Froot and Stein's (1991) analysis in which FDI in the United States was driven by the rise in foreign currencies relative to the dollar. Here it is the Japanese real estate and stock markets that raise the wealth of Japanese firms.

In studying FDI in Japan, it is well to keep in mind that we are examining a country that liberalized FDI only in 1980. We really want to know how the liberalized regime of the 1980s works, not the MITI-dominated regime of the 1960s and 1970s. The Japanese real estate and stock market booms of the last half of the decade may well be enough to explain why the stock of foreign acquisitions was so low at the end of the decade. By this reasoning, the recent collapse of the Nikkei should lead to more acquisitions by foreign firms and thus a reversal of present patterns.

Having introduced an alternative explanation for the low level of foreign acquisitions in Japan, let me review the strongest piece of evidence in favor of

Lawrence's explanation. Table 4.9 presents equations explaining the share of 1991 industry sales in Japan that is accounted for by majority-owned foreign affiliates. Lawrence explains the share with conventional variables such as concentration ratios and technological intensity. But he also adds a variable representing the share of sales by keiretsu in that industry. He finds statistically significant effects of these sales. That is, FDI sales are significantly lower in industries where *keiretsu* are important. This is important evidence.

There are some possible explanations for this finding which do not rely on conspiracy theories. It could be, for example, that *keiretsu* are concentrated in industries where foreign investment is undesirable for reasons unrelated to the *keiretsu* per se. (Lawrence mentions the possibility that some omitted factor explains these results). Or suppose that we take the statistical results at face value. It could be that industries where *keiretsu* dominate are less attractive targets for direct investment because acquisition might jeopardize beneficial ties among firms within the *keiretsu*. If so, then the existence of the *keiretsu* discourages acquisitions but not necessarily because firms in the *keiretsu* mount defensive operations to keep shares out of foreign hands. In any case, the statistical evidence buttresses Lawrence's case that it is Japanese behavior, whether intentionally designed to exclude foreigners or not, that discourages acquisitions.

Overall, Lawrence's paper provides a convincing case that FDI in Japan is different than elsewhere. Whether this is due to deliberate exclusionary practices or to other causes is still subject to debate.

References

Froot, Kenneth A., and Jeremy C. Stein. 1991. Exchange rates and foreign direct investment: An imperfect capital markets approach. *Quarterly Journal of Economics* 106 (November): 1191–217.
Graham, Edward M., and Paul R. Krugman. 1991. *Foreign direct investment in the United States.* Washington, D.C.: Institute for International Economics.

Discussion Summary

Kenneth Froot began the discussion by suggesting that differences in language and culture, rather than actual discrimination, may explain why there is so little FDI into Japan; geographic isolation may be a further explanation. Also, the *keiretsu* groups can marshall liquidity to defend against a hostile takeover of any member by an outsider.

Martin Feldstein observed that the high Japanese share prices have been a barrier to foreign acquisitions in recent years. Foreigners could not get the same price-earnings ratios and therefore could not justify the acquisition of a

Japanese firm. He suggested that a majority-owned wholesale trade company is likely to be just a marketing subsidiary of a U.S. manufacturer, and he pointed out that direct investment is fundamentally different from licensing. The latter is essentially static; the licensee obtains what is known at a point in time but does not share in the dynamic of change and does not get future products.

Raymond Vernon began his comments with a general statistical point about cross-country data sets. Because there is no "universe" of which the current observations are a sample, there is no meaning to the standard errors. It is appropriate therefore to look at the coefficients as descriptive material but to ignore the *t*-statistics. Since there are many individual cases of barriers to foreign investment that are known, the statistical estimates confirm the existence of these barriers. Any other finding would not have been believable. Also, there is a data problem associated with licensing fees for intrafirm transactions.

James Hines suggested expanding the sample beyond the OECD. He noted that Japanese tax rules would discourage foreign investment in Japan.

Deborah Swenson mentioned that acquisitions are frequently spin-offs that are not doing well, but there are not many of these in Japan. *Robert Lawrence* noted in response that this is not true in Japan, where the *keiretsu* takes over sick spin-offs.

Michael Adler asked what the welfare consequences are of FDI. *Lawrence* named three in response: japanese welfare is reduced by a reduction in FDI, rent shifting may benefit Japan, and asymmetry of bilateral pattern of FDI creates tension.

Karl Sauvant pointed out that if *global* production is key to a firm's ability to compete, closing a market to foreign firms hurts their ability to compete worldwide.

Peter Petri offered a further explanation of why U.S. firms do not invest in Japan: that U.S. firms may not have a comparative advantage in manufacturing. Japanese firms come to the United States because they have such a comparative advantage. *Richard Caves* added that there are a variety of other factors that may explain why there is so little FDI in Japan: distance, language, and so on.

Said *Geoffrey Carliner,* "There was a time when General Motors could have bought Toyota for less than it spent on direct investment in plant and equipment."

Robert Feenstra ended the discussion by commenting that *keiretsu* firms are a market for other members of the group. A foreign investor would not have this advantage. This also serves as a barrier.

5 Foreign Direct Investment in the United States: Changes over Three Decades

Robert E. Lipsey

5.1 Historical Background

As far back as there is any statistical record, and probably earlier also, it has been a characteristic of the United States' foreign investment history that, while inward investment was largely in portfolio form, outward investment was mainly direct investment. That is, the outward investment mostly involved control of foreign operations by U.S. firms, while the inward investment took the form of lending by foreigners to government agencies or enterprises that were U.S.-controlled.

The contrast between the two sides of the investment balance sheet is summarized in table 5.1, to the extent that the historical record permits the distinction to be made. The individual figures in the table often rely on weak statistical foundations, and the fluctuations in the ratios should not be taken very seriously. For example, the sharp rise in the share of direct investment in the U.S. outward total between 1929 and 1935 to a large extent reflects the fact that, in the data source, bond holdings were adjusted to market value in 1935, while direct investments were not, although they too must have fallen substantially in market value. The contrast between inward and outward investment is clear, however. Direct investment was almost always more than half the outward investment total but never more than a quarter of the inward investment.

The large decline in the share of direct investment on the outward side between 1919 and 1929 has had its counterpart in more recent years, as we discuss later. That decline reflected a tremendous expansion in portfolio lending, concentrated in Latin America to a much larger extent than ever before. Much of that portfolio investment disappeared in defaults and price depreciation during the 1930s.

The author is indebted to Qing Zhang for statistical and computer assistance and to Robert Lawrence, R. David Belli, and other conference participants for comments and suggestions

Table 5.1   Share of Direct Investment in Foreign Private Investment in the
United States and U.S. Private Investment Abroad: Selected Years,
1897 to 1960

	U.S. Private Investment Abroad	Foreign Private Investment in the U.S.
1897	93%	—
1908	65	—
1914	75	18%
1919	56	23
1924	50	24
1929	44	16
1935	59	25
1940	60	22
1950	62	19
1960	65	17

Sources: Lipsey (1988) and U.S. Bureau of the Census (1975), based mainly on data from Lewis (1938).

Since direct investment is a transfer more of technological or management skills than of capital, it may seem surprising that there was so little inflow into the United States during the nineteenth century, when several European countries must have possessed superior technology and skills. One explanation may be that the transfer of skills took a different form when transportation and communication were so slow and primitive compared to that in recent years. Because of the difficulty of controlling foreign enterprises from a home base, much of the transfer of knowledge took the form of human migration, either to establish enterprises in the United States or to manage them after they were first established. Also, as Mira Wilkins (1989) points out in her recent study of foreign investment in the United States before 1914, the distinction between direct and portfolio investment was not always a sharp one. Even portfolio investors sometimes intervened in the management of U.S. firms when things went badly. And many of the earlier direct investments in the United States were what she refers to as "free-standing" enterprises, differing from most U.S. direct investment in recent years in that they were owned by foreigners but not by foreign firms. They were not subsidiaries of multinational firms, as is typical now, although they were sometimes parts of loose networks trading with each other and sometimes sharing expertise in technical fields. Such enterprises were probably much more likely over time to turn into domestic U.S. firms with the migration of their owners or adaptation to local conditions in the United States than are the current subsidiaries of multinational enterprises.

5.2   The Magnitude of Foreign Direct Investment in the United States

5.2.1   The U.S. Share in the World's Stock and Flows

The dominant role of the United States as a supplier of direct investment to other countries before the 1970s is reflected in the fact that U.S. outward investment accounted for over half of the developed world's stock of direct investment in 1967 and 1971, with the next most important direct investor, the United Kingdom, owning only about 15–17 percent and no other single country accounting for more than 6 percent (United Nations, 1978, Table III-32). On the other side of the account, foreign direct investment in the United States was only 9 percent of the world's total stock in 1967 and 11 percent in 1975 (United Nations 1978, table III-33).

The U.S. share of direct investment outflows since the late 1960s is described in table 5.2. It was well over half the developed-country total in the 1960s and stayed at or close to half through the 1970s. In the second half of the 1970s, the United States was still responsible for almost half the developed country outflow and more than 40 percent of that of the whole world. Then, in the first half of the 1980s, U.S. direct investment fell to less than 20 percent of the world outflow and by the latest period had gone below 15 percent.

Table 5.2   **U.S. Share of Developed Countries' and World Direct Investment Inflows and Outflows, 1960 and 1965–1990**

	Outflows		Inflows	
	Developed Countries	World	Developed Countries	World
1960	57.6%		6.2%	
1965–66	64.9		2.2	
1967–69	56.8		16.7	
1970–72	51.9		10.4	7.2%
1973–75[a]	43.8		26.2	16.8
1973–75[b]	48.9		24.3	18.8
1975–80[c]	47.7		35.4	26.2
1975–80[d]		42.4%		24.5
1981–85		19.1		39.3
1980–84[e]		31.8		42.2
1985–89		17.1		46.0
1980–85[f]			50.4	37.6
1986–90		13.8	42.0	34.7

Source: Appendix table 5A.1.
[a]Comparable to 1970–72.   [c]Comparable to 1973–75.   [e]Comparable to 1985–89.
[b]Comparable to 1975–80.   [d]Comparable to 1981–85.   [f]Comparable to 1986–90.

The opposite change took place on the inflow side. The direct investment inflow to the United States was less than 10 percent of the total inflow to developed countries in 1960 and 1965–66, rose to 17 percent in 1967–69, and jumped to about a quarter in 1973–75 and over a third in 1975–80. The U.S. share of world inflows, only about 15 percent in the early 1970s, climbed to over a quarter in the late 1970s, around 40 percent in the first half of the 1980s, and over 45 percent in the late 1980s before declining somewhat.

The consequence of these declining U.S. shares of outflows and increasing shares of inflows can be seen in the shares of direct investment stocks. By 1988, the United States held 35 percent of the world stock of outward investment and 31 percent of the stock of inward investment. The U.S. share of outward investment would probably be considerably higher if either of the alternative valuations discussed below were used, since the U.S. investments are older than those of most other countries. And the U.S. share of inward investment would be considerably smaller if the reporting of inward investment by other countries were more complete.

These figures by themselves seem to imply that the United States has in recent years sharply cut back its former role as the major supplier of direct investment capital to the rest of the world. It has, instead, apparently come to absorb a very high proportion of the world's supply of direct investment capital.

While there is some truth to this summary, there are also some questionable aspects to it. Since the United States was the leading foreign direct investor in the early post–World War II decades, many of its holdings are well-established foreign firms, and the further flow of U.S. direct investment capital to foreign countries comes largely from the retained earnings of these companies. While the United States reports these retained earnings as flows of direct investment, many other countries do not, and the United States share in outflows is therefore probably exaggerated. Since many other countries fail to report the reinvested earnings in their inward investment accounts, the U.S. share on the inward side is probably also overstated.

5.2.2 . U.S. Inward and Outward Direct Investment Stocks and Flows

Since the United States was much more of an exporter than an importer of direct investment for many years, as described above, the stock of foreign direct investment in the United States was small compared to U.S. holdings abroad. In 1950, for example, the inward stock was less than 30 percent as large as the outward stock, measured by book values, and in 1966, after the rapid growth in U.S. outward direct investment, it was less than 20 percent (table 5.3). As foreign direct investment in the United States began to grow rapidly in the years after 1977, the book value ratio rose, to the point where in 1990 the foreign direct investment in the United States appeared almost as large as the U.S. direct investment abroad, a startling change in a little over a decade.

As this near reversal of the direct investment balance took place, along with the widely publicized story that the United States had gone from a major credi-

Table 5.3   Value of Stock of Foreign Direct Investment in the United States
                     as Percentage of the Value of the Stock of U.S. Direct Investment
                     Abroad: Selected Years, 1950 to 1991

	Book Value		Current Cost Total	Market Value Total
	Excluding Netherlands Antilles Finance Affiliates	Total	Current Cost Total	Market Value Total
1950	28.8%	28.8%		
1966	17.5	17.5		
1977	23.5	23.7	22.4%	
1982	54.7	60.0	45.7	57.5%
1985	73.5	80.2	59.7	58.0
1988	90.9	93.7	72.6	57.7
1990	93.0	93.5	74.8	74.9
1991	89.3	90.1	74.3	81.6

Sources: Appendix tables 5A.2 and 5A.4; Scholl, Mataloni, and Bezirganian (1992), table 3.

tor position to being "the world's greatest debtor" within a few years, a number of observers expressed skepticism about the significance of the book value data. These are basically historical cost valuations, but those for U.S. direct investment abroad are affected by exchange rate changes, since many book values are translated into U.S. dollars from foreign currencies using current exchange rates. Also, since U.S. direct investment abroad was much older on average than foreign investment in the United States, it seemed likely that it had been made at much lower than current prices and, for that and other reasons, was greatly undervalued (Eisner and Pieper 1990; Ulan and Dewald 1989). That impression was reinforced by the fact that foreign income from direct investment in the United States was much smaller than U.S. income on direct investment abroad, well under half in 1990 (e.g., Di Lullo 1991, table 5). In response to these doubts, the Bureau of Economic Analysis (BEA) undertook the calculation of some alternative measures. One, the "current-cost" method, is based on a revaluation of tangible assets. The main feature is a revaluation of plant and equipment, using a perpetual inventory calculation from past expenditures. Land and inventories are also revalued to a rough measure of current prices. The "market-value" method is a revaluation of the equity part of direct investment on the basis of movements in stock prices (Landefeld and Lawson 1991).[1]

Two aspects of the story seem fairly clear. One is that foreign direct invest-

1. Both of these adjustments are extremely crude. Even if they were not, there is no reason to expect them to give similar results. In the case of U.S. corporations, for which the data are far better, the adjusted book value, akin to the current value used here, ranged from more than 20 percent below to almost 90 percent above the market value of the equity derived from stock prices between 1929 and 1958 (Goldsmith and Lipsey 1963, table 25), and from 30 percent below to more than twice as high between 1954 and 1977 (Cagan and Lipsey 1978, table 2-3).

ment in the United States is still considerably smaller than U.S. direct investment abroad. The other is that the foreign investment in the United States grew much more rapidly than U.S. investment abroad after 1977, not only in percentage terms but, by some measures, in dollar terms as well. Thus, compared with the 1950s, 1960s, and 1970s, the United States was an exceptionally attractive location for foreign companies in the 1980s relative to the attractiveness of foreign locations for U.S. companies. This was the case despite the very high price of U.S. assets during part of this period, as the exchange value of the U.S. dollar reached its peak in 1984 and early 1985. However, the period after 1977 also includes two periods of low exchange values of the dollar, one around 1980 and one after 1985.

While the expected effects of exchange rate changes on trade by affiliates are clear (they are described below), the effects of investment flows are ambiguous. For example, a high exchange value of the U.S. dollar makes foreign production facilities more economical relative to those in the United States, but the incentive for a U.S. firm to invest in such facilities would be stronger if the product were very tradable than if it were a service or a relatively nontradable good. In addition, the high value of the dollar would reduce the price of a foreign facility in dollar terms, so that an increase in physical investment might be offset by the decline in the dollar price of the foreign assets and result in a decline in investment outflows denominated in dollars unless there were a high elasticity of demand for productive assets or a high elasticity of substitution between U.S. and foreign assets.

5.2.3   Foreign-owned Firms' Shares of the U.S. Economy

The rapid growth of foreign direct investment in the United States should be compared with some measures of the size of the U.S. economy. By some indicators, this comparison places the foreign operations in perspective as, even now, a small part of the economy. One such measure is the ratio of the stock of foreign direct investment to the assets of U.S. corporations (table 5.4). The stock of foreign direct investment looks small by this standard, but the rapid growth after 1977 does not stand out.

If we confine our attention to the nonfinancial sector, foreign direct investment appears more important. That is partly because foreign ownership is less important in finance and partly because the finance sector's assets include a large amount of holdings of the equity and debt of other sectors and of the finance sector itself. There is much less duplication, in this sense, in the nonfinancial sector's assets. The foreign share here more than doubled between 1950 and 1980 or 1960 and 1980, and then much more than doubled during the 1980s. Thus, the growth of the foreign investment share accelerated during the 1980s.

In a sense, this comparison between foreign investment and assets is a misleading one because the numerator and denominator are different concepts. More appropriate comparisons might be for shares of output or shares of inputs

Table 5.4   Book Value of Foreign Direct Investment in the United States as
                   Percentage of Assets of U.S. Corporations: Selected Years, 1950–1991

	All Corporations	Nonfinancial Corporations
1950	0.6%	.9%
1960	0.6	1.0
1966	0.5	1.0
1974	0.7	1.4
1977	0.7	1.3
1980	1.1	1.9
1982	1.4	2.4
1985	1.5	3.0
1987	1.8	4.0
1988	2.0	4.5
1989	2.1	4.9
1990	2.2	5.2
1991	2.1	5.1

Sources: Appendix tables 5A.3 and 5A.4.

into production, such as labor or capital, but these are more limited in their time spans.

Orr (1991) calculated the share of U.S. manufacturing industry assets under foreign control in 1980 and 1988. As part of the calculation, he estimated what the foreign share of motor vehicle industry assets would be if Japanese-owned auto production operations, listed under the wholesale trade industry in the Department of Commerce data, were transferred to the manufacturing category. An affiliate is listed in wholesale trade in the official data if its wholesale trade activities are larger than the manufacturing activity. Rather than value added, value of sales is the criterion. This method tends to put into wholesale trade affiliates that would be in manufacturing by a value added or employment criterion, because ratios of sales to value added or employment are much larger in wholesale trade than in manufacturing. Orr's estimates for the foreign share in manufacturing assets were 8.5 percent (1980) and 14.3 percent (1988). Even with the estimated motor vehicle industry assets added, the shares in the transportation equipment industry, 4.4 percent in 1980 and 5.9 percent in 1988, were well below the average for manufacturing.

A comparison of gross product, excluding banks, suggests slightly more than a doubling of the foreign share in U.S. output between 1977 and 1990 (table 5.5), somewhat slower than that indicated by the direct investment data. Another comparison, this time on the input side, for employment (table 5.6) shows that the levels are fairly small but the growth has been rapid: the ratio more than tripled between 1974 and 1990.

The employment shares of foreign firms vary greatly among sectors: they are much higher in goods production, particularly mining and manufacturing,

Table 5.5   Foreign Affiliate Share of U.S. Gross Product, excluding Banks:
                   Selected Years, 1977–1990

1977	1.9%
1982	3.3
1987	3.6
1988	4.0
1989	4.4
1990	4.4

Sources: U.S. Department of Commerce (1992a; 1992d, table 1).

Table 5.6   Employment in Nonbank U.S. Affiliates of Foreign Companies as
                   Percentage of U.S. Private Nonagricultural Employment: Selected
                   Years, 1974–1990

1974	1.6%
1977	1.8
1980	2.7
1982	3.3
1984	3.5
1987	3.8
1988	4.4
1989	5.0
1990	5.1

Sources: Appendix tables 5A.6 and 5A.7.

than in service sectors (table 5.7). The sector ratios are subject to the problem
that establishments are classified differently in the two sources. The aggregate
U.S. data are classified by industry of establishment, while the data for foreign
affiliates are consolidated into a total for all affiliates of a single firm and classified by the predominant industry of those affiliates.

For one year, 1987, new data provided by the combination of BEA and Census information permit us to make a much more exact calculation of foreign
shares on an establishment basis. The main difference is that on a consistent
establishment basis the foreign share is lower in goods production (6.9 percent
compared with 8.2 percent) and higher in finance and services (4.6 and 2.4
percent compared with 3.1 and 1.2 percent). Within goods production, the establishment data show that the foreign share is exaggerated by the enterprise
data in both manufacturing and mining, including petroleum, the latter by over
40 percent.

The development that has drawn the most public comment is the growth
of the foreign share in manufacturing, from minor levels in 1974 to over
10 percent of employment in 1989. What is equally notable is the perva-
siveness of the growth in foreign shares, which more than doubled in every
broad industry group shown here. While this growth is often viewed from the
U.S. perspective as a sign of U.S. weakness, it was also a part of a general

Table 5.7 Employment in U.S. Affiliates of Foreign Corporations as Percentage of Total U.S. Nonagricultural Private-Sector Employment, by Broad Industry Groups: Selected Years, 1974–1990

	1974	1977	1980	1982	1984	1987§	1988	1989	1990
Mining*	13.0%	10.4%	10.4%	12.3%	13.7%	16.2%	17.4%	21.2%	23.1%
Manufacturing	2.8	3.5	5.5	6.7	7.2	8.2	9.5	11.1	11.6
Goods production	3.2	3.9	5.8	7.1	7.6	8.6	9.9	11.6	12.2
Construction	0.2	0.3	1.0	1.3	1.0	1.0	1.1	1.4	1.4
Transp. and public utilities	1.0	0.5	0.7	1.1	1.2	1.8	2.4	3.4	4.2
Goods, construction, transportation and public utilities	2.5	2.9	4.3	5.3	5.5	6.1	7.1	8.4	8.9
Wholesale trade	2.8	3.2	4.1	5.3	5.2	5.5	6.1	6.4	7.0
Retail trade	1.0	1.0	2.0	2.6	2.8	3.0	3.5	4.1	3.8
Finance, insurance, real estate†	1.1‡	1.1	2.1	2.3	2.3	3.1	3.6	3.7	3.4
Other services	0.3	0.2	0.5	0.6	0.9	1.2	1.5	1.7	1.9
Trade and services†	1.0	1.0	1.6	2.1	2.2	2.5	2.9	3.2	3.2

Sources: Appendix tables 5A.6 and 5A.7; U.S. Department of Commerce (1992e), table 1.1.

*Including petroleum.
†Banking included in denominator but not in numerator.
‡Including banking, it would be 1.8 percent.
§By industry of establishment, foreign affiliate shares were:

Agricultural services, forestry, and fishing	3.7%
Mining	14.0
Manufacturing	6.9
Goods production	7.0
Construction	1.0
Transportation and public utilities	1.8
Wholesale trade	6.1
Retail trade	3.5
Finance, insurance, and real estate	4.6
Services	2.4
Services, broadly defined	2.7

move toward internationalization of production by firms all around the world, in which foreign firms began to imitate the internationalization that large U.S. firms pioneered in the 1950s and 1960s (Lipsey 1989). Even at the end of the period, the foreign share in U.S. manufacturing employment was not high compared to that in most developed countries except Japan and the Nordic countries.

The growth in the foreign share of U.S. manufacturing employment has affected all the main groups within the manufacturing sector, but it has gone much further in some groups than in others (table 5.8). Over the whole period, the foreign share of employment in chemicals has been much higher than that in any other industry group, a surprising fact in view of the strong position of U.S. chemical companies in world trade. In fact, the foreign shares among these industry groups do not seem to bear any relation to the competitive strength of U.S. companies; they are no higher in the groups in which U.S. firms are relatively weak, such as foods, metals, and miscellaneous manufactures, than in industries where U.S. firms hold strong positions, such as chemicals and machinery. It may be that the foreign shares are high in chemicals and machinery because the nature of these industries leads firms from all countries to be multinational, and that it would be higher if U.S. firms were not strong in these fields.

Two points should be made about particular industries. The fact that the

Table 5.8   **Employment in U.S. Manufacturing Affiliates of Foreign Corporations as Percentage of U.S. Manufacturing Employment, by Industry: Selected Years, 1974–1990**

	1974	1980	1987*	1989	1990
All manufacturing	2.8%	5.5%	8.2%	11.1%	11.6%
Food and kindred products	4.4	7.0	8.8	15.2	15.0
Chemicals	10.8	25.7	38.6	40.6	46.7
Metals	3.2	4.1	7.4	12.6	12.3
Machinery, except electrical	1.9	4.7	5.4	11.5	10.1
Electrical machinery and equipment	2.8	8.3	10.5	15.3	17.7
Transportation equipment	.3	3.4	2.7	3.6	4.2
Other manufacturing	2.0	2.9	5.8	6.9	7.0

Sources: Appendix tables 5A.6 and 5A.7; U.S. Department of Commerce (1992e), table 1.1.
*By industry of establishment, foreign affiliate shares were:

All manufacturing	6.9%
Food and kindred products	7.6
Chemicals	21.1
Metals	6.5
Machinery, except electrical	6.3
Electrical and electronic machinery and equipment	10.9
Transportation equipment	3.1
Other manufacturing	5.9

foreign share is so low in transport equipment and has not risen since 1980, although it clearly did increase before that, reflects two factors. One is the lack of foreign ownership in the aircraft industry. That may partly reflect the connection with national defense, but the international dominance of U.S. firms must also be a factor. A second reason for the low share, especially in view of the failure of the share to rise after 1980, may be a classification scheme that places some manufacturing employment by foreign car producers under wholesale trade because that is the predominant activity of the U.S. subsidiaries. However, the establishment data for 1987 do not suggest that such mismatching between establishment and enterprise classifications was a major problem in this industry.

The high foreign share in chemicals probably reflects the characterization of Du Pont as foreign-owned, although it is not owned by a foreign chemical company and is not part of a foreign-based chemicals network. It is different in this respect from other foreign-owned chemical operations, such as the Swiss-owned pharmaceutical firms and Hoechst-Celanese. The inclusion of Du Pont, if it is included, has a major effect: it would probably account for something in the neighborhood of 100,000 employees out of the reported 443,000. If all of Du Pont, including petroleum operations, is combined into this chemicals group, the degree of exaggeration is increased by the fact that employees in the petroleum operations are in the numerator but not in the denominator of the fraction. However, even without Du Pont, chemicals would still be the industry group with the largest foreign share, by a large margin.

The suspicion that Du Pont petroleum operations may be included in the enterprise figure for chemicals is strengthened by the apparent exaggeration of the foreign share in chemicals in those data; the establishment data put that share at 21 percent in 1987 rather than at 39 percent, still by far the highest of any manufacturing sector. However, table 5.7 indicates that the foreign share is overstated in mining and petroleum, as well as in chemicals, by the use of the enterprise basis.

The large role of foreign firms in the chemical industry has long historical roots, based on foreign (particularly German) companies' early lead in chemical technologies. Wilkins (1989) reported that "foreign direct investment had more impact on the pre–World War I American chemical industry than on any other U.S. industry. . . . In no other industry were Europeans so far in advance of Americans; in no other single industry was the foreign technological contribution so dramatic" (p. 383) and that "by 1914 few branches of the U.S. chemical industry were untouched by foreign direct investment. No other American industry was as influenced by European business enterprises" (p. 411). "In the pre-war chemical and dye industries, German interests were supreme" according to Lewis (1938, 102).

That large foreign, particularly German, role persisted despite the confiscation and sale to Americans of German patents and property by the Alien Property Custodian during World War I and a second round of confiscations during and after World War II. Among the German holdings before World War I, according to Wilkins (1989, chap. 11), where Rohm and Haas, Heyden Chemical, Merck & Co., Hoechst, and Bayer. During World War II, the Alien Property Custodian vested $51.4 million in enemy-owned property, mostly German, that included American Potash and Chemical Corp. and General Aniline and Film Corp. (U.S. Department of Commerce 1948, 93, 99) and, in the years after World War II, vested another $58 million, part of which consisted of "two large rayon manufacturing companies" (U.S. Department of Commerce 1950, 130–31, 160).

In 1989, almost a quarter of foreign firms' employment in chemicals (even with Du Pont's employment included, if it is; almost 30 percent if we assume it is included and remove it) was in German-controlled firms. These firms must possess some strong and persistent technological advantages to retain their position in the United States and to keep regaining it after it has been cut off.

Another view of the changing importance of foreign-owned affiliates in U.S. manufacturing is provided by shares in plant and equipment expenditures. While the employment measure in a sense overweights labor-intensive activities, the plant and equipment measure gives a high weight to capital-intensive activities and, possibly, to relatively new operations. The foreign affiliate shares may be exaggerated by the inclusion of intracompany transfers of plant and equipment that would not enter the denominator.

Since 1974, the foreign share in manufacturing plant and equipment expenditure appears to have multiplied greatly (table 5.9). In several respects, the capital expenditure data confirm the story in the employment data. The trend in the foreign share was very strongly upward, although not quite as steep. The rise in the importance of the foreign firms was evident in all the industry groups. The role of foreign-owned firms was highest in chemicals throughout the period. In general, the foreign role is greater in capital expenditures than in employment, but foods and electrical machinery were exceptions in this

Table 5.9   **Plant and Equipment Expenditures by U.S. Manufacturing Affiliates of Foreign Corporations as Percentage of Total U.S. Expenditure, by Industry: Selected Years, 1974–1989**

	1974	1980	1987	1989
All manufacturing	6.2%	8.9%	12.3%	16.3%
Foods	5.5	9.2	7.9	11.0
Chemicals	15.6	23.7	33.5	50.4
Metals	10.5	7.8	12.4	26.8
Machinery, except electrical		4.0	6.5	13.2
Electrical machinery and equipment	2.0	10.4	9.4	10.2
Transportation equipment		1.3	10.3	6.0
Other manufacturing	4.2	9.2	9.0	10.6

Sources: Appendix tables 5A.11 and 5A.12

regard. In the case of the chemicals industry, the possible inclusion of Du Pont in the 1987 and 1989 data could be a major part of the high ratios. In 1984, for example, Du Pont reported over $2 billion in plant and equipment expenditures in the United States, a large amount compared with the $4.5 billion for all chemical affiliates of foreign companies in Appendix table 5A.12. Du Pont reported $800 million of capital expenditures in oil and gas operations in the United States that year, but some may have been expensed and therefore not included in the capital expenditure figures.

5.3 Foreign-owned Affiliates in the United States and U.S. Trade

5.3.1 The Role of Foreign-owned Affiliates in U.S. Exports and Imports

By the end of the 1980s, foreign-owned affiliates had come to play a large role in U.S. merchandise trade. They exported $84 billion in goods from the United States and imported $170 billion, 23 percent of U.S. exports and over a third of imports. These amounts seem very large relative to the shares of foreign firms in U.S. production or employment, but they are so large because much of these firms' export and import activity is as intermediaries, trading in goods produced by other firms, not necessarily foreign. More than half of the foreign firms' exports, for example, are by foreign trading firms, classified as wholesale trade affiliates. They deal in metals and minerals and in farm products and other raw materials. The metals and minerals group is mainly Japanese, and the other is split between Japanese and French affiliates. In neither group is it likely that much of the exports comes from the foreign firms' own production. One might guess that while the foreign firms' intermediation provides some gains in efficiency, the exports would not change greatly if these trading operations were closed. On the other hand, the exports by wholesale affiliates in motor vehicles and machinery, mainly Japanese, could have been the output of manufacturing operations by the same firms in the U.S.

Imports by foreign-owned wholesalers are mostly of manufactured products that would probably be imported anyway. The importation via affiliates is presumably more efficient for the foreign manufacturers and probably adds to their profits or their market shares.

If we assume that the exports and imports of manufacturing affiliates are more related to their own production activities than are those of trade affiliates, the trade of the manufacturing affiliates may be more likely to reflect the effects of the direct investment. The amounts are still large, $32 billion of exports and $41 billion of imports by manufacturing affiliates in 1989 (U.S. Department of Commerce 1992c, tables G-5, G-6). The exports were more than 10 percent of our rough estimate of exports produced by the manufacturing sector and more than 12 percent of all exports in Standard International Trade Classification (SITC) groups 4 through 9. Not all of the trade by manufacturing affiliates is of manufactured products, but the 1987 data (U.S. Department of Commerce 1990b, tables G-10, G-16) suggest that only about 5 percent of exports and between 5 and 10 percent of imports are crude materials and fuels.

One contentious topic with respect to foreign firms' operations has been their impact, if any, on U.S. trade. A suspicion is often expressed, echoing earlier complaints against U.S. operations in Canada, for example, that foreign-owned firms are disinclined to export but have much higher propensities to import than U.S. firms do. It is not clear that such propensities, if they existed, would have any implications for U.S. trade in general, but we can ask whether the foreign operations are very distinctive in their trade behavior.

Foreign-owned manufacturing operations do export less than they import. In the earliest year for which we have data, 1974, their exports were about two-thirds of their imports. The ratio jumped to more than 100 percent in 1982, after a period of low U.S. exchange rates; dropped to 62 percent in 1986 after the high-dollar period; and then rose to 80 percent (Appendix table 5A.8). By 1989, exports were almost 80 percent of imports.

The trade behavior of the foreign affiliates should be viewed against the changes that took place in U.S. trade as a whole during these years. In 1974, U.S. exports and imports, other than those of foreign-owned affiliates, were equal. There was a strong downward trend in the export-import ratio, however, until by 1989 it was a little lower than the ratio for foreign manufacturing affiliates. Thus, to the extent that the data for nonaffiliates reflect the general macroeconomic circumstances of the United States, exports from the United States by foreign affiliates were facing unfavorable conditions.

5.3.2 Changing Exchange Rates and the Trade of Foreign-owned U.S. Firms

One possible explanation for the change in foreign affiliate export-import ratios is that the foreign affiliates have in some sense "grown up" and have become less dependent on their parent companies for supplies and components. That may be the case, but there are reasons to be skeptical. One is that foreign direct investment in the United States has been growing so fast that the average age of the foreign-owned enterprises is probably not rising. Another is that the time pattern suggests the influence of another factor: the U.S. exchange rate. The export-import ratio was highest in 1982, after the low point in the exchange value of the dollar, and the ratio was at a low point in 1986, after the peak in the value of the U.S. dollar. That influence of the exchange rate is at least mildly confirmed by equation (1), which relates the export-import ratio to the effective exchange rate of the dollar, lagged one year, and a time trend.

$$(1) \quad \left(\frac{EXAFF}{IMAFF}\right)_t = -12.91 - 4.29 \, EER_{t-1} + .007 \, YR \qquad \bar{R}^2 = .131$$
$$\qquad\qquad\qquad (0.76) \quad (1.98) \qquad\qquad (0.82)$$

where $EXAFF$ = Affiliate exports $\times$ 100; $IMAFF$ = Affiliate imports; EER = U.S. effective exchange rate as reported in the *Federal Reserve Bulletin,* $\times$ 1,000; and YR = Year; and t-statistics appear in parentheses.

The time trend is not significant, but it is positive, as we would expect from any maturing of the investments. The coefficient of the effective exchange rate variable is negative, as we expect, and statistically significant, as it would be if a high price of the dollar discouraged exports by these affiliates and encouraged imports by them.

If we suspect some J-curve effects on the import side, we might include both current and lagged exchange rate changes, as in equation (2).

$$(2) \quad \left(\frac{EXAFF}{IMAFF}\right)_t = -13.90 + 6.60\ EER_t - 9.28\ EER_{t-1} + .0075\ YR$$
$$ (1.02)\quad(2.71)\qquad(3.68)\qquad\qquad(1.09)$$
$$ \bar{R}^2 = .448$$

The use of both current and lagged effective exchange rates greatly improves the explanation of the changes in affiliate export-import ratios and suggests that both current and lagged responses to exchange rates are important. This evidence fits with the finding in Lipsey (1991) that foreign affiliates' exports-sales ratios to a large degree, and imports-sales ratios to a small degree, respond to effective exchange rate changes.

The movements of the effective exchange rate over this period, together with a time trend term, explain the export-import ratio of the United States, other than foreign affiliates, to a far greater degree than they do the affiliate trade ratios, as can be seen in equation (3).

$$(3) \quad \left(\frac{USEX}{USIM}\right)_t = 35.70 - 4.00\ EER_{t-1} - .017\ YR \qquad \bar{R}^2 = .897$$
$$ (6.75)\quad(5.96)\qquad\quad(6.49)$$

where $USEX$ = U.S. exports of merchandise $-$ exports by foreign affiliates in the United States; $USIM$ = U.S. imports of merchandise $-$ imports by foreign affiliates; and t-statistics appear in parentheses.

The effective exchange rate coefficient is about the same for foreign affiliates' trade (in equation 1) and for other U.S. trade (in equation 3), but the trends are very different; the U.S. trade ratio has a strong downward trend over this period. If we add the current exchange rate to the lagged exchange rate of equation (3), we find that the current rate has the expected negative coefficient but it is not statistically significant (equation 4). It does, however, improve the fit of the equation slightly.

$$(4) \quad \left(\frac{USEX}{USIM}\right)_t = 35.53 - 1.11\ EER_t - 4.84\ EER_{t-1} - .0173\ YR$$
$$ (6.85)\quad(1.20)\qquad(5.03)\qquad\qquad(6.59)$$
$$ \bar{R}^2 = .901$$

The ratio for nonaffiliate U.S. trade, incorporating the effect of lagged exchange rate changes in combination with a trend term, goes a considerable way toward explaining the trade ratio for affiliates (equation 5).

$$(5) \quad \left(\frac{EXAFF}{IMAFF}\right)_t = -62.9 + 1.33 \left(\frac{USEX}{USIM}\right)_t + .032 \, YR \qquad \bar{R}^2 = .444$$
$$\quad\quad\quad (2.91) \ (3.51) \qquad\qquad (2.93)$$

In this case, the time trend is again positive, implying that given the factors affecting nonaffiliate trade, or U.S. trade in general, the trade ratio for affiliates was rising; the trend for affiliates was toward typical U.S. behavior.

A stronger explanation of the affiliate trade ratio is achieved by adding the contemporary exchange rate to equation (5):

$$(6) \quad \left(\frac{EXAFF}{IMAFF}\right)_t = -78.4 + 1.83 \left(\frac{USEX}{USIM}\right)_t + .039 \, YR + 4.28 \, EER_t$$
$$\quad\quad\quad\quad (4.36) \ (5.22) \qquad\qquad (4.36) \qquad (2.76)$$
$$\quad \bar{R}^2 = .652$$

The positive contemporary exchange rate coefficient here suggests a J-curve effect, only for foreign-owned affiliates or larger for them than for other U.S. firms.

5.4 Country and Industry Composition of Foreign Direct Investment in the United States

5.4.1 Industry Composition of Investment

The longest continuous series on the industry composition of foreign direct investment in the United States is for the direct investment position. While that measure is related to the composition of sales, assets, employment, or other measures of activity, the relationship is not always close. A given amount of assets or employment can be financed mainly either by parent funds or by borrowing in the United States itself, and the extent of financing through borrowed funds can vary from industry to industry. In addition, the historical data on the U.S. position classify the origin of the investment by the country of direct, or immediate, foreign ownership rather than by the country of the ultimate owner, as in some of the recent data.

One shift in the industry composition of direct investment in the United States was the growth in importance of goods industries and decline in service industries from 1950 through the 1960s (table 5.10). That change was subsequently reversed, so that the shares in 1991 were between those of 1950 and 1960. Within these categories, petroleum first rose greatly in importance and then declined even more, ending up at less than 10 percent of the total. The decade and a half after 1960 also saw a rapid growth of wholesaling and a decline in finance investment, both of which were then partially reversed, leaving both groups at the end slightly below their importance in 1974. One consistent trend since 1974 has been a steady growth in investment in nonfinancial service industries, although they were still below 10 percent of the total in 1991.

If we compare the trends in the distribution of FDI in the United States with those of U.S. FDI, we can see several contrasts (table 5.10). One strong contrast is between goods and services, with a large shift toward services in U.S. direct investment and a corresponding decline in the role of goods industries, particularly petroleum. Transportation and public utilities almost vanished from FDI in both directions, although recent relaxations in host country rules against foreign ownership and the desire for capital investment and modernization may restore some of the past role of these industries in outward U.S. FDI. The major shift in U.S. outward direct investment was the growth in the finance sector, from about 4 percent in the 1950s to over 30 percent in 1991, from far below the share in foreign direct investment in the United States to well above the foreign share. The data suggest that U.S. financial firms must have gained in some respect on their foreign rivals over these thirty years.

A different view of the distribution of foreign-owned firms' activity in the United States, perhaps without some of the possible distortions of the investment position data, is given by the distribution of assets. Assets do have their own defects as an activity measure, giving greater weight to industries with high ratios of capital (including financial) to labor than do measures of output or comprehensive input measures. Assets will, therefore, give a high weight to affiliates in finance, even when banking is omitted. In addition, the financial assets are much more likely to be outside the United States than are fixed assets or labor. An advantage of the asset data is that they are available as far back as 1959 and thus give a view of the whole thirty years since then.

The most striking change in the distribution of assets of foreign affiliates in the United States is the enormous shift from goods industries to service industries, broadly defined to include trade and finance as well as other services (table 5.11). Goods industries accounted for over three-quarters of foreign affiliates' assets in 1959 and only a third in 1987. The sharpest fall was in the share of the petroleum industry, followed by that in manufacturing. The corresponding increase was not spread over service industries but was concentrated in finance, although some other service sectors did grow.

This shift in industry composition partly confirms the shift shown by the data on investment position (table 5.10), but the changes in the asset distribution were far larger and show a much larger financial sector, even though the investment position data include banking.

Orr's (1991) estimate of Japanese automobile production assets that were involved in manufacturing but listed under wholesale trade in the Department of Commerce data (discussed earlier) would roughly double the share of that industry in the total. The share would still be one of the lowest in our list.

A measure of labor input is provided by employment in foreign-owned af-

Table 5.10   **Distribution of U.S. Direct Investment Position, by Broad Industry Groups: Selected Years, 1950–1991**

	1950	1960	1966	1974	1982	1990	1991
	A. Foreign Direct Investment in the U.S.						
Agriculture, forestry, fishing, mining	—	—	—	1.7%	2.3%	2.7%	2.5%
Petroleum extraction and refining	11.9%*	17.9*	19.2%*	23.2	11.4	8.7	7.8
Manufacturing	33.6	37.8	41.8	31.1	35.3	39.7	40.2
Goods production	45.5	55.7	61.1	56.0†	49.1†	51.0†	50.5
Transportation, communication, and public utilities	—	5.9	—	1.3	1.1	1.1	1.0
Wholesale trade	—	9.2‡	—	15.7	14.8	12.8	13.1
Banking	} 31.4			1.9	6.3	4.7	5.1
Other finance		26.2	—	21.4	17.3	17.5	18.8
Other services	—	1.8	—	1.1	1.5	8.0	7.8
Services, broadly defined	54.5	44.3	38.9	44.0	50.9	49.0	49.5
Total, all industries	100.0	100.0	100.0	100.0	100.0	100.0	100.0
	B. U.S. Direct Investment Abroad						
Agriculture, forestry, fishing, mining	14.6	12.0	8.6	4.4	2.5	1.2	1.1
Petroleum extraction and refining	28.8*	25.7§	20.6	12.5	17.4	10.5	10.3
Manufacturing	32.5	31.5	42.2	42.1	36.6	38.6	38.6
Goods production	75.8	69.2§	71.4	59.0	56.6	50.3	50.1
Transportation, communication, and public utilities	12.2	8.4	4.5	1.5	1.0	1.6	1.8
Wholesale trade, excluding petroleum	4.6	4.6	6.3	9.5	9.1	9.0	9.5
Petroleum trade and services	—	10.0	6.7	8.6	7.9	2.8	2.7
Banking	} 3.9	0.5	0.6	3.0	4.5	4.6	4.1
Other finance‖		3.2	6.4	15.3	16.7	26.3	26.6
Other services	1.7	1.2	2.2	2.6	2.0	2.7	2.9
Services, broadly defined‖	24.2	30.8	28.6	41.0	43.4	49.7	49.9
Total, all indusries‖	100.0	100.0	100.0	100.0	100.0	100.0	100.0

Sources: Appendix tables 5A.2 and 5A.3.

*Total petroleum including trade and services.

†Including agriculture and mining; excluding petroleum trade and services.

‡Total trade, including retail.

§Including petroleum extraction and refining, but not trade and services. Figures comparable to 1950 are 35.8 and 79.5.

‖Excluding finance affiliates in the Netherlands Antilles.

Table 5.11   **Industry Distribution of Assets of Foreign-owned Firms in the United States, 1959–1987**

	1959	1974	1980	1987
Mining	2.5%	2.5%	2.3%	1.4%
Petroleum*	33.5	16.4	15.1	8.4
Manufacturing	40.9	15.0	28.0	23.7
Foods		2.2	2.8	2.5
Chemicals		4.5	8.9	8.2
Metals		2.6	3.5	2.5
Machinery		2.0	5.9	3.5
Nonelectrical			2.6	1.4
Electrical			3.3	2.2
Transport equipment		} 3.7	1.5	.8
Other manufacturing			5.2	6.1
Goods industries†	76.9	33.9	45.4	33.5
Wholesale trade		13.7	17.1	10.7
Retail trade	} 14.2	1.3	3.3	2.8
Finance (excluding banking), insurance, and real estate		48.6‡	30.3	47.7
Finance (excluding banking)			11.1	28.7
Insurance	9.0§		12.4	11.6
Real estate			6.8	7.4
Other services		} 2.5	1.5	3.5
Other industries			2.4	1.9
Services, broadly defined‖	23.2	66.1	54.6	66.5
Total	100.0	100.0	100.0	100.0

Source: Appendix table 5A.14.

*Includes petroleum trade and services, a little under 20 percent of the petroleum total in 1974.

†Mining, petroleum (including petroleum trade and services), and manufacturing.

‡The share including banking would be about 48 percent.

§Includes finance, other services, and other industries.

‖Includes agriculture, forestry, and fishing; transportation, communication, and public utilities (over 40 percent of the total in 1974); construction, hotels, and lodging places; and other services.

filiates. Unfortunately, the employment data cover only the second half of the period spanned by the data on assets and the direct investment position.

The employment data confirm the shift out of goods production and into service production after the mid-1970s, as well as the particularly large decline in employment in petroleum (table 5.12). The rising fields for foreign firms, according to the employment data, were retail trade and other services. However, the employment data do not show the rise in importance of nonbank finance indicated by the investment and assets data.

A comparison of the industry distribution of employment in foreign-owned affiliates with that of U.S. firms as a group shows a much slower shift from manufacturing on the part of the foreign firms but much more of a decline in

Table 5.12   **Industry Distribution of Nonagricultural Employment: Foreign Affiliates in the United States and All U.S. Firms**

	Foreign Affiliates				All U.S. Firms			
	1974	1982	1987*	1990	1974	1982	1987*	1990
Mining and petroleum	11.1%	6.7%	4.5%	4.3%	1.4%	1.8%	1.0%	.9%
Manufacturing	52.5	51.0	48.1	46.9	31.0	25.2	22.1	20.7
Foods	7.1	5.2	4.5	5.3	2.7	2.2	1.9	1.8
Chemicals	11.0	16.0	12.3	10.9	1.7	1.5	1.2	1.2
Metals	8.4	4.2	5.0	5.7	4.3	3.2	2.5	2.4
Mach. exc. electrical	4.1	5.4	3.4	4.5	3.4	3.0	2.4	2.3
Elect. mach. and equip.	5.3	6.3	6.8	6.3	3.1	2.7	2.4	1.8
Transp. equipment	0.5	2.9	1.7	1.8	2.9	2.4	2.4	2.2
Other manufacturing	16.1	10.9	14.4	12.3	13.0	10.2	9.3	9.0
Goods production	63.6	57.7	52.5	51.2	32.4	27.0	23.2	21.6
Public util. and transp.	4.3	2.3	3.0	5.2	7.4	6.9	6.3	6.4
Construction	.8	2.1	1.6	1.5	6.3	5.3	5.8	5.6
Wholesale trade	11.6	11.5	10.0	9.3	6.9	7.2	6.9	6.8
Retail trade	11.5	16.3	17.4	16.1	19.6	20.6	21.7	21.5
Finance, including banking					6.5	7.2	7.7	7.4
Finance, excluding banking	4.5	5.0	6.4	4.8				
Other services	3.9	5.0	9.0	11.4	21.0	25.8	28.4	30.8
Services, broadly defined	36.4	42.3	47.5	48.8	67.6	73.0	76.8	78.4

Sources: Appendix tables 5A.6 and 5A.7; U.S. Department of Commerce (1992e), table 1.1.

*The distribution of employment on an establishment basis was as follows:

	Foreign Affiliates	All U.S. Firms
Mining, including petroleum extraction and refining	3.6%	1.0%
Manufacturing	40.4	22.9
Foods	3.4	1.8
Chemicals	5.3	1.0
Metals	4.5	2.6
Machinery, excluding electrical	3.6	2.2
Electrical machinery and equipment	5.2	1.9
Transportation equipment	1.7	2.2
Other manufacturing	16.7	11.3
Goods production	44.0	23.9
Public utilities and transportation	2.9	6.1
Construction	1.6	6.1
Wholesale trade	10.6	6.8
Retail trade	19.4	21.4
Banking	3.3	2.0
Other finance	6.3	6.1
Other services	12.0	27.7
Services, broadly defined	56.0	76.1

petroleum, which includes some refining operations. The comparison also points up the much heavier concentration of foreign firms' employment in manufacturing and in goods production in general, more than twice the U.S. proportion by the end of the period. This comparison can be read as a sign of declining comparative advantage of U.S. companies in manufacturing, although not necessarily of the United States as a production location, since the foreign firms were choosing the United States as a manufacturing location. However, as shown elsewhere (Lipsey and Kravis 1987; Blomström and Lipsey 1989; Kravis and Lipsey 1992), there is no sign of any such decline in competitiveness of U.S. manufacturing firms in world export markets. The rising share of foreign firms in U.S. manufacturing may reflect mainly the increasing internationalization of the foreign firms.

The other side of this story is the much greater concentration of U.S. employment in services, with the foreign share growing but still far behind.

The comparison between foreign-owned and all U.S. firms on an affiliate basis somewhat deflates the apparent foreign firm concentration in manufacturing and goods production in general, reducing it to 40 percent in manufacturing and 44 percent in all goods production. That is still, however, almost twice the level for all U.S. firms. The affiliate data show employment in foreign affiliates much less concentrated in chemicals than is indicated by the enterprise data.

A somewhat different picture of the comparative advantages of firms appears if we compare foreign affiliates in the United States with U.S. parent companies. In this comparison, we are holding constant not only the location of production but also the multinationality of the firms. Both sets of firms produce in the United States and in foreign countries and are probably of similar size, while the total of U.S. firms in table 5.12 includes many smaller ones that are less likely to be making a choice of production location.

The distribution of employment by U.S. parents is given in table 5.13. U.S. parents are more concentrated in goods industries than are foreign affiliates, although parent employment too has shifted toward service industries. Manufacturing accounts for more of parent employment than of affiliate employment, but the margin has been decreasing, another suggestion that the comparative advantage of U.S. firms relative to foreign firms has been moving away from manufacturing. Among manufacturing industries, chemicals are the industry in which foreign affiliates are much more concentrated than are U.S. parents. Transport equipment is the industry in which U.S. parents are more concentrated than the foreign firms. In neither case is there any clear sign of a trend over these fifteen years. Outside of manufacturing, U.S. parents and foreign affiliates show the same rising shares of their employment in the narrowly defined service sector.

While labor input by foreign-owned affiliates receives the most attention, we may also wish to observe the distribution of these firms' additions to the physical capital stock of the United States. Some of the trends observed for

Table 5.13   **Industry Distribution of Employment by Nonbank U.S. Parent Companies: 1977, 1982, and 1989**

	1977	1982	1989
Petroleum	4.7%	6.6%	3.4%
Manufacturing	62.4	56.3	54.2
Foods	5.4	5.4	6.1
Chemicals	6.4	7.3	6.7
Metals	7.9	5.2	3.7
Machinery, excluding electrical	8.2	7.8	6.8
Electrical machinery and equipment	6.7	8.7	5.4
Transportation equipment	12.1	9.0	11.1
Other manufacturing	15.7	12.9	14.4
Goods production	67.1	62.9	57.5
Wholesale trade*	13.1†	2.1	2.3
Finance‡	4.6	5.4	5.8
Other services	3.9	5.3	9.2
Other industries	11.4	24.3†	25.2†
Services, broadly defined	32.9	37.1	42.5
Total	100.0	100.0	100.0

Source: Appendix table 5A.13.

*Includes agriculture, mining (except petroleum), construction, transportation, communication, and public utilities.

†Includes retail trade.

‡Excludes banking, insurance, and real estate.

labor recur in the capital expenditure data, particularly the steep decline in the shares of the petroleum and mining industries and the rise in the share of the finance sector, all always a much larger part of capital expenditure than of employment. There were also increases in the shares of retail trade in plant and equipment expenditure. This is an industry more important in employment than in capital expenditure (table 5.14). In manufacturing, there was something of a contrast between the employment and capital expenditure measures: a small decline in the industry's employment share but a rise in its share in capital spending. Those differences suggest more of a move to higher capital intensity among manufacturing affiliates than among those in other industries. Within the finance sector, the major growth was the jump in the share of the real estate industry during the 1970s. This is always, of course, an extremely capital-intensive industry, with a measured capital-labor ratio often inflated by the fact that the labor input involved is employed by other service industries, even when it contributes to the sales of the real estate sector.

The closest approach to an output measure for foreign-owned affiliates over thirty years is total sales, but we cannot deduct purchased inputs. In the earlier years, we cannot even deduct imports, although that would be possible for more recent years.

In 1959, the sales of foreign-owned affiliates in the United States were concentrated in goods industries, particularly manufacturing, to an extent never

Table 5.14   **Industry Distribution of Expenditures for Property, Plant, and Equipment by U.S. Affiliates of Foreign Firms: 1974, 1980, and 1987**

	1974	1980	1987
Mining	6.5%	2.2%	2.8
Petroleum	37.0	21.0	13.7
Manufacturing	30.6	31.0	34.6
Foods	2.3	2.6	1.9
Chemicals	11.5	11.6	12.0
Metals	6.7	3.2	3.4
Machinery, excluding electrical	} 2.8	1.7	2.0
Electrical machinery and equipment		3.9	3.1
Transportation equipment	} 7.2	1.0	3.8
Other manufacturing		7.0	8.4
Goods production	74.1	54.2	51.1
Wholesale trade	6.7	6.8	6.4
Retail trade	2.1	3.2	4.5
Finance (excluding banking), insurance and real estate	9.7	29.5	28.0
Finance (excluding banking)	—	1.0	2.1
Insurance	—	.9	1.4
Real esatate	—	27.6	24.5
Other services	} 7.4	2.3	6.1
Other industries		4.0	3.9
Services, broadly defined	25.9	45.8	48.9
Total	100.0	100.0	100.0

Source: Appendix table 5A.16.

repeated in later years (table 5.15). Manufacturing and petroleum accounted for more than half of all foreign affiliate sales.

By 1974, almost half the sales were by wholesale trade affiliates, and all goods industries combined accounted for only 40 percent of total affiliate sales. It is not clear whether there was a great change in the type of goods sold. There may have been only a change in organization, to separate sales from manufacturing activities, or possibly a change in the way the data were collected. Within the goods sector, the changes were smaller, but there was a shift from manufacturing to petroleum and, among manufacturing industry groups, out of foods and into metals.

After 1974, the changes were smaller, mainly the decline in petroleum evident in all the measures; an increase in the importance of manufacturing, in contrast to the employment record; and some shift to retail trade and the finance sector but no overall move into the broadly defined service sector.

5.4.2   Sources of Foreign Direct Investment in the United States

The historical data on the country of origin of direct investment in the United States are based on the location of the immediate owner. Only for 1977 and later years are there data on the location of the "ultimate beneficial owner,"

Table 5.15   **Industry Distribution of Sales by Nonbank U.S. Affiliates of Foreign Firms: Selected Years, 1959–87**

	1959	1974	1980	1987
Mining	0.9%	1.0%	0.8%	0.8%
Petroleum	16.5	18.0	13.6	9.7
Manufacturing	36.0	21.3	23.8	30.2
Foods	16.1	3.8	2.9	3.1
Chemicals	6.3	5.4	6.8	9.7
Metals	1.9	4.2	3.1	3.6
Machinery	5.1	3.0	5.1	5.4
Nonelectrical	3.0	—	2.2	1.8
Electrical	2.0	—	2.9	3.6
Transportation equipment	} 6.6		1.5	1.1
Other manufacturing		4.9	4.3	7.3
Goods industries	53.4	40.2	38.2	40.7
Wholesale trade	} 30.1	45.3	47.9	37.4
Retail trade		4.3	5.7	6.5
Finance (excluding banking), insurance, and real estate	13.2	7.7	5.5	10.4
Finance (excluding banking)			1.2	3.6
Insurance			3.4	5.3
Real estate			1.0	1.5
Other services	} 3.2		0.8	2.7
Other industries		2.5	1.8	2.3
Services, broadly defined	46.6	59.8	61.8	59.3
Total	100.0	100.0	100.0	100.0

Source: Appendix table 5A.15.

which can be different for various reasons including the tax treatment of earnings by host countries.

In 1960, foreign direct investment in the United States meant European and Canadian investment, with English-speaking countries alone accounting for over 60 percent (table 5.16). The majority of investments were in large enterprises long present in the United States, such as the branch lines of Canadian railroads, Royal Dutch–Shell petroleum interests, and Swiss chemical and pharmaceutical firms. The U.S. Department of Commerce (1962, 4) report for 1960 commented that "a sustained increase in the role of flow of foreign industrial capital to the United States has not yet developed" and "the Department of Commerce, and various States, are now developing programs to bring opportunities here to the attention of foreign industrialists and other investors." There is no indication here of any hostility toward inward investment or any fear of its consequences, but more of an interest in promoting its growth.

The country distribution of investment in 1991 presents some contrasts with the earlier one but some continuity also, and the later data are available by the country of the ultimate owner rather than by only the immediate foreign parent (table 5.17).

The U.K. share declined, but less than might have been expected from the overall decline in the position of the United Kingdom in the world economy. The importance of Canada decreased greatly, and Germany and France became fairly important sources of investment. The major new source is, of course, Japan, passing the Netherlands in importance and second only to the United

Table 5.16   **Country Distribution of Foreign Direct Investment in the United States, 1960**

Canada	28%
Europe, total	68
United Kingdom	33
Netherlands	14
Switzerland	11
Other areas	4

Source: U.S. Department of Commerce (1962), table 1.

Table 5.17   **Country Distribution of Foreign Direct Investment in the United States, 1991**

	Shares by Country of			UBO minus Parent ($ million)
	Parent	UBO*	UBO/Parent Ratio	
Canada	7.4%	10.0%	135%	$ 10,648
Europe	63.3	59.0	93	−17,531
United Kingdom	26.0	24.3	93	−7,169
Netherlands	15.7	10.3	66	−21,712
Germany	6.9	8.2	118	5,130
France	5.6	6.6	119	4,329
Switzerland	4.3	4.6	106	1,038
Latin America and other				
Western Hemisphere	4.3	2.4	56	−7,694
Brazil	1.6	1.5	93	−433
Panama	1.1	.2	20	−3,478
Netherlands Antilles	2.0	.2	8	−7,290
U.K. Islands, Caribbean	−.1	.1	−63	869
Middle East	1.2	2.4	208	5,169
Asia and Pacific	23.7	25.0	105	5,088
Japan	21.3	21.8	103	2,275
Australia	1.6	1.7	105	303
Hong Kong	.3	.9	276	2,243

Source: U.S. Department of Commerce (1992b), table 18.

*Ultimate beneficial owner.

Kingdom. A country that warranted only a line in the 1960 survey is now the second-largest investor of all.

The availability of data by the country of ultimate ownership reveals some interesting contrasts with those by the country of the immediate parent. The latter data are shown to exaggerate the decline in the importance of Canada and understate it for the Netherlands, because a change in Canadian tax laws caused some Canadian owners to shift nominal ownership to the Netherlands. Germany and France are shown to be more important as sources of investment than the parent country data indicate. A large part of the direct investment in the United States originating in the Middle East and in Brazil (and other South American countries) is apparently owned through intermediate subsidiaries based in Panama, the Bahamas, and the Netherlands Antilles. "Advantages to UBO's [ultimate beneficial owners] of holding their U.S. investments indirectly through these countries may include minimization of taxes, avoidance of regulatory constraint, and protection of privacy" (Belli 1981, 63).

The main conduits for direct investment in the United States, in quantitative terms, were the United Kingdom, the Netherlands, Panama, and the Netherlands Antilles. The main sources of investment carried out through other countries were Canada, Germany, France, Middle Eastern countries, and Hong Kong.

Some examples of Middle Eastern property holdings in the United States with intermediate parents established in the Netherlands Antilles are described in an article that also indicates that these intermediaries were shifted to the United States for tax reasons after the passage of the 1986 Tax Reform Act (Abu Dhabi's Links 1992).

The country distribution of sales in 1959 matched that of the direct investment stock in 1960 fairly well. Companies from Canada accounted for a little over 30 percent of sales, and almost all the rest were from affiliates of companies based in Europe (table 5.18). By 1974, only two-thirds of sales were from affiliates of Canadian and European firms, and that share was approximately the same in 1987. The very large share of the Netherlands in 1959, most of which was in the petroleum industry, was greatly reduced by 1974, while affiliates from Japan, largely in wholesale trade, became the largest in terms of sales. After 1974, the pace of change became much slower, the main shifts being a reduction in the Netherlands share and a rise in that of West German firms.

The country-of-origin distribution for manufacturing affiliates showed a little less change than that for all affiliates. The main difference was that Japanese manufacturing affiliates played a much smaller role, remaining behind those from the United Kingdom and West Germany. Also, in manufacturing, the European share remained higher in 1987 than it had been in 1959. The main shifts in country sources, however, matched those in the total: a large decline for Canada, mainly before 1974; a large and steady decline for Nether-

Table 5.18   **Distribution by Country of Ownership of Sales by All Foreign-Owned Affiliates and Foreign-Owned Manufacturing Affiliates in the United States: Selected Years, 1959–1987**

	1959	1974	1980	1987
	All Affiliates			
Canada	31.2%	10.9%	8.6%	12.0%
Europe	68.0	54.7	62.9	52.8
United Kingdom	17.9	18.5	22.9	17.6
Netherlands	36.2	11.7	9.4	7.0
France	1.2	8.7	9.9	5.9
Germany	0.6	5.9	11.1	10.0
Other Europe	12.1	9.9	9.6	12.3
Japan	0	27.3	20.4	25.1
Total	100.0	100.0	100.0	100.0
	Manufacturing Affiliates			
Canada	40.2	18.8	16.0	19.4
Europe	58.9	68.1	74.8	65.3
United Kingdom	24.0	24.5	18.2	21.3
Netherlands	15.1	12.4	8.7	6.6
France	1.8	6.4	12.8	7.5
Germany	0.9	8.1	19.5	13.6
Other Europe	17.0	16.7	15.6	16.3
Japan	0	4.2	4.1	6.9
Total	100.0	100.0	100.0	100.0

Source: Appendix table 5A.15.

lands affiliates; and major increases for those from France, West Germany, and Japan.

The distributions of sales by industry and investing country suggest what the directions of comparative advantage were for companies from different countries. For example, over 70 percent of U.S. affiliate sales by Netherlands-owned affiliates were in the petroleum industry in 1959, and the share declined but was still close to half in 1987, far above the average for other countries (Appendix table 5A.15). Affiliates from West Germany and the Netherlands had exceptionally large shares of their sales in chemicals. Japanese affiliate sales were extremely concentrated in wholesale trade affiliates because they were, to a large extent, involved in the distribution of products exported from Japan. Within manufacturing, however, the Japanese affiliates' sales were particularly large in transport equipment, reflecting the strength of Japanese motor vehicle producers. For the United Kingdom, the specialization in foods was above the average for all foreign firms.

Outside of manufacturing, Canadian firms had disproportionate shares of their sales in insurance, in real estate, and especially in mining. Aside from wholesale trade, finance also accounted for a relatively large share of sales for Japanese firms.

The sales distributions are an indication of the worldwide comparative advantages of firms based in different countries, but they may not reflect the advantages in producing in the United States, since large parts of the affiliate sales, varying widely among firms and countries, originate from production outside the United States. The employment distributions may reflect more clearly the advantages firms from different countries have in producing in the United States.

The concentration on chemicals among West German firms in 1974 stands out clearly in the fact that 36 percent of their affiliates' employment in the United States was in that industry, as against an average for all countries of under 11 percent. The only observable deviations of even close to this magnitude (many entries are missing) from the average distribution for the world are of Japanese firms in wholesale trade and U.K. firms in retailing.

By 1987, West German affiliates in the United States, while still more concentrated on chemicals than those of any other country, had diversified and were then of far more importance than average in nonelectrical machinery also. Canadian and French affiliates were much more heavily represented in machinery than were the world's enterprises, on average, and Japanese firms had become exceptionally concentrated in finance (except banking), as well as in wholesale trade.

5.5   Financial Aspects of Foreign Direct Investment in the United States

For many years, most of the additions to U.S. direct investment abroad have come from the reinvested earnings of U.S. companies already established in foreign countries. Even as early as 1966–76, almost 60 percent of the growth in the U.S. outward stock was from reinvestment. The trend has been very different for foreign direct investment in the United States (table 5.19). Almost half of the growth in the foreign position in the United States in the 1950s, and over 60 percent in the 1960s, was financed by reinvested earnings. In the 1970s, however, although reinvested earnings grew rapidly to over four times the level in the 1960s, they financed less than half of the growth in the stock, as equity and intercompany account inflows grew to eight times their level of the 1960s.

The 1980s were again a contrast to all the earlier periods. Equity and intercompany flows, particularly the former, grew explosively to over twelve times the 1970s level. At the same time, reinvested earnings almost disappeared, falling from $14 billion in the 1970s to virtually zero in the 1980s. In half the years of the 1980s, the reinvested earnings were negative, and they turned strongly negative with the onset of the recession, totaling a negative $42 billion in 1989–91. Thus, while U.S. direct investment abroad seems to have entered an era of mature self-financing, with few new firms entering the list of overseas

Table 5.19   **Reinvested Earnings of Foreign-Owned Affiliates in the United States and Change in Foreign Direct Investment Position ($ million)**

	Change in Position	Reinvested Earnings	Share of Reinvested Earnings*
1950–59	$ 3,483	$ 1,718	51.1%
1960–69	5,214	3,245	71.5
1970–79	40,372	14,607	43.5
1980–89	322,856	4,431	1.7
1980	28,584	5,177	18.1
1981	25,668	2,945	11.5
1982	15,963	−2,361	− 14.8
1983	12,384	−340	− 2.7
1984	27,522	3,105	11.3
1985	20,032	90	.4
1986	35,799	−239	− .7
1987†	42,980†	1,481	3.4
1987‡		579	
1988	51,360	1,963	3.8
1989	54,170	−7,390	− 13.6
1990	27,778	−15,316	− 55.1
1991	10,875	−18,924	−174.0

Sources: 1950–79 data: U.S. Department of Commerce (1984), tables 1, 4; position in 1949 was estimated as 1950 position minus capital inflow in 1950, from table 2; change in position and reinvested earnings for 1974 on the basis of 1959 survey are from Mantel (1975). 1980–81 data: U.S. Department of Commerce (1990a), tables 1, 4. 1982–91 data: U.S. Department of Commerce (1992b), tables 9, 17; 1987 change in position and reinvested earnings is from Nicholson (1991) and Scholl (1991).

*Averages of individual-year ratios.

†Based on 1980 benchmark survey; comparable to earlier years.

‡Based on 1987 benchmark survey; comparable to later years.

investors, foreign direct investment in the United States in the 1980s went through a period of wild growth, financed by inflows of new money, followed by a sharp drop in net income after 1988 and aggregate net losses in 1991 (U.S. Department of Commerce, 1992e).

The rapid growth of foreign direct investment in recent years has consisted mainly of acquisition of existing U.S. firms rather than the establishment of new firms. Comprehensive data from the U.S. Department of Commerce exist only for recent years, but they do show a continued move in this direction. In 1984–87, over 80 percent of inflows of foreign direct investment were for acquisitions. High as that was, the proportions for 1988–90 surpassed them, averaging close to 90 percent. The acquisition share was even higher in manufacturing, usually over 95 percent during these years. The only industry in which the establishment of new enterprises predominated was real estate, where 90 percent of investment flow in 1984–86 and 71 percent in 1987–90 consisted of the establishment of new enterprises. Even in this case, there was a trend toward acquisitions.

Another indication that the investment rush of the last decade has been very different from earlier foreign direct investment in the United States is provided by the collapse in the apparent profitability of such investment (table 5.20). While there are often good reasons to doubt published data on the profits of segments of enterprises, which is what these affiliates all are, the decline looks too large and too sudden to represent only a sudden rise in tax avoidance. The very newness of the recent investments may explain some of the decline. However, the predominance of acquisitions among recent foreign investments means that these are generally going concerns rather than start-ups; and on that ground alone, one might expect a more rapid attainment of normal profit rates.

The data for major industry groups show that the decline in profitability was quite general, but it was more severe in some groups than in others. Petroleum and manufacturing affiliates, after the sharp declines to the 1985–89 period, remained profitable in 1990–91. But equally sharp declines in finance and other industries (mining, wholesale and retail trade, and other industries) were followed in 1990–91 by even larger declines in profitability, to the point where affiliates reported net losses.

The geographic breakdown points up the relative stability of the profitability of U.K. investment. In the last period, levels of profits for European investments were far above those of firms from Canada and Japan (table 5.21). European investment was more concentrated in manufacturing than was Canada's and Japan's, the latter heavily invested in real estate and banking. But this broad industry breakdown does not tell the whole story; while most areas' manufacturing affiliates remained profitable in the late 1980s, Japan's had losses in both of the last two periods. Japan was also the country whose investment in the United States had accelerated most rapidly in the late 1980s, a hint of a possible connection between the rate of growth of investment and its profitability.

Table 5.20	Foreign Direct Investment in the United States: Income as Percentage of FDI Position,* by Industry Group, 1950–1991				
	All Industries	Petroleum	Manufacturing	Finance†	Other
1950–59	8.2	16.8	8.2	7.1	4.5
1960–69	7.2	11.3	8.2	4.5	4.2
1970–79	10.2	12.1	9.0	13.0	9.3
1980–84	7.7	18.7	4.5	8.5	5.4
1985–89	3.6	5.6	2.4	4.8	2.5
1990–91	−0.2	5.0	1.4	−2.9	−2.2

Sources: U.S. Department of Commerce (1984; 1990a; 1992b) and earlier articles in the same series.

*Income in year t as percentage of FDI position at end of year $t-1$.

†Finance, insurance, and real estate.

Table 5.21   **Foreign Direct Investment in the United States: Income as Percentage of FDI Position,* by Country of Origin, 1950–1991**

	Canada	Europe			Japan
		Total	United Kingdom	Netherlands	
1950–59	8.1%	8.6%	7.3%	18.0%	—
1960–69	3.4	7.7	6.8	11.0	13.3%
1970–79	7.3	10.2	10.3	11.4	4.8
1980–84	4.9	8.0	9.2	13.1	12.7
1985–89	1.5	5.0	6.3	5.3	4.5
1990–91	−3.7	1.1	4.4	0.4	−1.8

Sources: U.S. Department of Commerce (1984; 1990a; 1992b) and earlier articles in the same series.

*Income in year t as percentage of FDI position at end of year $t-1$.

Reports in the press (e.g., "How Japan got burned" 1992) suggest that the declining profitability of Japanese direct investment in the United States reported in the official data is not a mirage. A summary of a Japanese newspaper's survey of Japanese-owned U.S. affiliates stated that "80% of the 264 units weren't returning profits to parent companies and 63% cited earnings as their biggest concern" ("Japanese wary" 1992).

An examination of the low profitability of foreign affiliates in the United States relative to other U.S. firms, based on tax data for the late 1980s (Grubert, Goodspeed, and Swenson 1991) attributed half of the differential to characteristics of the affiliates and of the period. The two affiliate characteristics were the revaluation of target firm assets following acquisitions and the immaturity of the affiliates. Both were related to the headlong acquisition rate of that period. The main relevant characteristic of the period was the decline in the exchange value of the U.S. dollar.

Some part of the rest of the differential was attributed to foreign firms' income shifting to minimize taxes. That shifting was presumably responsible for the fact that the proportion of affiliates with zero profits was higher than the proportion among domestic firms. The part of the profit differential attributable to income shifting is, in a sense, illusory. In fact, it may represent an incentive for investment in the United States. However, the sharp decline in the direct investment inflow (particularly of equity capital) in 1991, to less than half the 1990 level, reinforces the picture of low and declining profits (U.S. Department of Commerce 1992b, table 5).

5.6 Summary

The major development in foreign direct investment in the United States over the past thirty years has been its enormous growth. That is the case whether one considers the absolute values or the shares of the world's direct investment flows and whether one considers book or market valuations. The United States, which had accounted for a greatly disproportionate share of the world's direct investment outflows in the 1960s, far above the U.S. share in the world's income or output even at its peak in 1950, by the late 1980s was accounting for almost half of the world's direct investment inflows. That share was even more disproportionate than the earlier outward share, given the reduced importance of the United States in the world economy.

One consequence of this huge inward flow is that the United States has become almost as much of a host to foreign companies as other countries are to U.S. firms. Foreign direct investment in the United States, formerly a quarter or even less of U.S. direct investment abroad, is now, even by current cost or market valuations, three-quarters as large.

The rapid growth of foreign direct investment in the United States has left foreign firms still controlling only a small part of total assets of U.S. firms and employing less than 5 percent of the U.S. labor force. However, the shares have become much more significant in manufacturing, quadrupling in the last fifteen years and reaching over 10 percent of employment. The most notable share of employment has been in chemicals, over 40 percent in 1989. But the industrial composition of foreign direct investment in manufacturing has been relatively stable; chemicals was the U.S. industry most heavily penetrated by foreign firms in 1974 and as far back as 1900, as well as at present. If we rank industries by degree of foreign control in 1974, no industry moved more than one rank by 1989 except electrical machinery, now the second highest at over 15 percent. The foreign, particularly German, role in chemicals, has a very long history. The level of German activity was high even before World War I and has remained high even though it was reduced twice by confiscations of alien property during the two world wars.

Another measure of the foreign role, the share in plant and equipment expenditure, shows an even higher share—over half—in chemicals but a much lower one in electrical machinery. The foreign operations may be entering relatively capital-intensive sectors of the chemical industry and relatively labor-intensive sectors of the electrical machinery industry.

The trends in the distribution of foreign firms' activity among broad sectors of the economy look different by different measures. The direct-investment position data show a large rise in the share of goods industries and then, after 1974, a shift back to services, leaving the goods share a little higher in 1990 than in 1950 and the service share a little lower. In the three decades between 1960 and 1990, however, there was some shift toward services. Data on total assets of foreign-owned firms show a much steadier and stronger shift from goods industries to service industries, mainly financial services. The time series on sales suggests a very large shift toward services between 1959 and 1974 but little change since then, while the shorter time series on employment indicates a substantial shift out of goods and into services between 1974 and 1989 despite the relatively small role they give to financial services. Another short series, on plant and equipment investment, also points to a shift in the direction of service activities by foreign firms, with real estate the major factor here.

Foreign-owned affiliates have continued to import more, relative to their exports, than have U.S. companies in general, but the trend appears to be toward foreign affiliates becoming more like other U.S. firms in this respect. The foreign affiliates are quite sensitive to exchange rate changes in adjusting the balance of exports and imports, but not more so than U.S. firms as a group.

Perhaps the most publicized change in inward direct investment in recent years has been its source. Japan, hardly mentioned in the 1960 discussion, now accounts for 20 percent of the stock of foreign direct investment in the United States, second only to the British share. Canadian investment has shrunk in importance. But aside from these two, there are many elements of continuity. The United Kingdom remains the largest investor, as it was in 160 and for many years before that. The Netherlands is next (after Japan), and the following three are Germany, France, and Switzerland, as in 1960, although the order has changed and Germany is now the leader among the three.

Data on shares of affiliate sales give a much larger role to Japan because of the importance of Japanese wholesale trade affiliates, and they give a comparatively small position to affiliates from the Netherlands. Within manufacturing, however, U.K. affiliates remain the largest single group, and affiliates from the two English-speaking countries account for over a third of total sales.

One of the largest changes in foreign direct investment in recent years has been in its financing. Whereas half or more of increases in investment in the 1950s and 1960s were financed from retained earnings, the proportion dropped almost to zero in the 1980s. The pace of new investment was too great to be financed by reinvested earnings in any case. It consisted, to a large and increasing extent, of new entries to the U.S. market through takeovers of existing U.S. firms. In addition, earnings fell and reinvested earnings were negative in many years during the 1980s. To some extent, the poor earnings reflected the deep recession of the early 1980s and that of 1990 also, but one may suspect that poor choices of investment targets, high prices paid for existing companies, and the willingness of foreign firms to pay heavily for access to U.S. markets may all have played a role. The steep decline in rates of return during the 1980s also points in the same direction, although affiliates from the Netherlands and Canada, two traditional sources of foreign investment, also suffered sharp reductions in profitability.

Appendix

Table 5A.1   **U.S., Developed Country, and World Direct Investment Inflows and Outflows: Annual Averages, 1960–1990 ($ million)**

	Inflows			Outflows		
	United States	Developed Countries	World	United States	Developed Countries	World
1960 (1)	$ 140	$ 2,271		$ 1,674	$ 2,906	
1965–66 (1)*	72	3,215		3,564	5,492	
1965–66 (1)	72	3,816		3,564	5,564	
1967–69 (2)†	923	5,298		5,173	8,358	
1967–69 (2)	923	5,534		5,173	9,101	
1970–72 (2)	926	8,902	$ 12,785‡	7,651	14,744	
1973–75 (2)	3,795	14,464	22,560‡	11,498	26,256	
1973–75 (3)	3,400	13,981	18,065	11,573	23,677	
1975–80 (3)	6,884	19,439	26,244	16,118	33,759	
1975–80 (4)	7,895	24,642	32,183	17,092	39,774	$ 40,278
1981–85 (4)	19,156	36,593	48,736	8,640	44,454	45,312
1980–84 (5)	19,000		45,000	14,000		44,000
1985–89 (5)	46,000		100,000	18,000		105,000
1970–79 (6)		17,300	22,000			
1980–85 (6)	18,742	37,179	49,813			
1986–90 (6)	51,878	123,582	149,673	22,800	160,000	165,600

Sources: (1) United Nations (1973), table 9. (2) United Nations (1978), tables III-34, III-43. (3) United Nations (1983), annex tables II.1, II.2. (4) United Nations (1988), tables A.1, A.2. (5) United Nations (1991c), table 10. (6) United Nations, annex tables 1, 2; text tables I.1, I.5.

Note: Numbers in parentheses indicate source.

*Comparable in coverage to 1960.

†Comparable in coverage to 1965–66 (Austria and Switzerland omitted).

‡Inflows of developed countries plus developed country outflows to developing countries.

Table 5A.2   U.S. Direct Investment Abroad, by Industry of Affiliate ($ billions)

	1950	1957	1966	1977	1982	1985	1987	1988	1989	1990	1991
Agriculture, forestry, and fishing	$ 589	$ 680	$ 348	$ 528	$ 504	$ 497	$ 551	$ 561	$ 523	$ 607	$ 558
Mining, excluding petroleum	1,129	2,361	4,109	5,998	5,210	4,916	4,745	4,850	4,236	4,652	4,555
Petroleum extraction and integrated refining and extraction	—	5,518	9,134	12,987	32,693	34,171	38,067	36,847	34,181	37,634	38,984
Primary production	—	8,559	13,591	19,513	38,407	39,584	43,363	42,258	38,940	42,893	44,097
Petroleum refining and petroleum and coal products	—	1,009	1,524	5,259	7,028	7,840	7,237	7,847	6,725	7,319	8,011
Petroleum, total	3,390	(9,055)[a]	(14,132)[b]	(28,030)	(57,817)	(57,695)	(59,774)	(57,807)	(51,393)	(56,957)	(59,160)
Manufacturing	3,831	8,009[a]	21,843[b]	62,019	83,452	94,700	131,645	138,725	144,679	164,466	175,413
Goods production	8,939[c]	17,577	36,958	86,791	128,887	142,124	182,245	188,830	190,344	214,678	227,521
Construction[d]		118	378	905	1,061	1,331	969	1,057	892	1,087	1,280
Transportation, communication and public utilities excluding petroleum	1,425	2,145	2,346	2,186	2,273	2,679	1,911	2,098	3,166	6,674	8,036
Petroleum tankers, pipelines, storage		1,198	1,154	5,108	1,648	1,602	1,359	1,431	1,422	1,659	2,051
Wholesale exclusive petroleum	542	1,156	3,271	14,011	20,788	22,790	31,847	34,054	35,319	38,217	43,218
Petroleum wholesale trade	—	1,212[e]	1,841[e]	5,380	10,835	8,048	8,365	8,078	5,372	6,882	6,431
Retail excluding petroleum	220	513	911	2,825	3,697	3,997	5,087	6,376	7,084	7,867	8,759
Petroleum retail trade[f]	—			272	222	215	189	221	479	540	659
Trade, excluding petroleum	762	1,669	4,182	16,836	24,485	26,787	36,934	40,430	42,403	46,084	51,977
Trade, including petroleum	—	—	6,023	22,488	35,542	35,050	45,488	48,729	48,254	53,506	59,067
Banking	} 463	131	286	4,370	10,317	14,461	18,027	19,109	19,077	19,783	18,756
Finance (excluding banking), insurance, and real estate		802	3,314	21,248	18,018	22,591	53,046	63,386	96,828	112,374	117,094

(continued)

Table 5A.2   (continued)

	1950	1957	1966	1977	1982	1985	1987	1988	1989	1990	1991
Netherlands Antilles[g]											
Holding companies[h]	56	111	789	−1,216	−20,089	−20,784	−14,496	−10,335	−6,879	−2,460	−3,919
Other services, excluding petroleum	199	293	1,139[i]	11,477	19,597	22,775	34,541	37,506	57,055	64,977	70,077
Oil and gas field services	—	117	479	3,870	4,615	4,683	6,706	7,869	9,222	11,401	13,368
Services, broadly defined[k]	2,849[j]	7,817	14,834	1,914	5,392	5,820	4,557	3,383	3,213	2,924	3,024
				60,414	98,954	108,910	146,558	157,398	188,954	211,868	226,594
Total	11,788	25,394[c]	51,792[b]	145,990	207,752	230,250	314,307	335,893	372,419	424,086	450,196
Total, excluding Netherlands Antilles[g]	11,788	25,394	51,792	147,205	227,841	251,034	328,803	346,228	379,298	426,546	454,115

Sources: 1950 and 1957 data: U.S. Department of Commerce (1960, 93–94, tables 5 and 6; 1982, table 1). 1966 data: U.S. Department of Commerce (1982, table A; 1975, table A-15). (Data are on an "allocated" basis; affiliates owned indirectly are classified by their country and indusry of operation rather than by the country and industry of the primary affiliates that are their intermediate owners; the largest effects are to increase the importance of petroleum wholesale trade and of manufacturing and to decrease the importance of holding companies.) 1977 data: U.S. Department of Commerce (1981), 10–11, table C; table I.W 3. 1982–91 data (unrevised): U.S. Department of Commerce (1992a, tables 5 and 18) and earlier articles in the same series.

[a] Figures comparable to 1950 are 26,278 for total investment, 9,106 for petroleum, and 8,414 for manufacturing.

[b] Figures comparable to 1957 are 54,799 for total investment, 16,222 for petroleum, and 22,078 for manufacturing.

[c] Includes all petroleum operations. Corresponding 1957 figure is 20,105.

[d] 1950 data included with other services.

[e] Includes petroleum retail trade (service stations).

[f] 1979 and 1960 data included with petroleum wholesale trade.

[g] We omit Netherlands Antilles finance affiliates after 1977 because they are almost entirely shell operations set up for tax reasons to borrow abroad and relend the proceeds to their parents.

[h] The operating companies owned by the holding companies are often outside the finance sector.

[i] Hotels, advertising and other business services, motion pictures, and all other, including inactive.

[j] Excludes petroleum trade and services. Corresponding 1957 figure is 5,178.

[k] All except goods industries.

Table 5A.3   **U.S. Corporation Financial and Fixed Capital Stocks: Selected Years, 1950–1991 ($ millions)**

| | Financial Assets | | | | Current Dollar Net Stocks of Fixed Capital | | | | |
| | | | | | | Corporate | | Corporate Nonfinancial | |
Year	Total Corporate* (1)	Nonfinancial Corporate Business (2)	Commercial Banking (3)	Private Nonbank Financial Institution (4)	Total† (5)	Non-residential (6)	Residential (7)	Total† (8)	Non-residential (9)
1950	$ 395.2	$ 102.4	$ 149.6	$ 143.2	$ 171.3	$ 166.6	$ 4.7	$ 167.9	$ 163.2
1959	738.5	178.7	218.6	341.2	314.1	308.0	6.1	297.9	291.8
1960	780.8	181.7	228.3	370.0	323.0	316.7	6.3	306.9	300.6
1966	1,249.5	272.3	361.9	614.1	450.1	439.2	10.9	434.0	423.1
1973	2,428.1	526.8	761.3	1,135.6	922.2	898.4	23.8	913.9	890.1
1974	2,440.1	516.7	794.9	1,128.5	1,107.4	1,081.9	25.5	1,058.2	1,032.7
1977	3,580.0	779.8	1,067.9	1,732.3	1,520.5	1,489.9	30.6	1,447.7	1,417.1
1978	4,110.7	907.9	1,221.1	1,981.7	1,723.6	1,690.1	33.5	1,637.5	1,604.0
1979	4,673.8	1,063.1	1,356.3	2,254.4	1,976.2	1,939.4	36.8	1,871.7	1,834.9
1980	5,277.7	1,191.2	1,482.9	2,603.6	2,277.8	2,238.1	39.7	2,151.4	2,111.7
1981	5,808.8	1,294.1	1,619.9	2,894.8	2,579.6	2,538.2	41.4	2,429.7	2,388.3
1982	6,400.6	1,322.2	1,732.4	3,346.0	2,756.9	2,714.8	42.1	2,587.3	2,545.2
1983	7,126.3	1,422.9	1,888.8	3,814.6	2,844.9	2,802.0	42.9	2,656.9	2,614.0
1984	7,990.1	1,506.5	2,128.8	4,354.8	2,993.2	2,949.2	44.0	2,780.0	2,736.0
1985	9,038.1	1,600.7	2,376.5	5,060.9	3,158.1	3,112.4	45.7	2,918.3	2,872.6
1986	10,344.1	1,765.9	2,617.2	5,961.0	3,317.2	3,269.4	47.8	3,043.1	2,995.3
1987	11,125.4	1,911.6	2,772.8	6,441.0	3,459.6	3,409.2	50.4	3,152.4	3,102.0
1988	12,115.2	2,074.0	2,951.7	7,089.5	3,681.1	3,630.8	50.3	3,333.4	3,283.1
1989	13,312.3	2,189.9	3,231.6	7,890.8	3,886.4	3,834.1	52.3	3,495.2	3,442.9
1990	13,758.8	2,310.7	3,336.4	8,111.7	4,083.9	4,030.2	53.7	3,659.0	3,605.3
1991	14,831.7	2,379.0	3,442.5	9,010.2	4,171.1	4,116.5	54.6	3,725.5	3,670.9

Sources: Financial assets—1950–59: Federal Reserve Board (1979); 1960–87: Federal Reserve Board (1992a); 1988–91: Federal Reserve Board (1992b).

Fixed capital: Musgrave (1992, 1992b).

*Column (1) = Column (2) + Column (3) + Column (4).

†Column (5) = Column (6) + Column (7).

‡Column (8) = Column (7) + Column (9).

Table 5A.4   **Foreign Direct Investment in the United States, by Industry of Affiliate ($ millions)**

	1950	1960	1966	1974A	1974B	1977
Agriculture, forestry, and fishing[a]	—		—	32[b]	—	
Mining, excluding petroleum	—	88	—	427	—	
Petroleum extraction and integrated refining and extraction	—	—	—	$ 6,153[c]	—	
Primary production	—	—	—	6,612	—	
Petroleum refining and petroleum and coal products	—	—	—	—	—	
Petroleum, total	$ 405	$1,238	$1,740	(6,354)	$ 5,614	$ 6,573
Manufacturing	1,138	2,611	3,789	8,242	10,387	14,030
Goods production				14,855		
Manufacturing and petroleum[d]	1,543	3,849	5,529	14,596	16,001	20,603
Construction[a]	—		—	36[b]	—	
Transportation, communication, and public utilities, excluding petroleum	—	408	—	347	—	
Petroleum tankers, pipelines, storage	—	—	—	232[e]	—	
Wholesale, excluding petroleum	—	—	—	4,153	—	
Petroleum wholesale trade	—	—	—	−52	—	
Retail, excluding petroleum[f]	—	—	—	425	—	
Trade, excluding petroleum	784[c]	634	—	4,578	5,613[c]	8,594[c]
Trade, including petroleum wholesale	—	—	—	4,526	—	
Banking	—	—	—	510	—	
Finance (excluding banking), insurance, and real estate	—	—	—	5,686	—	
of which holding companies	—	—	—	3,807	—	
Finance	1,065	1,810	2,072	6,196	3,530	5,398
Other services, excluding petroleum	—	121[i]	—	302	—	
Oil and gas field services	—	—	—	21	—	
Services, broadly defined	1,848	3,061	3,525	11,916	9,143	
Total investment minus goods production						13,992
Total investment minus goods production and excluding petroleum trade and services.						
Total	3,391	6,910	9,054	26,512	25,144	34,595

Sources: 1950, 1960, 1966, 1974B, 1977 data: U.S. Department of Commerce (1984), table 1; trade and finance data for 1950 and 1960 are from U.S. Department of Commerce (1962, 34, table 1). 1974A data: U.S. Department of Commerce (1976), tables 2, A-4 (these data have been revised in the source listed for 1977 and earlier years, but we used this source for its superior detail). 1980–91 data: U.S. Department of Commerce (1992e, 113–114, table 17) and earlier articles in the same series.

[a]1950 data included in other services.

[b]Investment in unincorporated affiliates in agriculture and construction is combined in the sources. We assumed that half was in agriculture, half in construction.

Table 5A.4   (continued)

1980	1982	1985	1986	1987	1988	1989	1990	1991
$ 773	$ 1,049	$ 1,106	$ 1,250	$ 1,250	$ 1,116	$ 1,350	$ 1,334	$ 1,235
1,320	1,876	4,039	5,090	5,591	7,440	4,741	9,230	8,802
10,229	14,199	24,305	24,225	33,151	30,806	31,033	32,876	30,177
12,322	17,124	29,450	30,555	39,992	39,362	37,124	43,440	40,214
39	44	21	58	687	764	1,964	1,515	1,701
(12,200)	(17,660)	(28,270)	(29,094)	(37,815)	(36,006)	(40,345)	(42,165)	(39,955)
33,011	44,065	59,584	71,963	93,865	122,582	150,949	157,431	162,853
45,372	61,233	89,055	102,576	134,544	162,708	190,037	202,386	204,768
45,211		4,037	3,602	1,345	1,519	2,407	2,519	2,706
522	3,692	1,934	2,292	3,136	3,576	4,528	4,504	3,920
774	1,379	501[e]	534[e]	609	1,007	1,038	1,077	1,578[e]
368[i]	457[i]	29,051	33,997	37,427	43,725	45,456	50,750	52,962
11,560	18,397	2,767	3,734	3,101	2,827	5,756	5,831	6,110
962	1,909	6,822	8,923	7,972	9,865	8,549	8,877	6,730
3,650	5,207		5	437	426	405		
15,210	23,604	35,873	42,920	45,399	53,590	54,005	59,627	59,692c
16,172	25,513	38,640	46,654	48,505[e]	56,854[e]	60,187[e]	65,863[e]	65,802
4,617	7,846	11,377	12,394	14,354	16,906	18,431	18,731	20,655
13,530	21,607	35,454	45,096	47,126	52,971	71,552	69,603	76,249
857	1,772	3,793	3,560	3,131	4,795	6,189	2,395	2,102
18,147	29,453	46,831	57,490	61,480	69,877	89,983	88,334	96,904
1,089	1,899	2,943	6,724	13,514	19,048	20,614	31,557	31,511
601	1,051	676	542	262	166	128	461	389
37,674	63,444			128,850	147,251	178,887	194,316	200,809
37,835		95,560	117,838					
83,046	124,677	184,615	220,414	263,394	314,754	368,924	396,702	405,577

[c]Includes petroleum refining and petroleum and coal products.

[d]Includes all petroleum; excluding agriculture, forestry, fishing, and mining.

[e]Includes petroleum retailing.

[f]1985 and 1986 data included in petroleum tankers, pipelines, storage.

[g]Trade, services, construction, transportation, communication, and public utilities.

[h]1991 data included in petroleum tankers, pipelines, storage.

[i]Includes agriculture and construction.

Table 5A.5   Total Assets of Nonbank Foreign Affiliates in the United States: 1959, 1973, 1977–1989 ($ billions)

Year	Total Nonbank Affiliates	Finance other than Banking	Total excluding Finance
1959	$ 9.6*	—	—
1973	93.5†	$ 26.3	$ 67.3
1977	143.5	33.8	109.7
1978	181.2	46.7	134.5
1979	228.6	58.9	169.7
1980	291.3‡	87.7	203.6
1981	407.0	110.2	296.8
1982	476.4	142.6	333.8
1983	531.7	179.2	352.5
1984	602.5	254.0	348.5
1985	741.1	355.7	385.4
1986	838.0	407.2	430.8
1987	943.7	469.9	473.8
1988	1200.8	574.9	625.9
1989	1402.2	641.8	760.4

Sources: 1959 data: U.S. Department of Commerce (1962), table 9. 1973 data: U.S. Department of Commerce (1976), table G1. 1977–80 data: U.S. Department of Commerce (1985), table B1. 1981–89 data: U.S. Department of Commerce (1991a, table B1) and earlier volumes in the same series.

*Includes banking.

†Banking affiliate assets were $40.6 billion.

‡Banking affiliate assets were $229.9 billion (U.S. Dept. of Commerce 1983, table 5).

Table 5A.6 Employment of Nonbank U.S. Affiliates of Foreign Corporations, by Industry of Affiliate (thousands of employees)

	1974	1977	1978	1979	1980	1981	1982	1983	1984	1985	1986	1987	1988	1989	1990
Agriculture, forestry, and fishing	8	9	10	10	10	11	11	11	9	10	11	14	15	22	21
Mining and petroleum	117	106	114	104	127	168	163	150	158	155	144	143	154	180	201
Manufacturing	551	686	804	1,006	1,105	1,300	1,242	1,321	1,382	1,455	1,412	1,543	1,829	2,139	2,197
Food and kindred products	75	72	84	111	120	128	126	139	148	151	160	143	177	251	250
Chemicals	115	198	224	261	284	414	390	398	407	430	377	396	391	437	510
Primary and fabricated metals	88	85	84	107	113	111	103	146	157	168	158	159	200	280	268
Machinery, excluding electrical	43	65	86	112	117	138	132	125	125	116	92	109	194	245	212
Electrical machinery and equipment	56	95	110	149	173	164	153	168	184	194	223	217	271	267	296
Transportation equipment	5	3	21	50	65	73	71	65	66	64	62	56	55	74	84
Other manufacturing	169	168	195	217	233	273	266	280	297	332	339	463	541	584	578
Goods production	675	800	928	1,120	1,242	1,479	1,416	1,482	1,549	1,620	1,567	1,700	1,998	2,341	2,420
Transportation, communication and public utilities	45	23	25	27	36	43	57	56	63	58	74	96	131	190	242
Construction	8	13	23	28	43	58	52	45	43	41	42	52	57	72	72
Wholesale trade	122	153	172	196	217	254	280	269	287	295	308	322	365	399	437
Retail trade	121	142	172	236	304	344	398	420	457	482	561	559	678	804	756
Finance, except banking and insurance	9*	10	11	13	25	18	25	37	43	47	56	84	99	95	54
Insurance	33	33	38	45	62	68	71	68	62	69	74	87	102	112	127
Real estate	5	8	11	22	20	29	26	27	27	31	32	34	36	38	46
Other services	41	37	51	66	85	124	123	143	184	219	224	290	379	461	534
Services, broadly defined†	382	419	502	633	792	938	1,032	1,065	1,165	1,242	1,371	1,524	1,847	2,171	2,286
Total all industries	1,057	1,219	1,430	1,753	2,034	2,417	2,448	2,547	2,714	2,862	2,938	3,224	3,844	4,512	4,705

Sources: 1974 data: U.S. Department of Commerce (1976), table 2. 1977–80 data: U.S. Department of Commerce (1985), table F-1. 1981–88 data: U.S. Department of Commerce (1991b, table F-1) and earlier volumes in the same series. 1989 and 1990 data: Bezirganian (1992), table 2.

*Banking: 26,000.

†All except goods production.

Table 5A.7   Private Nonagricultural Employment in the United States, by Industry: Selected Years, 1974–1990 (thousands of employees)

	1974	1977	1980	1981	1982	1983	1984	1985	1986	1987	1988	1989	1990
Mining and petroleum*	894	1,015	1,225	1,353	1,329	1,148	1,155	1,106	946	881	883	849	869
Manufacturing†	19,880	19,480	20,087	19,956	18,580	18,238	19,189	19,081	18,796	18,860	19,241	19,285	18,951
Food and kindred products	1,707	1,711	1,708	1,671	1,636	1,615	1,612	1,603	1,609	1,620	1,636	1,651	1,668
Chemicals	1,061	1,074	1,107	1,109	1,075	1,043	1,049	1,044	1,022	1,026	1,065	1,076	1,093
Primary and fabricated metals	2,747	2,765	2,755	2,712	2,349	2,202	2,320	2,273	2,175	2,148	2,205	2,223	2,179
Machinery, excluding electrical	2,208	2,175	2,494	2,498	2,244	2,033	2,198	2,174	2,053	2,008	2,082	2,130	2,095
Electrical machinery and equipment	1,968	1,878	2,091	2,094	2,008	2,013	2,208	2,197	2,116	2,069	2,070	1,747	1,673
Transportation equipment	1,868	1,872	1,900	1,898	1,735	1,747	1,901	1,9809	2,025	2,051	2,051	2,054	1,980
Other manufacturing	8,321	8,005	8,032	7,974	7,533	7,585	7,901	7,810	7,796	7,938	8,132	8,404	8,263
Goods production	20,774	20,495	21,312	21,309	19,909	19,386	20,344	20,187	19,742	19,741	20,124	20,134	19,820
Transportation, communication, and public utilities	4,725	4,713	5,146	5,165	5,082	4,954	5,159	5,238	5,255	5,372	5,548	5,644	5,826
Construction	4,020	3,851	4,346	4,188	3,905	3,948	4,383	4,673	4,816	4,967	5,125	5,187	5,136
Wholesale trade	4,433	4,708	5,275	5,358	5,278	5,268	5,555	5,717	5,753	5,844	6,029	6,221	6,205
Retail trade	12,554	13,808	15,035	15,189	15,179	15,613	16,545	17,356	17,930	18,483	19,110	19,549	19,683
Finance, including banking, insurance, and real estate	4,148	4,467	5,160	5,298	5,341	5,468	5,689	5,955	6,283	6,547	6,676	6,695	6,739
Other services	13,441	15,303	17,890	18,619	19,036	19,694	20,797	22,000	23,053	24,236	25,600	27,120	28,240
Services, broadly defined	43,321	46,849	52,854	53,817	53,820	54,944	58,128	60,938	63,090	65,449	68,088	70,416	71,829
Total all industries	64,095	67,344	74,166	75,126	73,729	74,330	78,472	81,125	82,832	85,190	88,212	90,550	91,649

Source: U.S. Department of Commerce (1992a), 45–47.

*Including petroleum and coal products.

†Excluding petroleum and coal products.

Table 5A.8 **Exports and Imports of Merchandise from and into the United States and Total Sales by U.S. Manufacturing Affiliates of Foreign Firms, 1974 and 1977–1989 ($ millions)**

Year	Exports	Imports	Sales
1974	$ 2,026	$ 3,059	$ 31,301
1977	3,557	5,624	50,489
1978	4,521	7,193	62,930
1979	6,548	8,668	81,245
1980	9,048	10,413	98,162
1981	13,590	13,226	139,439
1982	12,883	12,386	141,529
1983	12,045	14,021	158,115
1984	13,078	18,172	176,395
1985	12,849	18,635	185,895
1986	12,805	20,617	190,619
1987	14,890	23,420	220,702
1988	25,192	32,762	280,716
1989	31,281	39,227	347,023

Sources: 1974 data: U.S. Department of Commerce (1976). 1977–80 data: U.S. Department of Commerce (1985). 1981–89 data: U.S. Department of Commerce (1991a and earlier issues in the same series), tables E3, G3, and G6.

Table 5A.9 **U.S. Manufacturing Exports (U.S. $ millions)**

	Total	Food	Chemical	Metals	Non-Electrical Machinery	Electrical Machinery	Transport Equipment	Other Manufacturing
				United Nations Tape Data				
1966	$ 22,827	$ 1,985	$ 2909	$ 2,717	$ 4,759	$ 1,800	$ 4,480	$ 4,177
1977	94,889	7,236	11,452	7,139	19,803	9,487	22,466	17,306
1982	164,234	10,896	21,894	13,058	37,641	17,385	33,073	30,287
1983	157,005	10,798	21,682	11,237	32,754	17,517	34,047	28,970
1984	168,202	10,862	24,496	10,766	36,361	19,698	36,394	29,625
1985	169,220	9,925	22,013	9,759	37,028	18,554	42,717	29,224
1986	176,558	11,289	23,007	9,049	36,395	20,243	43,382	33,193
				Shortcut Method				
1986	170,080	9,076	23,680	6,408	36,971	18,891	43,544	31,511
1987	198,892	9,900	27,374	8,004	42,420	22,539	50,329	38,326
1988	248,294	12,613	33,406	11,311	53,614	29,757	59,178	48,415
1989	269,720	12,891	38,043	14,281	56,287	30,182	62,331	55,705

Sources: U.N. tape data: UN trade tapes. Shortcut method: United Nations (1991a, 1991b).

Table 5A.10   U.S. Total Manufacturing Shipments,* by Industry, 1966, 1977, 1982–1991 ($ millions)

	Total*	Food	Chemicals	Metals	Nonelectrical Machinery	Electrical Machinery	Transport Equipment	Other Manufacturing
1966	$ 518,579	$ 79,665	$ 40,569	$ 84,718	$ 47,417	$ 36,066	$ 72,500	$157,644
1977	1,263,714	192,913	120,905	193,205	122,749	77,845	166,954	389,143
1982	1,756,810	280,529	176,254	224,110	186,773	125,728	201,347	562,069
1983	1,882,776	289,314	189,552	232,323	178,446	136,138	245,392	611,611
1984	2,103,696	304,584	205,963	258,422	211,075	162,362	284,593	676,697
1985	2,157,882	308,606	204,790	255,533	218,408	163,951	307,380	699,214
1986	2,213,276	318,203	205,711	250,928	213,574	164,811	322,688	737,361
1987	2,345,492	329,725	229,546	267,615	217,671	171,287	332,936	796,712
1988	2,551,077	351,513	259,698	307,911	243,258	186,949	354,048	847,700
1989	2,693,954	379,543	275,187	333,600	260,805	195,225	372,436	877,158
1990	2,738,108	397,090	285,612	332,300	263,573	200,430	377,319	881,784
1991	2,696,261	398,110	288,018	309,105	250,080	205,789	375,221	869,938

Source: U.S. Department of Commerce (1992ᵃ), 11–12.
*Excluding petroleum and coal products.

Table 5A.11   U.S. Manufacturing Plant and Equipment Expenditures, by Industry, 1970–1989 ($ billions)

	Total Manufacturing*	Food	Chemicals	Metals	Non-electrical Machinery	Electrical Machinery	Transport Equipment	Other Manufacturing
1970	$ 23.54	$ 2.50	$ 3.06	$ 2.55	$ 3.29	$ 2.18	$ 2.04	$ 7.92
1971	22.86	2.49	3.25	2.44	2.59	1.82	2.34	7.93
1972	29.20	3.13	3.92	3.19	3.11	2.34	2.66	10.85
1973	32.56	3.11	4.46	3.43	3.42	2.84	3.12	12.18
1974	38.01	3.25	5.69	4.95	4.42	2.97	3.75	12.98
1975	38.06	3.39	6.11	5.83	4.67	2.42	3.36	12.28
1976	40.86	3.75	6.68	5.97	5.03	2.62	3.62	13.19
1977	46.29	4.18	6.83	5.69	5.76	3.28	5.32	15.23
1978	52.12	4.87	7.10	5.87	6.29	3.98	6.40	17.61
1979	62.30	5.06	8.56	6.57	8.41	5.17	7.75	20.78
1980	89.80	7.39	12.60	10.40	11.59	9.59	18.16	20.07
1981	101.66	8.41	12.62	11.39	13.09	11.07	18.79	26.29
1982	92.99	7.74	13.27	10.05	12.89	10.62	15.16	23.26
1983	88.05	6.60	13.28	8.61	12.35	10.90	13.02	23.29
1984	113.29	8.82	15.32	10.59	15.41	14.61	16.18	32.36
1985	126.47	10.29	16.45	11.29	15.97	15.57	19.29	37.61
1986	124.77	10.60	16.81	11.13	13.61	14.17	18.88	39.57
1987	128.52	11.04	16.37	12.63	13.77	15.26	16.74	42.71
1988	144.28	12.69	18.29	14.55	14.93	18.01	16.43	49.38
1989	153.70	15.90	18.50	12.00	14.60	20.50	18.70	53.50

Sources: Seskin and Sullivan (1988), and earlier articles in that series.
U.S. Bureau of the Census (1991), table 897.
*Manufacturing excluding petroleum.

Table 5A.12   **Property, Plant, and Equipment Expenditures by U.S. Manufacturing Affiliates of Foreign Firms, 1974 and 1977–1989 ($ billions)**

	Total Manufacturing	Food	Chemicals	Metals	Non-electrical Machinery	Electrical Machinery	Transport Equipment	Other Manufactuirng
1974	$ 2.36	$0.18	$0.89	$0.52	*	*	$0.22*	$0.55
1977†	2.95	0.25	1.18	0.37	$0.22	$0.20	—	0.72‡
1978†	4.04	0.39	1.71	0.47	0.26	0.25	0.04	0.92
1979†	5.72	0.47	2.49	0.67	0.34	0.59	0.13	1.03
1980	8.02	0.68	2.99	0.81	0.46	1.00	0.24	1.84
1981	10.45	0.53	4.73	1.18	0.66	1.03	0.39	1.93
1982	10.48	0.61	4.85	0.99	0.61	0.99	0.62	1.81
1983	9.05	0.67	3.88	0.87	0.56	0.78	0.40	1.89
1984	10.48	0.80	4.49	0.93	0.48	1.25	0.62	1.91
1985	11.30	0.74	4.80	1.30	0.53	1.35	0.45	2.13
1986	11.09	0.85	4.32	1.18	0.42	1.38	0.97	1.97
1987	15.82	0.87	5.49	1.57	0.89	1.44	1.72	3.84
1988	20.69	1.32	7.05	2.29	1.26	2.01	1.62	5.14
1989	25.10	1.75	9.32	3.22	1.93	2.10	1.12	5.66

Sources: 1974 data: U.S. Department of Commerce (1976), table I8, p. 123. 1977–80 data: U.S. Department of Commerce (1985). 1981–89 data: U.S. Department of Commerce (1991a and earlier volumes in the same series), table D 25, col. 1, or table D 29, col. 1.

*Figure in column (7) includes nonelectrical machinery, electrical machinery, and transport equipment.

†Plant and equipment expenditures only. Property, plant, and equipment expenditure was 8 percent higher in 1980.

‡Includes transportation equipment.

Appendix Table 5A.13 Employment of Nonbank U.S. Parent Companies, by Industry 1977, 1982–1989 (thousands of employees)

	1977	1982	1983	1984	1985	1986	1987	1988	1989
Petroleum, total	890.5	1,225.3	1,129.6	1,061.5	1,010.6	812.4	693.8	658.4	628.0
Manufacturing	11,775.0	10,532.8	10,403.1	10,660.4	10,502.8	10,431.0	10,195.9	9,819.9	10,138.4
Foods	1,016.7	1,011.2	986.7	1,003.5	1,092.4	1,215.5	1,158.2	1,067.9	1,135.5
Chemicals	1,207.7	1,364.6	1,368.3	1,328.6	1,291.4	1,265.6	1,258.7	1,189.2	1,253.4
Metals	1,484.2	976.2	858.0	825.7	737.2	667.1	674.1	666.3	690.6
Nonelectrical machinery	1,546.3	1,457.9	1,446.1	1,566.0	1,406.5	1,217.7	1,131.0	1,156.9	1,266.7
Electrical machinery	1,274.1	1,619.5	1,651.3	1,689.1	1,557.1	1,601.0	1,149.0	1,042.5	1,016.3
Transportation equipment	2,289.0	1,687.3	1,735.1	1,908.8	2,195.8	2,317.0	2,331.7	2,172.9	2,083.0
Other manufacturing	2,957.0	2,416.0	2,357.6	2,338.6	2,222.4	2,147.0	2,493.0	2,524.1	2,692.9
Goods production*	12,665.5	11,758.1	11,532.7	11,721.9	11,513.4	11,243.4	10,889.7	10,478.3	10,766.4
Wholesale, excluding petroleum	2,471.6†	396.7	378.9	372.7	367.5	317.6	314.7	341.8	423.7
Finance (excluding banking), insurance, and real estate	862.0	1,004.0	1,003.8	992.2	901.4	990.8	1,054.1	1,049.3	1,080.9
Other services, excluding petroleum	739.6	993.8	1,035.5	1,060.3	1,167.5	1,262.5	1,478.0	1,530.0	1,725.7
Other industries‡	2,145.8	4,551.9	4,448.6	3,983.8	4,162.7	4,017.6	4,249.3	4,338.3	4,724.2
Services, broadly defined§	6,219.1	6,946.5	6,866.8	6,409.0	6,599.2	6,588.4	7,096.1	7,259.3	7,954.6
Total all industries	18,884.6	18,704.6	18,399.5	18,130.9	18,112.6	17,831.8	17,985.8	17,737.6	18,721.0

Sources: 1977 data: U.S. Department of Commerce (1981), table II.S1, col. 1. 1982 data: U.S. Department of Commerce (1985), table II.O1, col. 1. 1983–89 data: U.S. Department of Commerce (1991a and earlier volumes in the same series), table 54, col. 8, or table 84, col. 1.

*Goods production including all petroleum.

†Including retail trade.

‡Including mining; agriculture; transportation, communication, and other public utilities; construction; and retail trade.

§Excluding petroleum service.

Table 5A.14   **Assets of U.S. Affiliates of Foreign Firms, by Industry and Investing Country 1959, 1974, 1980, and 1987 ($ millions)**

	World	Canada	France	West Germany	Nether-lands	United Kingdom	Japan
				1959			
All industries	$9,598	$2,575	—	—	$3,345	$1,481	—
Mining	237	66	—	—	—	171	—
Petroleum	3,220	288	—	—	2,784	13	—
Manufacturing	3,921	1,272	—	—	464	978	—
Wholesale and retail trade	1,359	350	—	—	72	201	—
Other industries	861	600	—	—	25	119	—
				1974			
All industries	$174,272	$23,856	$8,692	$8,201	$17,323	$32,226	$39,069
Mining	4,396	670	—*	—*	—*	1,937	0
Petroleum	28,499	1,638	—*	12	9,958	4,164	1,867
Manufacturing	26,213	4,936	1,483	2,347	2,909	6,550	1,384
Foods	3,864	1,597	—	5	299	603	142
Chemicals	7,895	164	412	1,503	1,134	2,046	—
Metals	4,542	950	—	130	363	1,289	—
Machinery	3,511	956	108	200	459	440	—
Other manufacturing	6,400	1,269	251	509	654	2,172	—
Wholesale trade	23,868	1,905	2,097	1,838	1,126	2,170	10,471
Retail trade	2,259	351	26	—*	—*	1,156	—*
Finance, insurance, real estate	84,758	13,393	4,500	3,856	2,085	15,428	24,360
Other industries	4,279	962	586†	148‡	1,245‡	822	987§
				1980			
All industries	$292,033	$47,879	$25,654	$31,196	$36,103	$56,594	$27,626
Mining	6,813	3,342	413	193	—	136	5
Petroleum	44,060	3,368	—	360	—	—	894
Manufacturing	81,684	13,140	9,253	17,766	6,132	14,646	3,885
Foods	8,203	2,636	235	94	161	2,714	355
Chemicals	26,086	553	1,793	10,347	3,023	5,502	311
Metals	10,277	1,869	1,704	1,288	—	1,141	1,194
Machinery, excluding electrical	7,645	} 3,966	} 311	1,045	} 2,278	1,664	501
Electrical and electronic equipment	9,782			1,433		1,053	399
Transportation equipment	4,476	} 4,116	2,521	1,560	4	7	} 1,125
Other manufacturing	15,214		2,689	1,999	—	2,565	

(continued)

Table 5A.14   (continued)

	World	Canada	France	West Germany	Nether-lands	United Kingdom	Japan
Wholesale trade	50,068	1,898	5,108	5,459	688	5,064	18,724
Retail trade	9,685	820	—	1,788	744	—	161
Finance, exclud-ing banking	32,291	5,051	—	495	1,061	4,706	2,082
Insurance	36,240	9,869	255	2,938	3,513	9,872	375
Real estate	19,872	7,764	416	1,153	2,056	1,938	654
Other services	4,372	409	785	148	452	765	567
Other industries	6,948	2,218	1,068	894	—	659	279
				1987			
All industries	$943,654	$142,506	$34,675	$61,168	$68,929	$159,525	$200,386
Mining	12,912	3,006	—*	892	—	3,302	26
Petroleum	79,666	3,364	4,415	1,134	—	25,387	906
Manufacturing	223,462	50,744	16,781	28,353	13,026	48,971	15,729
Foods	24,048	7,010	1,195	99	—	7,785	541
Chemicals	77,352	—	3,681	14,112	—	12,982	2,557
Metals	23,170	4,911	550	1,926	—	2,723	2,860
Machinery, exclud-ing electrical	13,062	} 3,228	3,499	5,753	—	2,482	2,851
Electrical and electronic equipment	20,372				—	2,735	1,796
Transportation equipment	7,689	—	2,791	510	—	998	2,406
Other manufacturing	57,770	—	5,065	5,953	—	19,265	2,719
Wholesale trade	100,740	4,040	5,769	11,333	1,173	13,557	46,561
Retail trade	26,748	9,514	461	3,982	4,235	2,547	635
Finance, excluding banking	271,044	8,976	3,463	4,345	1,483	27,878	119,789
Insurance	109,179	34,051	339	5,318	12,946	20,449	699
Real estate	69,682	23,033	410	2,493	4,067	9,091	10,147
Other services	32,572	1,727	1,147	2,063	495	6,260	4,070
Other industries	17,648	4,051	1,891‖	1,254	—	2,084	1,824

Sources: U.S. Department of Commerce (1962), table 9; (1976), table G-13; (1983), table B-7; (1990b), table B-5.

*Included in other industries.

†Includes mining and petroleum.

‡Includes mining and retail trade.

§Includes retail trade.

‖Includes mining.

Table 5A.15   **Sales of U.S. Affiliates of Foreign Firms, by Industry and Investing Country, 1959, 1974, 1980, and 1987 ($ millions)**

A. Country of Parent

			Europe					
	World	Canada	Total	France	Germany	Nether-lands	United Kingdom	Japan
				1959				
All industries	$14,354	$4,710	$8,653	—	—	—	$2,162	0
All industries, excluding finance	12,353	4,062	7,330	$360	$292	$3,131	3,061	0
Mining	122	53	69	0	0	0	0	0
Petroleum	2,356	160	2,196	0	0	2,102	9	0
Manufacturing	5,131	2,063	3,020	92	47	775	1,234	0
Foods	2,299	1,353	946	—	0	—	654	0
Chemicals	891	45	832	6	46	—	78	0
Metals	276	207	69	—	0	0	17	0
Machinery, excluding electrical	432	238	189	>0.5	0	0	52	0
Electrical machinery and equipment	289	1	288	—	0	—	52	0
Other manufacturing	944	219	696	—	1	—	382	0
Wholesale and retail trade	4,291	1,550	1,847	263	245	212	717	0
Banking[a]	115	52	44	—	—	—	15	0
Finance (excluding banking), insurance, and real estate	1,886	596	1,279	—	—	—	≥867	0
Other industries[b]	453	236	198	6	0	42	202	0
				1974				
All industries	$146,771	$15,934	$80,311	$12,796	$8,727	$17,106	$27,138	$40,106
Mining	1,409	≤468	941	≤31	1	330	579	0
Petroleum	26,350	≤3,087[c]	15,910	≤630	≤49	10,564–10,818	2,602	9,133[d]
Manufacturing	31,301	5,881	21,323	2,004	2,538	3,882	7,660	1,311
Foods	5,534	1,341	3,995	≤721	3	549	1,194	131
Chemicals	7,985	216	6,414	404	1,572	1,406	1,679	[e]
Metals	6,139	—[e]	3,357	513	227	282	1,996	554
Machinery	4,400	1,250	2,750	≤370	187	680	547	267
Other manufacturing	7,243	3,074[f]	4,807	285	550	964	2,244	359[g]
Wholesale trade	66,499	4,378	30,164	9,418	5,715	1,534–1,788	8,578	27,097
Retail trade	6,327	—[h]	3,800	29	25	180	3,116	—[h]
Finance (excluding banking), insurance, and real estate[a]	11,259	1,950[i]	6,377	650	316	152	3,757	2,163[i]
Other industries[b]	3,626	638[j]	1,796	≤57	≤57	210	849	402

(*continued*)

Table 5A.15   (continued)

			Europe					
	World	Canada	Total	France	Germany	Nether-lands	United Kingdom	Japan

B. Country of Ultimate Beneficial Owner

			Europe					
	World	Canada	Total	France	West Germany	Nether-lands	United Kingdom	Japan
				1980				
All industries	$412,390	$35,456	$259,414	$40,806	$45,620	$38,618	$94,410	$84,207
Mining	3,388	1,777	1,392	—	—	—	123	0
Petroleum	56,052	2,445	47,973	—	—	—	15,470	3,713
Manufacturing	98,162	15,686	73,416	12,548	19,180	8,584	17,850	3,990
Foods	11,956	2,644	8,182	202	101	—ᵉ	4,858	455
Chemicals	28,204	1,016	26,374	1,745	11,348	3,675	5,004	381
Metals	12,911	2,948	8,359	2,656	1,526	—ᵉ	1,214	1,068
Machinery, excluding electrical	9,089	4,261 }	6,332	368 }	1,320	3,717 }	2,151	523
Electrical machinery and equipment	11,977		6,944		1,207		988	678
Transport equipment	6,390	51	6,253	7,577 }	1,609	4	10	885 }
Other manufacturing	17,635	4,767	10,972		2,070	1,188ᵏ	3,625	
Wholesale trade	197,674	5,395	96,675	18,661	14,104	1,852	49,134	75,021
Retail trade	23,475	2,281	19,511	—	—	—	3,915–4,601	190
Finance, excluding banking	4,755	875	3,031	—	58	26	492	≤2,439 }
Insurance	14,197	3,106	9,440	111	910	—	4,883	
Real estate	3,933	2,255	1,027	124	178	294	281	107
Other Services	3,332	329	2,080	477	117	233	617	491
Other industriesᵇ	7,423	1,308	4,869	1,442	1,566	115	959–1,645	292–361

			Europe					
	World	Canada	Total	France	West Germany	Nether-lands	United Kingdom	Japan
				1987				
All industries	$744,617	$89,433	$393,132	$44,113	$74,259	$52,373	$131,233	$186,812
Mining	5,757	1,670	2,758	≤741	900	—	1,115	≤102
Petroleum	71,993	1,323	52,514	≤4,582	≤3,073	≤21,225	15,896	2,169
Manufacturing	225,079	43,705	146,878	16,906	30,676	14,832	47,975	15,496
Foods	22,862	3,174	17,967	1,106	116	—	8,201	612
Chemicals	72,105	—	≤42,803	2,091	14,941	—	12,811	2,134
Metals	26,658	5,954	9,372	669	2,984	116	2,795	3,600

Table 5A.15 (continued)

	World	Canada	Europe Total	France	Germany	Nether-lands	United Kingdom	Japan
Machinery excluding electrical	13,766	⎱ 4,191	9,405	⎱ 5,149	1,619	276	2,423	2,320
Electrical machinery and equipment	26,577	⎰	19,895	⎰	4,240	—	2,717	2,721
Transport equipment	8,384	—	5,737	3,618	542	2	1,239	
Other manufacturing	54,727	30,386[g]	≤41,699	4,273	6,234	912[i]	17,790	
Wholesale trade	278,843	8,786	105,596	18,556	23,132	2,917	39,270	151,000
Retail trade	48,433	13,720	30,847	1,355	10,943	6,799	4,419	642
Finance, excluding banking	27,008	780	11,406	317	345	131	3,524	11,765
Insurance	39,260	10,849	20,076	167	1,920	4,720	8,417	297
Real estate	10,907	4,588	3,358	151	411	689	1,446	745
Services	20,086	1,267	11,604	716	879	461	7,080	1,360
Other industries[b]	17,252	2,746	8,094	1,363–3,607	1,980–3,002	≥599	2,090	3,236

Sources: U.S. Department of Commerce (1962), tables 13 through 14; (1976), tables K-4 and K-5; (1985), table E-5; (1990b) table E-3.

[a]Gross income.

[b]Including transportation, communication, and public utilities.

[c]Including metals.

[d]Including retail trade.

[e]Included in other manufacturing.

[f]Including metals.

[g]Including chemicals.

[h]Included in petroleum.

[i]Total income, assumed equal to net sales.

[j]Including other industries' total income, assumed equal to net sales.

[k]Including metals and foods.

[l]Including foods, chemicals, and electrical machinery and equipment.

Table 5A.16   Expenditures for Property, Plant, and Equipment by U.S. Affiliates of Foreign Firms, by Industry and Investing Country, 1974, 1980, and 1987 ($ millions)

	All Countries	Canada	France	West Germany	Netherlands	United Kingdom	Japan
				1974			
All industries	7,716	893	370	373	2,295	1,388	721
Mining	505	110	4	—ᵃ	—ᵃ	278	0
Petroleum	2,858	—ᵃ	—ᵃ	3	1,842	438	—ᵃ
Manufacturing	2,358	313	158	224	291	457	299
Food	179	46	8	1	16	46	16
Chemicals	887	10	}114	158	139	148	32
Metals	520	78		11	60	93	NA
Machinery	218	34	8	15	34	30	49
Other manufacturing	555	145	28	39	41	140	NA
Wholesale trade	519	49	49	33	15	53	—ᵃ
Retail trade	160	—ᵃ	. 1	1	—ᵃ	61	16
Finance, excluding banking	748	165	—ᵃ	69	44	—ᵃ	—ᵃ
Other industriesᵇ	568	256ᶜ	158ᵈ	43ᵉ	103ᶠ	101ᵍ	406ʰ
				1980			
All industries	$25,713	$6,427	$1,883	$2,981	$4,048	$3,547	$1,452
Mining	567	284	78	12	—ᵃ	10	0
Petroleum	5,404	893	126	67	—ᵃ	—ᵃ	3
Manufacturing	7,971	1,407	733	2,024	460	1,301	516
Food	681	280	8	10	—	146	42
Chemicals	2,977	55	184	1,458	—	672	50
Metals	810	179	120	64	—	52	—
Machinery, excluding electrical	448	}313	}23	105	}228	91	—
Electrical and electronic equipment	1,004			93		85	—
Transport equipment	249	}580	128	99	1	1	—
Other manufacturing	1,802		270	196	23	254	—
Wholesale trade	1,750	83	—ᵃ	269	—ᵃ	193	412
Retail trade	823	100	—ᵃ	131	55	—ᵃ	27
Finance, excluding banking	254	—ᵃ	—ᵃ	1	0	14	—ᵃ
Insurance	235	—ᵃ	—ᵃ	23	—ᵃ	53	0

Table 5A.16   (continued)

	All Countries	Canada	France	West Germany	Netherlands	United Kingdom	Japan
Real estate	7,101	3,122	128	328	599	436	272
Other services	590	81	172	17	20	65	29
Other industries	1,019	457[i]	646[j]	109	2,914[k]	1,475[c]	193[l]
				1987			
All industries	45,647	9,324	1,613	3,731	4,472	7,140	9,587
Mining	1,258	—[a]	4	126	2	224	1
Petroleum	6,239	180	405	64	—[a]	—[a]	101
Manufacturing	15,819	4,117	806	1,816	670	2,808	2,607
Food	870	155	85	—	—	333	65
Chemicals	5,488	—	132	865	—	563	84
Metals	1,567	228	15	112	—	188	337
Machinery, excluding electrical	891			70		160	187
Electrical and electronic equipment	1,437			276		246	237
Transport equipment	1,723	—	}337	0	38	1,380	
Other manufacturing	3,844	—		—	26	1,319	317
Wholesale trade	2,907	183	93	560	49	272	1,326
Retail trade	2,057	459	57	279	636	171	36
Finance, excluding banking	947	82	18	6	—[a]	120	472
Insurance	640	—[a]	0	28	127	91	2
Real estate	11,198	3,188	30	452	—[a]	956	3,771
Other services	2,790	222	39	}400{	21	319	1,008
Other industries	1,801	893[m]	162		2,967[n]	2,179[o]	263

Sources: U.S. Department of Commerce (1976), table I-8; (1983), table D-9; (1990b), table D-27.

[a]Included in other indusries.

[b]Includes services.

[c]Includes petroleum and retail trade.

[d]Includes petroleum and finance, insurance, and real estate.

[e]Includes mining.

[f]Includes mining and retail trade.

[g]Includes finance, insurance, and real estate.

[h]Includes petroleum, wholesale trade, and finance, insurance, and real estate.

[i]Includes finance (excluding banking) and insurance.

[j]Includes wholesale and retail trade, finance (excluding banking), and insurance.

[k]Includes mining, petroleum, wholesale trade, and insurance.

[l]Includes finance (excluding banking).

[m]Includes mining and insurance.

[n]Includes petroleum, finance (excluding banking), and real estate.

[o]Includes petroleum.

Table 5A.17   Employment in U.S. Affiliates of Foreign Firms, by Industry of Affiliate and Investing Country: 1974, 1980, 1987 (thousands of employees)

A. Country of Foreign Parent

	All countries	Canada	France	West Germany	Netherlands	United Kingdom	Japan
				1974			
All industries	$1,083.4	$176.0	57.8	59.0	172.2	284.3	70.9
Mining	22.7	—a	—a	—a	6.0	8.1	0.0
Petroleum	93.7	—a	—a	—a	—a	11.3	—a
Manufacturing	550.6	92.3	33.7	41.8	86.3	132.6	21.3
Food	74.7	15.7	—	0.1	—	21.2	—
Chemicals	114.7	1.7	4.1	21.4	24.6	23.9	—
Metals	87.8	17.0	—	1.7	—	28.1	—
Machinery	99.6	23.2	3.4	4.0	19.2	12.4	7.0
Other manufacturing	173.8	34.8	5.3	14.6	29.0	47.0	5.0
Wholesale trade	121.9	19.0	8.4	9.7	14.1	17.5	23.4
Retail trade	120.5	—a	0.3	0.4	—a	61.0	—a
Finance (except banking), insurance, and real estate	72.6	9.5	1.9	4.2	1.2	27.3	4.8
Other industries	101.3	55.2c	13.5d	3.3d	64.6e	26.5	21.4e

B. Country of Ultimate Beneficial Owner

	All countries	Canada	France	West Germany	Netherlands	United Kingdom	Japan
				1980			
All industries	$2,033.9	$290.0	$206.4	$375.9	$186.7	$428.2	$115.3
Mining	25.2	11.9	1.2	—a	—a	1.0	—a
Petroleum	101.6	11.6	5.9	1.4	—a	—a	0.2
Manufacturing	1,105.0	152.8	119.0	239.0	102.6	224.0	36.2
Food	120.4	19.5	1.6	1.1	3.1	58.7	4.9
Chemicals	283.8	4.3	15.4	134.4	—	47.5	2.6
Metals	112.9	20.2	20.4	14.2	—	16.5	—f
Machinery, excluding electrical	116.9	20.6	2.8	17.4	}58.8	32.8	5.1
Electrical and electronic equipment	172.5	30.3	2.7	16.7		17.2	7.1
Transport equipment	65.1	0.7	}76.1			0.2	}16.5 ¹
Other manufacturing	232.6	57.1		55.2	4.3	51.2	
Wholesale trade	217.2	14.5	28.2	33.4	3.7	35.0	54.7
Retail trade	304.2	35.9	—a	—	21.1	—a	3.7
Finance, excluding banking	24.8	—a	≤5.2	0.3	—a	6.1	1.5
Insurance	62.3	8.4	0.2	2.9	8.6	27.8	—a
Real estate	19.7	13.6	0.3	0.2	0.7	1.1	0.4
Other services	85.3	10.3	5.5	2.6	3.5	11.7	10.4
Other industries	88.6	31.0g	46.1g	96.2h	46.5i	121.6e	8.2j

Table 5A.17   (continued)

	All Countries	Canada	France	West Germany	Netherlands	United Kingdom	Japan
				1987			
All industries	3,224.3	592.9	187.8	366.6	270.1	647.4	303.2
Mining	27.6	8.5	0.5	3.0	0.4	6.1	0.2
Petroleum	114.9	2.2	—a	1.1	—a	44.8	0.3
Manufacturing	1,542.6	275.1	110.1	193.9	93.5	391.2	86.9
Food	142.6	21.7	7.9	0.8	—	53.6	3.7
Chemicals	395.8	—a	12.0	76.2	—	88.0	11.3
Metals	159.3	33.5	4.1	16.1	1.0	20.6	17.8
Machinery, excluding electrical	109.3	33.6		47.2	2.9	21.8	16.3
Electrical and electronic equipment	216.8		36.4	35.0	—	31.7	12.5
Transport equipment	55.7	186.3k	20.6	3.3	0.0	13.5	7.7
Other manufacturing	463.0		29.0	50.4	7.8	161.9	17.6
Wholesale trade	321.9	18.3	29.0	50.3	7.8	45.8	108.6
Retail trade	558.7	185.7	13.6	92.2	110.0	47.8	8.2
Finance, excluding banking	83.9	1.9	0.5	0.6	0.5	12.4	44.0
Insurance	87.4	11.2	0.1	2.9	15.1	24.2	0.4
Real estate	33.9	20.9	0.1	0.4	1.4	3.3	1.0
Services	290.3	33.7	12.1	8.9	3.9	51.4	29.6
Other industries	163.1	35.4	21.8b	13.3	37.5b	20.4	24.0

Sources: U.S. Department of Commerce (1976), table L-4; (1985), table F-4; (1990b), table F-3.

[a]Included in other indusries.

[b]Includes services.

[c]Includes mining, petroleum, and retail trade.

[d]Includes mining and petroleum.

[e]Includes petroleum and retail trade.

[f]Included in other manufacturing.

[g]Includes finance, excluding banking.

[h]Includes mining and retail trade.

[i]Includes mining, petroleum, and finance.

[j]Includes mining and insurance.

[k]Includes chemicals.

[l]Includes metals.

References

Abu Dhabi's links with a powerful law firm present problem for Democrats on BCCI issue. 1992. *The Wall Street Journal,* 20 May.

Belli, R. David. 1981. U.S. business enterprises acquired or established by foreign direct investors in 1980. *Survey of Current Business* 61, no. 8 (August): 58–71.

Bezirganian, Steve D. 1992. U.S. affiliates of foreign companies: Operations in 1990. *Survey of Current Business* 72, no. 5 (May): 45–68.

Blomström, Magnus, and Robert E. Lipsey. 1989. The export performance of U.S. and Swedish multinationals. *Review of Income and Wealth* 35, no. 3 (September): 245–64.

Cagan, Phillip, and Robert E. Lipsey. 1978. *The financial effects of inflation.* NBER General Series no. 103. Cambridge, Mass.: Ballinger Publishing for the National Bureau of Economic Research.

Di Lullo, Anthony J. 1991. U.S. international transactions, third quarter 1991. *Survey of Current Business* 71, no. 12 (December): 60–85.

Eisner, Robert, and Paul J. Pieper. 1990. The world's greatest debtor nation? *North American Review of Economics and Finance* 1, no. 1.

Federal Reserve Board. 1979. *Flow of funds accounts: Financial assets and liabilities.* Annual revisions. Washington, D.C.: Board of Governors of the Federal Reserve System.

———. 1992a. *Balance sheets for the U.S. economy 1960–1991.* Washington, D.C.: Board of Governors of the Federal Reserve System, March.

———. 1992b. *Flow of funds accounts: Financial assets and liabilities.* Annual revisions. Washington, D.C.: Board of Governors of the Federal Reserve System.

Goldsmith, Raymond W., and Robert E. Lipsey. 1963. *Studies in the national balance sheet of the United States.* Vol. 1. Princeton, N.J.: Princeton University Press for the National Bureau of Economic Research.

Grubert, Harry, Timothy Goodspeed, and Deborah Swenson. 1991. Explaining the low taxable income of foreign-controlled companies in the United States. Unpublished paper. November.

How Japan got burned in the U.S.A. 1992. *Fortune,* 15 June, pp. 114–16.

Japanese wary on U.S. operations. 1992. *The Wall Street Journal,* 9 June.

Kravis, Irving B., and Robert E. Lipsey. 1992. Sources of competitiveness of the U.S. and of its multinational firms. *Review of Economics and Statistics* 74, no. 2 (May): 193–201.

Landefeld, J. Steven, and Ann M. Lawson. 1991. Valuation of the U.S. net international investment position. *Survey of Current Business* 71, no. 5 (May): 40–49.

Lewis, Cleona. 1938. *America's stake in international investments.* Washington, D.C.: Brookings Institution.

Lipsey, Robert E. 1988. Changing patterns of international investment in and by the United States. In *The United States in the world economy,* ed. Martin Feldstein, 475–545. Chicago: University of Chicago Press.

———. 1989. The internationalization of production. NBER Working Paper no. 2923. Cambridge, Mass.: National Bureau of Economic Research, April.

———. 1991. Foreign direct investment in the United States and U.S. trade. *Annals of the American Academy of Political and Social Science* 516 (July): 76–90.

Lipsey, Robert E., and Irving B. Kravis. 1987. The competitiveness and comparative advantage of U.S. multinationals, 1957–1984. *Banca Nazionale del Lavoro Quarterly Review* 161 (June): 147–65.

Mantel, Ida May. 1975. Foreign direct investment in the United States in 1974. *Survey of Current Business* 55, no. 10 (October): 36–42.

Musgrave, John. 1992a. Fixed reproducible tangible wealth in the United States, 1988–91. *Survey of Current Business* 72, no. 8 (August): 37–43.

———. 1992b. Fixed reproducible tangible wealth in the United States, revised estimates. *Survey of Current Business* 72, no. 1 (January): 106–37.

Nicholson, Robert E. 1991. U.S. international transactions, first quarter 1991. *Survey of Current Business* 71, no. 6 (June): 36–73.

Orr, James. 1991. The trade balance effects of foreign direct investment in U.S. manufacturing. *Federal Reserve Bank of New York Quarterly Review* 16, no. 2 (Summer): 63–76.

Scholl, Russell B. 1991. The international investment position of the United States in 1990. *Survey of Current Business* 71, no. 6 (June): 23–35.

Scholl, Russell B., Raymond J. Mataloni, Jr., and Steve D. Bezirganian. 1992. The international investment position of the United States in 1991. *Survey of Current Business* 72, no. 6 (June), 46–59.

Seskin, Eugene P., and David F. Sullivan. 1988. Plant and equipment expenditures, the four quarters of 1988. *Survey of Current Business* 68, no. 6 (June): 19–22.

Ulan, Michael, and William G. Dewald. 1989. The U.S. net international investment position: Misstated and misunderstood. In *Dollars, deficits, and trade,* ed. James A. Dorn and William A. Niskanen. Norwell, Mass.: Kluwer Academic Publishers for the Cato Institute.

United Nations.

    1973. *Multinational corporations in world development.* New York: Department of Economic and Social Affairs.

    1978. *Transnational corporations in world development: A reexamination.* New York: UN Center on Transnational Corporations.

    1983. *Transnational corporations in world development, third survey.* New York: UN Center on Transnational Corporations.

    1988. *Transnational corporations in world development, trends and prospects.* New York: UN Center on Transnational Corporations.

    1991a. *Commodity trade statistics, 1989.* Statistical Papers, series D, vol. 39 (1–11).

    1991b. *1989 international trade statistics yearbook.* New York: United Nations.

    1991c. *World investment report, 1991: the triad in foreign direct investment.* New York: UN Center on Transnational Corporations.

    1992. *World investment report, 1992: Transnational corporations as engines of growth.* New York: United Nations.

U.S. Bureau of the Census. 1975. *Historical statistics of the United States: Colonial times to 1970.* Washington, D.C.

———. 1991. *Statistical abstract of the United States, 1991.* Washington, D.C.

U.S. Department of Commerce.

    1948. *International transactions of the United States during the war, 1940–1945.* Washington, D.C.: Office of Business Economics.

    1950. *The balance of international payments of the United States, 1946–48.* Washington, D.C.: Office of Business Economics.

    1960. *U.S. business investments in foreign countries.* Washington, D.C.: Office of Business Economics.

    1962. *Foreign business investments in the United States.* Supplement to *Survey of Current Business.* Washington, D.C.: Office of Business Economics.

    1975. *U.S. direct investment abroad, 1966: Final data (benchmark survey).* Washington, D.C.: Bureau of Economic Analysis.

    1976. *Foreign direct investment in the United States: Benchmark survey, 1974.* Vol. 2, *Report of the Secretary of Commerce to the Congress in compliance with* the Foreign Investment Study Act of 1974. Washington, D.C.: U.S. Department of Commerce, April.

1981. *U.S. direct investment abroad, 1977 (benchmark survey)*. Washington, D.C.: Bureau of Economic Analysis.

1982. *Selected data on U.S. direct investment abroad, 1950–76*. Washington, D.C.: Bureau of Economic Analysis.

1983. *Foreign direct investment in the United States, 1980*. Washington, D.C.: Bureau of Economic Analysis.

1984. *Selected data on foreign direct investment in the United States, 1950–79*. Washington, D.C.: Bureau of Economic Analysis, December.

1985. *Foreign direct investment in the United States: Operations of U.S. affiliates, 1977–80*. Washington, D.C.: Bureau of Economic Analysis.

1990a. *Foreign direct investment in the United States: Balance of payments and direct investment position estimates, 1980–86*. Washington, D.C.: Bureau of Economic Analysis, December.

1990b. *Foreign direct investment in the United States, 1987 benchmark survey, final results*. Washington, D.C.: Bureau of Economic Analysis, August.

1991a. *Foreign direct investment in the United States: Operations of U.S. affiliates of foreign companies, preliminary 1989 estimates*. Washington, D.C.: Bureau of Economic Analysis, August.

1991b. *Foreign direct investment in the United States: Operation of U.S. affiliates of foreign companies, revised 1988 estimates*. Washington, D.C.: Bureau of Economic Analysis, August.

1991c. *Foreign direct investment in the United States: Review and analysis of current developments*. Washington, D.C.: Economics and Statistics Administration, Office of the Chief Economist, August.

1992a. *Business statistics 1963–91*. Washington, D.C.: Bureau of Economic Analysis, June.

1992b. Foreign direct investment in the United States: Detail for historical-cost position and balance of payments flows, 1991. *Survey of Current Business* 72, no. 8 (August): 87–115.

1992c. *Foreign direct investment in the United States: Operations of U.S. affiliates of foreign companies, revised 1989 estimates*. Washington, D.C.: Bureau of Economic Analysis, August.

1992d. Gross product of U.S. affiliates of foreign direct investors, 1987–90. *Survey of Current Business* 72, no. 11 (November): 47–54.

1992e. U.S. direct investment abroad: Detail for historical-cost position and balance of payments flows, 1991. *Survey of Current Business* 72, no. 8 (August): 116–44.

Wilkins, Mira. 1989. *The history of foreign investment in the United States to 1914*. Cambridge, Mass.: Harvard University Press.

Discussion Summary

Raymond Vernon led off the discussion by agreeing with *Robert Lipsey* that exchange rate movements might offer an important explanation of at least some of the FDI patterns. In addition, he feels that FDI may influence the impact of exchange rate movements on other economic variables such as exports: he conjectures that the *J*-curve phenomenon might be less pronounced in markets characterized by substantial FDI, since firms can adjust the trade between their own affiliates more easily and quickly than unaffiliated trading patterns could be changed.

Vernon offered three reactions to the low reported profit rates of foreign direct investors in the United States. First, he noted that firms may undertake FDI to attenuate certain other business risks; firms that do FDI for this reason may do so—wisely—even though the expected rate of return is low. Second, and similarly, foreign firms may undertake FDI in the United States to strengthen their competitive positions vis-à-vis other multinationals (including U.S. multinationals); such investment might make sense even though its measured U.S. profitability is low. Third, Vernon observed that measures of FDI profitability (and, for that matter, the stock of FDI capital) are inherently arbitrary and noisy; consequently, it might be a mistake to focus too much attention on the apparently low profit rates of FDI in the United States.

Robert Lipsey argued that the data, and the theories, that underlie profitability calculations for FDI subject the statistics to large standard errors and make them difficult to interpret. In addition, Lipsey emphasized that there is an important distinction between *mature* FDI, which is largely finance out of retained earnings, and *immature* FDI, which cannot be so financed (because FDI is frequently unprofitable in the early years).

G. Peter Wilson noted that the low profitability of FDI in the United States in the 1980s is probably too dramatic to represent tax avoidance exclusively.

Robert Z. Lawrence recommended that the trade flow equations be reestimated using real, rather than nominal, exchange rates. He observed that the estimated elasticities are quite high relative to those found elsewhere in the literature.

Lawrence then suggested that there are two hypotheses consistent with the profitability figures. One is that foreigners have paid too much for their investments in the United States. A second story is that foreigners receive a benefit to their FDI in the United States that does not appear in the data (one possibility is international portfolio diversification); if this second study is correct, then FDI in the United States may represent an efficient and mutually (to Americans and foreigners) beneficial way to finance the U.S. current account deficit.

Edward Graham observed that a recent study by Grubert, Goodspeed, and Swenson examines the profitability of FDI in the United States and finds it to be low after trying to correct for several factors such as the maturity of investments. Graham then conjectured that foreigners should be expected to overpay for their acquisition of U.S. firms, since there may be complementarities between foreign firms and the U.S. firms they acquire.

Geoffrey Carliner pointed out that not enough time has elapsed to evaluate fully the profitability of FDI in the United States in the 1980s, in particular since FDI is often concentrated in growth industries that may not mature for many years to come.

James Hines insisted that the Grubert, Goodspeed, and Swenson study represents the most careful examination of FDI profitability in the United States and that it makes a compelling case that FDI was not earning normal rates of return in the 1980s. He pointed out that this contrasts sharply with the profitability of outbound foreign investments of U.S. multinationals, which was quite high in the 1980s. He cautioned, however, against attributing these profitability differentials entirely to tax-induced transfer price manipulations, since there are many possible explanations, including that foreigners made mistakes in choosing their investments in the United States.

Martin Feldstein suggested that FDI in the United States in the 1980s may have been largely oriented toward buying market share and should not be expected to be very profitable in its early years. *Deborah Swenson* said that such a conclusion is consistent with some of her empirical findings about FDI.

David Yoffie pointed out that it is difficult to measure the profitability of new investments, especially when they may offer complementarities with existing investments. *Kenneth Froot* asked whether BEA could match its data with tax reform information in order to refine its profitability calculations. *David Belli* replied that BEA was prohibited from doing so.

Edward Graham complained that BEA suppresses a considerable amount of data for confidentiality reasons and claimed that, since foreign-owned firms file 10-K reports with the SEC anyway, there was no reason for the suppressions. *David Belli* pointed out that 10-Ks contain different information than that reported by BEA.

6   Mobile Exporters: New Foreign Investors in East Asia

Louis T. Wells, Jr.

Over the past five or so years, Indonesia has experienced a boom in the amount of foreign direct investment coming into the country.[1] Between 1986 and 1990, 50 percent more foreign investment projects were approved than were approved for the twenty-year period between 1967 and 1987. From 1987 to 1990, the number of approvals tripled. But it is not only the growth in foreign investment that is striking. Equally remarkable is the fact that the majority of recent foreign investors for manufacturing do not come from the countries that are usually thought of as sources of international investment—not from Japan, which is often touted as dominating regional investment, nor from the United States or Europe. Rather, they come from other developing East Asian countries. Although substantial flows of foreign investment from other developing countries are not totally new to Indonesia, the latest wave differs from the past in the markets toward which output is aimed. Rather than designing factories to supply the Indonesian market, more than half of these foreign firms plan to export most of their output from the host country. The phenomenon, documented and examined in this essay primarily for Indonesia, is occurring elsewhere in developing Asia as well. There is some slight evidence to suggest that such investment will also have important implications for other developing countries.

This paper has several goals: first, simply to identify and report on the size of the new wave of foreign investment; second, to examine why the flows are going to the particular countries that are receiving them; third, to explain in terms of widely accepted foreign investment theory why foreign direct investment is involved at all; and fourth, to examine some of the characteristics of the investment that might make it attractive or unattractive to the host country.

---

1. Unless otherwise indicated, all data for Indonesia in this paper are for *approvals* by the BKPM, Indonesia's foreign investment authority. They exclude petroleum and the financial sector, which are not subject to the jurisdiction of BKPM.

The new investments appear to reflect shifts in comparative advantage, as Indonesia has become a more attractive site for certain kinds of manufacturing activities. Yet, it is unlikely that local firms would have quickly taken up the new opportunities. Particular foreign companies held firm-specific advantages—especially in the form of reputation with buyers in the United States and Europe—that enabled them to respond to the new opportunities in ways that were not available to local firms or to foreign investors with only capital.

6.1   Developing Asia as a Source of Foreign Investment

For at least three decades, firms from the richer developing countries of Asia have been building manufacturing affiliates abroad. Already in 1963 and 1964, fifteen Hong Kong textile firms were establishing plants in Singapore. In the 1960s, Hong Kong firms built similar plants in Macao, Thailand, and the Philippines and eventually as far away as in Mauritius (Wells 1983, 74). However, those investors, were, in the main, different from the *mobile exporters* that have recently emerged in East Asia.

In Indonesia, foreign direct investment (FDI) from other Asian countries was already important by 1970. Although Japan accounted for a little more than half of the equity in foreign-owned manufacturing investment arriving in the period 1967 to 1977, other Asian countries accounted for a respectable 18 percent, more than either European or U.S. investors (Halverson 1991 [original source: Hill 1988]). The proportion from other developing countries declined substantially—to 6 percent—during the 1977–85 period, as Japanese investment dominated. But recent years have seen a sharp rebound as new types of investors from other Asian developing countries have increased their share of foreign investment flows into Indonesia.

The dramatic increase in the importance of flows from other developing countries is evident in recent data. In the period from January 1990 through July 1991, firms from East Asian developing countries accounted for 56 percent of the projects approved by BKPM, the Indonesian foreign investment authority (by value, a little more than half). When manufacturing alone is considered, the East Asian developing countries accounted for 65 percent of all such investment. Close to three-quarters of these East Asian firms were from Taiwan and Korea (see tables 6.1 and 6.2). Although Japanese firms are widely thought to dominate foreign investment in Southeast Asia, the developing East Asian countries in fact invested more than three and a half times what Japanese enterprises put into Indonesia.

The dominance of investment from Taiwan and Korea in the total of developing-country investors is also a recent phenomenon. For the 1967 to 1981 period, Korean and Taiwanese investment was overwhelmed by investment from Hong Kong. During that period, Hong Kong accounted for 12.6 percent of approved investment, Taiwan and Korea only 3.2 and 1.3 percent,

Table 6.1   **All Foreign Investment in Indonesia: Numbers of Projects and Total Investment, January 1, 1990–July 31, 1991**

Home Country	Number of Projects	Value of Total Investment (U.S.$ thousands)
East Asian developing countries	365	$5,754,961
Hong Kong	55	909,186
Taiwan	127	809,297
Korea	118	2,488,939
Singapore	59	1,507,159
Malaysia	6	25,300
Japan	122	1,597,123
United States	18	325,281
Other industrialized	74	1,802,570
Other	23	380,963
NA*	51	1,876,398
Total	653	11,412,015

Source: Calculated from BKPM data on approvals.
*Mixed nationalities, etc.

Table 6.2   **Foreign Manufacturing Investment in Indonesia: Number of Projects and Total Investment, January 1, 1990–July 31, 1991 (ISIC 3000s)**

Home Country	Number of Projects	Value of Total Investment* (U.S.$ thousands)
East Asian developing countries	315	$4,277,582
Hong Kong	39	693,971
Taiwan	120	780,872
Korea	107	2,176,970
Singapore	43	601,269
Malaysia	6	17,400
Japan	77	1,132,198
United States	12	132,054
Other industrialized	34	830,927
Other	13	227,369
NA†	34	881,601
	485	7,481,731

Source: Calculated from BKPM data on approvals.
*Includes domestic and foreign equity and borrowing.
†Mixed nationalities, etc.

respectively (Halverson 1991, 91 [from Thee 1984]).[2] In the recent period, a new trend has become clear: Taiwan and especially Korea have been taking over as the important sources of foreign investment in Indonesia.

In sum, the Indonesian experience shows a growth in investment from other developing Asian countries in recent years, both in absolute terms and in share of total foreign investment. More of that investment comes from Korea and Taiwan than in the past. Moreover, as the next section will show, the kind of investment that dominates has also changed; the new investors are coming for reasons that differ from those that were most common in the past.

6.1.1 Motivations for Investment

Round One

The earliest Third World manufacturing investors in the Southeast Asian region probably were firms driven abroad by export quotas at home. Thus, the fifteen Hong Kong textile plants in Singapore were producing there for markets in the industrialized countries because access to those markets from Hong Kong facilities had been restricted by quotas. Similarly, Hong Kong textile firms and firms from India eventually went as far as Mauritius to gain favored access to the European market, available to products from that country since it was an ACP nation.[3] Initially, such investments were in textiles, the first major labor-intensive industry to fall under voluntary export restrictions; later investors followed a similar pattern for other products that came under quotas, such as shoes. In some ways, these earlier foreign investors have a great deal in common with the mobile exporters that are now investing in Indonesia and elsewhere in developing Asia. Both groups went abroad to serve third markets—primarily in Europe and North America—that they had been serving from their home-country plants.

Strikingly, these round-one investors never reached Indonesia in any significant numbers. A dozen or so applied for approval in Indonesia in the early 1970s, but their applications were never approved. No functioning export-processing zones were available, and the government hesitated to allow special status for such investors, as it had for one U.S. electronics firm. No general duty drawback or exemption system functioned to allow components to be brought in for inclusion in exported products. Also, most or all of these early applicants were Chinese-owned firms, and ethnic sensitivities were high in Indonesia. Since the country placed little weight on manufactured exports at the time because oil was generating adequate foreign exchange, there was little

---

2. It is not clear whether the figures used are for total investment in projects that qualify as foreign investments or for the foreign equity in such projects. Unless the different nationalities use sharply different financing for their projects, the distinction is of little importance in the comparison just made.

3. ACP (Africa-Caribbean-Pacific) countries received preferred access to the European Community under the Lomé Convention.

pressure for compromise (Wells and Warren 1979, 83). This attitude was to change in the 1980s, as oil prices fell.

Although quota-driven investment has continued to expand, new production sites (e.g., Indonesia) have also fallen under quota restrictions, limiting the growth of such investment.

Round Two

These pioneer foreign investors were followed by a much larger stream of investors whose target markets were the host countries themselves. Tariffs and quotas in the poorer countries limited exports to those markets from Hong Kong, Taiwan, Korea, India, and so on. To escape those restrictions, Third World firms established plants in those markets, plants designed overwhelmingly to serve local customers. In many cases, parent firms had exported to the market before they invested. In this, they were like many of the multinationals from the industrialized countries, which had gone abroad to defend markets first captured by exporting. In other cases, market opportunities had been identified by Chinese in Indonesia and other parts of Southeast Asia and reported to relatives in Singapore, Hong Kong, or Taiwan; investments followed.

A similar round of investment occurred in Latin America, although the numbers seem to have been smaller. There, firms from Argentina, Brazil, and other industrializing Latin American countries established subsidiaries elsewhere in the region. A Brazilian firm, to cite just one example, manufactured bicycles in Bolivia and Colombia (Wells 1983). A few firms from both Asia and Latin America (especially Brazil) invested as far away as Africa.

This second wave of investment by Third World multinationals has by now been rather firmly established, documented, and described (Wells 1983; Lall 1983; Khan 1986; White, Campos, and Ondarte 1977). To a great extent, the investment was associated with small-scale, often second-hand plants; cost-minimizing technologies; and price rather than brand-name competition. There were, of course, exceptions. Inca Cola, for example, expanded abroad from Peru based on marketing skills. Until recently, in spite of the exceptions, it was the small-scale, cost-oriented investor serving local markets who accounted for most of the flow of foreign direct investment from developing countries to other developing countries.

Firms of the type just described are particularly attracted to markets that offer protection from imports. Such investors are still building plants in Southeast Asia, particularly in sectors where protection is offered. Some fifty of the recent developing Asian investors in Indonesian manufacturing indicated that they would export no more than 20 percent of their output (the number only increases to sixty if 50 percent exported is the cutoff point).[4] But trade policies

4. In fact, these figures probably overstate considerably the amount of manufacture destined ultimately for the local market. A number of the nonexporting manufacturers in fact produce for other firms that will export. For example, nonexporters include firms that make fish and shrimp food and fabrics that will be sold to other firms that export the final product.

have been reformed in a number of countries; as a result, formerly high rates of protection have given way, and such investment has received little encouragement.

Round Three: The Mobile Exporters

The majority of very recent investors are of a different type from those that dominated round two. They come to Indonesia, as did the early quota hoppers, to serve export markets that they have been serving from their home plants, rather than to serve the Indonesian market. Thus, close to half of recent foreign investment from other East Asian developing countries has been for export factories (a project is counted as being for export if 80 percent or more of its production is to be exported). And overall, more than two-thirds of all manufacturing output for all recent investors from developing countries has been destined for export. For investors from Korea, Hong Kong, and Singapore, a still larger part of the projects is aimed at the export market (see tables 6.3 and 6.4).

Unlike the first round of Third World investors, a large number of the new investors have come to Indonesia to produce products that are not subject to so-called orderly marketing arrangements or other forms of export quotas at home. Although textiles remain important and quotas play a role in investment decisions, sports shoes account for a large number of clothing projects. Managers in those plants do not claim to have invested for reasons of quotas. Beyond clothes, firms have invested to export a wide range of products: eyeglasses, speaker cabinets, furniture parts, nails, lead pipe, printed circuit boards, to name only a few.

Table 6.3   **Foreign Manufacturing Investment In Indonesia: Export-Oriented as Percentage of Total Approvals, January 1, 1990–July 31, 1991 (ISIC 3000s)**

	Number of Projects		Percentage
Home Country	Export-Oriented*	Total	
East Asian developing countries	146	315	46%
Hong Kong	25	39	64
Taiwan	21	120	18
Korea	69	107	64
Singapore	30	43	70
Malaysia	1	6	17
Japan	49	77	64
Other developed countries (including U.S.)	14	46	30
	209	438	48

Source: Calculated from BKPM data on approvals.

*Eighty percent or more of production to be exported.

Table 6.4   **Foreign Manufacturing Investment In Indonesia: Exports as a
Fraction of Production, January 1, 1990–July 31, 1991 (ISIC 3000s)**

Home Country	Export/Production (average for all projects)
East Asian developing countries	.71
Japan	.71
Other developed countries (including U.S.)	.53

Source: Calculated from BKPM data on approvals.

The bulk of the exports of these plants is to be sold in North America and
Europe. But other markets are also targeted. A number of plants manufacture
low-cost electronics and other products for Middle Eastern and African markets, for example.[5]

The mobile exporters indicate that they have sought new manufacturing sites
primarily to maintain low costs, rather than to escape quota restrictions. The
need to go abroad for lower costs has arisen for several reasons:

First, firms from Korea and Taiwan have been hit with currency revaluations,
raising the value of their home currencies against the currencies of their major
export markets. At the same time, the Indonesian rupiah has devalued against
the dollar and, of course, more sharply against the yen and European currencies. The relative decline in the value of the rupiah has not been offset by
inflation differentials.

Second, firms in Korea that have been manufacturing simple products claim
that they have difficulty hiring workers at home, even at the prevailing rates.
When industrialization makes other options available, workers are simply not
attracted to the repetitive, low-prestige assembly plants that make shoes and
other simple products. (These claims echo earlier claims of Taiwan pineapple
exporters that they could not hire workers even at premiums above prevailing
wages in Taiwan; the firms responded like today's manufacturers and developed plantations in Southeast Asia.)

Third, as manufacturers in Korea and Taiwan were hit by increasing costs
and labor shortages, those countries also lost special treatment for their exports
under the Generalized System of Preferences (GSP) in major industrialized
markets. Shipments of a wide range of goods from Korea and Taiwan, exempt
in the past, became subject to tariffs in the United States. In contrast, the industrialized countries still offered most Southeast Asian countries GSP treatment
in the early 1990s.

The cost drives were accompanied by liberalization of government rules in
Korea and Taiwan on outgoing capital movements. What had required cumber-
some approvals or illegal transactions in the past became much easier.

5. Information gathered in informal interviews.

As a result of all these changes, the Southeast Asian countries have become increasingly attractive manufacturing sites for firms from Korea and Taiwan that face severe price competition.

While firms from Korea and Taiwan have encountered rising costs from unfavorable movements in exchange rates, shortages of labor, and increased tariffs, Hong Kong manufacturers have similarly been confronted with wage increases but also with prospects of a mainland takeover in 1997. Consequently, Hong Kong manufacturers, unrestricted by capital controls, have likewise sought overseas manufacturing sites, for both cost and security reasons.

The current wave of investors, not surprisingly, has its antecedents. Costs mattered to some of the earlier investors. Many of the export-oriented, first-round investors from East Asia that had reached the Philippines and Mauritius were influenced in their site selection by the need for lower costs; quotas were not the only driving force. In a survey as early as 1979, managers of foreign plants in Mauritius and the Philippines indicated that low-cost labor was an important motivation for foreign investment (Busjeet 1980). Yet quotas seem to have been the dominant drive behind foreign investment for the exporters. For the majority of foreign investors from developing countries, it was local markets that counted; for these investors, labor and other production costs mattered much less than escape from the tariffs and quotas that limited opportunities to serve the local market from home sites.

6.1.2   Where to Invest

So far, the bulk of investment by mobile exporters from East Asian firms seems to have been directed toward Thailand and Indonesia, although reliable figures are not available for the entire region. These countries may have been chosen by investors largely by default. They meet the necessary condition of having low-cost labor, but so do other countries in the region, such as China, the Philippines, and Vietnam. Each of the alternatives, however, poses problems for would-be investors. The Philippines is viewed as being politically unstable. Vietnam is not yet an easy place for foreign firms to do business. China has attracted some such investment, but few investors want to bet their entire portfolio on China. Singapore and Malaysia are possible sites, but labor there is too expensive for investors that do not require the higher skills available in those countries. With Thailand and Indonesia as the attractive sites for low-wage manufacture, the early round-three investors seem to have preferred Thailand. As Bangkok grew more "crowded" with investors, Indonesia increased in popularity.[6]

Other preferences have also affected locational decisions. Taiwanese firms seem to have a preference for Thailand, while Korean investors appear particularly likely to go to Indonesia (see table 6.5). One can only hypothesize the reasons. The Chinese community in Thailand accounts for a larger part of the

---

6. Informal interviews with investors.

population and seems better integrated into the local community than do the Chinese groups in Indonesia; consequently, Chinese managers from Taiwan may feel more comfortable in Thailand. The exception seems to be Singapore investors. Though Chinese, many are in Indonesia. But close to 45 percent of the recent ones have located on Batam Island, a special enclave off the coast of Singapore, developed to attract Singapore firms. Of the rest, a large number are trading or consulting firms, real estate investors (hotels, largely), and manufacturers for the local market. For these firms, location in Indonesia is essential if the local market is to be served. Unlike the Chinese, the Koreans do not have large communities in either place. The lower costs of Indonesian labor may have proved more attractive to them, given no other reasons to prefer one country over the other.

Foreign investments by firms from East Asian developing countries have not been limited to Southeast Asia. Round-one investors went as far as Mauritius, as noted earlier. Korean and Hong Kong exporters were established in Sri Lanka, primarily for low-end textiles. Round-two investors, oriented toward domestic markets, were spread thinly across Africa by the mid-1980s.

Mobile investors may be driven farther afield for reasons beyond labor costs. Although the costs of labor and its availability in Costa Rica and Colombia may be somewhat more attractive than in Korea and Taiwan, the differences cannot be overwhelming, especially in comparison to the opportunities in Southeast Asia. Yet East African firms have invested in both countries. Investments by East Asian firms in Latin America are probably aimed more at reducing risks from trade barriers than at minimizing costs. These investments probably reflect managers' growing concerns with the prospects of Western Hemisphere trade preferences, from which Asian production sites would be

Table 6.5   **Foreign Investment by Country of Origin (percentage by value)**

Home Country	Host Country			
	Indonesia		Thailand	
	1/1990–7/1991	1989	1990	1991
East Asia	50.6%	28.1%	44.6%	25.6%
Hong Kong	8.0	6.0	26.3	6.7
Taiwan	7.1	15.1	10.2	13.2
Korea	21.9	2.6	3.0	1.2
Singapore	13.3	4.0	4.5	2.0
Malaysia	0.2	0.3	0.7	2.5
Japan	14.1	38.1	27.0	35.1
United States	2.9	3.9	6.4	14.1
Other	32.4	29.9	22.0	25.2
Total	100.0	100.0	100.0	100.0

Source: Provided by Peter A. Petri, from approvals data by the BKPM in Indonesia and the BOI in Thailand.

excluded. Like the Japanese, mobile exporters will probably show increasing interest in Mexico, as talks on a North American free trade area show progress.

Some African sites offer favorable access to European Community markets. Currently, most African countries face severe disadvantages, beyond distance, in attracting mobile exporters. Macroeconomic policies, particularly overvalued exchange rates and controls on profit remittances, are major hindrances to such investment. Yet the scattered East Asian investors producing for local African markets suggest that mobile exporters might also be attracted if policies are reformed.

Whatever the motivations for the scattered investments outside the region, so far the flows remain largely within-region. Firms from East Asian developing countries have invested first and foremost in countries within Southeast Asia in their search for low-cost and available labor.

6.2 Mobile Exporters and the Theory of Foreign Direct Investment

Two concepts are rather widely held among researchers concerned with foreign direct investment: (1) to survive abroad, a firm needs some kind of advantage over local competitors, and (2) a firm must have some reason to internalize that advantage through ownership rather than contracting with another firm.

In the case of the mobile exporters that are the focus of this study, the advantage brought by the firm is quite clearly market access. The firms have a track record of meeting the standards and schedules of foreign buyers. Most important, probably, is the management skill of the firm and the reputation built up with buyers for producing the required quality according to the promised delivery schedule. To some extent, the reputation might derive from technological skills. Whatever the source of the reputation on the part of suppliers, buyers are hesitant to shift large purchases to suppliers unknown to them.

The advantages accruing to investors from their buyer contacts are reinforced by the fact that some buyers have already established offices in the supplying countries—particularly in Korea and Taiwan. Korean and Taiwanese firms have built close relationships with those offices, and they can use those links even when they locate plants in Southeast Asia.

In theory, at least, the East Asian suppliers have an alternative to foreign direct investment when they seek lower-cost sites. A Korean or Taiwanese firm could simply contract with Southeast Asian plants to supply products that the firm then would sell to buyers it knows. But one can easily see why such arrangements would be unattractive to many exporting firms. Most important, the costs of a failure on the part of the contractee would be born by the parent enterprise, in the form of lost reputation with buyers. The negative impact may extend beyond the sales directly involved and could harm future sales even by the parent firm. A carefully built reputation can be at risk.

Theory might suggest contracts that would penalize foreign contractees severely for such failures. Yet it would be difficult to draw up such contracts and enforce them so that the Korean or Taiwanese firm would be adequately compensated for its total losses should the contractee fail to meet quality standards. Better, it would seem, to keep the transaction in-house, given the high risks to the parent firm if the contractee fails to deliver as required. Internalization seems the safer approach.

In sum, both conditions that usually characterize foreign direct investment hold: advantages in the hands of foreign firms and reasons for internalizing the transactions.

Foreign investors' advantages do not always last. Theories of foreign direct investment consider the concept of the "obsolescing bargain" (Vernon 1971, chap. 2). According to this concept, the strengths that the foreign investor has at the outset are often eroded with time. Where technology is the competitive advantage, local firms may eventually master the know-how, for example, leaving the foreign firm with no advantage unless it innovates and moves on to something new. With governments favoring local firms and with the inevitably higher costs that foreign management imposes, foreign investors are eventually driven out as their advantages erode.

There is some evidence that the advantages of mobile exporters can erode rather quickly. It seems that, at least in the case of athletic shoes in Indonesia, foreign buyers soon follow the subsidiaries and set up buying offices in the countries where new plants are located. The presence of enough foreign-owned suppliers has brought in the buyers. Thus, Nike, Adidas, and Reebok have all established offices in Indonesia. As a result, the "distance" between foreign buyer and prospective Indonesian suppliers declines. Before the arrival of the foreign firms, buyers rarely visited Indonesia; thus, it was difficult for local firms to establish the contacts that might lead to exports. Once buying offices have been established in the country, local firms approach the foreign buyers and offer to match the product quality and schedules of the Korean and Taiwan investors, at lower prices. The costs to the buyers of examining the prospective suppliers' factories and sample output, and experimenting on a small scale with a few orders, are not high once the buyers have established local offices. Domestic firms may thus erode the advantages with which foreign firms entered. This seems already to have happened in Mauritius, where Hong Kong textile firms established facilities some years ago and local firms have emerged as major competitors.

The product cycle models of international trade and investment also offer some understanding of the mobile exporters (Vernon 1966). Although the theory has become increasingly less useful in explaining trade and investment among the industrialized countries as their markets have converged and as multinational firms have established facilities in a number of countries, the theory still has some validity in explaining investment flows among countries with quite different income levels. Foreign investment moves, according to the theory, down the ladder of development as products mature. Thus, movement of investments from the richer developing countries of East Asia into the poorer countries of the region is consistent with the theory.

6.3   Benefits to the Host Country

In a simple world, with competition, market prices of resources that reflect shadow prices, no overwhelming scale economies, and no significant externalities, foreign investment that is profitable to the firm would be beneficial to the host country. But that simple world does not describe reality in Southeast Asia. Past studies have shown that import substitution policies, for example, lead to significant numbers of foreign investment projects that can be economically harmful to the host country (Encarnation and Wells 1986).

Indonesia has been dismantling the import barriers that were largely responsible for the discrepancy between private and economic returns. Yet it is widely believed that the market prices of labor do not reflect shadow prices. Unemployment remains high; wage levels seem to be higher than opportunity costs.

With large oil exports (accounting for some two-thirds of all export earnings when oil prices were high), Indonesia's exchange rate long remained too high to encourage labor-intensive manufactured exports. Oil and gas production, of course, generated little employment directly. Oil revenues (at times, about two-thirds of government revenue) accrued largely to the government. The focus of the government in investing these revenues was largely on "megaprojects" (capital-intensive plants such as steel, petrochemicals, and fertilizers), none of which generated many employment opportunities beyond the construction stage. Although Indonesia managed to avoid the excesses of Nigeria and Venezuela, its rapidly growing young population was finding few opportunities for work.

With current exchange rates, fewer distortions remain in the Indonesian economy. Yet experience in the past has made officials wary of reliance on oil or a few other raw materials for the bulk of foreign exchange earnings. Thus, investments that enable the country to diversify its exports are particularly valued. Due to the benefits of diversification, the shadow price of foreign exchange earned from nontraditional exports may be considered to be higher than the market price of such foreign exchange.

Moreover, it is increasingly popular in developing countries to look to foreign investment to provide capital, since other sources (e.g., foreign bank loans) have become scarce. In Indonesia, earnings from oil accrued to the government and were invested in industry. With lower oil revenues, the government has sought other sources of capital. Foreign investment offers an alternative.

6.3.1   Capital and Exports

In the case of Indonesia, the total amount of capital brought to the country by the new wave of investors is not huge, at least compared to total capital investment in the country. Yet the contribution of these firms to the recent rapid growth of nontraditional exports has been very important. But the net exports are, at least at the outset, less than any gross figures from such investors would suggest. After paying for imported components, dividends and interest, and expatriate management, the net foreign exchange earnings may not be large. With little local purchase of inputs, net foreign exchange earnings consist primarily of wages paid to Indonesian workers and taxes paid to the Indonesian government. Taxes may be quite small, even though Indonesia does not grant tax holidays. Export-processing investments offer possibilities for evading taxes by setting transfer prices such that profits are recorded largely elsewhere (Indonesia's corporate income tax rate is relatively low, at 35 percent; yet there may still be reasons for reporting profits in other jurisdictions. Hong Kong's rate is still lower, for example.)

One can estimate some orders of magnitude, at least for the labor payments. If all the export firms from East Asian developing countries that were approved in 1990 and the first half of 1991 actually commence production and have the work force indicated in their applications, some 87,000 Indonesians will be employed (the number would be much larger if firms were included that were exporting less than 80 percent of their output). At a wage rate of, say, $800 per year per worker, the wage bill would be roughly $70 million.

Although the direct contribution may be smaller than it first appears, such investment may be particularly welcome at a time when Japanese investment in the region is slowing.

6.3.2   Spillover as Catalyst

The capital associated with the investment and the direct exports may not be the most significant gains from the mobile exporters. From the point of view of the host country, local firms' access to the marketing channels from the industrialized countries may be the most important advantage offered. There is mounting evidence to suggest the important role that foreign firms in general play as catalysts for the development of local exporters (Rhee and Belot 1989). As described earlier, the mobile exporters often bring with them their buyers from the countries in which their products are sold. There is already a considerable amount of anecdotal evidence that Indonesian firms are taking advantage of access to these buyers to export directly and to sell components to foreign investors for inclusion in exports. Thus, the export diversification offered directly by the mobile exporters themselves may dramatically understate the actual contribution of these firms.

6.3.3   Labor Intensity

Although the total amount of capital brought by mobile exporters may be small, the number of jobs might be disproportionally large. In fact, a study of investors from other developing countries that invested in Indonesia between 1967 and 1975 shows that plants of investors from developing countries were considerably more labor intensive than those of their competitors from other countries. The capital-labor ratios for the advanced-country firms were about twice those of the developing-country investors. Japanese investors were even more capital intensive than other advanced-country firms (Wells and Warren 1979, 74). By the recent period (1990–91), those figures had changed significantly, even reversing themselves in some cases. Although the relatively few manufacturing firms from other industrialized countries were indeed much more capital intensive than the East Asian investors, the manufacturing investors from other developing countries were, by the recent period, twice as capital intensive as investors from Japan—the opposite of the old pattern (see table 6.6). But when only the exporting firms are compared, the differences between the developing-country firms and the Japanese investors disappear almost entirely.

How can one explain the differences and the changes? The early round of Japanese investors seems to have concentrated in capital-intensive protected industries (e.g., automobiles), while early developing-country investors invested in simpler, less capital-intensive activities, often using technologies especially suited to small scale. This adapted technology was labor intensive (Wells 1983). By the 1990s, Indonesia was on the road to a more liberal trade policy. As protection declined, the opportunities for investment in capital-intensive industries, behind import restrictions, were disappearing; the attractive ones had been made. The earlier yen revaluations seem to have led to more interest on the part of the Japanese in exporting from Indonesia. But Japanese investors appear to have made the shift toward more labor-intensive activities whether they were producing for the local market or for the export market. A small number of investors from other developed countries have not yet adjusted to the new policies. Like the second-round investors, they were building plants to secure what remained of a protected market. Similarly, European and U.S. investors were still responding to the old protected market with capital-intensive plants. Moreover, even when they were exporting, the plants of these investors tended to be capital intensive.

In the earlier period, there were other differences between developing-country investors and firms from the industrialized countries; the differences seem to have narrowed. For example, firms from developing countries em-

Table 6.6   **Foreign Manufacturing Investment In Indonesia: Capital Intensity, January 1, 1990–July 31, 1991 (ISIC 3000s)**

| | Investment per Indonesian Worker (U.S.$) | |
Home Country	All	Export Oriented*
East Asian developing countries	$ 33,088	$19,406
Japan	16,121	16,121
Other developed countries	122,385	91,408

Source: Calculated from BKPM data on approvals.

*Eighty percent or more of production to be exported.

Table 6.7   **Foreign Manufacturing Investment In Indonesia: Use of Expatriates,**
                   January 1, 1990–July 31, 1991 (ISIC 3000s)

	Indonesian Workers per Expatriate	
Home Country	All	Export Oriented
East Asian developing countries	31	35
All	30	35

Source: Calculated from BKPM data for approvals.

ployed more expatriates in the earlier period. Presumably, Taiwanese and Korean engineers and managers, for instance, were sufficiently inexpensive that there was little need to replace them with Indonesians. But by the early 1990s, the number of Indonesian employees per expatriate differed hardly at all between firms from the two kinds of countries; this was true whether all manufacturing firms were examined or only those oriented toward exports (see table 6.7). The increasing expenses of foreign managers and engineers, even from Korea and Taiwan, may partially explain this convergence.

Similarly, investments by firms from other developing countries in the early period were significantly smaller than those from the industrialized nations. But by the early 1990s, the differences were hardly noticeable. The average investment in a firm owned by an East Asian developing country was $15.8 million, the average for all investors $17.5 million.

Of course, high labor-capital ratios provide a measure of benefits that is of limited value in assessing the worth of foreign investment. Since the foreign capital involved may not be a scarce resource that would be available for other uses should the particular projects in question not materialize, more relevant is the labor utilized per unit of Indonesian capital employed or per unit of other scarce resources utilized. In terms of Indonesian capital, the labor-capital ratios are particularly high, since ownership of the export projects is predominantly foreign (more than 70 percent). Unfortunately, adequate data are not available to calculate employment per unit of total Indonesian resources.[7]

If, however, as seems to be the case, Indonesia and many other developing countries have a limited tolerance for foreign capital, then the number of jobs provided per unit of foreign capital may itself have some relevance.

The mobile exporters approved by Indonesia in the eighteen-month period under study would provide close to 90,000 direct jobs, not a number to be sneezed at. The actual number of jobs associated with exports by the foreign

7. Prior to the reforms in the mid-1980s, foreign investors would have been required to provide projections that allowed rough calculations of such figures. The lengthy questionnaire designed to allow analysts to do sophisticated economic cost-benefit calculations was dropped in an effort to make Indonesia a more attractive place for investment and in recognition of the fact that, in actuality, no one made the calculations that would have used the data requested.

manufacturers is considerably more: a number of the firms plan to export less than 80 percent of their output but still significant amounts; many firms that do not show their output being exported supply inputs to the mobile exporters; and then there are the jobs created indirectly.

In sum, the contributions to employment are likely to be significant. Given the low shadow price of labor, compared to market prices, the value to the host country of investment by mobile exporters may be greater than the value to the investors themselves would suggest.

6.3.4   Costs

Indonesia, and to some extent all the countries of Southeast Asia, face problems with ethnic diversity, especially the Chinese. Since a considerable number of the mobile exporters are Chinese from Taiwan and Hong Kong, the flows feed into these ethnic sensitivities. Yet the growing importance of Korean investment suggests that increasing diversity of sources may defuse some of the potential costs that seem in the past to have been associated with Third World investors in Southeast Asia.

In addition, the growth in manufactured exports associated with these investors, as attractive as it is for other reasons, increases the dependence of the host country on a few foreign markets. In Indonesia, this dependence has manifested itself in bilateral negotiations, particularly with the United States. Wary of the costs to its new success in exporting manufactured goods, for example, Indonesia caved in quickly to U.S. insistence on new intellectual property laws when it was confronted with threats to those exports. With the threat to its GSP status, and other penalties authorized under U.S. trade law (particularly under the so-called Super 301 provision), as well as European protectionist policies, Indonesia's growing exports of manufactured goods increasingly are hostage to the desires of market countries.

Although the gains associated with the new investments probably outweigh the costs, those costs should not be forgotten.

6.4   Investment Policies to Attract Mobile Exporters

From the oil boom of the early 1970s until very recently, Indonesia made little effort to attract foreign investors. Oil provided foreign exchange and capital, and it provided opportunities to borrow from international banks. As a result, in spite of interest in foreign direct investment between 1965 and 1973, other concerns took hold: for example, promotion of non-Chinese investment and the desire of some politicians and bureaucrats to be able to exercise control over the economy. Interest in encouraging foreign investment began to grow again after the collapse of oil prices in the 1980s. But that interest did not manifest itself in the usual ways—through tax holidays, investment promotion abroad, and so on.

Unlike its neighbors, Indonesia has since 1985 offered no tax holidays to foreign (or other) investors. Prior to 1985, the country did offer a complex set of tax holidays, the length of which depended on the location of the facility in Indonesia, its size (larger ones received more holidays), its market orientation, and so on. The entire system of tax holidays was abolished with the tax reform of the mid-1980s, which also lowered the corporate income tax rate.

The large inflows of foreign investment in recent years clearly indicate that tax incentives are not necessary for a developing country to attract foreign investment. Immediately following the elimination of tax holidays, investment approvals did drop off. But hindsight has revealed that the sudden decline resulted from investors applying in the previous year to gain the tax holidays *and* the lower rates, predating of approvals by the BKPM, and the impact of a major recession in the country. Foreign investment boomed as the economy picked up and as other changes were made that were more important to foreign investors.[8] The new, lower tax rate had offset the elimination of tax holidays.[9]

At the same time, Indonesia began to deal with its reputation for having a tedious bureaucracy. In the 1980s, some improvements were made; BKPM, which had to approve all incoming investment, simplified its application forms and promised quicker decisions. In the past, decisions had often taken one or two years. Reform reduced the decision time to a few months at most. In the reform, an effort was made to improve the predictability of the process. The government shifted from a "positive list," a rather unclear list of sectors in which foreign investment would be allowed, to a "negative list," a short and rather clear list of sectors in which foreign investment would not be allowed. Thus, a would-be investor could tell with a greater degree of certainty whether a proposal would be accepted or not. For small firms in particular, the increased certainty was attractive.

Another reform was especially important for the mobile exporters—in fact, probably an essential condition for the growth in such investment. In the past, Indonesia had struggled unsuccessfully with efforts to create export-processing zones. In general, nothing materialized; if it did, it was rife with corruption. Having decided that successful export-processing zones could not be created quickly, the government created an organization in the Ministry of Finance that was charged with providing duty exemptions and duty drawbacks for exporters. No longer would an exporter have to locate in an export-processing zone to qualify for duty-free imports.[10] If certain conditions were met, then the exporter could locate anywhere in the country without having to pay duty on imports required for exports. The procedures were designed

8. For research on the role of tax incentives in attracting foreign investment, see Guisinger et al. (1985). For an interpretation of the results of that study, see Wells (1986).

9. A careful study was done to compare the internal rate of return for foreign investment projects under the old, higher tax rate with tax holidays and various proposed new, lower rates without tax holidays. The rate chosen was one that meant little impact on the discounted rate of return on foreign investment, with the elimination of tax holidays.

10. In fact, special arrangements had existed earlier for certain exporters, primarily semiconductor firms.

to protect the national interest, assuring that duty-free imports did not leak into the country, but also to reduce the opportunities for corruption and to overcome the fears on the part of managers that usually accompanied drawback schemes: that the ministry of finance would be, at best, slow in rebating duties paid. The program proved extremely popular with export-oriented firms.

In addition, Indonesia created an investment area on Batam Island, just off Singapore, where export firms were exempt from Indonesian ownership requirements and other regulations. The site was designed to attract firms that found Singapore's labor costs too high but had need for resources located in Singapore, such as an attractive environment for managers to live in and financial facilities. But only a small number of the investors approved by Indonesia in 1990–91 were to build their plants on Batam Island. Mobile exporters were coming to Indonesia anyway.

Most important to the inflow were the resources that Indonesia had. Its large pool of inexpensive labor was, of course, the major attraction. Further, that pool was not limited to the capital city, as seemed to be the case in Thailand. Other urban areas, particularly Surabaya, offered industrial infrastructure and a large pool of labor should Jakarta's infrastructure become overburdened. Equally important, Indonesia imposed no currency controls. Firms could transfer profits abroad freely, and they could purchase foreign exchange for imports without constraint.

Even with the increased interest in foreign investment and the more attractive policies, Indonesia gave little more than lip service to foreign investment promotion. Investment promotion has been limited almost entirely to ineffective investment missions and seminars (Wells and Wint 1990). Although Indonesia once had a few offices abroad for the promotion of foreign investment, those have been closed. In 1991, there were plans to open an office in Brussels, but no plans existed to open offices in East Asian developing countries, where opportunities for promotion appeared most promising.

Indonesia was attracting large inflows of foreign investment without promotion. Expenditures on effective promotion could well be justified, given that employment and diversification of exports were more valuable to the economy than market prices would indicate. Yet Indonesia's resources and its policies seem to have been sufficiently attractive to mobile exporters, who sought stable, low-cost countries as export bases. In 1992, it appeared that the inflow of such investment was at a level close to the maximum that would be politically acceptable.

Some countries outside Southeast Asia have recognized the new wave of investors. For them, promotion will probably be essential if mobile exporters are to be attracted. Costa Rica, with one of the most effective promotion organizations in the developing world, has begun to recruit investors from Korea. Colombia, just starting its investment promotion efforts, has similarly recognized the prospects of bringing East Asian exporters to Latin America.

Costa Rica's success in attracting investors through promotion efforts has depended on personal selling, largely in the United States. Those efforts may be more difficult when the investors are to be attracted from East Asia: fewer promotion managers are likely to speak local languages; detailed business information is less easily come by; even official data provide little accurate information on which industries are already investing abroad. Approaches to promotion that work well in the United States will have to be adapted to work in East Asia. Yet, if such countries place large value on employment and diversification of exports, expenditures on effective promotion are justified.

References

Busjeet, Vinod. 1980. Foreign investors from less-developed countries. Unpublished doctoral dissertation. Harvard Business School.

Encarnation, Dennis, and Louis T. Wells, Jr. 1986. Evaluating foreign investment. In *Investing in development: New roles for private capital,* ed. Theodore M. Moran, 61–86. Washington, D.C.: Overseas Development Council.

Guisinger, S., and associates. 1985. *Investment incentives and performance requirements.* New York: Praeger.

Halverson, Karen. 1991. Foreign direct investment in Indonesia: A comparison of industrialized and developing country investors. *Law and Policy in International Business* 22 (1): 75–106.

Hill, Hal. 1988. *Foreign investment and industrialization in Indonesia.* Singapore: Oxford University Press.

Khan, Kushi, ed. 1986. *Multinationals of the South.* London: Francis Pinter.

Lall, Sanjaya. 1983. *The new multinationals.* Chichester, U.K.: John Wiley and Sons.

Rhee, Yung Whee, and Therese Belot. 1989. *Export catalysts in low-income countries: Preliminary findings from a review of export success stories in eleven countries,* World Bank Industry and Energy Department Industry Series Paper no. 5, PPR. Washington, D.C.: World Bank, November.

Thee, Kian Wie. 1984. Japanese direct investment in Indonesian manufacturing. *Bulletin of Indonesian Economic Studies* 20 (August): 190–207.

Vernon, Raymond. 1966. International investment and international trade in the product cycle. *Quarterly Journal of Economics* 80 (May): 58–60.

———. 1971. *Sovereignty at bay.* New York: Basic Books.

Wells, Louis T., Jr. 1983. *Third World multinationals: The rise of foreign investment from developing countries.* Cambridge, Mass.: MIT Press.

———. 1986. Investment incentives: An unnecessary debate. *CTC Reporter,* no. 22 (Autumn): 58–60.

Wells, Louis T., Jr., and V'Ella Warren. 1979. Developing country investors in Indonesia. *Bulletin of Indonesian Economic Studies* 15, no. 1 (March): 69–84.

Wells, Louis T., Jr., and Alvin Wint. 1990. *Marketing a country.* FIAS Occasional Paper no. 1. Washington, D.C.: Foreign Investment Advisory Service.

White, Eduardo, Jaime Campos, and Guillermo Ondarte. 1977. *Las empresas conjuntos Latinoamericanas.* Buenos Aires: Instituto para la Integracion de America Latina.

Comment   Peter A. Petri

Louis T. Wells's paper provides a timely and fascinating analysis of the recent wave of East Asian developing countries' foreign investment in each other. The Indonesian numbers cited are especially dramatic, but as table 6C.1 shows, the phenomenon has regionwide significance. Of foreign direct investments in East Asian developing countries, 39 percent have recently originated in the East Asian newly industrialized countries (NICs) and developing countries— nearly as much as came from Japan and the United States combined. Intriguing questions arise: Are these flows likely to be sustained? What theoretical mechanisms drive them? What accounts for their sharp surge in the late 1980s? What is their significance from empirical and theoretical perspectives?

Although the statistics are impressive, some words of caution are in order. The data analyzed in the paper and in table 6.1 deal with short time periods. In addition, Wells's discussion is largely based on data that tend to highlight rapid change. The value of *foreign projects approved* can show large year-to-year swings that may not show up with the same frequency or amplitude in actual *foreign investment flows.*

There are three reasons for this. First, since project approvals are akin to an option, they do not always result in investment flows. In volatile economic circumstances, such as the exchange rate movements of the mid-1980s, many firms become interested in identifying foreign production opportunities but then drop their foreign projects or wait to implement them until conditions are clearly favorable. Second, since the actual investments associated with a proj-

Table 6C.1   **Shares of Inward Foreign Direct Investment, Flow Data (percentage)**

Host Country	Year	East Asian Developing	Japan	United States	Other
		Investing Country			
NICs					
Hong Kong	1989	14.9%	29.9%	31.4%	23.8%
Korea	1988	3.9	52.8	28.1	15.2
Singapore	1989	5.4	30.7	33.2	30.6
Taiwan	1988	18.0	37.6	13.6	30.8
Average		10.6	37.8	26.6	25.1
Developing					
China	1988	69.8	16.1	7.4	6.7
Indonesia	1990	31.4	25.6	1.8	41.2
Malaysia	1990	54.6	23.9	3.2	18.3
Philippines	1989	10.0	14.5	55.7	19.8
Thailand	1988	29.5	51.7	11.3	7.5
Average		39.1	26.4	15.9	18.7

Source: United Nations, *World investment directory 1992.*

ect take place over several years (if at all), approvals affect flows with a distributed lag. Third, since approval statistics measure the total investments associated with a project, they are larger than the foreign inflows used to finance the project. For all these reasons, investment flows suggest more modest and more gradual changes than approvals.

Is the Indonesian experience discussed by Wells typical of regional trends? As table 6C.1 shows, Indonesia is not atypical; in fact, China and Malaysia have higher East Asian investment shares due to the key roles Hong Kong and Singapore, respectively, play in their economies. Table 6C.2 provides a time-series perspective by comparing recent data on project approvals from Thailand with Wells's Indonesian data. Intra–East Asian investment is clearly important in Thailand as well, but there it seems to have peaked in 1990, suggesting a temporary surge.

On the whole, Wells is ambivalent about the theoretical and empirical novelty of the East Asian investment phenomenon. On the one hand, he argues vigorously that today's "mobile exporters" are different from earlier waves of investors; on the other hand, he grounds their motivations in existing theory, which also suggests various historical precedents.

This is clearly not the first wave of foreign investment *in* East Asian developing countries. Previous investment waves have been motivated by trade barriers in host countries and by quota restrictions in their developed-country partners. The fact that today's investments are cost driven (that is, caused by the appreciation of the NICs' currencies in the 1980s) is not enough to make them novel; multinationals from developed countries have long used low-wage economies in East Asia and elsewhere as production platforms.

Table 6C.2   **FDI Inflows By Country of Origin, Approval Data (percentage of value)**

| | Host Country | | | |
| | Indonesia | Thailand | | |
Investing Country	1/1990–7/91	1989	1990	1991
East Asia	50.6%	28.1%	44.6%	25.6%
Hong Kong	8.0	6.0	26.3	6.7
Taiwan	7.1	15.1	10.2	13.2
Korea	21.9	2.6	3.0	1.2
Singapore	13.3	4.0	4.5	2.0
Malaysia	0.2	0.3	0.7	2.5
Japan	14.1	38.1	27.0	35.1
United States	2.9	3.9	6.4	14.1
Other	32.4	29.9	22.0	25.2
Total	100.0	100.0	100.0	100.0

Sources: Indonesia: Wells (chap. 6 in this volume). Thailand: BOI.

It is also not surprising that the NIC investors have chosen exporting industries. These investing firms come from intensely trade-oriented environments
and typically enjoy strong competitive positions in export-oriented industries.
Further, tradable-goods industries are especially sensitive to changes in relative
production costs, such as those occasioned by the exchange rate movements of
the 1980s.

Nor is this the first wave of investments *by* East Asian developing countries.
Hong Kong, Korea, Singapore, and Taiwan have been significant foreign
investors for some time. To be sure, their past investments had specialized objectives, such as establishing marketing channels in developed countries or
exploiting advantages derived from special family and business ties.

Could the novelty be that general factors (such as production cost) are becoming useful in explaining the outward investments of developing countries,
much as they have long helped to explain the investments of developed countries? On this point, though, the experience of the tigers is not very convincing—these economies are essentially industrial economies, as much as Japan
was twenty years ago.

If intra–East Asian investment flows are not intrinsically novel, their high
volume may be. Along with sharply rising intra–East Asian trade flows, these
investments could foreshadow rising regional economic interdependence (Petri
1993). They could also help to diversify regional linkages by balancing the
dominant role of Japan.

Whether the pace of recent investment flows can be sustained is unclear. It
can be argued that the investment wave of the 1980s is an artifact of the exchange rate cycle of the 1980s, which first built up and then rapidly diminished
the tigers' competitiveness in labor-intensive industries. With more stable currency markets, more moderate investment flows could follow, even if the tigers
continued to develop quickly compared to other countries.

Consider what it means for a firm to lose its competitive position *suddenly*—
for example, due to the sharp exchange rate changes that occurred in the
1980s—as compared to gradually, in the normal course of development. A
firm hit by a sudden shock may well have strong remaining assets in marketing,
technology, and management, which can be utilized regardless of its production advantage (assuming that the firm is willing to invest abroad). By contrast,
a firm that anticipates a gradual loss in its production advantage may find it
more economical to let its marketing and management assets depreciate
(alongside its physical assets) rather than to maintain these assets and invest
abroad.

According to this argument, a sudden change in costs will lead to large direct investment, while a gradual loss of similar magnitude will not. This story
is especially relevant to the 1980s wave of intra–East Asian investments. In the
late 1980s, East Asian investors found themselves with significant marketing
and other assets that made foreign investment worthwhile, even though these
advantages were not based on technological or managerial secrets that could

be long kept from host country firms. The fate of these investments is likely to follow that of Japanese garment firms established in Thailand in the 1970s: by the 1980s, most had been acquired by domestic managers. In the future, assuming relatively stable currency markets, NIC firms will provably avoid investments in assets that have a good chance of being useful only abroad and are easily appropriated by foreign firms.

In the meantime, host countries should be delighted by these inflows. Because intra–East Asian investments are in relatively low-technology industries, they are more relevant to the hosts' development than are investments by developed countries. Because the firm-specific advantages of the investing firms are weak, the prospects are better for assimilating or acquiring them. In sum, policymakers should do their best to encourage intra–East Asian investment flows, especially while investments from Japan remain hostage to that country's financial crisis. They should not assume, however, that these flows can be easily maintained at their recent high level.

Reference

Petri, Peter A. 1993. The East Asian trading bloc: An analytical history. In *Regionalism and rivalry: Japan and the United States in Pacific Asia,* ed. Jeffrey A. Frankel and Miles Kahler. Chicago: University of Chicago Press.

Discussion Summary

Most comments and questions focused on three related issues discussed in *Louis Wells*'s paper. First, how sophisticated are the mobile exporters' operations? Second, to what extent are their site choices explained by the mobile exporters' demand for local factors of production and their desire to locate where there are established Chinese communities? Third, what are the welfare effects of the mobile exporters' investments.

Several participants asked questions or made comments about the sophistication of the mobile exporters' operations. *Michelle Gittelman* asked Wells to specify the portion of the mobile exporters' value chain that is located in countries such as Indonesia. He replied that originally the Indonesian sites had assembled parts that were primarily from their home countries but that recently they have started using more local parts. *Dick Caves* stated that the earlier literature indicated a sharp dichotomy between Asian and other investments, in that the others brought intangibles to their foreign investments while Asians tended to have smaller, more labor-intensive operations. In response to Caves's inquiry as to whether this dichotomy persisted, *Wells* said it was still present but to a slightly lesser extent.

Bill Zeile suggested a reason why the recent Japanese investments in Indonesia are more labor intensive than investments by firms from other advanced nations (see text, sec. 6.3.3): these recent investors are Japanese suppliers following other Japanese firms that made earlier capital-intensive investments. *Monty Graham* asked why countries such as Korea use foreign direct investment in Indonesia but contracting relations in countries such as Bangladesh. *Wells* responded that it may be that the manufacturing processes in Bangladesh is lower-end and, thus, that the production process requires less adaptation to change. *Peter Petri* added that the Bangladesh operations originally had been foreign direct investment but that the Bangladesh managers, who had been trained by the Koreans, soon established competing firms. He emphasized that this evolution will probably occur in Indonesia in the near future because the production skills are readily acquired by local managers.

Participants questioned whether the mobile exporters' demand for local factors of production and their desire to locate where there are established Chinese communities fully explain their site choices. *Paul Healy* offered an alternative explanation for why Hong Kong and Taiwan have focused on Thailand while Singapore, another country with a large Chinese presence, has invested in Indonesia. He argued that Singapore, wishing to narrow the economic gap between itself and its neighbors, provides tax breaks to Singaporean companies that locate close to its borders. *Wells* agreed, indicating that many of the Singaporean companies are investing on the Indonesian islands closest to home. *Dara Monashi* asked whether there was an unusually large Chinese presence in the African countries where the East Asians have been locating and, if so, whether it would be reasonable to assume that there would be similar additional investments in other African countries with smaller Chinese populations. *Wells* responded that he has no knowledge about the Chinese populations of various African countries and that the African investments were primarily for import purposes. *Petri* asked whether the site choices were the result of being able to segment the production process and transport intermediate goods at low cost. *Wells* responded that transportation costs had come down recently in some Indonesian locations where international airports have been established.

With regards to welfare issues, *Kenneth Froot* asked whether Wells had data on the employment base or wage levels and, more generally, whether Indonesia views the recent investments positively. *Wells* responded that the Indonesian government viewed the employment effects very positively but he does not have data to formally address this issue. *Krishna Palepu* asked why investments were export oriented in a country such as Indonesia, where the market is so large. He suspects that Indonesia would be better off if it promoted manufacturing for its local economy. *Wells's* reply was that the recent investments were export oriented; however, earlier investments were import oriented, and the recent investments constitute a small portion of the total stock of foreign investments in Indonesia.

7   Foreign Direct Investment in Semiconductors

David B. Yoffie

Semiconductors were a "global" industry long before the term was fashionable. Many U.S. semiconductor firms aggressively invested abroad prior to being well established in their home market. The rationale and location of foreign direct investment (FDI) in semiconductors largely fit conventional theories of foreign investment: at different points in time, firms located overseas to take advantage of low labor costs, to overcome tariff barriers, to appropriate their intangible assets (intellectual property), and to reduce transaction costs and arbitrage costs of capital differences. However, the patterns of investment have changed dramatically over the last two decades. This raises a number of interesting theoretical issues.

I will argue that FDI in semiconductors can be roughly grouped into three waves. During the first wave, in the 1960s and 1970s, the world leaders in semiconductors (largely U.S. firms) invested heavily overseas in assembly and test facilities which exploited locational advantages (low labor costs in Southeast Asia), and they only invested in fabrication facilities that jumped tariff barriers (in Europe). The Asian investment was complementary to trade; the European investment was largely trade substituting. For the most part, inward FDI did not occur in Japan because of strict capital controls.

During a second wave, in the mid-1970s, FDI moved beyond greenfield investment in the final stage of manufacturing to mergers and acquisitions of entire firms; European firms, in particular, expanded their presence in the U.S.

This paper has benefited from research assistance by Harvard Business School research associate Jeff Cohn and the financial support of the Harvard Business School Division of Research. The author would also like to thank Lael Brainard, Geoffrey Carliner, Kenneth A. Froot, and other participants at the National Bureau of Economic Research conference on foreign directed investment for their useful comments. The historical analysis of foreign direct investment in the 1960s and early 1970s also borrows from a joint paper with Laura Tyson, "Semiconductors: From manipulated to managed trade" (Yoffie 1993).

market by buying U.S. companies. Acquisitions of non–start-up semiconductor companies in this second wave appear to have ended, at least temporarily, when political intervention prevented Japan's Fujitsu from buying a U.S.-based firm, Fairchild Semiconductor, which was owned by a French company, Schlumberger, based in the Netherlands Antilles.

A third wave of FDI started in the late 1980s and has continued into the early 1990s. This wave is characterized by significant FDI in greenfield front-end fabrication facilities, primarily by U.S. firms in Europe and Japanese firms in both the United States and Europe. With a few exceptions, most notably IBM and Texas Instruments (TI), core Research and Development activities on semiconductors have remained in the home base throughout the history of the industry.

The evolution of investment in these waves can be largely accounted for by political changes (e.g., the U.S.-Japanese Semiconductor Trade Agreement of 1986 and Europe's 1992 program) and changes in technology (i.e., declining labor intensity and rising scale economies). But the dynamics of change present some surprising puzzles. First, there has been stickiness to foreign investment in semiconductors. Despite radical changes in the economics of the industry, which largely negate the advantages of locating in low–labor cost countries, many historical investments in Southeast Asia have remained intact and been expanded. Second, there appears to be a lack of agglomeration in the new greenfield investments. While some theories might suggest that local externalities would produce investment in clusters (Krugman 1991; Porter 1990), significant portions of the greenfield FDI in the late 1980s and early 1990s have been widely dispersed in the United States and Europe. Third, there continue to be dramatic asymmetries between the style of investments by nonlocal firms in Japan and FDI in Europe and the United States. FDI in Japan is scarce, and the little investment which has occurred has been in the form of joint ventures, even though restrictions on FDI have been formally eliminated. Outside of Japan, by contrast, most Japanese and U.S. firms invest in wholly owned greenfield facilities outside of their home base.

The methodology for this paper relies heavily on relatively soft data and interviews. Unfortunately, systematic evidence on FDI in semiconductors is difficult to obtain: neither firms nor governments publish precise data on investment expenditures, overseas employment, or revenues. Even capacity numbers, which some firms disclose and which might be considered proxies for production, are unreliable because of variations in semiconductor yields. My primary source of data is from the industry, particularly Dataquest, which publishes plant locations, estimates of offshore production, and trade statistics. In addition, I have relied on interviews with managers in leading semiconductor firms in the United States, Japan, and Europe. The analysis is also confined largely to the merchant market for semiconductors and focuses primarily on the higher-technology, higher-growth segment of integrated circuits.

7.1.1   The Economics of Semiconductors—Past and Present

It is well known that semiconductors have some unusual economic characteristics. The production of semiconductors and, more specifically, integrated circuits (ICs) benefited more than any other product in industrial history from an amazingly steep learning curve. In 1964, a chip containing about sixty-four components was priced at around $32. By 1971, the price of a chip containing over a thousand components was about $1 (Yoffie 1987a; Borrus 1988). Between 1974 and 1988, there was a 635-fold reduction in memory prices per bit (Semiconductor Industry Association 1992). The rule of thumb in the industry was that costs generally fell 30 percent to 40 percent with every doubling in volume. Such steep learning economies occurred because semiconductor manufacturing routinely yielded more defective than sound chips. For complex new products, yields as low as 25 percent were quite common, while mature products might yield 90 percent. Although documentation is weak, producers also believed that there were intergenerational externalities: learning gained from making 1-Mb DRAMs, for instance, could be transferred to 4-Mb DRAMs.

In addition to learning economies, the semiconductor industry has been characterized by very high and growing economies of scale in front-end fabrication (fab) combined with extraordinary levels of research and development (R&D). In 1970, a minimum efficient scale plant required about $30 million in capital investment, and the output of that plant needed to generate roughly 3 percent of world sales to break even. By 1992, state-of-the-art plants cost an average of $650 million but could range from $200 million to as much as $1 billion; the cost varied with the complexity of the product and the desired volume. While overall world market share was no longer relevant, estimates suggested that a manufacturer would need $1.25 billion in annual revenue and 10–20 percent world market share within a particular segment to justify even a small fab.[1]

Also, unlike large, lumpy investments in other industries, which had long useful lives, physical plants became obsolete in only three to five years in the semiconductor business. There were several consequences of this economic feature. First, firms had to make significant ongoing capital expenditures.[2] Second, investments were generally sunk, with little or no after-market value. And a closely related third, the relatively thin market for capacity limited the options for FDI. Few firms wanted to buy competitors' fabs because of the rapid aging of the facility, plus variations in manufacturing processes between firms limited the general utility of any given firm's investment.

---

1. Interview with semiconductor executives.
2. While capital expenditures averaged only 10 percent of sales in 1990, they averaged over 30 percent in boom periods.

Beyond the economies of scale in manufacturing, semiconductors were also one of the most R&D-intensive industries, with R&D expenditures averaging more than twice the U.S. manufacturing average. In 1990, R&D was 12.8 percent of U.S. semiconductor revenues. Semiconductor technology also had a peculiar problem of being difficult to appropriate. Especially in the U.S. Silicon Valley, personnel tended to be highly mobile, and it was common for venture capital firms to lure away promising engineers from established companies. Most of the start-ups in Silicon Valley came from Fairchild and later Intel. The "leakiness" of technology and the significant infrastructure developed in Silicon Valley made it an attractive place for a new entrant to establish a business in the 1960s through the 1980s. At the same time, there were strong economies of agglomeration in R&D: very close coordination and communication among R&D facilities was desirable.

The cost structure of semiconductor firms has evolved over time. Variable costs, always small, have declined over the last three decades. The basic inputs into semiconductor production are sand (silicon) and electricity. Distribution and transportation costs are tiny (1–2 percent). By 1992, freight costs ranged from two–three cents for a commodity product packaged in plastic to ten cents for larger chips packaged in ceramic. With insignificant transportation costs, it was relatively simple in the 1960s and 1970s to physically separate the stages of production—especially fabrication versus assembly and test. By the 1980s, however, capital investment in automation dramatically reduced variable labor costs, virtually eliminating the cost penalty of colocating all stages of production in a high-wage location. A volume assembly facility in 1992 cost approximately $125 million–$130 million for the building (20 percent) and equipment (80 percent). One estimate suggested that direct labor per chip in 1992 was about ten–twenty cents in Southeast Asia versus twelve–fifty cents in the United States, depending largely on the product complexity.[3]

7.2   First Wave of FDI: Assembly and Test in Southeast Asia and Europe

The first wave of FDI in semiconductors was documented thoroughly by Kenneth Flamm (Flamm and Grunwald 1985). To summarize Flamm's argument, the first surge in foreign investment came in the 1960s from the pioneers in the industry, U.S. firms. The shift to offshore assembly operations became especially important between 1964 and 1972, driven by the aggressive moves of firms in the increasingly competitive industry to compete on cost. The natural division of production among wafer fabrication, assembly, and testing al-

3. Interview with industry executive. Since the final selling price of these chips could vary from $1 to $500, it is difficult to calculate direct labor as a percentage of sales. The assembly of the simple, low-priced memory chips, however, was much more automated. In addition, the added one–three cents in direct labor costs for simple chips in the United States could be offset by lower inventory costs.

lowed the assembly stage of production to be located at a different facility from fabrication without any significant impact on learning economies. And the assembly stage required relatively low-skilled labor that was available abroad at a substantial wage discount (as much as 90 percent), yielding up to a 50 percent reduction in total manufacturing costs. The difference in the final price of a chip could be as much as $1.50, versus $3.00 for memory products in the mid-1970s. Not for another decade could a high percentage of this labor cost be automated out of assembly.

The policies of both the United States and several newly industrializing countries also supported the offshore assembly strategy. Under items 807 and 806.3 of the U.S. Tariff Schedules as amended in 1963, imported articles assembled in whole or in part of U.S.-fabricated components became dutiable only to the extent of the value added abroad. This meant a substantial tariff break on the offshore assembly of chips. And beginning in 1967, the governments of Mexico, Taiwan, Singapore, Malaysia, and Korea established "export platforms" to encourage direct foreign investment. These platforms offered a wide variety of inducements to such investment, including tax-free exports, import tax reductions, and tax holidays. By 1974, the U.S.-based producers had established 136 operations overseas: 33 fabrication; 103 assembly, 69 of which were in developing countries in Latin America and Southeast Asia (see table 7.1). By 1978, more than 80 percent of the semiconductors shipped in the United States were assembled and tested overseas, mainly in these countries.

The second type of foreign direct investment—front-end fabrication to serve a local market—occurred mainly in Europe, where high tariff rates (17

Table 7.1   Overseas Operations of U.S.-based Semiconductor Companies, 1974

	Fabrication	Assembly	Total
North America	—	2	2
Canada	—	2	2
Europe	24	21	45
United Kingdom	9	7	16
France	5	3	8
Others	10	11	21
Latin America	1	24	25
Mexico	1	17	18
Others	—	7	7
Far East	8	56	64
Malaysia	—	14	14
Singapore	—	11	11
Hong Kong	—	11	13
Korea	—	9	9
Japan	6	—	6
Others	2	11	13
Total	33	103	136

Source: Finan (1975, 56–58).

percent of value), preferential procurement procedures, and pressure by the European governments (especially British and French) encouraged such investment to serve growing European markets. The first major period of investment in Europe occurred between 1969 and 1974, by which time 46 affiliates (18 engaged in complete manufacturing operations, including fabrication and assembly) had been established (Flamm 1990). In the absence of trade barriers, exports would have been the preferred mechanism for serving the European Economic Community market. The economies of scale in manufacturing and the added logistics costs of transferring designs and making the fabs "work" in Europe could only be justified economically if exporting was impossible. The least attractive option was to license technology to local firms. While cross-licensing was very common if two companies had patents that were mutually valuable, one-way licenses for money were less desirable because it was extremely difficult to appropriate adequate value from the technology.

Tariffs, quotas, and other forms of border protection also encouraged U.S. companies to consider foreign direct investment to serve the Japanese market. But the Japanese actively restricted such investment (in contrast to the Europeans, who actively encouraged it). The Japanese strategy was avowedly one of import substitution through the creation and promotion of indigenous suppliers, while the European strategy was one of import substitution, at least in part, through substituting the local production of U.S. companies for imports from them. Japan also restricted foreign purchases of equity in Japanese firms. High tariffs, restrictive quotas, and approval registration requirements were used to control imports. Approval was also required for all patent and technical assistance licensing agreements. As a result of controls on the acquisition of foreign technology, the Ministry for International Trade and Industry (MITI) acted as a monopsonist buyer of such technology and also controlled its diffusion among Japanese firms. These tight border controls held the U.S. share of the Japanese semiconductor market substantially below what it was in the rest of the world. By 1975, for example, U.S. firms had 98 percent of the U.S. market, 78 percent of the European market, and only 20 percent of the Japanese market.

The requirements posed by the Japanese government for investment were so unattractive that few firms chose to exercise this option.[4] Most leading U.S. firms chose the only avenue open to earn a return from the Japanese market: one-way licenses of technology. Through most of the 1970s, licensing fees amounted to almost 10 percent of Japanese sales (Braun and Macdonald 1982, 155). Only Texas Instruments (TI), by refusing to license its key integrated circuit patents to Japanese firms and by petitioning the U.S. government for trade protection based on patent infringement by the Japanese, was able to

---

4. Even after direct controls were abolished in 1978, non-Japanese firms found it difficult to invest in Japan.

Table 7.2   U.S. Participation in Foreign Semiconductor Markets

	Semiconductor consumption in France, Britain, W. Germany and Japan, Uncorrected Values ($ millions)	Percentage supplied by Direct Exports from the United States	Cumulative Number of U.S. Factories in These Countries	
			Assembly	Fabricating
1960	$134	11%	5	4
1961	151	15	6	4
1962	174	16	6	4
1963	208	17	7	5
1964	248	16	8	5
1965	323	23	8	6
1966	349	27	10	7
1967	390	32	11	7
1968	490	30	13	8
1969	660	37	24	15
1970	840	30	29	16
1971	875	25	30	18
1972	1,284	18	34	18

Source: Finan (1975, 120).

Note: Virtually 100 percent of U.S. supply to Japan was serviced by direct exports until 1970. And even TI's one local fab in Japan, jointly owned by Sony, did not have a material impaction these numbers through 1972.

extract permission from the Japanese government to establish a wholly owned manufacturing subsidiary in Japan in 1968.[5]

The implications this first wave of FDI had for international trade were unsurprising. Most FDI during this period was complementary to U.S. exports. Through the late 1970s, an estimated 80 percent of the fabrication by U.S. firms was still done in the United States; 20 percent was done abroad, mainly in Europe. The reverse numbers applied in assembly: about 80 percent of assembly by U.S. firms was performed abroad and only 20 percent at home. FDI in Europe, however, appeared to be largely a substitute for trade, at least during this early period. Direct U.S. exports to Europe declined between the late 1960s and the early 1970s, as the number of fabs more than doubled over a four-year period (see table 7.2). The combination of significant investment in assembly operations in Southeast Asia and investment in fabs in Europe reduced U.S. net export earnings, producing U.S. trade deficits as early as 1971 (table 7.3). Most U.S. imports until the late 1970s were assembled products

5. Initially, TI was only allowed to establish a 50–50 joint venture with Sony in 1968. Four years later, Sony sold out to TI. MITI finally agreed to TI's request for a wholly owned subsidiary only after TI threatened any Japanese exports of consumer electronics using TI's technology with an immediate patent infringement lawsuit. For more on the history of joint ventures in the semiconductor industry, see Steinmueller (1987).

Table 7.3   **Total U.S. Semiconductor Trade ($ millions)**

	Exports				Imports			
	Total	Integrated Circuits	Transistors, Diodes, and Rectifiers	Other*	Total	Integrated Circuits	Transistors, Diodes, and Non-Rectifiers	Other*
1966	$ 130.4	$ 8.9	$ 91	$ 30.5	$ 44.6		$ 28.7	$ 15.9
1967	152.4	26.5	81.4	44.1	46.5		26.7	19.8
1968	204.5	36.2	89.5	78.8	76.6		44.7	31.9
1969	345.7	72.4	138.6	134.7	111.2		59	52.2
1970	416.9	99.8	146.2	170.9	167.7	$ 69.4	59.8	38.5
1971	370.5	91.2	99.9	179.4	187	94.2	60.4	32.4
1972	469.6	103.5	126	240.1	328.8	180.5	100.1	48.2
1973	848.6	217.7	195.8	435.1	610.5	365.3	160.6	84.6
1974	1,247.5	313.5	215.6	718.4	953.5	606.3	235.9	111.3
1975	1,037	262.1	111.6	663.3	802	581.5	138.5	82
1976	1,385.9	320.4	120.3	945.2	1,098	813.7	153.1	131.2
1977	1,490.5	348.1	70.6	1,071.8	1,403.2	1,025	173.5	204.7
1978	1,521.4	471.9	85.4	964.1	1,827.4	1,405.2	179.1	243.1
1979	2,075.1	650.1	90.9	1,334.1	2,587.7	235.4	195	357.3
1980	2,782.3	833.5	95.2	1,853.6	3,395.6	2,780.4	212.2	403
1981	2,832.7	768.4	87.3	1,977	3,645.5	2,982.1	264	399.4
1982	3,058.9	836.3	81.8	2,140.8	4,397	3,501	263.9	632.1
1983	3,673.5	1,025.7	97.9	2,549.9	5,330.1	4,150.2	257.4	922.5
1984	4,651.5	1,391.3	118.8	3,141.4	8,284.2	6,125.8	345.9	1,802.5
1985	3,693.1	1,140.6	123.1	2,429.4	6,369.7	4,423.9	259.4	1,686.4
1986	4,185.4	1,148.1	138.8	2,898.5	6,685.7	4,539	303.7	1,843
1987	6,229	1,622.8	131.4	4,474.9	8,561.9	6,038.1	336.8	2,187
1988	8,035.4	2,588.5	168.4	5,278.5	12,089.8	8,767.6	452.2	2,896.9
1989	9,530.6				12,301.6			
1990	10,709.6				12,143.5			

Sources: 1966–72: U.S. Department of Commerce Publications #ES-2:15. 1973–76: U.S. Department of Commerce Publications #ES-2:17. 1977–82: U.S. Department of Commerce Publications #ES-2:19. 1983–86: U.S. Department of Commerce Publications #ES-2:20. 1987–88: compiled from U.S. Department of Commerce Publications #FT-246. 1989–90: Compiled from U.S. Department of Commerce statistics (breakdowns for 1989–90 were not available due to a change in classification from SIC to a harmonized system).

*Other semiconductor devices.

from U.S. affiliates located in the newly industrializing countries (NICs). U.S. exports of unfinished circuits were primarily to five Southeast Asian assembly locations for final assembly and packaging. These products were then either reexported to the United States or to Japan and Europe.

The one other area where FDI might have been trade substituting was TI's fab investments in Japan. TI's strategy was to service the Japanese market from its facilities in Japan. By the 1980s, even TI had become a net exporter from

Japan, importing virtually nothing from the United States.[6] While its initial investment might have been considered a complement to trade (since MITI strictly limited TI's imports), TI did not switch production back to the United States when imports restrictions were liberalized in the mid-1970s.

7.3 Second Wave: European Acquisitions of U.S. Firms

From the mid-1970s through the mid-1980s, the structure of the semiconductor industry changed, and so did the patterns of direct investment. The most obvious structural shift was the rise of Japanese competitors, accompanied by the virtual collapse of Europe and the relative decline of U.S. firms. Here again, the story is well known and need not be repeated in this paper. But accompanying this structural shift in competitive position was a change in investment patterns. FDI in assembly facilities in Southeast Asia continued and indeed expanded as Japanese firms also began investing in assembly operations in the region. There was also further incremental U.S. investment in fab capacity and design centers in Europe and Israel.[7] However, the most notable trend in FDI during this period was outright acquisitions or taking substantial ownership positions in leading U.S. firms.

A list of the major corporate acquisitions or investments can be found in table 7.4. Most of the explanations for these investments fit into the school of industrial organization motivations for FDI rather than the variety of macro-explanations associated with locational advantages, tax policies, cost of capital, protectionism, and so on. It is hard to attribute the trend to macroeconomics or macropolicies, because the pattern of acquiring U.S. semiconductor companies was so ubiquitous: the investors were large U.S. companies as well as non-U.S. firms based in a variety of locations in Europe, North America, and Asia. Although a few of the acquisitions could be traced to firms trying to diversify their existing business portfolio, such as Exxon's purchase of Zilog and Schlumberger's purchase of Fairchild, most of the acquiring firms were already in some part of the electronics business.

Until the end of the 1970s, small U.S. firms were the clear leaders in product and process technology. Many of these companies were willing recipients of foreign (or domestic) capital because of the rising capital and R&D expendi-

6. Interview with TI executives, 1986.
7. Israel was unusual because it was probably the only country where U.S. firms, such as Motorola and Intel, invested in R&D facilities that served the global market. The design centers in Israel, unlike most Japanese design centers in the United States or U.S. design centers in Europe and Japan, were not exclusively focused on local adaptation of products. Two firms, National Semiconductor and Intel, also invested in fabs in Israel. Israel was an attractive location because the government offered tax relief and some subsidies in addition to an abundant supply of highly qualified engineers and preferential tariff treatment for Israeli exports to Europe. Intel's decision to invest in a design center and then a fab was largely a consequence of a senior, highly valued Intel manager who wanted to return home.

Table 7.4   Selected Corporate Investments in U.S. Semiconductor Companies, 1975–1991

Date	U.S. Company	Corporate Investor	National Base	Equity Ownership (%)
1975	Maruman IC	Toshiba	Japan	100%
1975	Signetics	Philips	Netherlands	100
1976	Advanced Micro Devices	Seimens	West Germany	20
1976	American Microsystems	Robert Bosch	West Germany	12.5
1976		Borg Warner	United States	12.5
1976	Interdesign	Ferranti	United Kingdom	100
1976	Monolithic Memories	Northern Telecom	Canada	24
1976	MOS Technology	Commodore	Bahamas	100
1977	Exar	Toyo	Japan	53
1977	Frontier	Commodore International	Bahamas	100
1977	Intersil	Northern Telecom	Canada	24
1978	Electronic Arrays	Nippon Electric	Japan	100
1979	Fairchild	Schlumberger	Netherlands Antilles	100
1979	Inmos	National Enterprise Board	United Kingdom	100
1981	Advanced LSI Logic	Micrel	United States	
1985	Storage Semiconductor	California Devices	United States	Plants
1985	Storage Semiconductor	Zoran	United States	Plant
1986	Micron Technologies	Samsung	South Korea	22
1986	Comdial Technology	Orbit Instrument Group	United States	80
1987	Fairchild/Schlumberger	National Semiconductor	United States	100
1987	Monolithic Memories	Advanced Micro Devices	United States	Merger
1987	GTE's Comm Sys Division	California Micro Devices	United States	Microcircuits division

1988	AT&T	Silicon Systems	United States	Plant
1988	Zymos	Daewoo	South Korea	51
1988	GE Solid State Semicon	Harris	United States	100
1988	Honeywell Colorado Chip	Atmel	United States	100
1988	Micron Technologies	Amstrad PLC	United Kingdom	9.8
1988	Zoran	Synergy	United States	Plant
1988	Zymos	Saratoga	United States	Plant
1989	Silicon Systems	TDK	Japan	Plant
1989	Saratoga	Maxim	United States	Plant
1989	Vitelic	Oki Electronic	Japan	Minority stake
1989	Data General	Rohm	Japan	Plant
1989	Honeywell Solid State Division	Atmel	United States	Electronics division
1990	GegaBit Logic	Cray Computer	United States	Fabs
1990	Cypres Semiconductor	Altera	United States	Plant
1991	Tera Microsystems, Inc.	Mitsubishi	Japan	6.7
1991	Vitelic	Mosel	United States	Merger
1991	VTC	Cypress	United States	Plant
1991	Crystal Semiconductor	Cirrus Logic	United States	100
1991	Gigabit Logic	Triquint	United States	Merger

Source: The Wall Street Journal (various issues); New York Times (various issues).

tures required in the industry. While venture capital was plentiful for most of this period for start-up companies, intense Japanese competition beginning around 1976 limited access to debt and equity markets for small firms that wanted to expand their fab or assembly operations. Prevailing wisdom at the time was that a large, diversified parent corporation could solve the inherent cyclicality problems of the business.

If small U.S. firms were willing to be acquired, why did large European, some large Japanese, and even South Korean companies want to buy?[8] The answer has two parts. First, several of the acquired companies had significant technologies, patents, or cross-licenses. Even for firms not in the merchant semiconductor market, integrated circuit technology was perceived to be critical for downstream applications. There was a variety of externalities associated with ICs. As chips became more highly integrated, growing in capacity and complexity, they took on the characteristics of entire systems. To appropriate the value of the system, most major computer, telecommunications, and consumer electronics companies in the world believed that they would have to make semiconductors. Companies such as IBM, DEC, Hewlett-Packard, Siemens, and Philips, as well as all of the large Japanese electronics companies, integrated backward in the 1960s. In fact, several of these companies, particularly IBM and DEC, gained significant competitive advantages from their ability to design and make custom logic chips that were proprietary.

A second rationale behind these acquisitions was to learn the "secret" of U.S. success in semiconductors. For European firms in particular, partly because they had failed to become significant players on their own, acquiring or investing in small U.S. companies was attractive. Europe was a relatively small and fragmented market for semiconductors, compared to the United States, in the early 1970s. Dominated by national champions, none of the large European semiconductor manufacturers had established itself in a position of global leadership. By investing in U.S. companies, many of which had at least one generation of successful products, these European firms hoped to appropriate some of the externalities of being located in the leading market for innovations in semiconductors. Silicon Valley in California was an especially attractive region because of the leakiness in technology and mobility of personnel. As one European scholar reported from an interview with European semiconductor executives,

> Such a firm [the European acquisition] would rapidly discover what ingredients contributed most to success in the industry, would act as a training ground for non-American personnel and would be able to funnel information about processes and techniques to the parent firm or home country with

8. Korea's Samsung bought 22.1 percent of Micron Technology, a DRAM manufacturer, for $5 million in 1986. This particular horiozntal investment seemed to be targeted at getting across to DRAM patents and technology. Also in 1986, Daewoo bought controlling interest in a small semiconductor firm, Zymos, in a bid to enter semiconductors ("Overseas investments" 1991).

the minimum delay and the maximum effectiveness. (Braun and Macdonald 1982, 175–6)

None of the acquisitions, however, proved to be profitable for foreign (or even domestic) acquirers. Without exception, the European acquisitions were unsuccessful. Siemens, unable to gain leverage in its investment in Advanced Micro Devices, divested its holdings in 1991; American Microsystems, partly owned by Germany's Robert Bosch, no longer exists; Interdesign was absorbed by Ferranti, which remained a minor player in semiconductors; and Inmos dropped in market share to obscure levels. In the early 1980s, France's Thomson Semiconductor merged with Italy's SGS, which in turn bought Mostek from ITT. In the mid-1970s, Mostek was a significant DRAM supplier. By the late 1980s, Mostek facilities and product lines had virtually disappeared.

But the greatest failure of them all was Fairchild Camera, one of the pioneers of U.S. semiconductors. From the outset, Fairchild proved to be a cash drain for its parent, Schlumberger. Schlumberger entered a bidding war with a U.S. firm, Gould, for Fairchild in 1979. As a white knight, it paid $425 million in cash, which included $253 million in goodwill. Over the next seven years, Schlumberger invested another $1 billion in capital additions and research and development. While no public information on the profitability of Fairchild was ever released, Schlumberger accumulated for tax purposes net operating loss carryforward provisions of $600 million by 1986.[9] Prompted by these deep losses as well as a dramatic erosion in market share (Fairchild dropped from number two in the world in 1975 to number fourteen in 1985), Schlumberger tried to sell 82 percent of Fairchild to Fujitsu in 1986. The price was $225 million, but Schlumberger would keep the most valuable asset: the $600 million in tax losses. However, in the wake of several dumping suits filed against Japanese producers, U.S. Commerce Secretary Malcolm Baldrige opposed the sale. Five days after the secretary went public with his opposition, Fujitsu withdrew its bid. Six months later, Schlumberger sold all of Fairchild to a U.S. company—National Semiconductor—for $122 million.

Foreign and military policy considerations continued to stall foreign acquisitions of U.S. semiconductor companies. In 1987, the United Kingdom's Plessey sought to buy Harris Semiconductor, a manufacturer that focused almost exclusively on the government market, particularly military applications. When the Pentagon threatened not to buy chips from firms owned by non-U.S. capital, that deal also fell through (Ziegler 1991). Harris remained independent and a few years later expanded its semiconductor operations by buying General Electric's captive semiconductor subsidiary.

The Fairchild-Fujitsu deal was clearly the turning point for foreign acquisitions of non–start-up companies in the United States, especially from Japanese suitors. Fujitsu, which had no semiconductor investment in the United States

---

9. This brief discussion of Fairchild relies on MacKenzie de Sola Pool (1988); Rukstad and Wolfson (1989).

prior to 1986, was willing to pay a premium for Fairchild because Fairchild offered a strong patent position (dating back twenty years) that could give Fujitsu an entrée into new markets, especially U.S. defense markets. In addition, for the price of one fabrication facility, Fujitsu would have a base in the United States from which to expand and at least some of Fairchild's accumulated experience of working in Silicon Valley.[10] At a time of excess capacity in the industry, no U.S. firm could place a similar value on Fairchild's intellectual or physical assets. In the absence of political intervention, more such acquisitions might have been predicted. As discussed below, political events of the mid-1980s made locating fabrication in the United States suddenly more attractive for Japanese firms. However, Japanese firms seemed to have viewed the Fairchild incident and, to a lesser extent, the Harris decision as a signal that the U.S. government would prevent or forestall wholesale acquisitions of leading U.S. semiconductor companies. Acquisitions of very small (usually fabless) semiconductors have continued (see table 7.4), but unlike many of the earlier investments in U.S. capacity and market position, these investments have largely been purchases of technology.

7.4   Third Wave: New Greenfield Investment in Fabrication Facilities

The first wave of FDI was largely outflows from the United States, driven by the labor intensity of semiconductor assembly and the protectionism in Europe; the second wave of foreign acquisitions was largely European firms, driven by their failure to establish a successful base at home.[11] Throughout these periods, however, Japanese firms remained insignificant exporters of long-term capital. Prior to 1990, most large Japanese firms had assembly plants in Southeast Asia for very price-sensitive commodity products, but only four firms had fabrication plants outside of Japan, all (five fabs) in the United States and none in Europe. According to Dataquest, in a $60 billion worldwide market in 1989, Japanese companies accounted for more than 45 percent of world revenues but only 16 percent of the world's $6 billion in offshore production (Dataquest 1990).

Three events in the mid-1980s should have stimulated a renewed interest in FDI by all major players. Two events were political: the U.S.-Japanese Semiconductor Trade Agreement and Europe's 1992 program. The 1986 semiconductor trade agreement (hereafter referred to as the SCTA) was critical in enticing Japanese factories to the United States, while fears over the possibility of

---

10. At least some management could be expected to stay, since the deal with Schlumberger would have offered senior management an equity stake that would grow over time.

11. Some European firms continued to use an acquisition strategy. Phillips had the most success with its U.S. acquisition of Signetics. Philips was the only European to remain a top-ten semiconductor firm in 1991. While it was not believed to be a very profitable operation, it continued to make significant investments, including a majority ownership in Taiwan Semiconductor Company in 1989.

fortress Europe in 1992 encouraged both Japanese and U.S. companies to expand their presence within Europe. The third event was Japanese firms taking leadership in certain commodity products and, more important, Japan becoming the largest market for semiconductors in the world in 1986 with many of the world's leading semiconductor equipment vendors (USITC 1991). On the surface, FDI would have seemed more attractive, since Japan's market was now officially open. Japan consumed 50 percent of world production after 1986, and the SCTA sought to guarantee U.S. and other non-Japanese firms 20 percent of that market.

The SCTA was obviously important in stimulating Japanese investment in the United States because of its pricing provision. Immediately prior to the SCTA, the U.S. government found Japanese companies guilty of dumping DRAMS and EPROMs (another type of memory), with dumping margins of up to 188 percent for individual Japanese suppliers. As part of the SCTA, the United States agreed to suspend the dumping suits in exchange for the Japanese producers agreeing not to sell their products at prices below their (average) cost of production, plus an 8 percent profit margin, in the United States and third markets. The United States reserved the right to add or drop products from the monitoring arrangement in the future. It was anticipated that this arrangement would deter or prevent dumping of such products in the future. However, products manufactured in the United States would be exempt from the pricing guidelines.

Changes in European rules of origin on semiconductors provided similar incentives for FDI in Europe. In 1989, the commission fundamentally altered the definition of "made in EC."[12] Prior to 1989, chips would be considered European if the "last substantial process or operation that is economically justified was performed" in the EC. Assembly and test operations were counted as a "substantial process" under these guidelines. The new rules, however, stated that fabrication of wafers or diffusion was necessary to exempt the chips from duty. This change also influenced the antidumping rules in the EC. In the past, a manufacturer could move test and assembly to the European Community and be exempt from possible dumping sites. Since Japanese and Korean firms had been frequent targets of dumping suits in the electronics industry, the EC regulation was widely interpreted as an "antiscrewdriver" plant rule targeted at Asian producers.[13]

The combination of these two policy changes in Europe and the United States influenced a step-function change in the policies of Japanese firms toward FDI. By 1990, virtually every Japanese firm had announced plans for new facilities: eleven (ten of which were memory) were slated for the United States, and ten (eight memory) were proposed for Europe. In my interviews

---

12. Quoted from EC Regulation 802/68, article 5, in Flamm (1990, 271).
13. One Korean firm, Samsung, also invested in fab capacity for DRAMs in France. Since Samsung has excess capacity at home, politics can be the only explanation for this investment.

with Japanese firms, their managers argued that "in terms of costs, management of engineers, and the control of production, it was better to produce in Japan."[14] Nonetheless, these firms decided to invest abroad. The rationale most frequently cited for this decision was trade friction, but there were also other familiar rationales such as "being close to the customer," access to new engineering talent and technology, and access to foreign capital. Moreover, the pattern of investment by firms had striking parallels to Knickerbocker's hypothesis that smaller companies in oligopolistic industries often follow the industry leader overseas (Knickerbocker 1973). In semiconductors, the largest Japanese producer, NEC, pioneered investment in the United States in the late 1970s and was the first to invest in Europe (Scotland and later West Germany). The other large semiconductor firms—Hitachi, Mitsubishi, Matsushita, Toshiba, and Fujitsu—lagged a decade behind NEC in the United States but only two to three years behind in Europe. Smaller firms (e.g., NMB) generally eschewed building foreign fabrication facilities. In at least two instances, Japanese firms did buy existing capacity: Matsushita's production in Oregon was a small fab bought from National Semiconductor as part of the Fairchild acquisition, and Sony made a deal with AMD in the United States to have use of their fabs in Texas for making static RAMs. AMD, financial strapped, later sold Sony the capacity. The former AMD fab had forty times more capacity for SRAMs than Sony's 1991 semiconductor market share in the United States.

Few of the Japanese investments in the United States or Europe could be easily justified by strictly economic criteria.[15] The economics of production was the driving force behind the first wave of assembly FDI in Southeast Asia; the desire to appropriate some of the spillovers of semiconductors was the driving force behind the second wave of acquisitions. In this third wave, only the sale of some semiconductor products, particularly application-specific integrated circuits (ASICs), could benefit from closer links between the customer and the manufacturing location. All of Toshiba's U.S. operations, for instance, were small, "personalization" fabs that took mostly finished wafers from their Japanese factories and performed the final two or three (out of two hundred–plus) steps of production in the United States. They were relatively small investments for the purpose of local customization.

Politics was the driving force behind the vast majority of Japanese FDI in fabrication for memories, particularly DRAMs and SRAMs. Since these products were strictly commodities with huge economies of scale and virtually zero transportation costs, the best location for a DRAM plant was next to the R&D lab. Yet virtually all of the significant R&D for memory products of Japanese firms was kept at home.[16]

14. Interviews with Japanese firms, December 1989.
15. Toshiba, for example, announced plans to build fab capacity in Europe after the change in regulations but subsequently decided to postpone it indefinitely. They announced in 1991 that further new capacity could not be financially justified. Interview with industry executive, 1992.
16. It was common practice in the semiconductor industry for firms to have design centers in major markets. Japanese firms were no exception to this rule. Design centers, however, were not a

Another important attribute of Japanese fabs in the United States was that they were generally not using state-of-the-art technology in 1992. In Japan, the newest memory fabs used eight-inch wafers and 0.5-micron line width technology: the most advanced Japanese fab (NEC) in the United States had six-inch wafers with 0.7-micron line width; the majority of the fabs averaged around 1.0-micron line width.[17] Several of the plants in the United States (not including NEC, Hitachi, and Fujitsu) were built and equipped for under $100 million, suggesting they were largely pilot operations for small-volume business. NEC, which entered the market in 1978, was the only Japanese firm operating at very high volumes. The other leading Japanese firms had not fully ramped up production in the United States. In Europe, by contrast, most Japanese firms had committed bigger investments ($200 million–$400 million) in capital for large-scale memory production with six-inch wafers at 0.8-micron line widths.

There was a similar pattern, on a much smaller scale, of expanding fabrication facilities by U.S. companies in Europe. Since most U.S. semiconductor companies already had fabrication facilities in Europe, further FDI would only be likely if a firm needed to expand capacity for the European market. Excluding IBM, which entered a joint venture with Siemens in France for advanced memories, Texas Instrument was making the largest investment, with $1.2 billion, four-year project in Italy with heavy Italian government subsidies, including grants and loans. Three other U.S. firms decided to invest for the first time in Europe in the late 1980s and early 1990s: Intel, AT&T, and Analog Devices. Intel and Analog Devices built fabs in Ireland; AT&T built a large semiconductor fab in Spain. Among all U.S. semiconductor firms, only TI and IBM did significant R&D in Europe.

Despite what appeared to be obvious incentives for U.S. and European manufacturers to invest in Japan in the late 1980s, the rate of non-Japanese fab investment in Japan was virtually unchanged from the earlier periods. Point-of-sales affiliates, design centers, quality assurance and testing centers, and failure analysis centers expanded by more than a factor of two after the SCTA (Semiconductor Industry Associations 1989). None of these facilities, however, required significant capital investment. Prior to the SCTA, only four merchant "American" semiconductor companies (TI, Motorola, Fairchild, and LSI Logic) had fab or assembly facilities in Japan, but Schlumberger sold off Fairchild's Japanese fabs and only TI and Motorola expanded after 1986.[18] LSI Logic, an ASIC vendor with under $1 billion in revenue, located its first fab in

---

significant portion of total R&D spending for any semiconductor firm. Rather, a design center would take core products that came out of centralized R&D and adapt them for local needs. Sharp, for instance, built what it described as an R&D center in Washington State; however, the R&D was virtually all final-stage customization for the U.S. market.

17. Interview with industry executives, 1992.

18. This excludes IBM and AT&T. IBM had semiconductor facilities in Japan dating back twenty years, and AT&T entered into agreements with NEC on semiconductor technology in the latter half of the 1980s.

Japan. LSI needed capital, and Kawasaki Steel, looking to diversify, was willing to underwrite most of the investment ("A new emerging species" 1991).

Motorola entered the Japanese market after liberalization of capital controls in 1980. It went into a joint venture with a failing Japanese semiconductor company, (Aizu-Toko), which Motorola subsequently bought in 1982. After exiting from DRAMs in 1985, Motorola licensed some of its key microprocessor technology to Toshiba as part of a joint manufacturing in DRAMs in 1986. The joint venture also called for Toshiba to help Motorola with market access in Japan. (Motorola subsequently invested in a small fab in China in 1990 to serve the Chinese market, as well as new assembly test facilities in Hong Kong.)

TI adopted an aggressive strategy of new FDI in fab capacity in the late 1980s and early 1990s. While TI planned $2 billion in capital expansion, 50 percent of that investment was to be underwritten by foreign partners. In addition to its deal in Italy, TI planned to expand DRAM capacity in Japan, Singapore, and Taiwan. TI's major commitment of capital in Japan was done with a joint venture with Kobe Steel; in Taiwan, it was done with a joint venture with a PC clone company, Acer Computer. The Singapore joint venture included Canon, Hewlett-Packard, and the Singapore Economic Development Board, which collectively would invest $330 million for a facility to open in 1993.

FDI by European competitors was nonexistent in Japan in the latter half of the 1980s, while FDI in the United States was in a disinvestment mode: SGS-Thomson built a shell for a fab in the early 1980s in Phoenix but had not filled the building with equipment through 1992; Philips-Signetics was scaling back its operations, exiting from its older fab in Salt Lake City while retaining its plant in New Mexico; and Siemens had a very small pilot fab in Silicon Valley for sale.

7.5   Some Consequences of the Recent FDI

If one looks at the total FDI fab capacity invested in semiconductors in Europe, Japan, the United States, and developing countries in the 1980s, only U.S. investment in Europe significantly altered the global configuration of production of trade. As noted earlier, only an estimated 10 percent of world production took place outside of national firms' home bases by 1989 (see figure 7.1). Production was clearly "global," in the sense that products continued to be shipped to Southeast Asia for finishing and then reexported to the home and third countries. But by 1990, as figure 7.2 illustrates, Japanese firms had less than 4 percent of the fab lines in the United States and 3 percent of Europe, while TI and Motorola had only 8 percent of the lines in Japan.[19] The most

19. Fab lines are probably the most accurate measure of activities by nonlocal producers, but they do not equate to share of production. The Japanese had roughly 46 percent of world production in 1990 but only 29 percent of the semiconductor fab lines, because they have a narrower range of product offerings than do U.S. firms and larger, dedicated lines that produce higher volumes of chips than the average of U.S.-owned line.

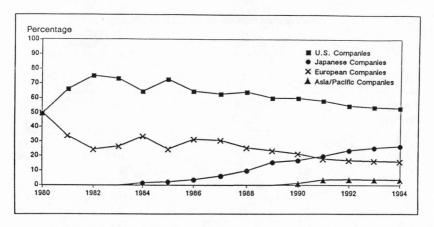

Fig. 7.1   Percentage of total offshore production by regional companies
Source: Dataquest (1990).

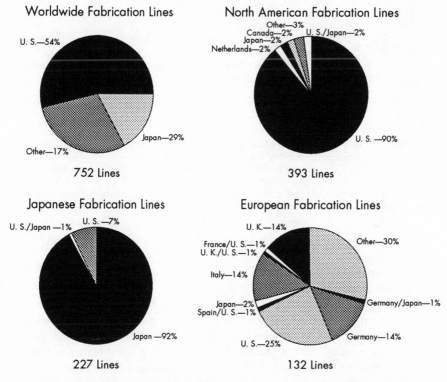

Fig. 7.2   Semiconductor fabrication lines: Location and ownership by major market and principal producers' share, 1990
Source: Semiconductor Equipment and Materials International.

Table 7.5   Total Japanese Semiconductor Trade ($ millions)

	Exports		Imports	
Year	Integrated Circuits	Total	Integrated Circuits	Total
1967[a,b]		$ 16.6	$ 5.0	$ 17.0
1968[b]		18.7	12.0	27.5
1969[b]		27.1	21.8	47.7
1970[b]		27.2	57.4	92.5
1971[b]		27.9	69.6	89.8
1972	$ 6.8	42.0	54.2	81.3
1973	9.5	84.3	122.5	181.8
1974	22.9	130.8	154.7	206.3
1975	45.5	140.8	134.9	182.9
1976	76.7	236.0	199.4	280.7
1977	117.9	309.4	207.6	291.7
1978	248.2	480.4	291.4	378.0
1979	494.5	753.8	449.6	556.2
1980	808.8	1,087.6	480.3	609.3
1981	904.9	1,236.5	517.8	686.7
1982	1,144.8	1,425.9	511.4	641.2
1983	1,784.2	2,150.0	642.4	785.9
1984	3,271.2	3,778.3	935.6	1,137.4
1985	2,439.7	2,920.9	693.8	836.3
1986	3,107.4	3,797.3	867.7	1,026.2
1987	4,096.6	5,005.4	1,125.4	1,307.6
1988	6,598.3	7,915.4	1,761.0	2,003.1
1989	8,313.0	9,681.1	2,246.9	2,547.0
1990	7,595.1	9,005.4	2,589.1	2,921.3

Source: Japan Electronics Bureau, JETRO.

[a]During the 1965–66 period, the Japanese exported only discrete semiconductor devices (DSDs); these included germanium transistors, silicon transistors, germanium diodes, silicon diodes, and silicon diodes for silicon rectifiers. (Thus, the data do not include integrated circuits for this period.)

[b]In the 1967–72 period, the Japanese began exporting integrated circuits (ICs). However, the data do no distinguish between ICs and DSDs.

material consequence of FDI has been felt in Europe, where U.S. firms had 25 percent of the total fab lines in production in 1990.

The implications of FDI in the 1980s and early 1990s had for trade and employment were relatively modest. Japanese firms continued to serve world markets largely through direct exports from Japan: the 10 percent decline in Japanese semiconductor exports in 1990 (table 7.5) was a result of collapsing DRAM prices, not trade substitution. Due to the limited ramping of U.S. production by Japanese fabs, Japanese imports were 82 percent higher in 1990 than in 1986. In the meantime, the United States continued to run trade deficits in semiconductors, but the bulk of imports into the United States—on the order of 65 percent to 70 percent—still originated from the foreign subsidiaries of U.S. companies.[20]

7.6 Implications of FDI in Semiconductors

There appear to be three possible anomalies in the evolving pattern of FDI in semiconductors. First, there has been a stickiness to FDI in semiconductors that is not purely economic in nature. Many U.S. firms invested aggressively in assembly and test facilities in Southeast Asia during the 1960s and 1970s. The impact of these historical investments continue to weigh heavily on the industry in the 1990s. If the semiconductor industry had started in this decade, with Japanese and U.S. firms holding the same competitive positions they held in 1990, the structure of world production would be vastly different. The volume of products shipped from Southeast Asia would be substantially reduced; direct U.S. exports would be much greater; and facilities in Ireland, Scotland, Israel, and various locations on the European continent might not even exist. Instead, most firms have, over time, expanded facilities in old locations, particularly in Southeast Asia. For the most part, organizational inertia appears to be the best explanation. Remember that only the physical plant, which accounts for about 20 percent of the capital costs of an assembly/test operation, is sunk: the equipment (80 percent of total costs) is mobile, and in the late 1980s and early 1990s, locating assembly and test next to the fabrication plant was more cost effective. Local assembly was especially cost effective for higher value-added logic products, which were increasingly dominating U.S. companies' product lines.

The second anomaly that appears in the data is the location of new FDI in fabrication facilities. The history of domestic investment in semiconductors in the United States and Japan clearly exhibits a clustering phenomenon: U.S. fabrication and R&D facilities clustered around three locations: California's Silicon Valley, Phoenix (Motorola's semiconductor headquarters), and Texas (TI's headquarters). In Japan, a similar clustering took place in the corridor between Tokyo and Yokohama and around Osaka. There was less clustering in Europe because of sovereign national boundaries. However, if one looks at the pattern of FDI in both the United States and Europe since the mid-1980s, investments have been widely dispersed. In Europe, new facilities have been built in Ireland, Scotland, England, Spain, Germany, Italy, France and (if one considers Siemens's non-German European investments) Austria (see figure 7.3). In the United States, Japanese FDI has gone to Washington, Oregon, and

---

20. One estimate by industry executives suggested that Japanese firms were producing roughly $1.5 billion worth of ICs in the United States in 1991, compared with roughly $5 billion in annual U.S. sales and $3.5 billion in imports. However, if the Japanese fully ramped their existing capacity in the United States, they could substitute more than half their exports for domestic production. Interview with industry executives.

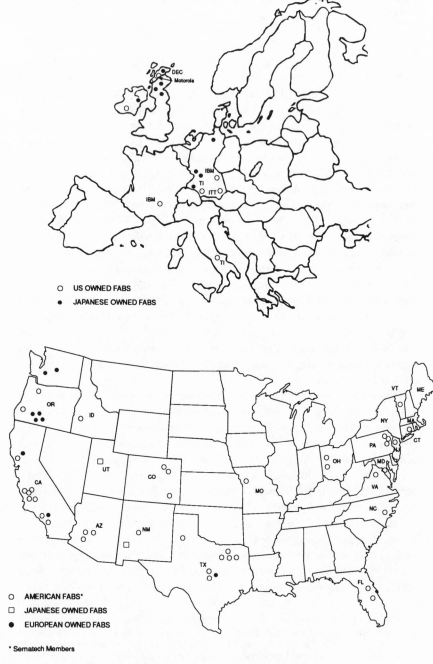

Fig.7.3   Location of FDI: United States and Europe, 1991

North Carolina, as well as to established clusters in Texas, California, Arizona, and New Mexico.[21]

There are at least two complementary explanations for these location decisions. First, and probably most important, there has been significant competition for FDI among states in the United States and even more intense competition among nations in Europe. Given the heavy capital intensity of fab investments, a variety of benefits—direct subsidies, interest-free loans, tax relief, free or subsidized land, and so on—provided by local governments have made some locations more attractive than others for investing firms. When the industry was in its infancy, subsidies in many instances would not have outweighed the benefits of clustering. Skilled labor was in short supply, and it was easier to hire those workers in established clusters, where they had more abundant job opportunities. The availability of the necessary infrastructure for constructing a complicated fab and a guaranteed power supply were also critical.[22] However, most of these inputs were available in the 1990s in many developed countries and most U.S. states. As a result, those specific benefits or positive externalities of clustering are less obvious to firms.

Second, some managers have interpreted the leakiness of semiconductor technology as a negative externality, which can be minimized by locating in places outside of existing clusters.[23] While countries and states are explicitly trying to replicate the dynamism of Silicon Valley by attracting foreign capital, firms are trying to avoid the negative consequences of Silicon Valley: the risks associated with state-of-the-art process and product technology leaking to competitors with facilities in the region. Building a fab in a new location does not guarantee that other firms will not locate there in the future, but there is a relatively low probability that a Spanish or Irish fab worker will end up in a competitor's factory in France or Germany. If firms continue to disperse their foreign investment activities and limit the scope of their foreign operations, the return on government subsidies for attracting FDI could be low indeed.

There also appeared to have been differences between the locational strategies of Japanese and U.S. firms. There is no dominant choice for a location within Europe, because demand for products is spread broadly across many European nations. Nonetheless, U.S. firms were more likely to be influenced by the size of the subsidy than were their Japanese counterparts. The biggest subsidies were offered by Spain, Ireland, and Italy, which enticed AT&T, Intel, and TI, respectively. NEC located in Scotland (large fab) and West Germany (small fab), while Fujitsu located in England. Japanese managers' greater comfort with English might be part of the explanation. Both regions offered financial incentives, though apparently much less than competing locations.[24]

21. Intel established a fab in New Mexico in the early 1980s.
22. Even minor power outages can be devastating to a semiconductor fab: a momentary outage can ruin up to $200,000 of work-in-progress per incident.
23. This insight came from interviews with managers of one U.S. firm's European operation.
24. Interview with industry executives.

Hitachi also opted to invest in West Germany, despite very limited government support.

A third anomaly, one difficult to explain, is the lack of significant new greenfield FDI in Japan; also, the little FDI which has taken place is almost exclusively in the form of joint ventures, despite fourteen years of "liberalized" capital flows. The primary driver behind FDI in Europe was the perception that, without a local presence, the market might become closed to Japanese and U.S. companies. A similar logic might have been applied to Japan, assuming that one believes being located behind any external barriers creates greater opportunity for sales. Japan, however, should have been a much more attractive market for FDI than Europe. Japan being the world's largest market for semiconductors, with much of the world's most advanced equipment suppliers, one might predict that non-Japanese firms would want to invest to take advantage of the externalities associated with local semiconductor production.

Some traditional explanations for the lack of FDI, such as the weak market for corporate control, cannot explain the lack of semiconductor FDI in Japan. Motorola, for example, was able to buy a Japanese firm to enter the market in the late 1970s. In addition, there is a market for fab capacity in Japan, even without buying an entire firm. High land prices in Japan have also been cited as a deterrent to entry, but some firms (e.g., Intel) who purchased adequate land in Japan more than a decade ago have still opted against FDI in fabrication or assembly. Moreover, joint ventures appear to be the dominant form of investment, even for firms with experience in Japan. Since the SCTA also gave Japanese firms additional incentives to buy non-Japanese semiconductors—up to 20 percent of the market—there were even greater incentives for FDI.

Without direct government subsidies or other benefits available to foreign investors in Europe or the United States, managers of U.S. and European firms continue to believe that the externality benefits of FDI in Japan do not offset the cost penalties associated with recruiting high-quality labor and the general high cost of operations in Japan. In addition, most non-Japanese firms continue to have difficulty recruiting the most talented engineers and selling products to large Japanese groups.

The experience of Motorola and TI, the two companies with ten–twenty years of experience in Japan, do not suggest to other U.S. competitors that FDI will provide positive benefits. Both companies have stated publicly their dissatisfaction with sales in Japan.[25] When TI entered the Japanese market, it was the undisputed technology and market share leader in the world. Despite twenty-four years of operating in Japan, TI has been unable to appropriate significant benefits from agglomeration: it dropped to number seven in world market share in 1991, with poor profitability. Motorola, number two in the world when it entered the Japanese market, has slipped less (to number five in

25. Motorola's travails are discussed in Yoffie (1987b); TI's public dissatisfaction with its position in Japan was quoted in The Wall Street Journal, March 9, 1991.

1991) but has been even more vocal about its inability to penetrate Japanese customers, despite local manufacturing and local partners committed to expanding Motorola's market access.

7.7 Conclusions

The broad pattern of FDI in semiconductors is generally consistent with many of the broader global patterns we observe in FDI. As one should expect from macrodata, the United States was a large net exporter of capital in the 1960s and 1970s in this industry, while Japan became a large net exporter of long-term capital in the late 1980s and early 1990s.

The motivations for FDI have also been fairly consistent with traditional explanations. In the early period, a search for the lowest labor costs and jumping tariff barriers dominated FDI. During the second wave of acquisitions, efforts to access the advantages of U.S. "dynamism" drove foreign investment. And during the most recent period, politics once again dominated the scene. As one U.S. manager noted, "Europe has been the most successful in blackmailing the world [to force investment in the community]";[26] but Japanese managers would probably suggest privately that the United States has not been far behind.

Despite the very global nature of the semiconductor industry, the experience of Japanese, U.S., and European FDI would not suggest that public policy officials would have any difficulty in answering Robert Reich's questions of "Who is us?" or "Who is them?" The vast majority of fabrication and an even larger percentage of research and development for semiconductors remain at home. Even though more nondomestic, especially Japanese, capacity will come on line over the next decade, the underlying economics will drive successful firms in semiconductors to keep R&D for core products closely coupled with advanced fabrication. Design centers will further spread around the world; more cross-national joint ventures to share the cost and risks of new technologies will evolve. But the heavy weight of history will also keep large employment for assembly in Southeast Asia.

The deeper examination of actual operations by Japanese firms in the United States also suggests that most FDI has been more symbolic than significant. The limited scale of Japanese plants, the slow ramping of production, and the use of second-generation technology in the United States could suggest that Japanese firms look at investments in the United States as options. By putting some capacity in place which can be fully ramped at a later date, Japanese firms retain flexibility to respond to possible protectionism without incurring the full cost penalty of large-scale non-Japanese production. At the same time, they reduce the incentives for protectionism in the United States, because they could ramp local production fairly quickly if duties or quotas were imposed.

26. Interview with a U.S. manager, 1992.

Only when the threat of protectionism is highly credible (as it has been for semiconductors in Europe or for cars in the United States), will firms make large-scale, irreversible capital commitments.

References

A new emerging species: Not many U.S. semiconductor houses can afford to manufacture; is competitiveness at risk? 1991. *Electronics,* July, p. 38.

Borrus, Michael G. 1988. *Competing for control: America's stake in microelectronics.* Cambridge, Mass.: Ballinger Publishing.

Braun, Ernest, and Stuart Macdonald. 1982. *Revolution in miniature: The history and impact of semiconductor electronics.* 2d. Cambridge: Cambridge University Press.

Dataquest. 1990. Semiconductor production: Truly global. *Research Newsletter* (SEMS newsletter), March.

Finan, William. 1975. The international transfer of semiconductor technology through U.S.-based firms. NBER Working Paper no. 118. Cambridge, Mass.: National Bureau of Economic Research.

Flamm, Kenneth. 1990. Semiconductors. In *Europe 1992: An American perspective,* ed. Gary Hufbauer. Washington, D.C.: Brookings Institution.

Flamm, Kenneth, and Joseph Grunwald. 1985. *The global factory: Foreign assembly in international trade.* Washington, D.C.: Brookings Institution.

Knickerbocker, F. T. 1973. *Oligopolistic reaction and multinational enterprise.* Boston: Harvard Business School Press.

Krugman, Paul. 1991. *Geography and trade.* Cambridge, Mass.: MIT Press.

MacKenzie de Sola Pool, Adam. 1988. A new American policy on foreign investment? An assessment of the public policy process in the Fujitsu-Fairchild takeover battle. Unpublished senior honors thesis. Massachusetts Institute of Technology, May.

Overseas investments: A ray of hope for Korea's economy. 1991. *Busines Korea* 8 (June): 32–34.

Porter, Michael E. 1990. *Competitive advantage of nations.* New York: Free Press.

Rukstad, Michael, and Mark Wolfson. 1989. *Schlumberger and Fairchild semiconductor.* Harvard Business School Case no. 9-389-133. Boston, Mass.: Harvard Business School.

Semiconductor Industry Association. 1989. *Three years of experience under the U.S.-Japan semiconductor agreement.* Third Annual Report to the President. San Jose, Calif.

———. 1992. *Semiconductors: Foundation for America's future.* San Jose, Calif., March.

Steinmueller, W. Edward. 1987. International joint ventures in the integrated circuit industry. Paper Series no. 104. Stanford, Calif.: Center for Economic Policy Research, Stanford University, September.

USITC. 1991. *Global competitiveness of US advanced manufacturing industries: Semiconductor manufacturing and testing equipment.* Publication no. 2435. Washington, D.C.: U.S. International Trade Commission, September.

Yoffie, David B. 1993. *Beyond free trade: Firms, governments, and global competition.* Boston: Harvard Business School Press.

———. 1987a. *Global semiconductor industry, 1987.* Harvard Business School Case no. 9-388-052. Boston: Harvard Business School.

———. 1987b. *Motorola and Japan (A).* Harvard Business School Case no. 9-388-056. Boston: Harvard Business School.

Ziegler, Nicholas. 1991.Semiconductors. *Daedalus* 120, no. 4 (Fall): 155–82.

Comment   S. Lael Brainard

Given the ambiguities in the aggregate data, it is refreshing to examine some of the unresolved questions about foreign direct investment (FDI) in a specific industry, and the semiconductor industry provides a particularly rich case. David Yoffie analyzes the evolution of FDI in the semiconductor industry by taking a careful look at industry data combined with anecdotal evidence from extensive interviews. I will restate his argument in somewhat different terms and then suggest issues that it raises.

The implicit argument is that the "natural" pattern of cross-border activity would consist entirely of trade flows. The economics of the semiconductor industry are consistent with each of a few firms establishing neighboring R&D and fabrication facilities (fabs) at a single location, operating at high volume, and exporting globally. This hypothesis is premised on significant plant-level economies of scale and steep learning curves, combined with low transport costs. Due to considerable interfirm, intraregional spillovers and high R&D content, these oligopolistic firms should cluster in one or a few locations with a high density of engineering and scientific skills. In the early years of the industry, the combination of high labor intensity in the final stages of production and an easily separable production structure made it optimal to locate assembly and test facilities in areas with low labor costs. More recently, automation has permitted colocation of testing and assembly with fabrication in areas with higher labor costs. Throughout, internalization of fabrication, assembly, and testing within a unified ownership structure has been warranted by considerable proprietary process technology.

Instead of exclusive reliance on trade, Yoffie argues, there has been extensive FDI and some licensing, which he attributes primarily to trade restrictions in the first case and to a combination of trade and investment restrictions in the second. His analysis presumes a clear ranking of the modes of cross-border market penetration: exporting is most profitable, followed by direct investment, with licensing or joint ventures the least desirable options.

Yoffie distinguishes three phases in the evolution of FDI in the semiconductor industry. The first, from the 1960s to the early 1970s, was characterized by U.S. dominance. Consistent with the natural pattern, industry leaders based in the United States made investments in Asia to tap into low labor costs for assembly and testing. They also made direct investments in the EC in response to tariff barriers. The activities of U.S. firms in Japan were largely confined to licensing, due to a combination of investment and trade restrictions.

The second half of the 1970s was characterized by a number of foreign acquisitions of U.S. semiconductor firms. Yoffie describes the acquisition activity as defensive attempts on the part of several European firms to boost flagging competitiveness.

The third phase stretches from the late 1980s to the present. It has been characterized by investment in greenfield fabs by both Japanese and U.S. firms in the EC and by Japanese firms in the United States. Yoffie describes the EC investments as a response to trade barriers and changes in domestic content regulations, and the U.S. investments as an "option" to hedge against potential trade barriers.

Cross-Border/Cross-Industry and Within-Border/Within Industry Evidence

Given the paucity of firm-level data, an evaluation of the argument comes down to a choice of whether it fits the mostly anecdotal evidence better than plausible alternatives do. The argument would be strengthened considerably by bringing to bear evidence on cross-border investment flows in other industries and on within-border flows in the semiconductor industry.

Thus, for instance, the paper would be more persuasive in discussing Japanese FDI in the United States if it were to incorporate evidence across a range of industries, to distinguish the features that are unique to the semiconductor industry. It is possible that wealth effects associated with the depreciation of the dollar (Froot and Stein 1991) or the Japanese land and stock price bubbles in the latter half of the 1980s explain Japanese investment in the U.S. semiconductor industry no less than in other industries. Indeed, the increase in FDI in semiconductors may have been low in comparison to other industries.

Similarly, Robert Lawrence's finding (chap. 4 in this volume) that there are implicit barriers to inward investment in Japan across a broad cross section of industries might lend support to Yoffie's argument that foreign firms continue to encounter barriers to investment in the Japanese semiconductor industry despite liberalization.

Further, a comparison of cross-border merger and acquisition activity with domestic activity might shed some light on the foreign acquisitions of U.S. semiconductor firms in the late 1970s. Indeed, without such a comparison, it is difficult to dismiss a hypothesis that the acquisitions were driven by internal industry dynamics such as the expansion beyond start-up, or the shift to very large scale integration (VLSI)—rather than declining competitiveness in Europe. Yoffie also notes that all of the European acquisitions from this period subsequently failed. Again, the argument would be strengthened by comparing the foreign failure rate with the domestic failure rate.

Lastly, data on the domestic configurations of semiconductor firms could be used to help determine whether the decentralization of production within firms has been forced by cross-border restrictions or is simply a natural by-product of the industry's evolution. If barriers are the prime driver, there should be more dispersion of production across borders than within borders.

The "Natural" Pattern of Trade

The argument that trade rather than investment would prevail in the absence of barriers slightly begs the question of the natural pattern of trade, which in turn has implications for the pattern of investment. This oversight permeates much recent literature on FDI: although multinational production is widely understood as an alternative to exporting when proximity and internalization advantages exist (Dunning 1988; Caves 1982), rarely is there explicit consideration of the type of trade for which it substitutes.

Depending on the underlying impetus for trade, different predictions for the pattern of investment might emerge. For instance, two distinct models based on differentiated goods might be appropriate for different segments of the industry. A model based on factor proportions (Helpman 1984; Helpman and Krugman 1985) would yield predictions largely consistent with Yoffie's explanation of U.S. investments in the commodity chip segment in Asia in the 1970s. A model emphasizing a trade-off between proximity and concentration advantages for each stage of the business system (Brainard 1992) would predict two-way trade in segments such as microprocessors, with two-way investment occurring only where proximity to customers or suppliers overrides scale considerations.

A third alternative is a model with an intraindustry, intranational learning curve, such as that used by Baldwin and Krugman (1990) in their analysis of the 16K RAM semiconductor segment. In this case, we might expect to see FDI even in the absence of trade barriers to tap into local learning.[1] This might, for instance, explain Yoffie's second wave.

External Economies and the Industry Life Cycle

A third question is applicable to the literature on high-technology industries generally. Yoffie's essay shares with many others in this area a slight fuzziness on the question of what needs to be close to what. Specifying the nature of key externalities more precisely, and analyzing how they change over time, might explain some of the puzzles Yoffie encounters.

There frequently is confusion as to the distinction between innovation resulting from R&D and learning curves—and the extent to which the latter is plant-specific as opposed to firm-specific. Thus, for instance, the prediction that the optimal configuration entails a single fabrication facility is premised on a learning curve that is plant specific within a generation, but it is unclear whether learning is transferred between generations and, if so, whether such transfers are possible across plants. Similarly, the prediction of geographic concentration is premised on agglomeration economies, but it is unclear whether these occur in R&D or learning. If the answer is R&D, is it more important to put R&D facilities close to related R&D labs, fab facilities, or customers? Further, the relative importance of these externalities may shift over time. The recent migration of plants away from Silicon Valley may be a response to changes in external economies over the product life cycle, rather than a contradiction of agglomeration economies. In many industries, geographic

---

1. The extent to which foreign firms can tap into "home market advantages" via direct investment is an unresolved issue. See Porter (1990).

spillovers between firms are critical in the early stages, which are characterized by high rates of innovation and interfirm learning facilitated by high turnover and spin-off activity. As such industries mature, however, proximity to specialized factors, to supplier industries, or to dense concentrations of customers may increase in importance and eventually dominate,[2] unless externalities between R&D labs continue to be critical or plant investment is long lived. In the semiconductor industry, the latter explanation seems unlikely, since the plant and equipment are obsolete in three to five years.[3]

Indeed, it was surprising to find no reference to vertical linkages in the discussion of location and agglomeration patterns. There is substantial evidence of vertical externalities in the semiconductor industry, both upstream and downstream. The newspapers are full of articles alleging that EC and U.S. semiconductor firms have been handicapped by delayed access to new equipment since Japanese companies gained dominance of the equipment market. There is also extensive downstream integration; it has been prevalent in Japan since the industry's inception and has increased substantially in the United States in recent years.

This is important for two reasons. It is possible that the seeming anomalies in recent fab locations are explained by changing industry economics in which vertical externalities increasingly dominate horizontal externalities. A comparison of the geographical configurations of vertically integrated firms with those of merchant firms might shed light on whether recent location choices were driven by strategic considerations as opposed to barriers. It would be useful to examine whether there is significant colocation of upstream and downstream R&D, and the extent to which downstream activities are themselves dispersed across borders.

Second, in line with Lawrence's analysis (chap. 4 in this volume) of *keiretsu* ties as implicit barriers to investment in Japan, the extensive degree of vertical integration of Japanese semiconductor firms might help to explain the low level of foreign investment into the Japanese semiconductor industry.

The Three Puzzles

Yoffie leaves us with three puzzles; I will comment on each in turn. First, he notes that there is a surprising lack of agglomeration in recent greenfield investments. As suggested above, it is possible that the lack of agglomeration in recent investments is better explained by the shift to VLSI, which has favored vertical integration and large scale over the high turnover and interfirm spillovers associated with agglomeration.

Agglomeration was never a significant factor for the Japanese semiconduc-

2. The importance of these factors may also vary among product segments.
3. The rapid obsolescence is also hard to reconcile with the option interpretation of recent Japanese investment.

tor industry. Many industries are concentrated in the Tokyo-Yokohama corridor and Osaka; this is not unique to the semiconductor industry. Further, there is a sharp difference in the market structures of the Japanese and U.S. semiconductor industries. The Japanese market has never been blessed, or afflicted, by the high rates of entry and exit, employee turnover, and interfirm leakage of technology that have characterized the U.S. market. Instead, the Japanese industry is characterized by stable relationships between semiconductor manufacturers and suppliers, buyers, and financiers, frequently through long-term contracts or ownership, and is dominated by large, diversified industrial conglomerates (MIT 1989).

Second, Yoffie notes that investments in Southeast Asia have been maintained and expanded, even though the automation of assembly and test processes has diminished the importance of access to low-cost labor. However, over the same time period, substantial downstream production (consumer electronics and automobiles) has shifted to this region, and the industrial infrastructure has expanded. It is possible that continued operation in the region is a sensible response to shifts in global production patterns, rather than a sign of inertia.

Third, Yoffie contends that it is surprising to see little FDI into Japan despite liberalization of FDI regulations and implementation of the semiconductor trade agreement (SCTA). This is correct with respect to the liberalization of FDI and corroborates evidence in other industries, as noted above. However, there is no reason to expect increased fabrication investment in response to the SCTA. The SCTA essentially targets the U.S. share of Japanese purchases of semiconductors. Implementation of the agreement would be consistent with rising imports from the United States by Japan, given large-scale economies and low transport costs. And, as Yoffie notes, investment in activities complementary to trade, such as marketing, distribution, and customization, has doubled.

Policy Implications

I conclude by turning briefly to policy implications. If Yoffie is correct, in the absence of barriers to trade, industry economics would imply domination by a few global players concentrated in a few geographical clusters, and there would be no FDI. If we take global share as a proxy for welfare,[4] then the ranking of different policies (in the absence of retaliation) would appear to be (1) joint trade and investment restrictions, (2) no restrictions, and (3) trade restrictions alone. Clearly, this is overstated. Yet, if trade and investment barriers have as deep and lasting an effect on firm configurations as Yoffie's analysis suggests, it is critical for U.S. policymakers to address barriers to both trade and investment in negotiations over semiconductors.

---

4. This is clearly incorrect, but it reflects the priorities articulated in policy debates.

References

Baldwin, Richard, and Paul Krugman. 1990. Market access and competition: A simulation of 16K RAMs. In *Rethinking international trade,* ed. Paul Krugman, 199–225. Cambridge, Mass.: MIT Press.

Brainard, S. Lael. 1992. A simple theory of multinational corporations and trade with a trade-off between proximity and concentration. MIT Sloan School Working Paper no. 3492-92-EFA.

Caves, Richard. 1982. *Multinational enterprise and economic analysis.* Cambridge: Cambridge University Press.

Dunning, John. 1988. *Explaining international production.* London: HarperCollins.

Froot, Kenneth, and Jeremy Stein. 1991. Exchange rates and foreign direct investment: An imperfect capital markets approach. *Quarterly Journal of Economics* 106:1191–219.

Helpman, Elhanan. 1984. A simple theory of international trade with multinational corporations. *Journal of Political Economy* 92:451.

Helpman, Elhanan, and Paul Krugman. 1985. *Market structure and foreign trade.* Cambridge, Mass.: MIT Press.

MIT, Commission on Industrial Productivity. 1989. The US semiconductor, computer, and copier industries. *Working Papers of the MIT Commission on Industrial Productivity.* Cambridge, Mass.: MIT Press.

Porter, Michael E. 1990. *The competitive advantage of nations.* New York: Free Press.

Discussion Summary

Robert Feenstra began the discussion by noting that a large fraction of FDI in semiconductors was undertaken by multinationals in order to have manufacturing capacity inside trade walls. It would be interesting to compare the experience of other industries where FDI occurred in response to the erection of trade barriers—for instance, autos. The United States rejected local content rules for autos but erected trade barriers while maintaining free access for FDI. *Feenstra* asked whether these two sets of policies have similar effects.

Someone else asked whether semiconductor FDI into low-wage areas continued because there is still a demand for old-fashioned, labor-intensive products. Why does Malaysia still attract FDI? *David Yoffie* answered that organizational inertia seems to explain this type of FDI. The labor input in these operations is now very small, and equipment, which constitutes 80 percent of the capital, can be moved. Only 20 percent of the capital is immobile plant. The most efficient location for testing and assembly operations in the late 1980s and early 1990s is next to the fabrication facility (fab).

Kenneth Froot asked why geographic agglomerations no longer seem to be important. That is, why do firms put fabs in Ireland and North Carolina instead of Silicon Valley? Saloner and Rotemberg have a model in which firms can hire workers and persuade them to make industry-specific investments in human capital if there are other firms in the area. This model implies that semiconductor firms should continue to locate in Silicon Valley.

Lael Brainard offered another reason for agglomerations: externalities with suppliers. The close ties which Japanese firms have with their suppliers give their fabs a comparative advantage over other fabs. So why are they willing to locate fabs outside Japan?

Yoffie explained that fabs only employ a small number of workers. Therefore, it is inexpensive to find good workers by paying them a premium. In locations outside traditional areas of semiconductor investment, these workers are less likely to quit to go to other fabs. Since labor turnover is very bad for high yields, firms have a strong incentive to locate fabs away from their competitors. *Yoffie* also argued that the benefit of locating near suppliers has declined. Japanese firms are willing to forgo these benefits in order to have production capacity inside actual or potential trade barriers in the United States and Europe.

Robert Lipsey noted that Japanese buyers of semiconductors are all in *keiretsu* and typically buy only from other firms in the *keiretsu*. Thus, demand for the output of merchant firms in Japan is much lower than demand for such output in other countries, and the advantage to foreign firms of investing in Japan in order to sell to the local market is less than the incentive to invest in other countries.

Raymond Vernon asked if foreign firms could, by locating in Japan, establish better contacts with Japanese suppliers and thus obtain the latest technology. He also asked what Texas Instruments (TI) and IBM do? *Yoffie* answered that IBM produces in Burlington for its own use throughout the world. TI has had great difficulty selling to Japanese customers and obtaining the latest technology from Japanese suppliers.

Krishna Palepu asked why governments give subsidies to FDI in semiconductors. *Yoffie* answered that they think there are large externalities but they are wrong. All they get is a little employment for local engineers, but so far no backward or forward linkages. In recent years, suppliers and customers of the semiconductor industry have not followed fabs to new locations.

Martin Feldstein asked whether increased tax revenues will eventually be large enough to pay for the investment incentives. *Froot* noted that persuading the second firm to invest in an area may be cheaper and easier than attracting the first, since the second can steal workers from the first.

Yoffie replied that it is too soon to say whether governments will recoup their tax subsidies but that they probably will not. A modern fab that costs $500 million to build and receives $150 million in investment incentives has perhaps forty workers. Almost all the $500 million is for imported equipment, and almost all the downstream work will continue to be done elsewhere. Governments see that spillovers occurred in Silicon Valley and want to duplicate that experience. But this is no longer happening. Ireland and Italy are only succeeding in spending huge amounts of money bribing firms away from each other.

Richard Marston observed that Compaq's facilities in Silicon Glen in Scotland now supply most of the EC with their computers. This is an example of an assembly operation which took some time to follow the initial fab. Maybe it takes time for downstream spillovers to come.

Feldstein suggested that corruption could also explain why governments give investment incentives to semiconductor firms.

James Hines reported that Puerto Rico gave $140,000 in tax subsidies to manufacturing firms for each $10,000-a-year job that was created. There was no measurable effect on local wages.

Someone else observed that subsidies of lost tax revenues do not cost governments anything, since the multinationals would not have invested in the subsidizing country without the tax benefits. The lost tax revenues come from the country where the investment would otherwise have gone.

Geoffrey Carliner asked if international coordination could prevent multinationals from playing one country off against another. He also asked why the United States does not apply countervailing duties against these types of subsidies.

8 International Corporate Equity Acquisitions: Who, Where, and Why?

Paul M. Healy and Krishna G. Palepu

In this paper we provide evidence on international equity investments among eleven of the leading industrial nations during the period 1985 to 1990. Our purpose is to document which countries have been the largest target nations and which have been the most active acquirers. We also examine factors that restrict and encourage equity investments between countries.

We find that international equity investments grew tenfold between 1985 and 1990 and currently account for about 30 percent of all corporate equity investments. In dollar terms, the United States is by far the largest target country for international equity investments and accounted for 60 percent of all international investments between 1985 and 1990. However, when we control for differences in country size, the United States ranks only third among target countries (behind the United Kingdom and Canada). At the other extreme, the Japanese equity market is effectively off limits to foreign investors. There were few significant foreign equity investments in Japan in the study period.

The United Kingdom is the most active acquirer nation, both in dollar terms and adjusting for country size, and accounts for 26 percent of all international acquisitions. U.S. French, and Japanese companies are also large acquirers in dollar terms, and each country accounts for about 14 percent of worldwide equity investments. However, when we control for country size, the United States ranks tenth out of eleven countries in investments abroad.

International activity in target countries is explained in part by (1) regulations that seek to deter foreign investment, (2) differences across countries in

This research was funded by the International Financial Services Center and the NTU-MIT Research Fund at the Massachusetts Institute of Technology and by the Division of Research at Harvard University. The authors are grateful to Philip Hamilton for assistance in data collection and to Michael Adler, Andrew Alford, Ravi Bhushan, Kenneth Froot, and participants at the National Bureau of Economic Research conference on foreign direct investment for comments on the paper.

ownership structure and corporate control markets, and (3) target countries' recent growth. Neither changes in real exchange rates between target and acquirer countries nor growth rates of acquirer countries are important factors explaining international investment patterns.

The chapter is organized as follows. Section 8.1 describes the data used in the study. International equity investment patterns among target countries and the factors explaining the level of investments in target countries are reported in section 8.2. In section 8.3 we present a summary of the most active acquirer nations, and in section 8.4 we present tests of factors that explain changes in international investments between the target and acquirer nations. Our conclusions are presented in section 8.5.

8.1 Data

The data for our analysis are from Securities Data Company's (SDC) database of intercorporate worldwide investments. SDC compiles a list of these transactions from U.S. and foreign news sources, including source documents from government agencies, surveys from foreign stock exchanges and investment banks, and reports from *Financial Times, International Financing Review, Reuters, Dow Jones News Services, The Wall Street Journal* (Asian and U.S. editions), and the *New York Times*. The database covers intercorporate equity investments, regardless of the percentage of ownership acquired. Portfolio investments by mutual funds are not reported.

To be included in our sample, transactions are required to be completed deals announced in the period January 1, 1985, through December 31, 1990. The transactions include investments by both public and private companies in other public or private companies. The investments range from acquisitions of noncontrolling equity interests to transactions that transfer complete control to the acquirer.[1]

The SDC database provides information on the country of the acquiring firm, the target firm country, and the dollar value of each acquisition at its completion date (expressed in U.S. dollars at that date). There is some question as to how to classify target and acquirer firms' nations when the entity considered is owned by another firm headquartered in a different nation. We identify

1. To corroborate the accuracy of the SDC data, international acquisitions of U.S. equity reported in the database from 1985 to 1990 are compared with the U.S. Bureau of Economic Analysis (BEA) data on international acquisitions of equity stakes exceeding 10 percent in U.S. firms. While there are some differences between BEA and SDC estimates for individual years, the aggregate acquisitions during these six years are remarkably close. The BEA reports acquisitions of $266.8 billion, whereas SDC estimates for investments by eleven countries examined in this study are $247.8 billion. There are two important differences between the databases. First, the BEA acquisitions are classified by year of completion, but we classify SDC acquisitions by announcement year. Second, the BEA covers all international equity investments in U.S. firms exceeding 10 percent ownership, whereas we examine all equity investments by ten industrialized countries.

Table 8.1   **International and Domestic Intercorporate Equity Investments, by Year, 1985 to 1990**

Year	Equity Investments (U.S. $ millions)			Percentage of Total	
	International	Domestic	Total	International	Domestic
1985	$ 10,139	$ 113,739	$ 123,878	8%	92%
1986	36,121	245,185	281,306	13	87
1987	65,334	209,868	275,202	24	76
1988	86,987	305,302	392,289	22	78
1989	117,152	351,644	468,796	25	75
1990	98,421	237,842	336,263	29	71
1985 to 1990	414,155	1,463,580	1,877,735	22	78

such a transaction by the parent company's country rather than by the acquirer's or target firm's country. For example, the acquisition of Jaguar by Ford Europe, a company with a U.S. parent, is classified as a U.S. company investment in the United Kingdom.

In our analysis, we consider investments in or by firms in the following countries: Australia, Canada, France, West Germany, Italy, Japan, the Netherlands, Spain, Sweden, the United Kingdom, and the United States. These eleven countries account for the bulk of intercorporate investments worldwide. Table 8.1 reports data on aggregate international intercorporate investments in these countries during the period 1985 to 1990. To provide a benchmark, data on domestic intercorporate investments are also reported. International equity investments have steadily grown in importance throughout the sample period. In 1985, they were valued at about $10 billion and increased tenfold to approximately $98 billion in 1990.[2] In contrast, domestic intercorporate equity investments in the eleven countries studied increased only twofold during this same period. In 1985, only 8 percent of worldwide equity investments were international. This percentage increased steadily in the succeeding five years and reached 29 percent by 1990.

8.2 Target Countries

This section examines investment levels in target company countries in the period 1985 to 1990. We then investigate institutional factors that explain differences in intercorporate investments across these countries.

2. While we focus on both controlling and noncontrolling international equity acquisitions, the bulk of the acquisitions are for control, where control is defined as acquisition of ownership of 51 percent or more. During the 1985 to 1990 period, controlling acquisitions account for 86 percent of all international intercorporate investments.

8.2.1   Investment Levels by Target Country

To analyze investment activity by target country, we compute the aggregate dollar value of international investments in each of the eleven industrialized countries in the period 1985 to 1990. Table 8.2 reports this aggregate amount, as well as international equity investments in each country as a percentage of the total for all countries. By far the largest target nation for intercorporate equity investments is the United States, which accounts for 60 percent of all international activity. The United Kingdom and Canada are also important target countries, with 16 percent and 8 percent of the total investments. Together, these three countries are targets of most of the international equity investments in the sample period. At the other extreme, there were few international equity acquisitions in Japan during this period.

To examine whether there has been a change in international investment activity by target market between 1985 and 1990, we estimate the value of international investments each year for four major regions (Europe, North America, Japan, and Australia). Figure 8.1 shows the annual international investments in these target regions. In 1985, North America (primarily the U.S.) made up 90 percent of the target market, with Europe the other 10 percent. The major trend over the following five years was a steady decline in the relative share of activity in North America and an increase in international acquisitions in Europe. By 1990, the target markets in the two regions were approximately equal in size.

The above findings do not control for differences in economy sizes across countries. We therefore deflate international equity acquisitions in each country during the period 1985 to 1990 by its total gross domestic product (GDP)

Table 8.2   **International Intercorporate Equity Investments, by Country of Target Firm, 1985 to 1990**

Target Country	International Equity Investments		
	Value (U.S. $ millions)	Percentage of Total	Percentage of Gross Domestic Product
Australia	$ 9,325	2.3%	0.6%
Canada	32,648	7.9	1.1
France	17,032	4.1	0.3
Italy	7,802	1.9	0.1
Japan	2,066	0.5	0.0
Netherlands	8,926	2.2	0.6
Spain	7,357	1.8	0.3
Sweden	3,764	0.9	0.3
United Kingdom	68,329	16.5	1.3
United States	247,789	59.8	0.9
West Germany	9,117	2.2	0.1
Total	414,155	100.0	

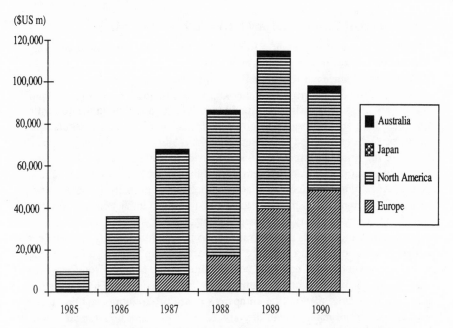

Fig. 8.1   **International intercorporate equity investments, by target market, 1985 to 1990**

in the same period (translated to U.S. dollars using average exchange rates for the year, as reported by the International Monetary Fund [IMF]). These statistics also appear in table 8.2. Controlling for size reduces the disparity among countries in international activity. While the United States, the United Kingdom, and Canada remain the dominant target nations, their rankings change. The United Kingdom is the largest target market, with international activity of 1.3 percent of GDP. Activity in Canada is 1.1 percent of GDP; in the U.S., it is only 0.9 percent. Australia and the Netherlands also emerge as important target nations, with international investments of 0.6 percent of GDP. Once again, Japan is the lowest-ranked target nation.

The evidence in table 8.2 shows significant differences in international activity across target nations. Two factors potentially explain these differences. Differences in government regulations and tax policies on intercorporate investments and differences in equity ownership across countries affect the relative feasibility of intercorporate equity investments in general. Further, many of the eleven countries studied have regulations which favor domestic investments over international activity. Below, we discuss the impact of each of these factors on international equity investments.[3]

3. Even though we discuss these factors as exogenous, it is likely that corporate control market, regulation, and ownership structures are simultaneously determined in a corporate governance system.

8.2.2   Effect of Corporate Control Market in Target Countries

There are several important differences in the nature of the intercorporate investment market in each of the eleven countries studied. First, differences exist across countries in the regulation of intercorporate investments. For example, government antitrust regulations in some countries restrict intercorporate equity investments which are likely to reduce competition in the domestic market. There are differences in government and stock exchange regulations on the procedures required for tender offers for majority control contests. Also, there are important differences across countries in the way these antitrust and tender offer regulations are administered. Finally, tax law differences across countries are likely to affect the relative attractiveness of intercorporate investments. These regulations are likely to have a significant impact on both international and domestic equity investment activity.

A second factor that is likely to influence international equity investments is the nature of ownership structure of corporations. In some of the countries examined, ownership of equity is concentrated in the hands of long-term investors, such as banks, founding families, and the government. These investors typically are represented on the company's board of directors, enabling them to monitor current management directly. As a result, these investors are more likely to replace poorly performing management themselves, reducing the role for hostile acquisitions as a disciplining mechanism. Further, concentrated ownership which is friendly to incumbent management is likely to resist the attempts of outside investors to wrest control of a corporation in an unfriendly transaction. In contrast, in financial systems where stock ownership is disperse, hostile acquisitions are likely to play an important role in changes in corporate control.

Differences in the nature of equity markets across countries impact both international and domestic investment activity. We therefore analyze cross-country differences in domestic investment activity to measure the effect of differences in the general nature of the intercorporate investment market.

Table 8.3 reports domestic intercorporate equity investment activity for each of the sample countries in the period 1985 to 1990, including the aggregate dollar value of domestic investments and domestic equity investments for each country as a percentage of the total for all countries. As with international investments, domestic activity is largest in the United States, accounting for 75 percent of all domestic activity. The United Kingdom has the second most active domestic market. Japan, which as previously noted is the target of few international acquisitions, has domestic activity comparable in dollar value to that of Australia, France, Italy, and Canada.

To control for differences in economy sizes across countries, we again deflate domestic equity investments for each country during the period 1985 to 1990 by its total gross domestic product measured in U.S. dollars in the same period. These statistics are reported in table 8.3. Controlled for size, countries

Table 8.3   **Domestic Intercorporate Equity Investments, by Country of Target Firm, 1985 to 1990**

Target Country	Domestic Equity Investments		
	Value (U.S. $ millions)	Percentage of Total	Percentage of Gross Domestic Product
Australia	$ 36,822	2.5%	2.6%
Canada	55,047	3.8	2.0
France	30,003	2.0	0.4
Italy	21,995	1.5	0.4
Japan	31,526	2.2	0.2
Netherlands	5,442	0.4	0.3
Spain	5,684	0.4	0.2
Sweden	15,812	1.1	1.2
United Kingdom	156,976	10.7	3.3
United States	1,096,159	74.9	3.9
West Germany	8,114	0.6	0.1
Total	1,463,580	100.0	

with the largest domestic investment markets are the United States, the United Kingdom, Australia, and Canada. As in the case of international activity, Japan and West Germany have very low levels of domestic intercorporate investments.

To examine whether differences in the intercorporate investment market explain both domestic and international investments equally, we estimate the correlation between the two types of investment in each country. The cross-country correlation between domestic and international investments as percentages of GDP is 0.81. The correlation between country ranks for international and domestic investment adjusted for GDP is 0.77. Both these correlations, which are highly statistically significant, support the hypothesis that the nature of the intercorporate investment market explains a significant proportion of the cross-country variation in international investments.

Differences in Government Regulations

As discussed above, the differences in the intercorporate investment market are potentially driven by differences in government regulations on corporate takeovers and investments. Table 8.4 presents a summary of takeover regulations for the sample countries in the period 1985 to 1990. The regulations examined include government antitrust regulations relevant to intercorporate investments, and government and exchange regulations of tender offers.[4]

Most nations have antitrust regulations that require government approval of

4. The primary sources of this information are manuals on mergers published by Westminster Management Consultants Limited (1990), and Economist Publications (1988).

Table 8.4   Summary of Special Regulatory Restrictions on Takeovers and
                     Equity Investments, by Country, 1985 to 1990

Country	Description
Australia	Mergers resulting in dominant market position must be approved by the government. A tender offer must be made once an investor acquires 20 percent of the voting stock.
Canada	Mergers are subject to antitrust regulations. Investors with more than 10 percent of the outstanding stock must publicly disclose their position. Tenders offers must treat all shareholders and convertible holders equally. A tender offer must be made once an investor acquires 20 percent of the voting stock.
France	Mergers are subject to antitrust review if they result in specified market share and sales levels. Investors that own 5 percent of a listed company have five days to disclose their position. All shareholders and convertible holders must be treated equally, and public offers must be made once an investor acquires 33 percent of the voting stock of a listed company.
Italy	No significant antitrust restrictions on mergers. Investors with more than 2 percent of a listed company's stock have thirty days to disclose their position. Regulations of public offers are by the stock exchanges and are minimal.
Japan	Mergers must be approved by Fair Trade Commission under the Anti-Monopoly Law. Tender offers must be filed with and approved by Ministry of Finance.
Netherlands	Few antitrust restrictions on mergers exist. Investors with 10 percent of shares in a listed company must disclose their position in the next prospectus or interim report. Regulation of public offers is by the stock exchange and is minimal.
Spain	Mergers are subject to antitrust review if they result in specified market share and sales levels. Investors with 10 percent of a listed company's shares must disclose their position immediately. Public offers, which are regulated by a government commission, must treat all shareholders and convertible holders equally. A tender offer must be made once an investor acquires 50 percent of the voting stock.
Sweden	No significant regulations exist governing intercorporate investments, including corporate takeovers. Investors with 10 percent of a company's shares must disclose their position the next day.
United Kingdom	Mergers are subject to antitrust regulations. Investors with more than 3 percent of the outstanding stock must publicly disclose their position. Investors that own 3 percent of a public company's capital have two business days to disclose their position. Tender offers must treat all shareholders and convertible holders equally. A tender offer must be made once an investor acquires 30 percent of the voting stock.
United States	Mergers are subject to antitrust regulations, though enforcement has been rare in recent years. Tender offers

Table 8.4   (continued)

Country	Description
	must be open for at least twenty days, and shareholders can withdraw tendered shares for fifteen days.
West Germany	Mergers are subject to antitrust review if they result in specified sales levels. Investors that own 25 percent of a company must disclose their position immediately. There are no significant government regulations on public offers.

mergers between large companies or ones that lead to highly concentrated markets. In addition, although not reported in table 8.4, most countries have restrictions on mergers in certain sensitive industries, notably in the airline, banking, defense, insurance, and media industries. Most countries also have statutory or stock exchange regulations on disclosure of ownership when specified levels are exceeded and on tender offer procedures. The tender offer regulations typically include equal treatment of shareholders, required tenders once prespecified ownership levels are achieved, and mandatory periods during which offers must remain open. There is considerable overlap in the nature of regulations across countries, implying that differences in regulations are unlikely to explain differences in international equity investments across target nations. Indeed, if anything, it appears that regulations are more severe in countries where intercorporate equity investments are common. For example, there are fewer regulations governing intercorporate investments in West Germany, Italy, the Netherlands, and Sweden than in the United States, Canada, or the United Kingdom. This is not surprising, since the demand for regulation is likely to arise only when acquisition activity is high.

Differences in tax laws across countries could also explain differences in intercorporate investments. Scholes and Wolfson (1990) argue that in the United States the 1981 and 1986 Tax Acts had important effects on merger activity. The 1981 tax bill permitted very rapid depreciation under the accelerated cost recovery system, encouraging domestic activity and discouraging international investments. The 1986 act repealed the accelerated depreciation write-offs and thus eliminated the bias against foreign equity investors. While Scholes and Wolfson report evidence consistent with this prediction, cross-sectional evidence is less clear. Graham and Krugman (1989, 39) argue that "tax considerations alone would have led one to expect a decline in the relative share of Japan and the United Kingdom and a rise in the relative share of Canada and the Netherlands from 1981 to 1986, followed by a reversal; in fact no such clear pattern is visible." In this paper, we focus on nontax factors to explain differences in intercorporate investments across target markets.

Differences in Corporate Governance

Intercorporate investments could also be explained by differences in the way companies are financed. There are significant differences in ownership structures in the countries examined. In Australia, Canada, the United Kingdom, and the United States, ownership is disperse. While financial institutions play a significant role in equity markets, they typically do not participate in corporate management. Financial institutions are also willing to trade their ownership positions, facilitating changes in corporate control through takeovers. In Japan, and for large publicly held companies in West Germany, corporations have established long-term interlocking ownership relations with banks and suppliers. These owners are reluctant to divest their stakes, presenting a barrier to new intercorporate equity investors, especially those seeking changes in corporate control, for both foreign and domestic companies. Public companies in the Netherlands typically separate the voting rights of stock from rights to receive dividends and return of capital. Voting rights are transferred to a foundation, which is friendly to management, and are usually not traded. Finally, in France, Italy, Spain, and Sweden, ownership is concentrated in the hands of founding families or government, again making corporate control transactions less likely.

Among the eleven countries examined, Australia, Canada, the United Kingdom, and the United States, which have diverse and liquid ownership, have the four highest ratios of domestic and international investments to GDP. The average levels of international and domestic equity investments as a percentage of GDP for this group of countries are 1 percent and 3 percent, respectively. In contrast, in France, West Germany, Italy, Japan, the Netherlands, Spain, and Sweden, where there are ownership impediments to takeovers, the average levels of international and domestic investments as a percentage of GDP are only 0.2 percent and 0.4 percent. This evidence suggests that the differences in corporate ownership structure across countries have an important influence on both domestic and foreign intercorporate investments.

In summary, variations in international equity investments are explained to some extent by the nature of the corporate control market. Differences in ownership structure, rather than general takeover regulations, appear to be the dominant factor influencing cross-country variation in domestic and international equity investments.

8.2.3   Effect of Discriminatory Restrictions against Foreign Acquisitions

As discussed earlier, a second force that influences international equity investments is regulatory barriers that favor domestic over foreign investments. Whereas differences in the nature of the corporate control market affect both foreign and domestic intercorporate investments, regulations on foreign investment affect only international activity. To explore whether there are regulatory barriers to international equity investments, we examine foreign equity investments laws for the eleven countries. A summary of these restrictions by country is presented in table 8.5.[5]

5. The primary sources of this information are manuals on mergers published by Westminster Management Consultants Limited (1990), and Economist Publications (1988). Our discussion is

Table 8.5   **Summary of Special Regulatory Restrictions on Foreign Intercorporate Equity Investments, by Country, 1985 to 1990**

Country	Description
Low Regulatory Barriers	
Canada	The only significant restrictions on foreign investment involve acquisitions of companies in sensitive industries, notably defense, financial services, and oil and gas companies.
Italy	No significant restrictions exist except for investments in the aircraft and banking industries.
Netherlands	No significant legal restrictions on foreign investment exist.
Spain	No restrictions exist for noncontrolling investments. Controlling investments are subject to administrative review, which is generally a formality. Prior government approval is required for acquisitions in restricted indusries, including defense, broadcasting, and air transportation.
United Kingdom	No significant restrictions exist except for investments in the media industry.
United States	No restrictions existed prior to 1988. After 1988, investments with national security implications are subject to administrative review.
West Germany	No significant legal restrictions to foreign investment exist.
Regulatory Barriers	
Australia	Administrative approval is required for foreign ownership exceeding 15 percent for a single investor and 40 percent for two or more foreign parties.
France	Government approval for non-EC members, and prior notification for EC members, is required for investments exceeding 20 percent voting control.
Japan	Government notification and approval is required for stakes exceeding 10 percent. Once approved, a transaction has to be completed within thirty days through a Japanese broker.
Sweden	Foreign investors can only buy nonrestricted, or "free," shares. Investments of up to 20 percent of voting shares can be made with government approval.

Canada, West Germany, Italy, the Netherlands, Spain, the United Kingdom, and the United States do not have any significant regulations that discriminate between domestic and foreign investments, except in those few industries deemed to have national security implications. The remaining countries have some form of discriminatory regulations. Australia requires administrative approval for foreign ownership exceeding 15 percent for a single investor and 40 percent for two or more parties. France distinguishes between investments by members of the European Community EC and other foreign investments and requires prior government approval for non-EC investments that exceed 20 per-

---

based on regulations in 1990. During 1991, new EC regulations were adopted by member countries, liberalizing acquisitions within the community.

cent of the voting control of a corporation. Japan requires government notification and approval for foreign acquirers of stakes exceeding 10 percent. Once approved, a transaction has to be completed within thirty days through a Japanese broker. Finally, Sweden permits foreign investors to freely purchase only nonvoting shares. Investments in voting shares can only be made with government approval.

As noted above, while international activity is influenced both by the nature of the corporate control market and by discriminatory foreign investment regulations, domestic activity is affected by the corporate control market alone. The ratio of international to domestic equity investments in each country thus provides a measure of the marginal effect of discriminatory regulations on international investments. In Canada, West Germany, Italy, the Netherlands, Spain, the United Kingdom, and the United States, countries with few discriminatory regulations, international investments average 81 percent of domestic investments. In contrast, the average ratio of international to domestic investments is only 28 percent for Australia, France, Japan, and Sweden, indicating that the discriminatory regulations in these countries succeed in discouraging foreign investment.

In summary, there is compelling evidence that cross-country variation in equity investments by target countries is driven by differences in corporate control markets and equity ownership that affect both domestic and international equity investments and by equity investment regulations that discriminate against foreign investors.

8.3   Acquirer Countries

This section examines which countries have been the most active international acquirers in the period 1985 to 1990 and explores the role of domestic activity on countries' propensity to invest abroad.

We compute the aggregate dollar value of international investments made by each sample country in 1985 to 1990. The findings are reported in column (1) of table 8.6. Column (2) reports international equity investments by each country as a percentage of the total for all countries. The United Kingdom is the largest acquirer nation, representing 29 percent of all international acquisitions. France, the United States, and Japan account for approximately 14 percent each of all international acquisitions. Companies in Spain, Italy, Sweden, and the Netherlands undertake very few international acquisitions.

To examine whether there has been a change in international investment activity by acquirer market between 1985 and 1990, we estimate the value of international investments each year for the four major regions (Europe, North America, Japan, and Australia). Figure 8.2 shows the annual international investments by acquirer regions. Europe (primarily the United Kingdom) is consistently the largest acquirer region throughout the five years. There is a significant decline in the importance of North American and Australian acquirers

Table 8.6   **International Intercorporate Equity Investments, by Country of Acquirer Firm, 1985 to 1990**

	International Intercorporate Equity Investments				International Equity Investments in Country as Percentage of International Investments by Country (5)
Acquirer Country	Value (U.S. $ millions) (1)	Percentage of Total (2)	Percentage of Gross Domestic Product (3)	Percentage of Acquirer Country's Domestic Equity Investments (4)	
Australia	$ 27,700	6.7%	2.0%	75%	34%
Canada	34,801	8.4	1.2	63	94
France	57,884	14.0	0.9	193	29
Italy	8,599	2.1	0.2	39	91
Japan	51,462	12.4	0.3	163	4
Netherlands	14,350	3.5	1.0	264	62
Spain	1,288	0.3	0.1	23	571
Sweden	13,893	3.4	1.1	88	27
United Kingdom	120,674	29.1	2.5	77	57
United States	56,857	13.7	0.2	5	436
West Germany	26,647	6.4	0.4	328	34
Total	414,155	100.0			
Average			0.5	28	100

and a growth in Japanese and European acquirers. In 1985, Europe constituted 51 percent of the acquirers, North America had a 31 percent share, Japan 1 percent, and Australia 16 percent. By 1990, Europe's share increased to 65 percent, North America was only 15 percent of the acquisition market, Japan 16 percent, and Australia 4 percent.

Once again, we control for differences in economy sizes across countries by deflating international equity investments by each country during the period 1985 to 1990 by its total GDP expressed in U.S. dollars in the same period. These statistics appear in column (3) of table 8.6. Controlled for size, the United Kingdom, Australia, Canada, Sweden, and France are the most active international acquirers. Interestingly, the United States is one of the least active international acquirers once we control for the size of its economy.

Table 8.6 also reports two other summary statistics on equity investments abroad for the eleven countries. The first, shown in column (4), deflates international equity investments for acquirer countries by domestic investment. High values of this ratio for a particular country indicate that its firms are more active acquirers abroad than domestically. Controlling for domestic equity investments, France, West Germany, Japan, and the Netherlands are the most active equity investors abroad, and the United States, Spain, and Italy are the least active. As discussed earlier, corporate ownership structures in France,

($US m)

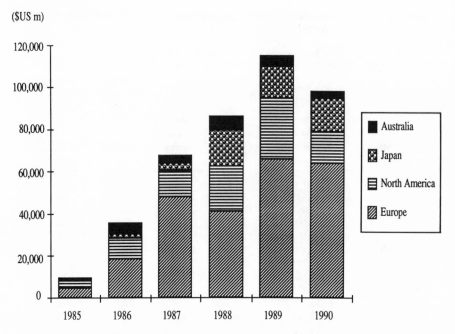

Fig. 8.2   International intercorporate equity investments, by acquirer market,
1985 to 1990

West Germany, Japan, and the Netherlands discourage intercorporate equity
investments by domestic (and foreign) firms. Apparently, the lack of developed
corporate control markets in these countries does not represent a significant
barrier to intercorporate investment abroad. The experience that firms in countries with active domestic markets have in negotiating equity acquisitions and
in integrating acquired companies does not appear to provide them with a comparative advantage over Dutch, French, West German, or Japanese companies
(which have no such domestic experience) in investing abroad. Certainly, companies in France, Germany, Japan, and the Netherlands can obtain bidding expertise for equity investments abroad by hiring experienced investment bank-
ers. There is also little evidence that United States acquirers, who operate in
one of the most active domestic markets, have developed expertise in profitability integrating acquired companies.[6]

The second measure, reported in column (5) of table 8.6, deflates international equity investments into a country by its equity investments abroad. Values of this ratio that differ from 100 percent indicate a mismatch between

6. Jensen and Ruback (1983) surveyed studies of stock returns to acquiring firms at mergers.
They concluded that, on average, acquiring firms only break even on mergers and acquisition
investments.

equity investments into and out of the country. There is a relatively high inflow of equity investments into Spain and the United States. Companies in France, West Germany, Japan, and Sweden are active acquirers abroad relative to foreign investments in their domestic market. As noted earlier, Japan and Sweden both have restrictions on foreign equity investments by outsiders. In addition, France, West Germany, Japan, and Sweden all have ownership impediments to takeovers and intercorporate equity investments. Thus, the high equity investment outflows for these four countries arise because they have equity markets that are effectively off limits to foreign investors, but they impose few restrictions on international activity by their own investors. In contrast, the U.S. equity market is characterized by high liquidity and dispersed stockholders, making equity investments by outsiders relatively straightforward. However, it is less obvious why U.S. firms are so reluctant to invest abroad. Also, the high equity inflows into Spain and Italy cannot be explained by the market for corporate control or foreign investment regulations in these countries.

8.4   Factors Explaining International Intercorporate Equity Investment Activity

In this section we use a multivariate model to examine factors that influence intercorporate equity investments between countries. The dependent variable in our analysis is the annual level of international investment between pairs of countries, deflated by the GDP of the acquirer country to adjust for its size. We explain cross-country and time-series variation in this variable, using a number of independent variables drawn from our earlier discussion and prior literature.

Earlier discussion suggested that countries with closely held companies are expected to have low levels of foreign equity investments. We use two measures to test this hypothesis. The first is an indicator variable that takes the value of one for countries with disperse ownership structure (Australia, Canada, United Kingdom, and United States), and zero for other countries (France, West Germany, Italy, Japan, Spain, and Sweden). The second variable is the level of domestic equity investment (deflated by target country GDP), which itself is influenced by corporate ownership structure within the target country. Of course, domestic equity investments are also affected by other factors, such as tax effects, antitrust regulations and enforcement, and tender offer regulations. Thus, domestic equity investments reflect a broader set of factors than the ownership dummy variable. Both the ownership dummy and domestic investment are expected to have a positive relationship with international investment levels.

To examine whether regulations that discriminate against foreign investors effectively reduce international equity investments into a country, we form a dummy variable that is one for target countries with severe discriminatory regulations against foreign acquisitions (Australia, France, Japan, and Sweden), and zero for other countries. We expect this dummy variable to have a negative relationship with the level of foreign equity investments.

A third variable that we examine is the relative size of the target and acquirer countries. Purely as a result of scale difference, small target countries are likely to attract less acquirer investment than do large target nations. Consequently, this variable is expected to have a positive relationship with acquirer country international investments.

We also examine the effect of changes in real exchange rates on international equity investments. In an earlier study, Froot and Stein (1990) argue that, because of informational imperfections in global capital markets, external financing of intercorporate investments is more expensive than internal financing. Consequently, appreciation of a country's currency increases its companies' relative wealth, raising their internal financing capability and lowering their cost of acquiring foreign firms. We test this hypothesis by examining the relationship between annual levels of international investments between acquirer and target countries, and contemporaneous and lagged percentage changes in average real exchange rates for the target and acquirer countries. Annual real exchange rate changes are measured using the International Monetary Fund index of the value of the dollar relative to the target and acquirer countries' currencies and relative changes in consumer prices in the two countries. Froot and Stein's model suggests that foreign investment is positively related to changes in real exchange rates for acquirer countries relative to target nations.

Finally, we explore whether economic growth in the target and acquirer nations affects international investments. We estimate contemporaneous and lagged annual economic growth rates for acquirer and target countries, using annual percentage change in real GDP index, reported by the IMF.

There are several reasons why acquirer country growth rates are likely to be related to international acquisitions. First, countries with high economic growth may have developed a comparative advantage in managing certain assets. If this knowledge is transferable to other countries, companies in high-growth countries have incentives to make investments abroad.[7] Economic growth in the acquirer nation could also be relevant to international investment if companies face free cash flow problems. Jensen (1986) hypothesizes that moral hazard problems make managers reluctant to pay out free cash flows to stockholders. Instead, they prefer to invest in zero or even negatively valued projects, such as equity investments. Consequently, companies in countries with high economic growth, which are likely to have high levels of free cash flows, are more likely to make equity investments abroad (as well as domestically). Finally, if there are market imperfections that restrict firms' abilities to raise external capital for profitable new investments, companies in countries

---

7. See Graham and Krugman (1989) for a summary of the literature on industrial organization reasons for international investments.

with high economic growth, and high internal cash flows, will have access to cheaper funding for new investments, including those in other countries. Each of these hypotheses implies a positive relationship between acquirer country economic growth and changes in international equity investments. However, there are also factors that would cause the relationship to be negative. If high economic growth in a country provides significant new investment opportunities within the country for both domestic and foreign firms, domestic firms will tend to concentrate on home-country investments rather than investing abroad. Because these conflicting hypotheses are not mutually exclusive, it is difficult to make predictions on the sign of the acquirer growth coefficient.

Target country economic growth is included to test whether foreign equity investors are attracted to countries which have high growth prospects or whether they are more attracted to countries which have underperformed and where there may be opportunities to turn around poorly performing companies.

We test the above hypotheses using panel data to estimate the relationship of annual levels of international equity investments between a given acquirer and target country (deflated by acquirer country GDP) in the years 1985 to 1990 to the above independent variables. The findings are reported in table 8.7. Model 1 is estimated using the ownership dummy variable, whereas model 2 uses domestic equity investments in the target country instead of the ownership dummy.

The results are consistent across the two models. Model 1 has an adjusted R^2 of 19 percent and statistically is highly significant. Four variables—the ownership dummy, the foreign regulation dummy, lagged acquirer growth, and the relative size of the target and acquirer nations—have statistically significant relations with international equity acquisitions.[8]

To understand the economic implications of the reported coefficients, we note that the average investment between a pair of countries in the sample is 0.09 percent of the acquirer country's GDP. The coefficient on the ownership variable implies that, at the margin, disperse equity ownership increases international equity investments by 0.16 percent of acquirer GDP. The dummy variable for discriminatory restrictions on foreign investment is −0.07 percent, implying that countries with such restrictions are effective in dampening foreign investment. The coefficient on lagged target growth is positive, indicating that high-growth countries tend to attract foreign investment. A one percentage point increase in real GDP target growth increases international equity acquisitions by 0.02 percent of acquirer GDP. Finally, the relative size of the target and acquirer is important in determining the level of international investment between the two countries.

The coefficient on exchange rate changes is insignificant, suggesting that

---

8. Because the models have several contemporaneous and lagged independent variables, we examine whether our findings are influenced by multicollinearity. The results are unchanged when we reestimate the models, using contemporaneous and lagged variables in separate regressions.

Table 8.7   **Relationship of Annual Intercorporate Equity Investments between Acquirer and Target Countries, as a Percentage of Acquirer GDP in the period 1985 to 1990, to Target Domestic and Acquirer Country Characteristics**

	Coefficient	
Independent Variable*	Model 1	Model 2
Target country GDP as a percentage of acquirer country GDP	2.24†	1.97†
Dummy variable for target countries with restrictions on foreign investments	−0.07†	−0.08†
Dummy variable for target countries with disperse equity ownership	0.16†	
Contemporaneous target country domestic equity investment as a percentage of target GDP		0.07†
Contemporaneous change in exchange rate between acquirer and target countries	−0.003	−0.03
Lagged change in exchange rate between acquirer and target countries	0.003	−0.06
Contemporaneous percentage change in real GDP growth for acquirer country	−0.80	−0.55
Lagged percentage change in real GDP growth for acquirer country	0.12	−0.74
Contemporaneous percentage change in real GDP growth for target country	−1.52	−0.88
Lagged percentage change in real GDP growth for target country	1.84‡	0.69
Intercept	0.01	0.02
Adjusted R^2	0.19†	0.24†
Number of observations	658	658

*The dependent varible is the annual change in intercorporate equity investments between acquirer and target countries as a percentage of acquirer GDP in the period 1985 to 1990.

†Significantly different from zero at the 1 percent level, using a two-tailed test.

‡Significantly different from zero at the 6 percent level, using a two-tailed test.

there are not serious informational imperfections across countries for equity investments. These results differ somewhat from those in other studies (see Froot and Stein 1991; Caves 1989; Dewenter 1992). Differences in samples, variable definitions, and the scope of the countries studied make it difficult to directly compare our results with these studies. However, to assess the robustness of our results, we repeat our analysis by (1) allowing the exchange rate coefficient to vary by country, (2) introducing exchange rate changes with one more lag, (3) changing the dependent variable to changes in international investment rather than levels, and (4) changing the independent variable to an index representing the level of exchange rates between the acquirer and target countries. The exchange rate coefficient remains insignificant in these specifications.

Finally, there is no significant relationship between changes in international activity and contemporaneous and lagged acquirer country growth. There are two interpretations for this finding. One interpretation is that acquirer growth rates do not play an important role in determining international equity investment flows. Alternatively, as discussed above, the insignificant coefficients are a result of conflicting effects of acquirer growth on international investment.

Model 2, which replaces the ownership dummy with domestic equity investments in target nations, generally reinforces the above findings. The coefficient on domestic investments is positive and highly significant. This is consistent with the hypothesis that the nature of the corporate control market has an important effect on international equity investments. This coefficient probably also captures other factors, such as growth opportunities, that make target countries attractive to acquirers. There is some evidence of this. The adjusted R^2 increases from 19 percent in model 1 to 24 percent in model 2, and the effect of lagged target growth, which no longer has a significant coefficient, appears to be subsumed by the domestic investment variable.

8.5 Conclusions

This paper examines international intercorporate equity investments among eleven of the leading industrial nations during the period 1985 to 1990. We find that these investments grew tenfold in the sample period and currently account for about 30 percent of all equity investments. In dollar terms, the United States is by far the largest target country for international equity investments and accounts for 60 percent of all international investments between 1985 and 1990. However, when we control for differences in country size, the United States ranks only third among target countries (behind the United Kingdom and Canada).

The United Kingdom is the most active acquirer nation, both in dollar terms and adjusting for country size, and accounts for 29 percent of all international acquisitions. U.S., French, and Japanese companies are also large acquirers in dollar terms, and each accounts for about 14 percent of worldwide equity investments. However, when we control for country size, the United States ranks tenth out of eleven countries in investments abroad.

International activity in target countries is in part explained by (1) regulations that seek to deter foreign investment, (2) differences across countries in ownership structure and corporate control markets, and (3) target countries' recent growth. Neither changes in real exchange rates between target and acquirer countries nor growth rates of acquirer countries is an important factor explaining international investments patterns.

References

Bureau of Economic Analysis, 1991. *Survey of Current Business.* Washington D.C.: Bureau of Economic Analysis, May.

Caves R. E. 1989. Exchange-rate movements and foreign direct investment in the United States. In *The internationalization of U.S. markets,* ed. D. B. Audretsch and M. P. Claudon, 199–228. New York: New York University Press.

Dewenter, K. L. 1992. Evidence for and against Froot and Stein's imperfect capital markets model of foreign direct investment. Working Paper. Chicago: University of Chicago.

Economist Publications. 1988. Directory of world stock exchanges. London: Economist Publications.

Froot, K., and J. Stein. 1991. Exchange rates and foreign direct investment: An imperfect capital markets approach. *Quarterly Journal of Economics* 106 (November): 1191–217.

Graham, E., and P. Krugman. 1989. *Foreign direct investment in the United States.* Washington, D.C.: Institute for International Economics.

Jensen, M. 1986. Agency costs of free cash flow, corporate finance and takeovers. *American Economic Review.* no. 2 (May): 323–29.

Jensen, M., and R. Ruback. 1983. The market for corporate control. *Journal of Financial Economics* 11(1): 5–50.

Scholes, M., and M. Wolfson. 1990. The effects of changes in tax laws on corporate reorganization activity Part 2. *Journal of Business,* 63(1): s141–64.

Westminster Management Consultants Limited. 1990. A practitioner's guide to European takeover regulation and practice. Woking, Surrey: Westminster Mangement Consultants Limited.

Comment   Michael Adler

Paul Healy and Krishna Palepu's paper makes a contribution by drawing attention to and confirming a point we have long suspected and possibly even known to be true: that regulatory or structural restrictions on takeovers and foreign ownership can significantly reduce foreign direct investment (FDI) into those countries that have them. The authors make this point, among others, in connection with data from a sample of developed, primarily (with the exception of Australia) Northern Hemisphere, nations.

Most northern policymakers, however, no longer view FDI as a policy problem, aside from national security concerns in specific industries and the challenge of leveling competitive conditions between Japan and the rest. Healy and Palepu's (H&P's) demonstration, in tables 8.2 and 8.3, that foreign and domestic intercorporate equity purchases are a much larger fraction of GDP in the English-speaking countries than in the more restrictive EC is therefore unlikely to raise either eyebrows or hackles in the North. Nor is their table 8.6 result that France, Germany, the Netherlands, and Japan have invested abroad proportionally much more than they have absorbed. North-North political-economic relations are unlikely to be greatly affected by the revelation of these imbalances.

H&P's point matters much more in the context of the ongoing difficulties over resource transfers between North and South and between West and East. Debtor countries in Latin America, Eastern Europe, Asia, and even Africa currently are being encouraged by their creditors to reconstruct their economies to attract voluntary FDI as a substitute for aid. One implication of H&P's work is that removing barriers to intercorporate takeovers in the debtor nations can assist this process. A second, indirect, and more problematic implication follows from observing that Germany and Japan, the most successful postwar economies, are among those with the highest barriers to takeovers. One may wonder about cause and effect. Are the debtors being well advised?

Appropriately enough, H&P have nothing to say regarding these wider issues. Their technical concern is with the pattern of facts that can be obtained from exploiting Securities Data Company's new database on international acquisitions between January 1985 and December 1990. The model they estimate in table 8.7 is not a test of any theory of FDI. It seems instead to be a preliminary attempt to see whether barriers to FDI, modeled by dummy variables for ownership structure and the presence of discriminatory regulations, properly belong in the specification of such a theory. Their methodology is not described in detail. It seems to consist of a pooled time-series, cross-section regression analysis that stops short of being an event study.

Their results confirm, as noted above, that the FDI barrier variables have the right signs and are significant at the 1 percent level. Large target markets attract more FDI than do smaller markets. And, echoing Caves's (1989) investigation of FDI in the United States, FDI is positively related to GDP growth in the acquiring country but not to growth in the target. Perhaps what is missing here is a stock market or comparable relative wealth variable. Caves has the intuitively appealing result that FDI into the United States between 1979 and 1986 had a strong negative correlation with U.S. stock prices. This effect, one surmises, should be quite general: purchases of foreign firms should go down as their prices rise.

The chief surprise in the H&P paper is that the contemporaneous and lagged exchange rate variables turned out not to be significant. However, this may be less of a surprise than one might think. Keep in mind that the empirical evidence of a strong association between FDI and exchange rates pertains almost exclusively to FDI into the United States. This is true of Caves (1990), who was first to report a significant negative correlation between the strength of the dollar and inward FDI. It is equally true of Froot and Stein (1991), who offered an attractive, imperfect-markets explanation of why this result is to be expected, as well as of Harris and Ravenscraft (1991), Swenson (chap. 9 in this book), and Dewenter (1992). However, Froot and Stein could not find any association between outward U.S. FDI and the exchange rate. Neither could Dewenter, who found also that Japan and the United Kingdom were the only countries whose FDI into the United States was negatively correlated with dollar strength. FDI outflows to the United States from Germany and the Netherlands were uncorrelated with the dollar exchange rate. They were, however, correlated with stock market measures of relative wealth.

The evidence, even in the case of the United States as target, seems somewhat mixed. The relationship between FDI and exchange rates (proxying imperfectly for shifts of relative wealth) may differ across acquiring countries and possibly also between time periods. The H&P sample, however, also includes FDI flows between non-U.S. country pairs. Whereas the dollar lost 50 percent of its value against other major currencies between 1985 and 1990, the cross-rates were much less volatile. The wave of intra-European mergers and acquisitions that began to form in the mid 1980s must therefore have been prompted less by exchange rate changes within the European Monetary System (or by U.S.-type buyout fever) than by other factors such as the EC's movement to a unified market and the resulting potential for scale economies. The inclusion of intra-European transactions could be expected to reduce the average sensitivity of FDI to exchange rates. In addition, effective structural and regulatory barriers to FDI into Europe from the English-speaking countries and Japan, or from all countries into Japan, would tend to have the same effect: effective barriers should reduce the average sample correlation between FDI and relative wealth changes. All told, the absence of significant exchange rate coefficients in H&P's results is no more than one would expect.

In summary, Healy and Palepu provide a necessary addition to the FDI literature. They contribute by showing that imperfections other than informational asymmetries in financial markets that produce wealth effects, also affect FDI takeovers. We are still far from a complete model of FDI. The work can usefully continue.

References

Caves, R. E. (1989) Exchange-rate movements and foreign investments in the United States. In *The internationalization of U.S. markets,* ed. D. B. Audretsch and M. P. Claudon, 199–228. New York: New York University Press.
Dewenter, K. L. 1992. Do exchange rate changes drive foreign direct investment? Working Paper. Chicago: University of Chicago, January 10 version.
Froot, K. A. and J. C. Stein. 1991. Exchange rates and foreign direct investment: An imperfect capital markets approach. *Quarterly Journal of Economics* 106, no. 4 (November): 1191–217.
Harris, R. S., and D. Ravenscraft. 1991. The role of acquisitions in foreign direct investment: Evidence from the U.S. stock market. *Journal of Finance* 46 no. 3 (July): 825–44. (Papers and Proceedings).

Discussion Summary

Kathryn Dewenter pointed out that she found foreign acquisitions in the United States were, on average, larger transactions than were U.S. domestic acquisitions. Would the results on the relative importance of foreign acquisitions be affected by taking size into account? *Dewenter* suggested that it would be easy enough to determine the answer, as it is possible to get data on the number of transactions.

Bob Lipsey suggested that *Healy* and *Palepu* attempt to compare their data on cross-border equity purchases with U.S. data on foreign acquisitions in the United States. This comparison might help determine how comprehensive SDC data are. In addition, *Lipsey* questioned the meaning of several of the explanatory variables in the Healy-Palepu regressions. For example, why should the GDP of the headquarters country of the acquirer be important? Why is the exchange rate of the headquarters country important? Presumably, if these firms earn profits in several other countries, then the GDPs and exchange rates of these other countries should be important, not those of the headquarters country.

David Belli noted that he had already examined the SDC data. He had found that it was good at picking up some of the transactions missing from the U.S. International Trade Commission data on foreign investment in the United States. However, the SDC data also omitted a number of important transactions.

Michael Dooley wondered whether the increase in FDI in the United States was somehow related to the leveraging process that at large portion of the corporate sector experienced in the late 1980s. If foreigners were randomly involved in these takeovers, that would lead to an increase in FDI.

9   Foreign Mergers and Acquisitions in the United States

Deborah L. Swenson

Foreign direct investment expenditures in the United States peaked in 1989 at $123.4 billion. While $71.2 billion of this investment represented new foreign enterprises created through acquisitions of existing U.S. assets or establishment of U.S. operations, fully 84 percent of the new business value occurred through acquisition. Compared with the quadrupling of foreign investment during the 1980s, the recent decline in foreign direct investment is slight. If there is any puzzle in these numbers, it is the prominence of acquisition in foreign investment activities and its dramatic increase during the 1980s.

Most theories of foreign direct investment (FDI) posit that firms invest abroad either to rationalize activities which are more effectively controlled within a single firm or in response to imperfect markets. Most variants of these arguments are based on the notion of firm decisions (e.g., internalization of transactions, or foreign direct investment as a step in the product life cycle). Implicit in these theories is the assumption that the investing firm possesses some superior abilities that enable it to pursue expansion across national borders.

Recent foreign direct investment experience in the United States is difficult to explain using these theories of the firm. We have to modify our understanding of firm motivations to encompass firm motivations for acquisition and the implications of changes in corporate control. Foreign acquisition may reflect changes in world markets that require foreign firms to acquire abilities, technologies, or firm structures which they need for effective worldwide competition but which are more costly to develop internally. Alternatively, if we assume that many acquisitions are disciplinary in nature, the prevalence of acquisition may imply that foreign acquisitions occur in cases where the foreign firms have superior control abilities.[1]

---

1. Baldwin and Caves (1991) studied Canadian firms, finding evidence consistent with their hypothesis that foreign acquisitions are motivated by issues of firm operation rather than by differential abilities at control.

In order to explain the complexities of foreign direct investment which are obscured in the aggregate statistics, this paper analyzes a panel of U.S. mergers and acquisitions that occurred between 1974 and 1990. More than 30 percent of the transactions involved the purchase of U.S. firms by foreign bidders. The benefit of comparing foreign and domestic transactions is that one can distinguish where foreign transactions are different and can use these differences to better understand the current and evolving motivations guiding foreign investments. Two particular aspects of the domestic and foreign acquisitions are used as evidence: target shareholder wealth gains in domestic and foreign acquisitions, and the financial information of domestic and foreign targets.[2]

In order to assess the importance of increased acquisition activity, this paper proceeds as follows. Section 9.1 examines the importance of foreign acquisitions relative to overall foreign direct investment in the United States and relative to the universe of acquisition activity in the U.S. market. Following aggregate descriptions, section 9.2 describes the creation of the acquisition sample which is used to analyze foreign acquisitions. The second section also presents some comparative financial information and transactions details involving the targets of foreign and domestic acquisitions. Section 9.3 concerns the measurement of shareholder gains in corporate control contests and documents the presence of a premium in foreign transactions. Finally, section 9.4 uses premium information and target firm characteristics to explain how foreign acquisitions differ from domestic acquisitions and how this accords with theories of foreign direct investment. Section 9.5 provides a brief conclusion.

9.1   Foreign Activity in the U.S. Market for Corporate Control

Although the flows of foreign direct investment to the United States abated somewhat at the close of the 1980s, the new levels far exceeded FDI expenditures of previous decades. When we look at statistics on FDI expenditures in the United States, a few patterns emerge. These patterns are not just evident in the aggregate but hold when the FDI expenditures of individual countries are examined independently. As table 9.1 indicates, the primary form of investment in terms of dollar value is acquisition of existing U.S. assets, as opposed to greenfield investments. The second notable feature of FDI directed toward the United States is that acquisition expenditures have expanded tremendously during the 1980s, while greenfield expenditures have not shown a similar increase. Japan is the one exception; Japanese expenditures on new establishments rose dramatically after 1985. Nonetheless, as was true for the other major investors, Japanese investors spent substantially more on acquisition than

---

2. Kogut and Chang (1991) and Harris and Ravenscraft (1991) consider the influence of target industry conditions on the propensity of foreign investment and on the shareholder gains in foreign acquisitions. Neither study considers the actual operational or financial information of the target firm.

Table 9.1   **Foreign Direct Investment in the United States, by Investor Country and Investment Type, 1980–1990 ($ millions)**

	Canada		France		Germany	
	ACQ*	EST†	ACQ	EST	ACQ	EST
1980	$ 1,743	$213	$ 516	$ 83	$ 1,186	$ 238
1981	5,100	984	801	104	800	349
1982	914	282	359	124	315	285
1983	718	354	167	128	378	206
1984	2,185	402	145	186	476	210
1985	2,494	420	593	161	2,142	127
1986	6,091	708	2,403	88	1,167	184
1987	1,169	107	1,949	96	4,318	347
1988	11,162	198	3,691	508	1,849	241
1989	4,196	206	3,295	174	2,216	219
1990	1,675	201	10,771	114	2,003	159
	Netherlands		United Kingdom		Japan	
	ACQ	EST	ACQ	EST	ACQ	EST
1980	$ 783	$867	$ 2,793	$ 273	$ 521	$ 75
1981	408	163	5,309	869	469	147
1982	139	191	2,002	1,126	137	450
1983	360	132	1,448	918	199	193
1984	460	102	2,964	751	1,352	454
1985	579	192	6,023	708	463	689
1986	4,406	295	7,699	872	1,250	4,166
1987	204	188	14,648	494	3,340	3,666
1988	2,067	147	22,237	321	12,232	3,956
1989	3,351	279	21,241	1,806	11,204	6,206
1990	2,189	177	12,200	898	15,875	4,584

Sources: U.S. Department of Commerce (1988, 1991), Bureau of Economic Analysis supplements to *Survey of Current Business,* May.

*ACQ = Value of acquisition activity.

†EST = Value of establishment activity.

on establishment in most years, and their cumulative expenditure through the decade was heavily directed toward acquisition purchases.

The prominence of acquisitions is now widely known. It is also well known that the number of acquisitions between U.S. firms expanded greatly in the 1980s. However, the relative importance of foreign acquisition in the U.S. market for corporate control remains to be examined. It might be the case that foreign firms will always be present in a certain percentage of all acquisition activity in the United States. If this were true, then foreign acquisitions could be explained by aggregate takeover activity alone. On the other hand, if foreign acquisitions are a changing percentage of the U.S. market for corporate control, we must seek explanations for these fluctuations. The most probable explanations lie either in the economic conditions prevailing at the time of takeover or in industry conditions of the target industries.

Table 9.2 investigates the role of foreign acquisitions, first as a percentage of the number of domestic transactions announced, and second as a percentage of the value of domestic transactions. The percentage of foreign takeover announcements relative to domestic announcements ranges from a low of 1.9 percent in 1972 to a high of 15.7 percent in 1988. When we compare cumulative transaction value of foreign acquirers as a percentage of the transaction value of domestic acquisitions, the low of 6.4 percent is found in 1985 and the peak is found in 1990, with a value of 44.1 percent. In all but one year, the percentage value embodied in foreign transactions has been higher than the percentage of transactions undertaken by foreign acquirers, indicating that foreign acquirers purchase targets that are, on average, larger than the targets of domestic acquirers.

Table 9.2 highlights two important aspects of foreign direct investment. First, foreign firms do not play a constant role in the U.S. merger and acquisition market. In the early 1970s, foreign acquirers were virtually absent from the market for corporate control. They were larger players in the periods spanning 1978–81 and 1987–90. In general, these two periods correspond to times when the U.S. dollar was relatively weak. The extent of fluctuations in the percentage of foreign activities even in the various subperiods, however, suggests that we must search for explanations in many areas besides exchange rates. The second notable feature of foreign takeover activity is the extent to which expanded acquisition activity reflects a trend toward very highly valued transactions. Over time, the increase in transaction value is far more pronounced than the increase in the number of transactions.

Aggregate statistics demonstrate the changing composition and nature of foreign investment. Not only do foreign acquisitions play a larger role in overall foreign direct investment, but foreign firms are also responsible for an increasing portion of the total U.S. market for corporate control. In order to explore the meaning of these changes, we now examine a set of domestic and foreign acquisitions in the United States. By looking at the specifics of a large number of individual transactions, we search for patterns which are responsible for the broad trends seen in aggregate measures of foreign direct investment.

9.2   Data

Initial firm identification began with the quarterly takeover rosters from the publication *Mergers and Acquisitions* between the years 1968 and 1990, although the final sample only includes acquisitions taking place between 1974 and 1990.[3] With the exception of management buyouts, all transactions which

---

3. Between 1968 and 1974, there were almost no listed foreign acquisitions of U.S. firms, and those listed did not meet the other selection criteria. As a result, the analysis in this study begins with 1974.

Table 9.2   **Comparison of U.S. Acquisition Activity of Domestic and Foreign Acquirers, 1972–1990**

	Number of Transactions		Number with Value > 100 M		Number with Value > 1,000 M		Total Value of Transactions (1987 $ billions)		Relative Value of Foreign Transactions	
	DOM*	FOR†	DOM	FOR	DOM	FOR	DOM	FOR	Number‡	Value§
Year										
1972	4,713	88	15	—	—	—	$ 43.0	—	1.9%	—
1973	3,892	148	23	5	—	—	40.4	—	3.8	—
1974	2,688	173	11	4	—	—	27.8	—	6.4	—
1975	2,113	184	12	2	1	—	20.7	$ 3.3	8.7	15.9%
1976	2,098	178	34	5	1	—	33.6	4.6	8.5	13.4
1977	2,062	162	38	3	—	—	33.6	5.5	7.9	16.4
1978	1,907	199	63	17	1	—	46.3	10.4	10.4	22.5
1979	1,892	236	72	11	3	—	57.5	8.9	12.5	15.5
1980	1,702	187	72	22	4	—	51.9	9.9	11.0	19.1
1981	2,161	234	89	24	8	4	80.9	23.8	10.8	29.4
1982	2,192	154	101	15	6	—	58.2	6.0	7.0	10.3
1983	2,408	125	128	10	10	1	77.0	6.8	5.2	8.8
1984	2,392	151	177	23	16	2	117.7	16.6	6.3	14.1
1985	2,804	197	249	21	33	3	179.0	11.5	7.0	6.4
1986	3,072	264	295	51	24	3	153.3	25.3	8.6	16.5
1987	1,812	220	239	62	26	10	123.3	40.4	12.1	32.8
1988	1,951	307	292	77	33	12	184.2	53.4	15.7	29.0
1989	2,081	285	245	83	27	8	167.1	36.9	13.7	22.1
1990	1,808	266	125	56	13	8	66.5	29.3	14.7	44.1

Sources: Merrill Lynch Business Brokerage and Valuation, *Mergerstat*SM *Review; Economic Report of the President.*

*DOM = Domestic acquirers.

†FOR = Foreign acquirers.

‡Numerical comparison computed by dividing each year's number of foreign takeover announcements by the number of domestic takeover announcements.

§Value computed by dividing each year's dollar volume of foreign transactions by that year's dollar volume of domestic transactions.

listed buyer nationality and the acquisition price paid per share were included. Two other information criteria had to be met for the firm to be included in the sample of acquired firms. Calculation of target shareholder gains required listing of the acquisition announcement date in *The Wall Street Journal* and daily stock returns information for each target. All firms with insufficient or nonexistent Center for Research in Securities Prices (CRSP) daily stock return information were eliminated from the sample.[4]

Table 9.3 provides details regarding the 703 transactions that met the infor-

---

4. Most of the deletions were over-the-counter stocks not included on the CRSP tapes. A few other firms were omitted because their stock was delisted within the event window used for analysis.

Table 9.3   **Time and Country Distribution of Acquisitions in the United States, 1974–1990**

A. Time Distribution

Number of Acquisitions

Year	Domestic	Foreign	Total
1974	2	2	4
1975	6	7	13
1976	18	4	22
1977	26	21	47
1978	33	18	51
1979	36	25	61
1980	20	13	33
1981	28	17	45
1982	17	10	27
1983	28	6	34
1984	53	11	64
1985	44	7	51
1986	51	16	67
1987	30	20	50
1988	48	24	72
1989	29	15	44
1990	8	10	18
Total	477	226	703

B. Country Distribution

Acquirer	Total Acquisitions
United States	477
United Kingdom	85
West Germany	24
Canada	23
France	17
Japan	16
Netherlands	15
Switzerland	12
Australia	7
Sweden	6
Italy	6
Hong Kong	3
Belgium	3
Other foreign*	9
Total	703

*Includes two acquisitions each performed by firms from Saudi Arabia and New Zealand and one acquisition by firms from Kuwait, Bermuda, Taiwan, Denmark, and Ireland.

mational requirements of this study. Panel A displays the data set representation of foreign and domestic acquisitions across time. The trends seen in the sample broadly reflect aggregate trends in foreign acquisitions in the United States. In the aggregate, foreign acquisition activities were most intense in the late 1970s to early 1980s and again in the late 1980s. This trend appears in the sample too, with more transactions appearing during these time periods.[5]

Of the 703 observations in the sample, 477 (68 percent) involve the acquisition of U.S. firms by another domestic firm. The nationalities of the remaining 226 acquisitions are presented in panel B. In the sample, foreign acquisitions were completed by bidders from nineteen different countries. Among the foreign bidders, British firms are most heavily represented in the sample, followed in importance by West German and Canadian firms.

Table 9.4 displays the characteristics of foreign and domestic acquisitions in the sample, and tests whether differences in the foreign and domestic samples are statistically significant. In each comparison, we provide a t-statistic and an industry-adjusted t-statistic. The first t-statistic tests whether the difference between the foreign and domestic populations is statistically significant. The industry-adjusted value tests whether the domestic and foreign groups are different after controlling for industry effects.

Panel A of table 9.4 concentrates on the transaction characteristics of foreign and domestic acquisitions. In most regards, the transactions are very similar. Both foreign and domestic acquirers used tender offers in more than 45 percent of all transactions. In the acquisitions sample, the total cost of domestic acquisitions was somewhat larger than that for foreign acquisitions, but the difference was not statistically significant, even after controlling for industry. Finally, for the 148 acquisitions where the information was known, foreign bidders were in possession of a greater percentage of shares at the time of bid placement than were the domestic firms. The 5 percent difference, however, is not significant.

Although foreign takeover efforts were similar in execution to domestic takeovers, panel B shows that the competitive environment in foreign acquisitions was different than the environment surrounding domestic acquisitions. To begin, successful foreign acquirers faced competing bids less often than domestic bidders. Domestic acquirers faced competitors in 27.4 percent of all transactions, compared with only 17.7 percent of all foreign acquisitions. Foreign acquirers were also less likely to be challenged by the Justice Department, Federal Trade Commission, Internal Revenue Service, or other government agency. The only similarity in competitive environment is in the frequency of hostile reaction by the target firms. Both foreign and domestic bidders faced hostile reactions in slightly more than 10 percent of their acquisitions.

5. Changes in the process of acquisitions caused the later years to be less well represented in the sample. Over time, an increasing number of transactions involved the purchase of divisions as opposed to entire firms, and an increased proportion of activity involved the purchase of corporate assets which were not traded on any of the stock exchanges.

Table 9.4   **Comparison of Foreign and Domestic Transactions, 1974–1990**

A. Transaction Characteristics

	Tender	% Stock Owned	Total Acquisition Cost ($ millions)
Domestic	46.5%	16.9%	$421.5
Foreign	50.0	21.0	349.7
t-stat	0.85	1.81	−0.76
Industry-Adj t-stat	0.81	1.08	−0.98

B. Competitive Environment

	Competitors	Hostile	Government Challenge
Domestic	27.4%	11.5%	14.0%
Foreign	17.7	10.1	9.3
t-stat	−2.83	−0.53	−1.78
Industry-Adj t-stat	−2.89	−0.54	−1.80

C. Target Firm Characteristics

	Sales*	Asset Size*	P/E Ratio	D/E Ratio	Int % Sales	4-Year Gr Rate
Domestic	$511.4	$388.7	10.94	1.13	1.82%	0.11
Foreign	431.2	509.9	13.05	1.19	1.72	0.17
t-stat	−0.61	0.89	2.25	0.92	−0.77	1.67
Industry-Adj t-stat	−0.66	0.88	2.01	1.29	−0.77	1.92

Notes: t-stat = t-statistic for the test that there is no difference in the foreign and domestic levels of the variable of interest. Indusry Adj t-stat = t-statistic for the tests for equality of domestic and foreign levels, controlling for industry.

Panel A: Tender = Percentage of transactions for which the bidder used a tender offer. % Stock Owned = Percentage of stock held by the bidder at the time of announcement; only known for 148 transactions. Total Acquisition Cost = Total payment by the bidder to effect the transaction.

Panel B: Competitors = Percentage of foreign and domestic transactions facing one or more competing bids. Hostile = Number of transactions opposed by the target. Government Challenge = Percentage of transactions opposed by the Internal Revenue Service, Justice Department, Federal Trade Commission, or any other government agency.

Panel C: All panel C variables generated by Compustat, based on the author's sample. P/E ratio = Price-earnings ratio. D/E Ratio = Debt-equity ratio. Int % Sales = Interest payments as a percentage of sales in the year prior to acquisition. 4-Yr Gr Rate = Growth of the respective targets in the 4 years preceding the takeover.

*Millions of dollars.

Panel C compares target firm characteristics of foreign and domestic transactions. Despite firm-size similarities, there were differences in the financial composition and in levels of growth of foreign and domestic targets. The price-earnings ratio of foreign targets is found to be almost 19 percent higher than that for domestic targets. This would imply market expectation that foreign targets would generate greater earnings growth than would the targets of domestic acquisition. In the sample, foreign targets are also characterized by a relatively high growth rate in the four years preceding the acquisition.

9.3   Premium Measurement and the Foreign Premium

In section 9.4, the value of changes in corporate ownership is approximated by target shareholder gains. This section discusses the measurement of target shareholder wealth gains and comments on the information they contain. When their firm is purchased by a foreign bidder, target shareholders realize an additional 9 percent gain relative to preacquisition share prices.

9.3.1   Measuring Target Shareholder Gains

Although we compare average abnormal returns on the event days surrounding the announcements of foreign and domestic takeovers, the analysis concentrates on cumulative abnormal returns. Constructing measures of average abnormal returns or cumulative abnormal returns begins with the standard market model. For each stock, the market model is estimated on returns data in the interval 250 to 21 trading days prior to the takeover announcement date, ($t = 0$). R_{it} represents the return to the individual stock i on trading day t, while R_{mt} represents returns to the market portfolio on trading day t.

$$R_{it} = \alpha + \beta_i R_{mt} + \varepsilon_{it}, \, t = (-250, -21)$$

To compute shareholder gains associated with acquisition announcement, the estimates of each firm's α_i, and β_i are applied to the market model during the acquisition event window. Both average abnormal returns (AR) and cumulative abnormal returns (CAR) accent the change in the traded value of target shares caused by the announcement of takeover intentions. Average abnormal returns for the domestic and foreign portfolios for each date t relative to the *Wall Street Journal* announcement date are calculated as follows:

$$AR_t = \frac{1}{N}\sum_{i=1}^{N} (R_{it} - \alpha_i - \beta_i R_{mt})$$

where N equals the number of firms in each portfolio.

The average abnormal returns for the foreign and domestic portfolios are presented in table 9.5, panel A. On the day before and the takeover announcement date itself, the foreign portfolio generated returns 3.9 and 2.9 percent greater in absolute value than the domestic portfolio returns of 11.6 and 6.0 percent. In other words, the announcement of a foreign acquisition resulted in target shareholder gains almost 39 percent greater than those created by the announcement of a domestic acquisition.

We generated cumulative abnormal returns to expand the analysis over a longer event window. The cumulative abnormal returns measure target shareholder wealth gains as they accrued in the period beginning twenty days prior

Table 9.5   **Abnormal Returns around the Merger Announcement Date ($t = 0$),
as Distinguished by Buyer Nationality, 1974–1990**

A. Daily Abnormal Returns

Event Day	N_{Dom}	AR_{Dom}	Z-stat	N_{For}	AR_{For}	Z-Stat
−20	477	0.001	1.219	226	0.005	3.813
−15	477	0.001	4.241	226	0.002	1.843
−10	477	0.003	4.196	226	0.007	5.758
−5	477	0.003	3.658	226	0.009	7.279
−4	477	0.011	11.031	226	0.011	8.031
−3	477	0.015	13.984	226	0.016	11.015
−2	477	0.015	16.806	226	0.026	16.028
−1	477	0.116	115.214	226	0.155	95.715
0	477	0.060	59.567	226	0.089	62.338
1	477	0.006	6.458	226	0.007	5.171
2	477	0.001	4.855	226	0.010	9.075
3	477	0.006	1.712	226	0.006	3.148
4	477	0.002	3.924	226	0.006	3.721
5	477	0.001	1.517	226	0.000	0.691
10	477	0.002	2.507	226	0.002	1.267

B. Cumulative Abnormal Returns

Event Day	N_{Dom}	CAR_{Dom}	Z-stat	N_{For}	CAR_{For}	Z-Stat
−20	477	0.001	1.156	226	0.005	3.040
−15	477	0.016	3.780	226	0.015	4.322
−10	477	0.027	4.076	226	0.041	7.155
−5	477	0.053	6.403	226	0.080	11.524
−4	477	0.064	7.778	226	0.091	12.605
−3	477	0.079	9.221	226	0.107	14.187
−2	477	0.095	11.019	226	0.133	16.677
−1	477	0.211	23.041	226	0.288	33.424
0	477	0.271	28.041	226	0.377	37.730
1	477	0.278	27.013	226	0.384	36.422
2	477	0.282	26.555	226	0.394	36.011
3	477	0.283	26.158	226	0.401	35.250
4	477	0.287	25.752	226	0.407	34.753
5	477	0.288	25.171	226	0.407	34.032
10	477	0.301	23.912	226	0.409	31.900

Note: AR is the abnormal returns, and CAR is the cumulative abnormal returns on the domestic ($_{Dom}$) and foreign ($_{For}$) portfolios.

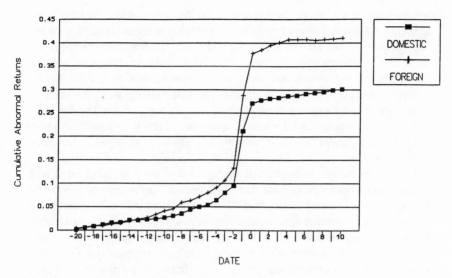

Fig. 9.1   Foreign and domestic cumulative abnormal returns

to the acquisition announcement and through the five trading days following the last announcement.

$$CAR = \sum_{t=annc-20}^{bid+5} [\frac{1}{N}\sum_{i=1}^{N} (R_{it} - \alpha_i - \beta_i R_{mt})]$$

The cumulative abnormal returns experienced in foreign and domestic acquisitions are shown in table 9.5, panel B. The evolution of cumulative abnormal returns is also displayed in figure 9.1. The gains on the foreign portfolio of targets are most pronounced on days −1 and 0, during which shareholders earned abnormal returns of 6.8 percent above those earned on the domestic portfolio. But the difference in total gains is noticeable across the entire event window.[6]

In aggregate, cumulative abnormal returns accruing to target shareholders indicate that target shareholders benefit more when their firm is subject to foreign takeover. We now compare the cumulative abnormal returns created by foreign and domestic transactions as we examine more disaggregated industry groupings. Table 9.6 displays foreign and domestic premiums disaggregated at the two-digit industry level for the manufacturing sector. Direct comparisons

6. The comparison and subsequent analysis is not sensitive to the length of the event window. We find that foreign transactions command higher shareholder wealth gains across all event windows.

are possible for sixteen of the manufacturing industries. While the cumulative abnormal returns in foreign acquisitions are higher in the average manufacturing transaction, they are not absolutely higher across all manufacturing industries. The foreign premium is higher than the domestic premium in eleven of the manufacturing sectors and lower in five. It is interesting to note that the industries experiencing high foreign acquisition activity were the same as those industries undergoing heavy domestic acquisition activity. The similarity of emphasis in foreign and domestic acquisitions seems to indicate that underlying industry factors may have precipitated consolidation in particular manufacturing sectors.

Initial information indicates that foreign acquisitions are associated with greater shareholder wealth gains than are domestic acquisitions of U.S. firms. However, the result may be due to differences in target industries, numbers of outside bidders, or other situational differences unrelated to buyer nationality. In the following sections, we control for circumstances associated with premium fluctuations to learn whether higher foreign payments arise from firm- or industry-level influences that are common determinants in all transactions or if the premiums are the outcome of unique factors facing foreign acquirers.

9.3.2   Evidence of A Foreign Premium

Before concluding that the premium measured in the foreign subsample is unique to foreign transactions, one must ascertain whether the high foreign premium represents foreign purchases of assets that would command higher payments regardless of buyer nationality. Although the bulk of wealth gains accruing to target shareholders have never been completely described, it is true that some industry and transaction characteristics are known to influence the level of the premium paid. To analyze the level of target shareholder wealth gains associated with the presence of foreign bidders, we use the following standard regression:

$$PREMIUM_i = \alpha + \beta_1 * FOREIGN + \beta_2 * COMPET + \beta_3 * MFG + \beta_4 * CASH + \beta_5 * CHALL + \varepsilon_i$$

In each regression, we describe target shareholder wealth gains as a function of bidder identity, transaction characteristics, and industry characteristics. The dependent variable *PREMIUM* is the cumulative abnormal returns accruing to target shareholders in each individual transaction. To determine the effect of foreign acquirers on shareholder gains, a dummy variable, *FOREIGN*, was created and set equal to one if the buyer was foreign and to zero if the buyer was a domestic firm. We expect the coefficient on foreign will be positive if foreign firms create additional synergy gains in their U.S. acquisitions or benefit from the arbitrage of cross-border asymmetries. Although it is difficult to provide

Table 9.6   Cumulative Abnormal Returns: Manufacturing Industries as Distinguished by Buyer Nationality, 1974–1990

	United States		Foreign	
	Premium	N	Premium	N
Food and kindred products	0.366	16	0.346	14
Tobacco products	—	0	0.595	1
Textile mill products	0.326	5	0.368	1
Apparel and other textile products	0.485	12	1.077	1
Lumber and wood products	0.374	5	—	0
Furniture and fixtures	0.348	7	—	0
Paper and allied products	0.372	14	0.385	4
Printing and publishing	0.431	11	0.619	8
Chemicals and allied products	0.392	25	0.419	21
Petroleum and coal products	0.476	2	0.179	2
Rubber and miscellaneous Plastic products	0.518	13	0.479	7
Leather and leather products	—	0	0.007	2
Stone, clay, and glass products	0.528	11	0.352	9
Primary metal industries	0.246	7	0.708	3
Fabricated metal products	0.397	25	0.469	3
Machinery, except electrical	0.449	47	0.621	35
Electric and electronic equipment	0.315	35	0.573	13
Transportation and equipment	0.358	15	0.423	3
Instruments and related products	0.359	28	0.352	14
Miscellaneous manufacturing industries	0.321	6	0.787	2
Total	0.386	284	0.486	143

economic arguments for irrationality, the coefficient on *FOREIGN* will also be positive if foreign firms were systematically overpaying.[7]

The variables *COMPET* and *CASH* are included because previous studies have shown them to be significant determinants of wealth effects. *COMPET* is a dummy variable set equal to one if there were other competing bidders who announced their intention to acquire the target. The coefficient on the competition dummy should be positive, since the presence of competing bids forces the winning bidder to meet the bid or lose the contest for control in most cases. Previous studies have also shown that transactions completed with cash command higher shareholder gains than those that do not. Consequently, all transactions that were completed entirely by cash payment are indicated by setting the dummy variable *CASH* equal to one. For all other transactions, the value of the *CASH* dummy is set to zero.

7. See Roll (1986) for an overpayment hypothesis. However, it would be hard to explain why manager nationality should influence this propensity.

Two other variables are used in the regressions describing target shareholder gains. First, there is a variable used to capture any differences in the bids made for manufacturing and for nonmanufacturing assets. Target firms were classified as manufacturing firms if the Standard Industrial Classification (SIC) code for their primary line of business was between 2000 and 3999. The dummy variable *MFG* was set equal to one for all targets that had SIC codes in this range. Second, we test for the influence of a government challenge on the wealth gains of target shareholders. The dummy *CHALL* was set equal to one if any government agency challenged the takeover transaction. The most common challenges were presented by the Federal Trade Commission, Justice Department, and Internal Revenue Service.

Table 9.7 displays the results of the benchmark regressions. As the first regression indicates, the premium paid in foreign transactions exceeded the premium paid by domestic purchasers by 10.9 percent. Relative to shareholder gains in domestic contests, the wealth gains associated with the presence of a foreign bidder are more than 40 percent larger than the gains in domestic contests. The presence of competing bidders augmented premium payments by 9.2 percent. Government challenge was also associated with an increase in the cumulative abnormal returns earned by target shareholders, although the coefficient is not statistically significant at conventional levels. In comparison, the returns to target shareholders of manufacturing assets commanded a significant premium 9 percent larger than the premium of nonmanufacturing assets.[8] The second regression augments the first by including a dummy variable representing takeovers effected by cash. When the *CASH* dummy is added, the estimated values of the other regressors are reduced. Nonetheless, the value of foreign bidders remains highly significant and is estimated to increase target shareholder gains by 9.3 percent.

The third regression of table 9.7 investigates the importance of time specification. Sixteen year dummies were included to capture the variations in shareholder cumulative abnormal returns that were the result of yearly changes in economic conditions or in the market for corporate control. The results show that the time dummies do reduce the value of the other regressors. However, the character and magnitude of the variables are not changed significantly. The data were also tested to see if time effects could be captured by a trend effect. However, the premiums received by target shareholders displayed no apparent trend between 1974 and 1990.

---

8. The premium on manufacturing assets could arise from one of many factors. Most likely, the difference represents the different elasticity of demand for shares in the manufacturing sector. As James and Weir (1987) show for the banking sector, the premium received by shareholders is positively related to the number of potential purchasers of the target. If there are more potential buyers of manufacturing assets, then competition for the assets may allocate more of the gains to target shareholders, leaving less of the surplus to the purchaser. The finding of a significantly higher premium could also be a proxy for other firm characteristics. However, inclusion of regressors such as research and development expenditures as a percentage of sales or other financial or operating statistics was unsuccessful in reducing the manufacturing dummy.

Table 9.7   Regression of Shareholder Gains on Merger Characteristics, 1974–1990

Dependent Variable	FOREIGN	COMPET	MFG	CHALL	CASH	YEAR	IND	CONSTANT	Obs	Adj. R^2
1. PREMIUM	0.1086[a] (0.0329)	0.0921[a] (0.0357)	0.0979[a] (0.0312)	0.0672 (0.0462)				0.2521[a] (0.0281)	703	0.036
2. PREMIUM	0.0930[a] (0.0345)	0.0686[c] (0.0375)	0.0760[b] (0.0330)	0.0349 (0.0494)	0.1464[b] (0.0611)			0.1490[b] (0.0582)	645	0.035
3. PREMIUM	0.0765[b] (0.0350)	0.0550 (0.0375)	0.0744[b] (0.0330)	0.0330 (0.0495)	0.1463[b] (0.0616)	YES		0.4480[a] (0.1062)	645	0.060
4. PREMIUM	0.0936[a] (0.0347)	0.0662[c] (0.0378)		0.0429 (0.0496)	0.1346[b] (0.0615)		YES	0.1398[b] (0.0786)	645	0.034
5. PREMIUM	0.0759[b] (0.0352)	0.0515 (0.0378)		0.0418 (0.0497)	0.1369[b] (0.0621)	YES	YES	0.4342[a] (0.1177)	645	0.060
6. PREMIUM 1974–81	0.1545[a] (0.0521)	0.1412[a] (0.0601)	−0.0066 (0.0530)	0.0797 (0.0728)	0.1873 (0.1993)			0.1260 (0.1985)	246	0.038
7. PREMIUM 1982–86	−0.0389 (0.0587)	0.0333 (0.0566)	0.0953 (0.0491)	0.0248 (0.0787)	0.1997[b] (0.0817)			0.0812 (0.0764)	219	0.035
8. PREMIUM 1987–90	0.0903 (0.0756)	0.0187 (0.0808)	0.1467[b] (0.0732)	−0.0592 (0.1125)	0.1050 (0.1079)			0.2115[b] (0.0998)	180	0.025

Notes: *PREMIUM* is cumulative abnormal returns accruing to target shareholders. The *COMPET* dummy was set equal to one if one or more competitors declared their intention to acquire the target. *MFG* is a dummy varibale for manufacturing sector targets. The dummy *CHALL* was set equal to one for any transaction facing challenge by a government agency. The *CASH* dummy was set equal to one for all transactions done entirely by cash payment. *YEAR* is a set of year dummies. *IND* is a set of industry dummy variables. Standard errors are in parentheses.

[a]Significantly different from zero at the 99 percent level.
[b]Significantly different from zero at the 95 percent level.
[c]Significantly different from zero at the 90 percent level.

Table 9.7's fourth and fifth regressions consider the influence of more detailed industrial heterogeneity on shareholder wealth gains. In the benchmark regressions, we limit the distinction to manufacturing and nonmanufacturing targets. However, we may learn that foreign firms tended to purchase firms which were from higher-premium sectors. If this were the case, the coefficient on the foreign dummy would disappear when a more comprehensive set of industry dummies were included. This specification with industry dummies rather than a single manufacturing dummy variable adds no information on the wealth effects of takeovers. This is also confirmed by regression five, which includes a set of industry and time dummies. The effect of foreign bidders remains as large and significant as in previous regressions. The robustness of the foreign premium to the inclusion of industry dummies and proxies for the competitive environment show that the foreign premium is not the simple outcome of foreign purchases concentrated in high-premium industries.

The final three regressions in table 9.7 test the benchmark regression on subperiods of the 1974 to 1990 time span. When the time periods of 1974 to 1981, 1982 to 1986, and 1987 to 1990 are used, it becomes apparent that the coefficients of the benchmark regression change markedly across the different time periods. Most notable for the paper is the instability of the foreign coefficient. Even if the time periods are split differently, it is apparent that the foreign premium was highest in the 1970s, fell in the early 1980s, but increased again in the late 1980s. These results cast doubt on the overpayment hypothesis. If it were true that firms became more sophisticated in their abilities in the U.S. acquisition market, we would expect a declining foreign premium, as is seen by comparison of the first and second time periods. But the resumption of the influence of foreign bids in the late 1980s contradicts the notion of ongoing learning. However, these results do suggest that there are some very important time-varying effects that influence the gains of target shareholders. We will return to these explanations in the next section.

9.3.3   Measurement Issues and the Foreign Premium

To the extent that individual premiums reflect the value of transaction-specific opportunities, premium variations may be used to evaluate the sources of value in foreign and domestic transactions. Unfortunately, the premium payment will not be an exact measure of the transaction's value, due to measurement concerns which must be noted.

As recognized in Hall (1988) and Malatesta and Thompson (1985), a current stock price reflects the expected value of a firm's discounted current and future profits. This value incorporates expectations of the stock's value under current management, as well as the incipient value of the firm under new management, weighted by the expected probabilities of each outcome. Takeovers will not occur unless the bidders expect to produce gains which cannot be realized without a change in control. As long as investors believe that their firm could become a takeover target, a fraction of potential takeover gains will be capitalized in the current stock price.

$$P_{stock} = E(P_{stock}|\text{foreign takeover})*[\text{prob(foreign takeover)}]$$
$$+ E(P_{stock}|\text{domestic takeover})*[\text{prob(domestic takeover)}]$$
$$+ E(P_{stock}|\text{no takeover})*[\text{prob(no takeover)}]$$

If there is any anticipation that a firm may be acquired, the observed effect of the takeover announcement will be less than the economic value of the event itself.

A second issue that influences the observed payment is the division of the gains between target shareholders and the bidding firm.[9] Following Hall (1988), one assumes that stochastic changes in the world create changes which favor changes in corporate ownership. The assumption of stochastic changes is important. Otherwise, investors could predict each firm's time path of ownership and each firm's precise value. Takeovers would command no shareholder gains, because stock prices would already reflect the value of all future changes in control. Each firm x has a valuation, V_{yx}, for target y's assets. Of the potential acquirers, the bidder with the highest valuation for the target makes the purchase. In order to purchase the target, the winning firm x' has to pay at least as much as the firm with the second-highest valuation would be able to pay.

$$\text{Max}_{x \neq x'} V_{yx} \leq P_{paid} \leq V_{yx'}$$

It is assumed that the valuation of firm, V_{yx}, exceeds the current market value of the target firm.[10] Since the price paid lies between the valuations of the highest and the second-highest valuing firms, the closer the valuation of the second bidder to the first bidder, the higher the minimum price the first firm must pay in order to gain control. If the highest bidder is uncertain about other firms' valuations, he may offer a larger bid. If the firm knew all other firms' valuations with certainty, it would only offer marginally more than the target was worth to the next-highest bidder.

Since the division of gains is not likely to be divided between the bidder and target in a systematic fashion, target shareholder gains are an imperfect measure of total value created by the acquisition. The empirical evidence on this issue will be considered in the next section.

9.4 Evidence from Foreign Acquisitions in the United States

In this section we search for explanations of the foreign premium in U.S. acquisitions. We begin with tests for the influence of exchange rate fluctuations on foreign premium payments and later try to ascertain the importance of firm

9. The degree to which target shareholders capture merger gains is controversial. Grossman and Hart (1980) suggest complete capture. Subsequent research has shown that informational asymmetries and costs of information gathering and shareholder heterogeneity will result in incomplete capture by target shareholders.

10. No bid will be placed if the current market value of the target firm, V_y, exceeds the firm's value under the ownership of another firm x. This ignores the possibility that management, enhancing its own perquisites, may place bids which are harmful to shareholder interests. See Roll (1986); Morck, Shleifer, and Vishny (1990).

explanations of foreign investment by gauging whether shareholder gains are influenced by the aspects of the target firm sought by foreign purchasers, or by the foreign firms' approach to the bidding.

9.4.1   Exchange Rates and Shareholder Gains

There are many potential avenues by which the exchange rate may influence the level of foreign acquisitions in the United States and the payments accompanying the activity. A couple of the channels, including country-specific interest rates, provide no aggregate predictions because their impact is firm specific.[11]. Exchange rate effects transmitted by changes in supply and demand are also indeterminate because their effects depend on the method of competition in relevant output and factor markets.

Exchange rate effects driven by wealth effects or worries of protection have more-direct predictions regarding the feasibility of specific acquisitions.[12] Most easily predicted are wealth effects induced by exchange rate movements, as explained in Froot and Stein (1991). When foreign firms are constrained in credit markets, competition among foreign bidders for U.S. targets should cause the enhanced ability to pay dollars to be translated into higher premiums. If the foreign bidder did not increase its premium offer, another foreign bidder, who also benefited from exchange rate-induced wealth effects, would offer a slightly higher bid and acquire the assets. It is true that foreign firms' willingness to pay should never exceed the expected present discounted value profits. And, unless the profit stream is influenced by the level of the exchange rate, the foreign perception of the dollar value of the assets does not fluctuate. However, if imperfect lending markets create borrowing constraints which prevent firms from bidding as much as their willingness to pay, the foreign premium may increase to the degree to which exchange rate movements relax the bidding constraints faced by foreign firms.

Even though some argue that a weak dollar facilitates the foreign purchase of domestic assets at bargain prices, the strength of the dollar will only influence the amount paid by the foreign bidder when dollar fluctuations create differential wealth effects for foreign and domestic bidders. The strength of the dollar will not create bargains, because depreciation reduces the value of the expected foreign currency profit stream at the same time that the foreign currency price of the U.S. target falls.[13]

---

11. Cushman (1985) models the foreign direct investment decisions of risk-averse firms and their response to the level and variability of the exchange rate. Since the real interest rate facing each firm is determined by its location of sales, source of production inputs, and location of financing, firm reactions are uniquely determined by each firm's multinational structure.

12. We do not analyze the protection argument here. A firm with lucrative export sales to the United States might choose to acquire U.S. assets to transfer production to the United States if it feared that large U.S. current account deficits might spur protection against its exports. If a strong dollar aggravates the current account deficit, then a strong dollar could promote foreign acquisitions. However, how much time will elapse before the onset of protection or the firm decision to invest is unclear.

13. Klein and Rosengren (1991) find that exchange rate effects on FDI are caused by wealth effects rather than by exchange rate effects on relative wages.

Table 9.8   The Effect of the Exchange Rate Level or Changes on the Foreign Premium, 1974–1990

	(1)	(2)	(3)
Competitors	0.0676[b]	0.0612[c]	0.0661[b]
	(0.0373)	(0.0373)	(0.0375)
Challenge	0.0311	0.0399	0.0390
	(0.0492)	(0.0491)	(0.0494)
Manufacturing	0.0686[b]	0.0696[b]	0.0731[b]
	(0.0330)	(0.0329)	(0.0331)
Cash	0.1493[a]	0.1502[a]	0.1481[b]
	(0.0609)	(0.0607)	(0.0611)
Constant	0.1515[a]	0.1509[a]	0.1493[a]
	(0.0580)	(0.0579)	(0.0581)
Foreign Dummies			
Strong-$ year	0.0133		
	(0.0476)		
Weak-$ year	0.1474[a]		
	(0.0411)		
$ depreciation		0.1592[a]	
		(0.0411)	
$ appreciation		−0.0031	
		(0.0474)	
Future $ appreciation			0.0550
			(0.0449)
Future $ depreciation			0.1272[a]
			(0.0432)
Obs	645	645	645
Adj. R^2	0.042	0.047	0.036

Note: Standard errors in parentheses.
[a]Significantly different from zero at the 99 percent confidence level.
[b]Significantly different from zero at the 95 percent confidence level.
[c]Significantly different from zero at the 90 percent confidence level.

To test whether the movements or the value of the exchange rate influence target shareholder wealth gains, we try a number of specifications that incorporate either the level of the exchange rate or its changes. In each of these tests, the foreign dummy is split to reflect the value of the U.S. dollar when the bid was placed for the U.S. target. The results of these tests are displayed in table 9.8.

In the first column of table 9.8, we test whether the cumulative abnormal returns measured in foreign acquisitions vary with the strength of the U.S. dollar. The first column classifies foreign purchases as having occurred during strong- or weak-dollar years.[14] The results show that target shareholder wealth

14. Dollar classification is based on real effective exchange rates published in the *OECD Main Economic Indicators.* Each observation was dated according to the date of its acquisition announcement. We then compare the value of the dollar to its average over the 1974–90 time period. If the value exceeded the average, it was classified as being a strong-dollar period. Weak-dollar periods indicated that the value of the dollar was below the 1974–90 average.

gains in foreign acquisitions are much larger in weak-dollar years. In fact, there are no additional wealth gains for target shareholders in foreign acquisitions during strong-dollar years. In addition to the results reported in table 9.8, the effects of dollar strength were also tested by adding the real value of the dollar to the benchmark regression. The continuous variable confirms our previous findings that the value of the foreign premium increases when the dollar is weak.

While the classification of foreign bidders according to strong- or weak-dollar years indicates the importance of the current exchange rate, we also test for the influence of exchange rate changes on the foreign premium. In the second column of table 9.8, we categorize foreign firms on the basis of dollar changes in the period prior to the foreign acquisition. The variable "$ depreciation" is a dummy variable representing all foreign firm purchases that occurred in a year following dollar depreciation, while the "$ appreciation" variable represents all foreign acquisitions that occurred in years following dollar appreciation.[15] Similar to the results involving the level of the exchange rate, the wealth gains in foreign acquisitions are found to be higher in years following dollar depreciation. In contrast, the wealth gains in years following dollar appreciation are found to be nonexistent.

Further exchange rate tests were performed to learn whether the finding that dollar depreciation enhances foreign bids was unique to foreign mergers or whether the finding reflected underlying economic changes which influenced all mergers. Since the value of the dollar reflects expectations regarding the U.S. economy, one might be concerned that the exchange rate results actually measure merger response to macroeconomic trends in the United States. These could include interest rates, as determined by the levels of saving and investment demand, or the rate of growth in the U.S. economy. Accordingly, the test was repeated to include division of the domestic sample on the basis of dollar appreciation or depreciation as well. If the relevance of the exchange rate coefficient was based on economic factors of importance to all mergers, then one would expect that the domestic premiums would also be higher in periods of dollar depreciation. However, the division of U.S. transactions is not justified by the data. Exchange rate classification of the domestic dummy yielded a coefficient small in magnitude and indistinguishable from zero.

Although unlikely, a second alternative exchange rate timing argument would posit that mergers are timed to anticipate future exchange rate movements. If foreign firms could time their purchases perfectly, they would choose to crowd purchases into periods before dollar appreciation.[16] Despite the problems with the argument, we use the third column of table 9.8 to test whether

15. The classification of appreciation or depreciation was based on the movement of the dollar in the year before the announcement of the takeover.
16. There are many difficulties with the argument that foreign firms might time their purchases to beat dollar appreciation. First, there is no reason to believe that firms should have better estimates of future exchange rate changes, and to the extent that exchange rate movements present

there is any different in target wealth gains in periods before dollar changes. The foreign dummy is split into two dummies, one for foreign purchases before dollar appreciation and another for foreign purchases occurring before dollar depreciation. The values of the two foreign variables are not statistically different, though the estimated value of the foreign variable in periods preceding depreciation is slightly higher than the variable indicating foreign purchases in periods preceding appreciation. If there were any reason to believe that firms timed purchases to beat future exchange rate changes, we would have expected the values of the two foreign variables to be the reverse of their estimated values.

9.4.2   Strategic Bidding and the Division of Takeover Gains

As was demonstrated in section 9.3, the level of the takeover premium depends in part on the division of gains between the bidding firm and target shareholders. In addition to the strategies pursued by bidders, the division depends on information, relative learning costs, and the competitive environment for particular targets. In this section, we examine whether foreign and domestic acquirers appear to pursue similar bid strategies.

Fishman (1988, 1989) explains why firms may place high initial bids or offer cash as strategic devices to preempt the entry of other bidders. Learning about the merit of various targets is costly, and one way in which firms can learn is observing the placement of bids by other firms.[17] If the initial firm places a sufficiently high bid, other firms will be deterred from assessing the value of the particular target, because their expected gain is smaller than the learning costs they would incur in deciding whether to place a competing bid.

In order to test whether foreign firms are bidding in a manner consistent with preemptive bidding, we separate the effect of competitors in domestic and foreign acquisitions. The results are shown in table 9.9. The unconstrained estimate is superior and shows that, while the presence of competitors significantly augments shareholder gains in domestic contests, the presence of competitors has no measurable influence on the premiums paid by foreign acquirers.[18] This finding is consistent with the possibility that foreign firms practice preemptive bidding. If foreign bidders place preemptively high bids, the entry of other bidders should have less influence on target shareholder gains

---

business risks, we would expect these firms to use futures contracts to protect themselves. Additionally, if many foreign firms decide to buy in the current period to avoid price increases caused by future dollar appreciation, then asset demand should bid up current-period asset prices, eliminating the advantages of current-period purchases.

17. As long as there is positive correlation in firms' evaluation of potential targets, one firm's bid signals to other firms that the target could be valuable to them as well.

18. A variable was created representing the presence of foreign competition in the bidding process. Its value could not be distinguished from the dummy variable for domestic competitors. The failure was not unexpected, because only 2 percent of the acquisitions in the sample faced public competition from a foreign bidder.

Table 9.9   **Regression of Target Shareholder Gains on Acquisition Characteristics: 1974–1990**

	(1)	(2)	(3)
Foreign	0.1065[a]	0.0586	0.0612
	(0.0389)	(0.0668)	(0.0512)
Challenge	0.0333	0.0708	0.0456
	(0.0494)	(0.0993)	(0.0671)
Manufacturing	0.0784[b]	0.0122	0.0668
	(0.0331)	(0.0671)	(0.0468)
Cash	0.1427[b]	0.1298[b]	0.1248
	(0.0613)	(0.1039)	(0.0768)
Competitors		0.0322	0.0775
		(0.0635)	(0.0481)
Domestic *	0.0863[b]		
Competition	(0.0441)		
Foreign *	0.0229		
Competition	(0.0711)		
Relative intangibles		−0.0668[b]	
		(0.0044)	
Foreign * Relative		0.0121	
intangibles		(0.0092)	
Relative market			−0.0545
			(0.0656)
Foreign * Relative			0.3799
market			(0.2575)
Constant	0.1461[a]	0.2182[a]	0.1804[b]
	(0.0583)	(0.0980)	(0.0728)
Obs	645	167	383
Adj. R^2	0.034	0.015	0.028

Note: Standard errors in parentheses.
[a]Significantly different from zero at the 99 percent confidence level.
[b]Significantly different from zero at the 95 percent confidence level.
[c]Significantly different from zero at the 90 percent confidence level.

than would be the case for domestic bids which have not been set at a preemptive level. In the presence of a competing bidder, the first bidder may increase his initial bid or drop out of the contest.[19] If foreign firms attempt to set preemptive bids, their initial bids are set closer to their estimated value of the target firm. These firms have less ability to increase their payments when competitors enter, since payment increases are bounded above by the bidder's estimate of target value.

This evidence agrees with the summary statistics presented in table 9.2 which show that foreign takeover bids face competitors 35 percent less often than do domestic transactions. The differences in foreign and domestic merger processes could be linked to relatively high foreign bids, which deter potential competition.

19. Target management may recommend the acceptance of the lower bid.

Less clear is why foreign firms should place more-frequent preemptive bids. Preemptive bids may be placed by foreign firms in an effort to mitigate the adverse publicity associated with resistance to foreign ownership. If preemptive bids reduce competition and speed the acquisition process, then foreign firms may find the extra costs worth the gains of reduced public attention and hostility. Resistance to foreign ownership might also exist at the shareholder or worker level. The argument that shareholders cared would require that shareholders value not only the financial returns of the underlying stock but also the continuation of U.S. control. This condition, however, seems rather unlikely, especially in light of the empirical facts that foreign takeovers were not any more likely to face hostile opposition than domestic takeovers were and that foreign purchases were less frequently subject to governmental challenge. In order to test if foreign firms were concerned with resistance at the worker level, a variable to measure labor intensity was included in the standard regressions.[20] Employment intensity, however, had no relation to shareholder gains in foreign transaction.

Our evidence can not resolve the presence or absence of preemptive bidding on the part of foreign acquirers. Nonetheless, the evidence is intriguing and worth further inquiry.

9.4.3   Evidence from Target Firm Operational Data

There is some suggestion that foreign firms are pursuing particular types of firms in the United States.[21] If foreign and domestic acquirers target different firms, we would expect that the shareholder gains would reflect firm differences. In fact, the appearance of preemptive bidding could be created by the differences in the assets sought by domestic and foreign bidders. Nonetheless, it is difficult to ascertain whether foreign firms seek different assets. It is plausible that certain U.S. targets are particularly attractive to firms expanding their global operations. While we would expect these U.S. assets to be subject to foreign interest, they would most likely be of interest to domestic multinationals as well. In this vein, we test whether certain target characteristics explain the large shareholder gains in foreign acquisitions.

One variable that does produce interesting results is the effect of intangibles. A ratio variable, "relative intangibles," was created by dividing the target firm's intangibles by the average level of intangibles in its industry. A second variable was created by multiplying the first variable by the foreign dummy variable to learn if intangible assets played a symmetric role in foreign and domestic transactions. Column 2 of table 9.9 indicates the influence of including the two variables. The foreign dummy is reduced significantly. The results indicate that the presence of intangibles results in higher wealth gains in foreign trans-

---

20. Measures tried were employment/sales and employment/assets.
21. Harris and Ravenscraft (1991) claim that foreign firms make purchases in industries that are more research and development intensive.

actions than would be the case for the same level of intangibles in a domestic acquisition. In other words, part of the high premiums in foreign transactions appears to reflect foreign bidders' willingness to pay for intangible assets.

A second test of intangibles involves the influence of market share on the premiums paid by bidders. In table 9.9, the variable "relative market" measures sales by the target in its primary line of business relative to the industry as a whole. The second variable "foreign*relative market" multiplies the relative market by the foreign dummy. In the estimation presented in column (3) of table 9.9, the measure of market share is found to have no influence on merger premiums in general but to increase the premiums paid by foreign bidders. At the same time, the value of the foreign dummy is lower than it is in the benchmark regressions. Like the previous test of intangibles, the inclusion of market share variables suggests that higher foreign bids are caused in part by foreign firms' willingness to pay for market share. This finding is consistent with theories that foreign firms will pursue acquisitions when it is more costly for foreign firms to develop market share in the United States.[22]

9.4.4   Other Motivations for Foreign Investment

The primary advantage of multinationals over uninational firms is often claimed to lie in multinational firms' ability to surmount barriers to the minimum-cost international flow of goods and finances. The benefits of being multinational range from use of the form as an alternate to individual international portfolio diversification, to such firms' ability to exploit country financial differences.[23] The results here cannot be claimed to apply to all foreign investment, because the current study concerns only acquisition, and the applicable restrictions/barriers may be more frequently avoided by means of joint venture, purchase of only a division rather than whole firm, or the establishment of a new business in the United States.

At the individual level, either capital market segmentation or large transactions costs could inhibit international portfolio diversification (see Agmon and Lessard 1977; or Errunza and Senbet 1981). Two possible tests are suggested by the implication that multinationals may provide international diversification at lower cost than international diversification created by individual investors. Assuming that target shareholders capture a portion of bidder gains, the foreign premium should be higher when the foreign firm's acquisition significantly

---

22. In addition to the reported tests, we also tested the benchmark findings for their sensitivity to the inclusion of target firm financial variables or to the addition of relative performance variables. When added to the analysis, these do not contribute to our understanding of foreign premium payments.

23. Numerous other explanations are possible involving the arbitrage of trade, tax, or other barriers. However, without a measure that indicates which restrictions are actually binding, answers cannot be found. Analysis of these issues could be much better captured by comparisons of pre- and postacquisition performance of the acquiring firm in target markets.

increases the foreign exposure of the multinational.[24] To this end, regressions were performed to see if the foreign premium was any higher for foreign firms which had no previous real operations in the United States.[25] However, when foreign bidders were distinguished according to their presence in the U.S. market, no differences in target shareholder wealth gains were found. We next tested an alternative method of determining foreign firm involvement in the U.S. market. Rather than classifying involvement as the presence or absence of U.S. subsidiaries, we classified involvement in the U.S. market according to the financing of the foreign firm. We might expect that the foreign firm gains the most international diversification when it had not previous financing in the United States.[26] However, the prior financial status of foreign acquirers had no influence on the level of the foreign cumulative abnormal returns.

The results display no evidence confirming the value of multinationals as vehicles for diversification; neither do the results alone refute the existence of those gains. Even if diversification gains resulted, it is not clear that target shareholders could appropriate those gains.

A second possible barrier, which would incline foreign firms toward foreign investment, is the presence of trade barriers against sales of their products in the United States. Unless the foreign products have distinct advantages or characteristics relative to their domestic competitors, the trade barriers will be just as likely to encourage domestic as foreign investment. A clean test would relate target shareholder gains to the level of barriers levied against specific products. Unfortunately, due to the small number of transactions in each industry and to uncertainty as to the degree to which the various restrictions are actually binding, the current data is not suited to this inquiry. As a first pass, the manufacturing dummy was split into separate foreign and manufacturing dummies. Assuming that barriers would particularly inhibit the flow of finished goods, one might expect that foreign purchases of manufacturing firms might generate a higher premium than domestic purchases of manufacturing assets would. However, beyond the inclusion of the foreign dummy variable on all foreign transactions, distinction of the manufacturing dummy on the basis of nationality was not warranted by the data.

24. Doukas and Travlos (1988) studied U.S. firms making acquisitions abroad. They found that abnormal returns to the bidding firms are largest when the firm makes a new entry or undertakes new activities, especially when the country entered is more dissimilar to the United States. They stress corporate multinationalism, rather than portfolio diversification, as the source of additional shareholder gains.

25. Determination of previous real operations was based on information contained in *Moody's International*. A dummy variable was created to indicate presence of the foreign firm in the U.S. market, at the time that the bid was placed. If the firm had any U.S. operations or subsidiaries, the variable was set equal to one.

26. Of the foreign firms in the sample, 25 percent had dollar-denominated debt, while 30 percent of the foreign firms had stocks issued in the United States prior to their bids. Most of the foreign stock issues were American depository receipts sold through investment banks. Fourteen percent of the foreign firms had both financial instruments.

9.5 Conclusion

While domestic and foreign acquirers have both expanded their activity in the U.S. market in the 1980s, certain differences in the characteristics of their transactions distinguish their efforts. The most pronounced difference arises in the target shareholder wealth gains in domestic and foreign acquisitions. Foreign acquisitions generated target shareholder wealth gains almost 10 percent in excess of those in similar domestic acquisitions. The robustness of the finding to controls for the method of payment, the competitive environment, and the presence of government or target management resistance indicate that high returns in foreign transactions are not simply caused by the concentration of foreign purchases in high-return sectors.

Other differences between foreign and domestic acquisitions are worthy of mention. To begin, foreign firms have acquired targets which are more rapidly growing and which have significantly higher price-earnings ratios than do the targets of domestic acquirers. In their contests for control, foreign firms are less likely to encounter competition from other bidding firms or challenge from government agencies. Finally, foreign acquisitions are more sensitive to exchange rate movements in a manner consistent with imperfect capital market explanations of foreign direct investment.

The presence of higher payments in foreign acquisitions seems indicative of additional value creation opportunities based on operational, financial, and transactions-based opportunities unique to cross-border acquisition. We find that part of the higher foreign payments is explained by foreign firms' payments for intangible assets. The specific causes of these differences and the particular asset characteristics should be the subject of further study.

References

Agmon, T., and D. Lessard. 1977. Investor recognition of corporate international diversification. *Journal of Finance* 32 (September): 1049–55.

Baldwin, John R., and Richard E. Caves. 1991. Foreign multinational enterprises and merger activity in Canada. In *Corporate globalization through mergers and aquisitions,* ed. Leonard Waverman, 89–121. Calgary: University of Calgary Press.

Brown, S. J., and J. B. Warner. 1980. Measuring security price performance. *Journal of Financial Economics* 8:205–58.

————. 1983. Using daily stock returns: The case of event studies. *Journal of Financial Economics* 14:3–31.

Cushman, David O. 1985. Real exchange rate risk, expectations, and the level of direct investment. *Review of Economics and Statistics* 67, no. 2 (May): 297–308.

Dewenter, Kathryn L. 1992. Evidence for and against Froot and Stein's imperfect capital markets model of foreign direct investment. Working Paper. Chicago: University of Chicago.

Doukas, John, and Nickolos G. Travlos. 1988. The effect of corporate multinationalism on shareholders' wealth: Evidence from international acquistions. *Journal of Finance* 43, no. 5 (December): 1161–75.

Dunning, John H. 1981. *International production and the multinational.* London: Allen and Unwin.

Errunza, Vihang R., and Lemma W. Senbet. 1981. The effects of international operations on the market value of the firm: Theory and evidence. *Journal of Finance* 35 (May): 401–17.

Fishman, Michael J. 1988. A theory of preemptive takeover bidding. *Rand Journal of Economics* 19:88–101.

————. 1989. Preemptive bidding and the role of the medium of exchange in acquistions. *Journal of Finance* 44 (March): 41–57.

Froot, Kenneth A., and Jeremy C. Stein. 1991. Exchange rates and foreign direct investment: An imperfect capital markets approach. *Quarterly Journal of Economics* 106 (November): 1191–217.

Grossman, S., and O. Hart. 1980. Takeover bids, the free rider problem, and the theory of the corporation. *Bell Journal of Economics* 11(1): 42–64.

Grossman, S. J., and J. E. Stiglitz. 1980. On the impossibility of informationally efficient markets. *American Economic Review* 70, no. 3 (June): 393–408.

Hall, Bronwyn H. 1988. The effect of takeover activity on corporate research and development. In *Corporate takeovers: Causes and consequences,* ed. Alan J. Auerbach. Chicago: University of Chicago Press.

Harris, Robert S., and David Ravenscraft. 1991. The role of acquisitions in foreign direct investment: Evidence from the U.S. stock market. *Journal of Finance* 46, no. 3 (July): 825–44.

Huang, Yen-Sheng, and Ralph Walkling. 1987. Target abnormal returns associated with acquisition announcements: Payment, acquisition form, and managerial resistance. *Journal of Financial Economics* 19, no. 2 (December): 329–49.

James, Christopher M., and Peggy Weir. 1987. Returns to acquirers and competition in the acquisition market: The case of banking. *Journal of Political Economy* 95, no. 2 (April): 355–70.

Jensen, M. C., and R. S. Ruback. 1983. The market for corporate control: The scientific evidence. *Journal of Financial Economics* 11, nos. 1–4: 5–50.

Klein, Michael W., and Eric Rosengren. 1992. The real exchange rate and foreign direct investment in the United States: Relative wealth versus relative wage effects. NBER Working Paper no. 4192. Cambridge, Mass.: National Bureau of Economic Research, October.

Kogut, Bruce, and Sea Jin Chang. 1991. Technological capabilities and Japanese foreign direct investment in the United States. *Review of Economics and Statistics* 73, no. 3 (August): 401–13.

Malatesta, Paul H., and Rex Thompson. 1985. Partially anticipated events: A model of stock price reactions with an application to corporate acquisitions. *Journal of Financial Economics* 14(2): 237–50.

Morck, Randall, Andrei Shleifer, and Robert W. Vishny. 1990. Do managerial objectives drive bad acquisitions? *Journal of Finance* 45, no. 1 (March): 31–48.

Roll, R. 1986. The hubris hypothesis of corporate takeovers. Part 1. *Journal of Business* 59, no. 2 (April): 197–216.

Vernon, Raymond. 1966. International investment and international trade in the product cycle. *Quarterly Journal of Economics* 83(1): 190–207.

Comment   Donald Lessard

Deborah Swenson's paper raises a number of fascinating questions regarding the motivations for foreign direct investment and employs company-level transaction data that have the potential to answer many of these questions in ways that are not possible with aggregate data.

Swenson's main focus is on measuring and explaining foreign premiums, the difference in the premiums paid in acquisitions by foreign firms versus those paid by domestic firms. While the behavior of these premiums may be viewed by some as capital markets arcana, they involve central questions: Why are certain activities worth more to foreign firms than to domestic firms? How do these differences vary across industries, types of activities, time, financial systems, macroeconomic circumstances, and so on?

Although acquisition data are partial relative to the FDI aggregates usually employed, they have some clear advantages. Firm-level explanations emphasize economies of scale, scope, and learning and therefore depend on the nature of the assets acquired and the way in which they are integrated into the acquiring firms' networks. Industry-level arguments vary with industry structure (global, continental, national, as well as degree of rivalry, etc). Financial system arguments often turn on differences between "inside" versus "outside" capital and asymmetries in information or in access to markets for corporate control, all of which are likely to vary across firms as well as countries. Even macroeconomic motives are likely to apply differentially to firms in different industries.

Swenson's primary explanation of the existence of foreign premiums is that, due to informational differences, foreign firms are more likely than domestic firms to engage in preemptive bids and thus pay higher prices on average. The reasons provided for this behavior, however, are not very convincing. Further, even if different groups of firms are willing to pay different prices, some bidding/equilibrium structure must be assumed to result in their having to pay more!

An alternative explanation might be that domestic and foreign firms bid for different populations of target firms. Consider two types of acquisition targets: (1) mispriced and/or mismanaged companies that essentially can be valued on a stand-alone basis, and (2) companies in industries with substantial potential global scale/scope economies whose value depends on the characteristics of the global network of the acquiring firm. Domestic firms should dominate bidding for the former group, while firms that are culturally and geographically distant from the United States should in general only be interested in the latter group, since they typically will have higher costs of gaining information about the United States, and so on. Dick Caves's unpublished results, which he referred to in the discussion, suggest that the difference in premiums is in fact associated with differences in target rather than acquirer characteristics. Why one group of targets should command greater premiums, however, still requires an explanation.

In order to answer a number of these questions more precisely, it is necessary to be more specific about the nature of the asset being acquired. Some direct foreign investments, whether by acquisitions or not, are essentially portfolio investments where the acquired asset is not integrated into the acquiring firm's network and its management and operations are not changed to reflect the skills, operating principles, and so on, of the acquiring firm. The acquisition of Rockefeller Center is an example. In those cases where the investment is incorporated into the acquiring firm's network, it is important to know whether this is largely a locally oriented investment (e.g., buying "downstream" activities in order to sell products in the United States that are designed and produced elsewhere) or whether it is an upstream investment that seeks to exploit U.S.-based activities for global purposes, such as the case of Genentech. Under these different situations, one might expect quite different value creation as well as value transfer. In addition, it would be helpful to know whether the target is stronger or weaker in R&D or advertising than the acquiring firm, based on ratios of R&D and advertising to sales, levels of patent activity, or nature of employees.

In all, this is a very interesting study at a level of analysis that has the potential to differentiate between competing hypotheses regarding FDI, and Swenson is to be commended for having opened up what I expect will become a major domain of FDI research.

Discussion Summary

The discussion opened with *Kenneth Froot*'s observation that this paper represents an important yet subtle change in the emphasis of FDI research, away from quantities and toward prices.

During the discussion, several comments were made on the specific results and arguments presented. Some people questioned the preemptive bidding hypothesis and why it should only (or, predominantly) hold for the foreign bidders. *Krishna Palepu* asked if the length of the abnormal return window affects the results, noting that preannouncement "leakage" may vary depending on the bidder. *Deborah Swenson* confirmed that she had tried several different specifications, but they did not alter the findings. *Palepu* also noted that the existence of foreign bidders in any given transaction would alter the distribution of expected bids, leading to higher expected shareholder wealth gains in transactions with foreign bidders, regardless of any other factors. (The higher number of potential competing bidders would increase the share of gains going to target shareholders.)

Several extensions to *Swenson's* work were suggested. *Robert Feenstra* observed there may be an option value to these investments for those foreign companies worried about potential trade restrictions (as in Bhagwati's quid pro quo investments). Since this fear only applies to a handful of industries, this hypothesis could be tested by comparing foreign takeover premiums across industries. The selection of appropriate industries could be based on trade protection filings with the FTC. *Froot* suggested trying to separate out the wealth effect from the exchange rate effect by looking at other shocks to corporate wealth, such as changes in stock prices.

Kathryn Dewenter mentioned three related results she has acquired in similar research: only shareholder wealth gains for the largest foreign acquisitions appear to have any exchange rate sensitivity; within the chemical and retail industries, shareholder wealth gains are not significantly higher for foreign buyers; and the pattern of foreign versus domestic wealth gains appears to depend on whether or not the target and buyer product lines are closely related. All of these findings suggest that moving toward more transaction detail, as recommended by *Donald Lessard,* is warranted and likely to provide richer insights.

Biographies

Michael Adler is professor of finance at Columbia University, Graduate School of Business.

S. Lael Brainard is assistant professor of applied economics at Sloan School of Management at the Massachusetts Institute of Technology and a faculty research fellow of the National Bureau of Economic Research.

Geoffrey Carliner is executive director of the National Bureau of Economic Research.

Richard E. Caves is professor of economics and business administration at Harvard University.

Kathryn L. Dewenter is assistant professor of finance and business economics at the University of Washington.

Michael Dooley is professor of economics at University of California, Santa Cruz, and a research associate of the National Bureau of Economic Research.

Robert C. Feenstra is professor of economics at the University of California, Davis, and associate director of the International Trade and Investment Program at the National Bureau of Economic Research.

Martin Feldstein is George F. Baker Professor of Economics at Harvard University and president of the National Bureau of Economic Research.

Kenneth A. Froot is professor of business administration at the Graduate School of Business, Harvard University, and a research associate of the National Bureau of Economic Research.

Edward M. Graham is senior fellow at the Institute for International Economics.

Paul M. Healy is Nanyang Technical University Senior Professor of Management at the Sloan School of Management, Massachusetts Institute of Technology.

James R. Hines, Jr., is associate professor of public policy at the John F. Kennedy School of Government, Harvard University, and a faculty research fellow of the National Bureau of Economic Research.

Paul R. Krugman is professor of economics at the Massachusetts Institute of Technology and a research associate of the National Bureau of Economic Research.

Robert Z. Lawrence is Albert L. Williams Professor of International Trade and Investment at the John F. Kennedy School of Government, Harvard University, and a research associate of the National Bureau of Economic Research.

Donald Lessard is professor of international management at the Sloan School of Management, Massachusetts Institute of Technology.

Robert E. Lipsey is professor of economics at Queens College and the Graduate Center, City University of New York, and a research associate of the National Bureau of Economic Research.

Richard C. Marston is James R. F. Guy Professor of Finance and Economics at the Wharton School of the University of Pennsylvania and a research associate of the National Bureau of Economic Research.

Rachel McCulloch is Rosen Family Professor of Economics at Brandeis University and a research associate of the National Bureau of Economic Research.

Krishna G. Palepu is professor of business administration at the Graduate School of Business Administration, Harvard University.

Peter A. Petri is Carl Shapiro Professor of International Finance and director of the Lemberg Program in International Economics and Finance at Brandeis University.

Karl P. Sauvant is chief, Research and Policy Analysis Branch, Transnational Corporations and Management Division, United Nations Department of Economic and Social Development.

Deborah L. Swenson is assistant professor of economics at the Fuqua School of Business, Duke University.

Raymond Vernon is Clarence Dillon Professor of International Affairs Emeritus at the John F. Kennedy School of Government, Harvard University.

Louis T. Wells, Jr., is Herbert F. Johnson Professor of International Business Management at the Graduate School of Business Administration, Harvard University.

G. Peter Wilson is associate professor of business administration at the Graduate School of Business Administration, Harvard University.

David B. Yoffie is professor of business administration at the Graduate School of Business Administration, Harvard University.

William Zeile is an economist in the Research Branch, International Investment Division, Bureau of Economic Analysis, U.S. Department of Commerce.

Contributors

Michael Adler
418 Uris Hall
Columbia University
116th Street and Broadway
New York, NY 10027

S. Lael Brainard
Sloan School of Management
Massachusetts Institute of Technology
50 Memorial Drive
Cambridge, MA 02139

Geoffrey Carliner
National Bureau of Economic Research
1050 Massachusetts Avenue
Cambridge, MA 02138

Richard E. Caves
Department of Economics
Littauer Center 210
Harvard University
Cambridge, MA 02138

Kathryn L. Dewenter
Department of Finance and Business
    Economics, DJ-10
University of Washington
Seattle, WA 98195

Michael P. Dooley
Economics Board
Crown College, Room 226
University of California, Santa Cruz
Santa Cruz, CA 95064

Robert C. Feenstra
Department of Economics
University of California
Davis, CA 95616

Martin Feldstein
National Bureau of Economic
    Research
1050 Massachusetts Avenue
Cambridge, MA 02138

Kenneth A. Froot
Graduate School of Business
Harvard University
Soldiers Field
Boston, MA 02163

Edward M. Graham
Senior Fellow
Institute for International Economics
11 DuPont Circle, N.W.
Washington, D.C. 20036

Paul M. Healy
Sloan School of Management
Massachusetts Institute of Technology
50 Memorial Drive
Cambridge, MA 02139

James R. Hines, Jr.
National Bureau of Economic
    Research
1050 Massachusetts Avenue
Cambridge, MA 02138

Paul R. Krugman
Department of Economics
Room E52-383
Massachusetts Institute of Technology
Cambridge, MA 02139

Robert Z. Lawrence
John F. Kennedy School of Government
Harvard University
79 John F. Kennedy Street
Cambridge, MA 02138

Donald Lessard
Sloan School of Management
Massachusetts Institute of Technology
50 Memorial Drive
Cambridge, MA 02139

Robert E. Lipsey
National Bureau of Economic Research
269 Mercer Street
Eighth Floor
New York, NY 10003

Richard C. Marston
Department of Finance
The Wharton School of Management
2300 Steinberg-Dietrich Hall
University of Pennsylvania
3620 Locust Walk
Philadelphia, PA 19104

Rachel McCulloch
Department of Economics
Brandeis University
Waltham, MA 02254

Krishna G. Palepu
Graduate School of Business
Harvard University
Soldiers Field
Boston, MA 02163

Peter A. Petri
Department of Economics
Brandeis University
Waltham, MA 02254

Karl P. Sauvant
Research and Policy Analysis Branch
TNC and Management Division
Department of Economic and Social
    Development
Room DC2-1254
United Nations
NY, NY 10017

Deborah L. Swenson
The Fuqua School of Business
Duke University
Durham, NC 27706

Raymond Vernon
John F. Kennedy School of Government
Harvard University
79 John F. Kennedy Street
Cambridge, MA 02138

Louis T. Wells, Jr.
Graduate School of Business
Harvard University
Soldiers Field
Boston, MA 02163

G. Peter Wilson
Graduate School of Business
    Administration
Morgan Hall 415
Harvard University
Boston, MA 02163

David B. Yoffie
Harvard Business School
Morgan Hall, Room 247
Boston, MA 02163

Author Index

"Abu Dhabi's Links," 138
Adler, Michael, 56, 111
Agmon, T., 278
Aliber, Robert Z., 42n9
"A new emerging species," 214
Auty, Richard M., 73

Baldwin, Richard, 225, 255n1
Belli, R. David, 138, 172, 253
Belot, Therese, 185
Bergsten, C. Fred, 38
Bezirganian, Steve D., 117t, 153t
Bhagwati, Jagdish, 42n11
"Biter Bitten," 105
Blomström, Magnus, 133
Borrus, Michael G., 199
Bower, Anthony G., 76n17
Brainard, S. Lael, 84, 225, 229
Braun, Ernest, 202
Buckley, Peter J., 22n3
Business Week, 63n6
Busjeet, Vinod, 180

Cagan, Philip, 117n1
Campayne, Paul, 68n12
Campos, Jaime, 177
Carliner, Geoffrey, 111, 171, 230
Casson, Mark C., 22n3, 75
Caves, Richard E., 1, 38, 40n6, 42n8, 43n12,
    48n22, 49n26, 80, 82, 84, 111, 195, 225,
    248, 251, 255n1
Chandler, Alfred D., 59

Chang, Sea Gin, 71, 256
Coase, Ronald, 22
Contractor, F. J., 64
Curhan, Joan P., 59n1, 96, 97t, 101t
Cushman, David O., 272n11

Dataquest, 210, 215f
Davidson, William H., 59n1, 62
Dewald, William G., 117
Dewenter, K. L., 248, 251, 253, 284
Di Lullo, Anthony J., 117
Dodwell Marketing Consultants, 103t
Dooley, Michael, 253
Doukas, John, 279n24
Drake, Tracey A., 80
Dunning, John H., 65n7, 70, 72, 73, 225

Economist, 71, 105
Economist Publications, 237n4, 239n5
Eisner, Robert, 117
Encarnation, Dennis, 70, 86, 90, 94, 184
Errunza, Vihang R., 278
European Commission, 67

Federal Reserve Board, 149t
Feenstra, Robert, 36, 83–84, 111, 228, 284
Feldstein, Martin, 36, 110–11, 172, 229, 230
Finan, William, 201t, 203t
Financial Times, 68nn10,11, 72n16
Fishman, Michael J., 275
Flamm, Kenneth, 200, 202, 211n12
Flowers, E. B., 67

Franko, Lawrence G., 39n4, 65
Froot, Kenneth A., 4, 27, 33, 42n8, 84, 109, 110, 172, 196, 224, 228–29, 246, 248, 251, 272, 283, 284

Galbraith, Craig S., 75
Gittelman, Michelle, 70, 72, 195
Goldsmith, Raymond W., 117n1
Gomes-Casseres, Benjamin, 64
Goodspeed, Timothy, 143
Goyder, D.G., 66
Graham, Edward, 32, 36, 39n5, 46n18, 48n22, 51n32, 76n17, 84, 85, 108, 171, 172, 196, 239, 246n7
Grossman, Gene M., 50n27, 75
Grossman, S., 271n9
Grubert, Harry, 143
Grunwald, Joseph, 200
Guisinger, S., 189n8

Hall, Bronwyn H., 270
Halverson, Karen, 174, 176
Harris, R. S., 251, 256n2, 277n21
Harrison, Ann, 56
Hart, Oliver, 22, 271n9
Healy, Paul, 196
Helpman, Elhanan, 75, 225
Hexner, Ervin P., 58
Hill, Frank Ernest, 59
Hill, Hal, 174
Hines, James, 111, 172, 230
Holloway, Nigel, 92
Horst, Thomas, 38
"How Japan Got Burned," 143

International Monetary Fund (IMF), 37n1, 91
Ito, K., 60
Ito, Takatoshi, 69

James, Christopher M., 268n8
Japan Economic Institute, 86, 92, 93t, 94n7, 95t, 103t
Japan Economic Journal, 85
"Japanese wary," 143
Jensen, Michael, 23, 244n6, 246
JETRO, 85, 86, 216t
Julius, Dee Anne, 16t, 32

Kay, Neil M., 75
Kester, W. C., 71, 72
Khan, Kushi, 177
Klein, Michael W., 272n13

Knickerbocker, Frederick T., 60, 67n9, 81, 212
Kogut, Bruce, 41n7, 71, 256n2
Kojima, Kiyoshi, 70
Kravis, Irving, 39n4, 59, 133
Kreinin, Mordechai E., 71
Krugman, Paul R., 32, 39n5, 46n18, 75, 76n17, 85, 108, 198, 225, 239, 246n7

Lall, Sanjaya, 57, 177
Landefeld, J. Steven, 117
Lawrence, Robert Z., 51n32, 102, 104, 111, 171
Lawson, Ann M., 117
Leonard, Jonathan S., 46n18
Lessard, Donald, 84, 278, 284
Lewis, Cleona, 114t, 123
Lewis, Jordan D., 64
Lewis, W. Arthur, 25
Lipsey, Robert E., 36, 37n1, 39n4, 42n10, 46n17, 56, 59, 63, 73, 114t, 117n1, 122, 127, 133, 171–72, 229, 253
Lorange, Peter, 64
Lynch, Robert Porter, 64

McCulloch, Rachel, 36, 39n3, 46n18, 56
Macdonald, Stuart, 202
Mackenzie de Sola Pool, Adam, 209n9
Malatesta, Paul H., 270
Marston, Richard, 230
Mason, Mark, 86, 94
Mataloni, Raymond J., 117t
Meckling, William, 23
"Mergers and acquisitions," 95
Mergstat Review, 96t
Michalet, Charles-Albert, 66
Milner, Helen V., 81
Ministry of Finance, Japan, 103t
Ministry of International Trade and Industry (MITI), 100t
Ministry of International Trade and Industry (MITI), Japan, 103t
MIT Commission on Industrial Productivity, 227
Monashi, Dara, 196
Moran, Theodore H., 38
Morck, Randall, 40n6, 271n10
Musgrave, John, 149t

New York Times, 61n2, 206–7t
Nicholson, Robert E., 141t
Nippon 1991, 61n2

Ondarte, Guillermo, 177
Organization for Economic Cooperation and
    Development (OECD), 18t, 19t, 47n19
Orr, James, 119, 129
"Overseas investments," 208n8

Palepu, Krishna, 196, 229, 283
Parkhe, Arvinde, 64
Penrose, Edith T., 24n4
Petri, Peter, 84, 102, 103t, 111, 194, 196
Pieper, Paul J., 117
Pomfret, Richard, 49n24
Porter, Michael E., 198, 225n1
Prestowitz, Clyde, 31

Ravenscraft, D., 251, 256n2, 277n21
Ray, Edward John, 88
Rhee, Yung Whee, 185
Roll, R., 267n7, 271n10
Rosengren, Eric, 272n13
Ruback, R., 244n6
Rukstad, Michael, 209n9

Sanbet, Lemma W., 278
Sauvant, Karl, 35–36, 111
Saxonhouse, Gary, 101t
Scharfstein, David, 35
Scholes, Myron, 28, 239
Scholl, Russell B., 117t, 141t
Schwartz, Jacob T., 63
Semiconductor Equipment and Materials Inter-
    national, 215f
Semiconductor Industry Associations, 199,
    213
Seskin, Eugene P., 156t
Shleifer, Andrei, 271n10
Stein, Jeremy, 4, 27, 33, 35, 42n8, 109, 224,
    246, 248, 251, 272
Steinmueller, W. Edward, 203n5
Stekler, Lois, 37n1
Stern, Robert, 101t
Stevens, Guy V. G., 37n1
Stocking, George W., 58
Sullivan, David F., 156t
Suri, Rajan, 59n1
Swenson, Deborah, 28, 111, 143, 172, 251,
    283

Taylor, William, 38n2
Teece, David J., 63, 75
Thee, Kian Wie, 176
Thompson, Rex, 270

Thomsen, Stephen, 16t
Tolchin, Martin, 31
Tolchin, Susan, 31
Travlos, Nickolos G., 279n24

Ulan, Michael, 117
United Nations, 115, 146t, 155t, 192t
U.N. Center on Transnational Corporations
    (UNCTC), 13, 15t, 18t, 53, 55, 57, 61,
    62n5, 70n13, 71n14, 85, 106
U.S. Bureau of the Census, 114t
U.S. Congress, 63, 71n15
U.S. Department of Commerce, 91t, 98t, 101t,
    120t, 121t, 122t, 124, 125–26, 132t, 136,
    137t, 141t, 142t, 143, 147–48t, 150–51t,
    152t, 153t, 154t, 155t, 156t, 157t, 158t,
    159–60t, 161–63t, 164–65t, 166–67t,
    204t, 257t
U.S. International Trade Commission
    (USITC), 90–91, 211

Vaupel, James W., 62nn3,4, 96, 97t, 101t
Vernon, Raymond, 1, 36, 56, 62, 111, 170–71,
    183, 229
Viner, Aaron, 94–95
Vishny, Robert W., 271n10

Wall Street Journal, 206–7t
Warren, V'Ella, 177, 186
Watkins, Myron W., 58
Webber, Alan, 38n2
Weir, Peggy, 268n8
Wells, Louis T., Jr., 174, 177, 184, 186,
    189n8, 190, 193t, 195–96
Westminster Management Consultants Lim-
    ited, 237n4, 239n5
White, Eduardo, 177
Wilkins, Mira, 25, 59, 69, 72, 114, 123, 124
Williamson, Oliver E., 22, 75
Wilson, G. Peter, 171
Wint, Alvin, 190
Wolfson, Mark, 28, 209n9, 239

Yeung, Bernard, 40n6
Yoffie, David, 172, 199, 220n25, 228, 229–
    30
Yoshino, Michael Y., 70
Yoshitomi, Masaru, 101, 102
Yu, C. J., 60

Zeile, William, 84, 195–96
Ziegler, Nicholas, 209

Subject Index

ACP (Africa-Caribbean-Pacific) countries, 176n3
Acquired firms. *See* Acquisitions
Acquiring firms: division of takeover gains with shareholders, 275–77; effect of home country growth rates on, 246; home countries of, 242–45
Acquisitions: as alternative to greenfield investment, 7; characteristics of foreign and domestic U.S., 261–62; discrimination against foreign, 240–42; foreign and domestic spending in United States on, 256–58; incentives for foreign firm, 278; of international equity investments, 231; in Japan, 7; by Japanese firms offshore, 7, 99; premiums paid by foreign firms, 11; in semiconductor industry, 205–10; shareholder gains, 263–71; shareholder gains with exchange rate changes, 272–75; trend in United States in foreign, 260–61; of U.S. firms by foreign firms, 141–42. *See also* Mergers and acquisitions (M&A)
Affiliates, foreign: assets in United States, 159–60t; employment in U.S. firms of, 119–25, 129, 131–32, 134, 144, 153t, 166–67t; exports from United States, 125–26, 145, 155t; home countries of firms in United States, 128–40; relations with *keiretsu* firms, 102–4, 110; total assets in United States of, 152t; in U.S. chemical industry, 123–24, 132–33, 144;

in U.S. manufacturing sector, 124–25, 144; in various U.S. industries, 128–29
African countries, 182
Agglomeration: considerations in semiconductor industry, 9, 225–27; lack in semiconductor greenfield investment, 198, 228; in semiconductor R&D, 200

Balance of payments: FDI financing of current account imbalances, 14–17, 18, 31; world FDI on basis of, 13
Banking sector, 20–21
Barriers to entry: effect on FDI, 42–43; in Japan for foreign direct investment, 6–7, 87, 90–92, 104; by *keiretsu* firms, 100–101. *See also* Regulations; Trade policy

Canada, 20–21
Capital stock: from direct investment in United States, 116–18; from FDI spending in Japan, 87, 108; foreign affiliate sources of financing of, 140–41; spending of foreign affiliates to U.S., 133–35, 164–65t; U.S. corporation, 149
Chemical industry: capital stock spending of U.S.-based foreign affiliates, 144; employment in U.S.-based foreign-affiliate firms, 123–24, 132, 144; foreign affiliates in U.S., 133; role of U.S. and foreign firms in, 122–25
Colombia: FDI in, 181; recruits investors, 190

Comparative advantage: as factor in FDI, 246; increasing similarity of, 80; of multinational corporations, 40–41; sales of foreign affiliates as indicator of, 139–40

Competition: in bidding to acquire a firm, 11, 275–77; as catalyst for old-style offshore investment, 58–61; differences in foreign and domestic U.S., 261–63; FDI as element of, 6, 44–45; impact of FDI on, 47–48; trade and FDI in large firm, 39. *See also* Premiums; Shareholder gains

Competitive advantage: of custom logic chip making, 208; in decision to invest offshore, 1–2; of mobile exporters, 174, 182–83; of multinational corporations, 40–41

Costa Rica: FDI in, 181; recruits investors, 190–91

Currency, 41–42. *See also* Exchange rates

Data sources: for analysis of firm acquisition in United States, 258–59; for analysis of foreign direct investment surge, 13, 15–17; for analysis of *keiretsu* effect, 102, 103–4; balance-of-payments accounts as, 15–17, 18; for equity investment analysis, 232–33; Harvard Multinational Enterprise Project, 66, 67; limitations of foreign-firm ownership in, 15, 17–18; for semiconductor industry investment analysis, 198

Developing nations: foreign direct investment by, 56; foreign direct investment in, 8, 14, 181, 190–91

Direct investment inflow: to Indonesia, 174; to United States, 2, 4, 18–19, 37–38, 115–16, 144, 146t

Direct investment inward, 48

Direct investment outflow: composition of U.S. industries as, 129; from United States, 4, 7, 37, 115–16, 144, 146t, 147–48t; motivation in, 179–80

Discrimination, Japan, 7, 240–42

East Asian countries: as foreign investors, 176–82; protection as motive for FDI, 177–78, 184, 192–95; as sources of FDI in Indonesia, 173–76

Employment: effect of FDI on aggregate, 45–47; FDI impact on industry and region, 45–47; in foreign-owned affiliates in United States, 119–25, 129, 131–32,

134, 144, 153t, 166–67t; by U.S. companies, 154t, 158t

Equity investments, international: countries (and firms) targeted for, 231, 234–35; factors influencing, 236–42; growth of, 231; incentives for, 231–32, 246–47

European Community (EC): firm strategy with common market, 66; outflows of FDI from, 53

European nations: direct investment in United States, 20–21; investment flows into southern, 20; Japanese direct investment in, 20–21. *See also* Firms, European

Exchange rates: as factor in FDI decisions, 5, 10, 41–42, 126–27, 170–71, 249, 251–52, 272; as factor in FDI surges, 27, 31; influence on foreign affiliate trade behavior, 126–28, 145. *See also* Valuation

Export platforms, 201

Exports: FDI in developing countries oriented to, 8; by foreign-owned affiliates in United States, 125–26, 145, 155t; U.S. manufacturing, 155t. *See also* Mobile exporters

FDI stock. *See* Capital stock

Financial markets changes, 30, 34

Financing: of current account imbalances, 14–17, 18, 31; of foreign affiliates, 8, 140–41. *See also* Reinvestment

Firm location decisions: components of, 44–45; factors influencing, 2–3, 40–41; mobile exporter criteria for, 180–82; in or out of home economy, 62–65; in semiconductor industry, 9, 197, 200–201, 214–16, 217–21; substitutability in, 6

Firms, European: investment in U.S. semiconductor industry, 205–10; post–World War II subsidiaries, 65–66; protection in pre–World War II environment, 65; subsidiaries and cross-border mergers of, 66–68. *See also* Affiliates, foreign

Firms, Japanese: hostile takeovers of, 92–94; sales to foreign firms, 95. *See also* Affiliates, foreign; *Keiretsu*

Firms, U.S.: alliances in international multinational networks, 64; European subsidiaries of, 66–68; investment in joint ventures, 89–90; investment in wholesale trade, 90–91; trade in semiconductors, 202–4

Foreign direct investment (FDI): alternatives

to, 88–92; balance of payments basis for world, 13; compared to licensing, 88–89; composition in U.S. industry sectors, 128–40, 150–51t; by country, 19t; defined, 1, 15–16, 43; financing of U.S. current account imbalances, 14; flows of developed countries, 18–19tt; foreign-affiliate countries as sources of, 135; of G5 nations (after 1985), 13–14; growth of (1985–89), 3–4; home countries of firm affiliates in United States, 128–40; influences on, 5; Japanese acquisitions, 99; key facts about trends in, 21; market occurrences of, 5; restrictions against, 240–42; suggested international regulation of, 55; surges or waves in, 4–5, 21, 24–34; theories of, 182–83; U.S. firm reinvestment, 140; world stocks and flows inward and outward, 14–15. *See also* Acquisitions; Direct investment inflow; Direct investment inward; Direct investment outflow; Equity investments, international; Mobile exporters

General Agreement on Tariffs and Trade (GATT), 48, 50, 55
General Agreement on Trade and Services (GATS), 55
Government role: in control of multinationals, 73–74, 80–81; in GATT negotiations, 50, 55, 81; in investment policy, 49–51, 53–55, 210–14; in regulation of FDI (Japan), 94–100
Greenfield investment: decline in, 3–4, 34, 45; in Japan, 7, 99, 100t; 91–92, 96–100, 108–9; by Japanese firms, 20; levels in United States, 256; in semiconductor industry, 9, 198, 210–14
Group of Five (G5) nations: foreign direct investment flows of, 13–14; foreign-owned firms in, 15–16

Imports: by foreign-owned affiliates in United States, 125–26, 145, 155t
Import substitution: deters foreign investment, 43; Japanese, 202; to maximize domestic firm profits, 49–51; as motive for East Asian foreign investment, 177–78, 184
Incentives to invest: Costa Rica and Colombia, 190–91; in developing countries, 184; encouraged for debtor countries,

251; for semiconductor firms, 219–20. *See also* Investment policy
Indonesia, 173–76
Investment: distinction between portfolio and direct foreign, 114; growth in United States of foreign, 116–18; influence of domestic pattern on FDI, 236–37; mergers and acquisitions as, 45–47. *See also* Acquisitions; Direct investment; Equity investments, international; Greenfield investment; Mergers and acquisitions
Investment policy: to attract mobile exporters, 188–91, 195; government role in, 48–51, 53–55, 210–14; international organization role in, 55; requirement for and effect of, 49–51, 53–55, 105–6. *See also* Semiconductor Trade Agreement (SCTA), U.S.-Japan

Japan: barriers to foreign direct investment, 90–91; as competitor in semiconductors, 205, 208; defense of *keiretsu*, 101–2; destinations of direct investment, 20–21; FDI in semiconductor industry in, 9; hostile takeovers in, 92–94; import substitution for semiconductor industry, 202; inward and outward foreign direct investment, 2, 19–20, 85–87, 104; lack of semiconductor FDI in, 220; licensing by U.S. firms in, 88–89; licensing in semiconductor industry, 202–3; purchases of foreign and Japanese firms, 95; restricts direct investment, 202–3; U.S. foreign direct investment in, 87; world share of outward FDI flow, 37–38, 53
Joint ventures, Japan, 89–90, 100t, 108–9

Keiretsu: analysis of effect, 102–3; as barriers to investment, 7, 87, 100–101; Japanese arguments for, 101–2
Korea, 174–76, 180–81

Latin America, 177
Licensing: as alternative to direct investment, 6, 88–89, 108; compared with foreign direct investment, 88–89; in semiconductor industry, 202–3, 208, 223. *See also* Joint ventures
Lomé Convention trade preferences, 176n3

Manufacturing sector, FDI in, 20–21; foreign investment in East Asia, 176–82; invest-

Manufacturing sector (*continued*)
    ment by foreign firms: Indonesia, 174–
    76, 178. *See also* Chemical industry; Mo-
    bile exporters; Semiconductor industry
Manufacturing sector, U.S.: capital stock
    spending of domestic firms, 156t; capital
    stock spending of foreign-affiliate firms
    in, 7–8, 157t, 164–65t; companies with
    foreign share in, 122, 124–25, 142–44;
    employment in foreign-affiliate firms,
    129–34, 144, 166–67; export-import be-
    havior of foreign affiliates in, 125–26,
    155t; growth in foreign share of, 120–22;
    sales by foreign-affiliate firms in, 155t
Market convergence, 25–26
Mauritius, 180, 181, 183
Mergers and acquisitions (M&A): determi-
    nants of cross-border, 10; effect of *kei-
    retsu* firms on, 104; effects of and incen-
    tives for, 25–26; as FDI in United States,
    10; growth of investment in, 3–4, 34; in
    Japan, 92, 104–5, 109; in semiconductor
    industry, 9, 197–98. *See also* Acquisitions
MNCs. *See* Multinational corporations
    (MNCs)
Mobile exporters: benefits to host country,
    184–88; growth of investment from, 8,
    178–80; investment criteria of, 180–82
Multinational corporations (MNCs): advan-
    tages of, 5, 278; factors in spread of,
    73–77; growth of (1980s and 1990s), 4–
    5, 61; long-run trends in, 24–26; motiva-
    tion for structure as, 5–6, 25–26; net-
    works within countries of regions, 65–68,
    69–73; rationale for old- and new-style
    offshore investment, 58–65, 82–83. *See
    also* Affiliates, foreign; Comparative ad-
    vantage; Competitive advantage; Firm lo-
    cation decisions; Firms, European;
    Firms, Japanese; Firms, U.S.

Newly industrialized countries (NICs): FDI ac-
    tivities of, 8; FDI in East Asian devel-
    oping countries, 192–95. *See also* Devel-
    oping nations

Obsolescing bargain theory, 183
Organization for Economic Cooperation and
    Development (OECD), Code of Liberal-
    ization of Capital Movements, 94

Premiums: in acquisitions by foreign firms in
    United States, 263–80; incentives for for-
    eign firm payment of, 277–78. *See also*
    Shareholder gains
Product cycles theory, 183
Production, internationalized, 120, 122
Profitability: impact of FDI on, 47–48; of
    U.S.-based foreign affiliates, 8, 142–43,
    171–72
Protection: effect of declining East Asian
    country, 186; impact on levels of trade,
    25; locational advantage created by, 43,
    177–78, 184, 186; measures to achieve,
    48; as motive for East Asian foreign in-
    vestment, 177–78. *See also* Barriers to en-
    try; Import substitution; Regulations;
    Trade policy
Public policy. *See* Government role; Invest-
    ment policy

Real estate industry, 20
Regulations: discriminating against foreign ac-
    quisitions, 240–42; as factor in cross-
    border investment, 10, 236–39, 250
Reinvestment: as engine of foreign investment
    in Japan, 87; by foreign affiliates in
    United States, 140–41; by U.S. firms
    abroad, 140–41
Risk management: as motivation to invest off-
    shore, 6, 30; of multinational corpora-
    tions, 58–65
Royalty earnings, 88–89

SCTA. *See* Semiconductor Trade Agreement
    (SCTA), U.S.-Japan
Semiconductor industry: anomalies in pattern
    of FDI, 217–21; foreign acquisition or in-
    vestment in U.S., 205–10; front-end fabri-
    cation, 201–2; Japanese, 210–22; off-
    shore investments in, 197–98; shift to
    off-shore assembly, 197, 200–201
Semiconductor market: in Japan, 220; U.S.
    participation in, 202–3
Semiconductor Trade Agreement (SCTA),
    U.S.-Japan: effect of, 210–11; incentives
    for Japan in, 220
Service sector: employment in foreign-affiliate
    firms in United States, 132–33, 144; FDI
    in, 21; U.S. firms in multinational net-
    works, 64–65
Shareholder gains: with acquired firm intan-
    gible assets, 277–78; effect of exchange
    rate fluctuation on, 272–75; resulting
    from bidding by foreign firms, 275–77;
    from stock ownership in acquired firms,
    263–71

Sri Lanka, 181

Structural Impediments Initiative, U.S.-Japan, 101

Taiwan, 174–75, 180–81

Takeovers: Japanese hostile, 92–94; prevention in Japan of foreign firm, 94–95

Tax policy: as deterrent to foreign investment, 28, 30–31; as factor in equity investment, 236, 239

Thailand, 180–81

Theory of the firm, 21–24

Trade: FDI effects on industry and region, 45–47; relation of international investment to, 24–25; role in large firm competition, 39

Trade policy: as determinant of FDI, 28–29; effect of restricted, 42–43; effect with barriers, 176–77; influence on FDI of barriers in, 5. *See also* Import substitution; Protection

Trade preferences: given ACP countries, 176n3

Trading blocs, regional, 73–74

United Kingdom, 20. *See also* Firms, European; Multinational corporations (MNCs)

United States: assets of foreign-affiliate firms in, 159–60t; employment in foreign-affiliate firms in, 129–34, 144, 166–67t; FDI growth in, 118, 126, 143–44; FDI in (by industry), 150–51t; industry composition of foreign affiliates in, 128–29; inflows of direct investment, 2, 4, 18–19, 37–38, 53, 115–16; Japanese semiconductor fabrication in, 212–13; mergers and acquisitions as FDI in, 10–11; outflows of direct investment, 4, 7, 37, 115–16, 144, 146t, 147–48t; sales of foreign-affiliate firms in, 161–63t; sources of FDI in, 20–21, 135–40, 145; spending of foreign-affiliate firms in, 164–65t; stock of FDI, 116–18; world share of outward FDI flow, 7, 37, 51, 53

Valuation: of currency in international capital transactions, 41–42; effects on FDI, 27–28, 33–34, 41–42; maximizing by following leader, 35